MOBILITIES, BOUNDARIES, AND TRAVELLING IDEAS

Mobilities, Boundaries, and Travelling Ideas

Rethinking Translocality Beyond Central Asia and the Caucasus

Edited by Manja Stephan-Emmrich and Philipp Schröder

OpenBook
Publishers

https://www.openbookpublishers.com

This work is part of the research project 'Translocal Goods — Education, Work, and Commodities between Tajikistan, Kyrgyzstan, Russia, China, and the Arab Emirates' [grant number: Az. 86870], which has been funded by the VolkswagenStiftung (Volkswagen Foundation), 2013–2017.

ISBN Paperback: 978-1-78374-333-9
ISBN Hardback: 978-1-78374-334-6
ISBN Digital (PDF): 978-1-78374-335-3
ISBN Digital ebook (epub): 978-1-78374-336-0
ISBN Digital ebook (mobi): 978-1-78374-337-7
DOI: 10.11647/OBP.0114

Cover image: Road between Nurek and Hubuk (2016). Photo by Hans Birger Nilsen, CC BY-SA 2.0. Flickr, https://www.flickr.com/photos/110608682@N04/30283802874
Cover design: Anna Gatti.

All paper used by Open Book Publishers is SFI (Sustainable Forestry Initiative), PEFC (Programme for the Endorsement of Forest Certification Schemes) and Forest Stewardship Council(r)(FSC(r) certified.

Printed in the United Kingdom, United States, and Australia
by Lightning Source for Open Book Publishers (Cambridge, UK)

Contents

Preface   1

Foreword   5
Nathan Light

Introduction: Mobilities, Boundaries, and Travelling Ideas   27
Beyond Central Asia and the Caucasus: A Translocal Perspective
Manja Stephan-Emmrich and Philipp Schröder

Part 1: Crossing Boundaries: Mobilities Then and Now

1. Emigration Within, Across, and Beyond Central Asia in the   61
   Early Soviet Period from a Perspective of Translocality
   Kamoludin Abdullaev

2. Crossing Economic and Cultural Boundaries: Tajik   89
   Middlemen in the Translocal 'Dubai Business' Sector
   Abdullah Mirzoev and Manja Stephan-Emmrich

Part 2: Travelling Ideas: Sacred and Secular

3. Sacred Lineages in Central Asia: Translocality and Identity   121
   Azim Malikov

4. Explicating Translocal Organization of Everyday Life: 151
   Stories From Rural Uzbekistan
   Elena Kim

5. A Sense of Multiple Belonging: Translocal Relations and   177
   Narratives of Change Within a Dungan Community
   Henryk Alff

Part 3: Movements from Below: Economic and Social

6. 'New History' as a Translocal Field   205
   Svetlana Jacquesson

7. Informal Trade and Globalization in the Caucasus and   229
   Post-Soviet Eurasia
   Susanne Fehlings

8. The Economics of Translocality — Epistemographic   263
   Observations from Fieldwork on Traders In(-Between)
   Russia, China, and Kyrgyzstan
   Philipp Schröder

Part 4: Pious Endeavours: Near and Far

9. iPhones, Emotions, Mediations: Tracing Translocality in   291
   the Pious Endeavours of Tajik Migrants in the United Arab
   Emirates
   Manja Stephan-Emmrich

10. Translocality and the Folding of Post-Soviet Urban Space in   319
    Bishkek: Hijrah from 'Botanika' to 'Botanicheskii Jamaat'
    Emil Nasritdinov

Afterword: On Transitive Concepts and Local Imaginations —   349
Studying Mobilities from a Translocal Perspective
Barak Kalir

Notes on Contributors   361

Index   365

Preface

This book marks the end of a very pleasant intellectual journey for us. It began in spring 2013, when we started our research project with the admittedly technical title *Translocal Goods — Education, Work, and Commodities Between Tajikistan, Kyrgyzstan, Russia, China, and the Arab Emirates*. We aspired to explore new ways in which the exchange relations of mobile actors from Central Asia redefine their own (emic) as well as our (analytic) understanding about identity, ethnicity and Islam as they extend beyond common 'containers' of local community, nation state and regional setting. Within that conceptual frame, three individual scientific efforts each dealt with quite distinct themes:

- *Studying Islam Abroad — Students' Mobility, Life-Chances and Translocal Muslim Practice in-between Tajikistan and the Arab World* (Manja Stephan-Emmrich)

- *The 'China-Business' — An Ethnography of Kyrgyz Traders and their Translocal Livelihoods in-between 'Home', China, and Russia* (Philipp Schröder)

- *Translocal Hijab — The Producing, Distributing and Consuming of Religious Clothing in-between Tajikistan and the United Arab Emirates* (Abdullah Mirzoev)

We have presented in detail the concepts and empirical data associated with these projects in an earlier publication (Schröder and Stephan-Emmrich 2014), as well as in the introductory chapter to this volume. But academia can only thrive to the degree it is supported by a generous institutional structure. In that regard, we could not have found a better partner than the Volkswagen Foundation (VolkswagenStiftung), and

 https://doi.org/10.11647/OBP.0114.12

in particular the program *Between Europe and the Orient — A Focus on Research and Higher Education in/on Central Asia and the Caucasus*. Until 2017, the funding provided by the Volkswagen Foundation enabled us not only to conduct our individual ethnographic fieldwork in Central Asia, Russia, China and the United Arab Emirates, but also to engage actively within various circles of the scientific community.

One such key event was a workshop held in Bishkek (Kyrgyzstan) in April 2015, which we jointly organized with our main local partner, the American University of Central Asia. Over three days, our group of participants intensively discussed draft papers that approached the notion of 'translocality' from all kinds of disciplinary, theoretical and methodological angles.

Since then these early texts have been developed into full-fledged chapters, due in no small part to our invited discussant, Barak Kalir of the University of Amsterdam in the Netherlands. As someone who shares our interest in mobility studies, but also draws from extensive research experience outside of Central Asia, his intuitive commentary provided the authors with a fresh perspective, challenging them to think beyond conventional approaches in their disciplines or focus areas. We are very grateful that Barak agreed to condense his thoughts on the contributions gathered here into a remarkable afterword.

At the beginning of this book you will find a foreword by Nathan Light of Uppsala University in Sweden. We appreciate his thoughts as a senior scholar of Central Asian studies, because they allow us to situate our authors' contributions within the wider perspective of (trans-) regional historic development. In this way, we believe, the fore- and afterwords complement the introduction in interesting ways: in the latter we could focus on the immediate conceptual issues of translocality as addressed by our authors, precisely because the fore- and afterword develop such invaluable contextual knowledge in regard to both area and mobility studies. Finally, we are grateful to all contributors, who all worked hard to meet the various expectations and shifting deadlines we set them.

As this volume is an unusual assembly of authors for whom English is not their native language, we are particularly thankful to our language editor, Tricia Ryan. Due to her own background in social science research in Central Asia, her timely remarks improved the manuscript beyond grammar or style.

We are indebted once more to the Volkswagen Foundation for agreeing to provide additional funds to support the publication of this research in Open Access format. In that regard, many thanks also to Alessandra Tosi of Open Book Publishers, whose patience and careful management were invaluable during this book's production process. Furthermore, we are grateful to Bianca Gualandi and Lucy Barnes, also from OBP, for supporting us in matters of visual design and language-editing. Nora Bernhardt, Karin Teuber and Fiona Smith of Humboldt-Universität of Berlin have been crucial assets to our project since 2013, and their enthusiastic support for our common research-and publishing-efforts is very much appreciated.

Finally, we do not see the present volume as an end to our exploration of translocality, but rather as a new beginning. We believe that beyond this collective contribution, presented on the following pages, translocality has much more descriptive and analytical potential to be uncovered. Examples of such potential include conceptual innovation in the field of 'new area studies', the anthropology of emotions, internet studies, or philosophical approaches to mobility and place, as is outlined in the foreword, introduction and afterword of this volume.

Berlin, February 2018
Philipp Schröder and Manja Stephan-Emmrich

Foreword

Nathan Light

The present volume brings together a valuable range of contributions that develop the analysis of translocality and mobilities. This research perspective is particularly important in Central Asia and the Caucasus because people in these regions have a long history of movement and engagement with surrounding regions. Adopting a translocal perspective helps reveal the ways researchers from elsewhere have shaped these regions' histories by emphasizing, on the one hand, enduring occupation of stable regions in the Caucasus and, on the other, mobile lives along the 'Silk Road' of Central Asia: in contrast, people living in these regions have long created more complex histories and cultural relations along both imagined and practical dimensions. Another important contribution made by this volume is to stimulate diverse perspectives through collaboration among researchers from the Caucasus, Central Asia, and abroad. In what follows I point to some ways that Central Asian and Caucasian realities can inspire new insights into the developing theoretical paradigms of research on translocality and mobility practices.

Social science and humanities studies on globalization, transnationalism, and mobility began as somewhat novel themes in the 1980s, and have expanded rapidly since. In social and cultural anthropology in particular this research area became popular and more diverse in the 1990s. Mobility is now a well-established interdisciplinary research perspective, as evidenced by such landmarks as the journals *Mobilities* founded in 2006 and *Transfers: Interdisciplinary Journal*

 https://doi.org/10.11647/OBP.0114.13

of Mobility Studies in 2011, and the *Routledge Handbook of Mobilities* published in 2014. Translocality or translocalism has emerged more slowly into the academic limelight, being overshadowed by the more established paradigms of globalization and transnationalism with their emphasis on larger-scale transformations.

Mobility and translocality and the theories, models, and methodologies linked to them have been dominated by ideas about the contemporary expansion and acceleration of movement across the globe. Nevertheless, the conceptual framework used to research mobility and translocality facilitates investigation of past movements of people and things as well. The modernization and globalization paradigms deploy a linear sense of ongoing acceleration, broadly aligned with the aspirational economic expansion institutionalized within many national and international governmental practices. This contrasts with more nuanced research on translocal mobilities focusing on varying patterns of historical and contemporary movement and circulation under the shifting constraints and aspirations of mobile subjects.

The increasing attention given to mobility and translocality in the social sciences over the past twenty-five years has extended to topics such as transport, migration, refugees, tourism, borders, and exile. With an initial emphasis on changing relationships among people, communities, and the nation state, researchers examined how globalizing economic activities, tourism, and migration were leading to novel transnational practices and identities. On the one hand, situations were treated as ethnographically distinctive in order to highlight emergent and shifting practices, such as commodity chains, mobile capital, or new patterns of labour migration, while on the other hand, researchers also pointed to broader trends in which increasing mobility and global connections led generally to postnational social dynamics that required new theories and methodologies. Usually rooting their narrative in Benedict Anderson's (1983) discussion of the rise of the nation state and its social, political, and territorial institutions to become a twentieth century universal, anthropologists such as Arjun Appadurai (1990), Liisa Malkki (1995), and Aihwa Ong (1999) suggested that the nation state was being superseded in ways that required new concepts, theories, and methods to understand.

Emergent transnationalism and globalization were identified as new conditions calling for new ways of thinking. Fewer scholars sought ways to use these new models to examine past mobility practices. At the extreme, the focus on novel conditions has led to studies emphasizing radical change and disruption such as Marc Augé's *Non-Places: An Introduction to Supermodernity* (2008), Thomas Eriksen's *Overheating. An Anthropology of Accelerated Change* (2016), or Steven Vertovec's 'Super-Diversity and its Implications' (2007). Such titles point to a broad narrative of modern lives being swallowed up by ever-increasing activity, rather than allowing for shifts, eddies, or deflations that might complicate such inexorable increase.

The underlying notion of a great divide emerging in late modernity has been difficult to deny. The emphasis on the 'acceleration of everything' — or 'time-space compression' as David Harvey (1989:284–307) aptly puts it — points to real processes, but raises many of the same problems as other great divide theories, such as stadialism in nineteenth-century cultural evolutionism (Meek 1976), or the posited oral-literate divide (Collins 1995). There is much room to debate whether or not people are experiencing radical changes or ruptures that call for entirely new ways of thinking. Both historians and anthropologists have tended to find more multidirectional shifts and practices, such as 'vernacular modernities' (Knauft 2002) and 'multiple literacies' (Street 1993) that undermine generalizations about the effects of new technologies, while sociologists tend to focus on the broader changes characterizing postmodern life.

Despite continuing consideration of acceleration and emergent mobilities and complexities, more recent studies generally make fewer claims about radical novelty, and expend more effort comparing transformations and examining long-term and ongoing processes. These approaches consider both ruptures and continuities, as well as considering earlier studies of mobility in order to enhance theories about it.

Mobility has arguably always been a key aspect of scholarly habitus itself, due to the importance of travel for research, cooperation, publication, and jobs (with equivalents in classical or medieval periods, and in Asia, North Africa, and the Middle East). Other economic activities have likewise long involved workers, managers, capital, raw materials, equipment and products moving in distinctive ways along widely varying circuits. All over the world, people move and carry ideas and objects with them and pass them along to others. These are fundamental to social processes, historical narratives, and cultural expression, but their centrality has often been overlooked due to what might be termed methodological localism. The contemporary expansion of the variety and extent of movement has prompted more careful attention, and challenged researchers to consider the qualitative changes caused by such mobilities. However, assessing the scale of movement and the degree of qualitative change requires deeper understanding of the prevalence and varieties of mobilities in the past.

Disciplinary genres and models

Disciplinary research often fits within what might described as typical chronotopes: sociologists generally emphasize large-scale transformations, while anthropologists often seek criss-crossing temporal connections, rather than embracing linear concepts of a present emerging from and diversifying upon the past. Anthropologists tend to discover more varied social formations, and, at least since the work of Eric Wolf (1982) and Johannes Fabian (1983), they have exhibited less of a tendency to view people as travellers in culturally-assigned positions along convergent historical paths. Changes, including shifts in mobilities and translocal practices, are more varied in the diverse social formations that anthropologists study. Earlier generations of anthropologists have explored cyclic (e.g., oscillations between *gumsa* and *gumlao* described by Edmund Leach 1954) and multidirectional histories. Historians, on the other hand, are less inclined to subsume activity within models of cycles or linear processes, and focus more on unique paths, avoiding both linear and cyclic chronotopes. In yet another pattern, economists are prone to identifying developmental stages, but also find a variety of cycles of development and decline within such stages. Economists thus tend to subordinate cycles to longer-term linear transformations of economic systems.

Disciplinary chronotopes and models emphasize different dimensions when making sense of mobility and translocality in their contemporary forms. Most sociologists, geographers, anthropologists, political scientists, historians, and cultural studies scholars continue to work with somewhat different understandings of mobilities, but a few specialists have been making productive connections among these evolving theoretical models. These include Peter Adey (2017), Tim Cresswell (2006), and Peter Merriman (2007) in geography, John Urry (2007) in sociology, Noel Salazar (2010) and Salazar and Nina Glick-Schiller (2013) in anthropology, Peter Greenblatt in literary studies (Greenblatt 2009), and Ulrike Freitag and Achim von Oppen (2010) in history.

Although historians have a longer tradition of studying regional networks and interactions, and generally focus on particularities, the limits of methodological regionalism have led to the subordination of translocal connections under the broader perspective of 'world history'. Between the levels of world and regional history, historians and cultural studies scholars have produced important new frames for understanding 'connected histories' involving many local processes, such as the Black Atlantic (Gilroy 1993, Thornton 1998), the Indian Ocean world (Anderson 2012, Freitag 2003), Indian merchants (Dale 2002, Markovits 2000), and studies of the Islamicate, Persianate, and Sanskrit ecumenes (Hodgson 1974, Pollock 2006). The large-scale sociopolitical perspective of civilizational analysis has also become increasingly popular (Árnasson 2003, Arjomand 2011), but should be informed by more studies of cosmopolitan subjectivities and mobilities (Kia forthcoming).

Dominant concepts within scholarly institutions strongly influence the ideas and research perspectives taken up within them. Patrick Manning's (2003) suggestive history of scholarship on the African diaspora shows how the study of interregional connections has been limited by institutional commitments towards more geographically-defined specializations. Recent critiques of the limits of area studies has led to a 'new area studies' paradigm that seeks to overcome its earlier narrowness and rigidity (see particularly Mielke and Hornidge 2014, and the discussion by Stephan-Emmrich and Schröder in this volume's introduction). But the most radical innovation will be to integrate the study of individual translocalism and the larger processes that dominate research.

Philosophical approaches

Although philosophical work has inspired important thinking across methodological and disciplinary frames, relatively few philosophers have written relevant works, principally Michel de Certeau (1984) and Gilles Deleuze and Félix Guattari (1987). Deleuze's extravagant analysis of 'the fold' (1993) has not been widely used to theorize movement, but offers valuable suggestions about how to understand non-linear connections among times and places. Emil Nasritdinov elegantly takes up the fold in his contribution to the present volume, and develops its potential for understanding mobility in spiritual terms. The abstractions expounded by Deleuze are slippery: his is a Baroque theory of the Baroque, and its complexity and flexibility makes it difficult to apply. But Nasritdinov suggests that the concept of the fold can help us understand Islamic beliefs and practices in both their complexity and rigidity, and their creativity and rapid transformation. According to him, through the mobile religious practice of *davaat*, people attain transformative experiences that make them more devout, but without a stable logic or structure for this transformation. He suggests that the fold connects multiple 'movements'. Including dreaming, pilgrimage, and remembering, which are crucial to Muslim spiritual transformation.

De Certeau, Deleuze, and Guattari all suggest that the dominant focus on stable concepts in Western philosophy has restricted consideration of interactions between disorder and boundaries, or among movement, assemblage, and entanglement. In short, the logic of capturing stable truths promotes the search for bounded entities and their characteristics, rather than investigating the interplay of chance, planning, and routine in shaping complex trajectories such as those that emerge in mobility.

The discussion of place and space is closely linked to that of mobilities and translocality, but connects to the larger philosophical literature that I will not attempt to review comprehensively here. Two important contributions are the work of Tim Ingold (2011) in anthropology, and Edward Casey in philosophy, both working on phenomenological accounts of places and ways of moving among them. Casey cites anthropological research extensively and has in turn been widely cited by anthropologists. His phenomenological analyzes of imagination (1976) and memory (1987) stimulate thinking about transtemporal connections, while his efforts to recuperate place as a central category of life from the spatializing tendencies of rationalizing modernity (1993, 1997) have been important for thinking about space and place in recent humanities and social science research.

Casey examines the role of movement among places at some length (1993:271–314) but does not explore connections to his earlier work on imagination and memory, and suggests that mobility is subordinate to place. He takes up many strands in his discussion, but his prevailing approach to place follows Heidegger, writing that 'For Heidegger, place and the self are intimately interlocked in the world of concrete work' and thus 'place and self are thoroughly enmeshed' (2001:684). Expanding from the idea of work to Bourdieu's broader concept of habitus, Casey proposes that 'habitus is a middle term between place and self, and, in particular, between lived place and the geographical self. This self is constituted by a core of habitudes that incorporate and continue, at both psychical and physical levels, what one has experienced in particular places' (2001:686). Although he does hold that places and journeys are mutually constituting, writing that 'places introduce permanency into journeys' and 'journeys bring out what is impermanent and continuously changing when we are in place itself' (1994:289), his treatment of the practices related to journeys and movement is limited, and a sense of attachment to essentialized and materialist concepts of place prevails in his work, reifying place as the foundation underlying human embodiment and activities.

Casey's extensive analysis of the treatment of place in philosophical tradition raises important issues and suggests how practices embed people into places, but he downplays the importance of movement and activity in the constitution of places. In order to promote a contrasting perspective, I would argue that human experience is founded upon and emerges within motion, whether constrained movement around a room, field, or workspace, or within larger ambits, which should be considered part of the investigation of translocal practices. Attention to subjects in places should recognize their activity within a phenomenology of movement, with psychic or physical confinement or constraint as dimensions to be accounted for, but not absolute bounds of emplacement.

Examination of the role of translocalism and movement in the constitution of subjects can take several directions. A recent treatment developed by Tim Edensor is based on Henri Lefebvre's concept of rhythmanalysis. Edensor suggests that 'rhythmanalysis elucidates how places possess no essence but are ceaselessly (re)constituted out of their connections. For instance, cities are particularly dense spatial formations containing a complex mix of multiple, heterogeneous social interactions, materialities, mobilities and imaginaries which connect through twists and fluxes of interrelation'. He continues, 'As Lefebvre says, '(There is) nothing inert in the world', which he illustrates with the examples of the seemingly quiescent garden that is suffused with the polyrhythms of 'trees, flowers, birds and insects' […] and the forest, which 'moves in innumerable ways: the combined movements of the soil, the earth, the sun. Or the movements of the molecules and atoms that compose it' (Edensor 2011:190, citing Lefebvre 2004).

Tim Ingold (2011) also focuses more on motion than place, and rejects either bounded places or beings in favour of a more fluid 'meshwork'. Ingold's suggestion that neither the subject nor the path are bounded entities helps disrupt assumptions about how to do fieldwork on mobilities. Phenomenologically informed fieldwork can investigate mobility practices even within everyday places. In their recent edited volume, Salazar, Elliot, and Norum (2017) suggest that there are many ways to investigate mobility while remaining 'in place' and that understanding people's activities within mobility formations and infrastructures calls for a broad range of perspectives and methods.

Categories

Questions of time, space, and place have been widely developed in philosophy and the social sciences, but mobile people have been investigated more as distinct types or figures: flaneurs, commuters, tourists, nomads, foragers, hunters, traders, itinerants, vagabonds, and pilgrims have been subject to particularistic consideration, as Noel Salazar (2017) points out in the introduction to a recent special issue entitled *Figures of Mobility*. Space and time are treated as continua, while commoditized mobilities, distinct ways of passing through space and time, are seen typologically as categories for labelling people and things (e.g., first class, posh, express, or even the ironic term for the Midwest in the US: the 'flyover zone'). Travel typologies can be used to distinguish modern from pre-modern, or even civilized from primitive. The very technologies that provide mobility across boundaries are themselves segregated and differentiated because they are commoditized products. Social stratification within transport allows elite travellers to isolate themselves and alleviate some of the travails of mobility, and divides the spectrum of mobility practices into socioeconomic categories. Elite spaces, such as airport club lounges and limousines, are inaccessible to those on non-elite trajectories.

Communication media also invite typological distinctions, making it more difficult to identify similarities and continuities of practice as new technologies become part of people's lives. Smartphone technology, with apps such as WhatsApp, provides for convenient and cheap communication and the sharing of digital images when travelling or living abroad, but there are important functional similarities in their use to create mementoes for oneself or images that can be circulated to significant others. Photographs and letters sent by post, phone calls, and SMS texts serve similar purposes regardless of their prominent differences. Technology may change rapidly but it participates in a complex balance of transformation and continuity: people adopt technologies that serve existing goals more readily than they adapt themselves to technologies by discovering and taking up novel goals and practices.

Questions persist about how to recognize and evaluate the ways new technologies and mobility practices are changing people and their social relations. Transport is undeniably faster and more ubiquitous, consuming more energy and other resources despite improving technologies, and taking people farther and more often. But are people spending more time and effort travelling? And does that travel isolate them from their community and lead to weaker social ties? Or are communication technologies making it possible to stay in touch, and facilitating mobility, allowing people to compensate for distance by alternative connections? Do community-based trust networks expand more easily to distant places through more versatile communication technologies? Such questions have to be carefully addressed by exploring how practices compensate or interact with one another, potentially reducing the effects of acceleration and complexity through connectivity and communication.

In a somewhat different direction and one that has been more extensively researched, online bulletin boards and discussion lists promote broader dialogue among members of ethnolinguistic groups and keep people in touch with developments affecting people, both in their home country as well as in foreign communities (Wilson and Peterson 2002, Bernal 2006). As with the role Benedict Anderson (1983) identified for print capitalism in shaping ethnic and national consciousness, online discussions can also lead to stronger identification with a community despite distance. Although print also enabled ongoing connections, it depends upon more localized production and distribution while internet access allows the community to stretch much more widely.

In my own research, I find Kyrgyzstani villagers using digital media to circulate information about each other despite wide displacement around the globe, but I am not sure that much of this information would not have been similarly distributed, if more slowly, through face-to-face encounters and postal communications in the past. In any case, it is clear that technology offers capacities that serve people's aspirations and values more than to reshape them. For example, villagers feel it is important to document ritual events, but usually do this through hiring a specialist to make high quality video recordings and edit them for distribution and replay. Cell phone videos are too low quality to preserve important events, so at least during the past ten years I have found that Kyrgyz rely upon local videographers and editors who create highly professional videos that people then circulate as physical recordings. Of course, the rapid shifts from black-and-white still photography in the Soviet period, to color photography after 1991, and then VCR and DVD videos does show an increasing rate of change, with new technologies giving young technology buffs the opportunity to become local professionals. Nonetheless, the most successful technology business in one village where I work remained, even in 2016, a photographer who uses camera, computer and printer to produce and edit digital color images for local customers.

Cosmopolitan connections

A wide variety of studies have taken up questions of cosmopolitan lifestyles and mobilities in Eurasia, including studies of connections among South Asia, the Middle East, Europe, and Central Asia. Cosmopolitanism has a long history throughout Eurasia, and reflects continuities within mobility practices such as trade and pilgrimage. Work by Engseng Ho (2006), Caroline Humphrey and Vera Skvirskaja (2012), Scott Levi (2002), Magnus Marsden (2008, 2016), Madeleine Reeves (2014), Jonah Steinberg (2007), Rian Thum (2014), and Pnina Werbner (1999, 2006) and many others have helped refine our knowledge of cosmopolitan mobility practices in this region.

Many of the works mentioned above, as well as chapters in this volume, can be seen as part of the broader study of Muslim mobilities. Important works in this field include Eickelman and Piscatori (1990) and Gelvin and Green (2014). Muslim translocal practices are widely reflected in Islamic literary tradition, with scholars, traders, and geographers leaving more than a millennium of written documents reflecting the circulation of people within the Islamic ecumene and beyond (e.g., Miquel 1987). Relevant to Central Asia is Wennberg's (2014) study of Bukharan literati reflecting upon acceleration, travel, and temporality in the late nineteenth century. Emphasizing the mobility of cosmopolitan Persianate literati, Mana Kia (forthcoming) describes the ideals of conduct known as *adab* as a mobile ethos that facilitates interaction among Muslims who encounter each other far from home.

Cosmopolitan activities were also an important aspect of the Soviet Union's ideology of progress, and included travel for professional and trade education, military service, and the participation of young workers in national projects such as the Baikal-Amur Mainline railway and hydroelectric construction projects. These efforts brought people together from many parts of the USSR and helped create pan-Soviet social experience and shared ideology and values. Such Soviet-era activities, along with tourism and long-distance trade, provided a foundation for ongoing connections in post-Soviet contexts, as well as shaping cosmopolitan aspirations and practices that motivate translocal mobility.

Post-Soviet translocal practices seem to be shaped more by economic motivations than the long distance or interethnic social ties that developed under socialism, and are characterized by regional patterns and asymmetric movement: Central Asians from poorer states (Kyrgyzstan and Tajikistan) move to Russia and Kazakhstan as workers and students, but few come from other post-Soviet states to Kyrgyzstan and Tajikistan to work or study. Instead, migrating workers and students come to Kyrgyzstan from China and South Asia.

Post-Soviet travel infrastructure perpetuates patterns established during the Soviet period. Travel by plane is usually through Moscow, regardless of where one is going in the post-Soviet space, but few people move among the economically lesser developed regions: cross-border mobility is well-developed among Central Asian states, and between Russia and Central Asia, but there is far less between the Caucasus and Central Asia. Members of Caucasian Muslim ethnic groups such as Chechens who were exiled to Central Asia around World War Two dominate movement between these two regions. For example, during numerous flights I have taken between London and Bishkek on British Airways flights that stopped in Yerevan, Armenia, I never saw someone board in Yerevan to travel to Bishkek or vice versa. In fact, many of the Armenians I met were travelling between Yerevan and Los Angeles, where roughly forty percent of Armenian Americans live (Wikipedia). Nonetheless, people from different parts of the Soviet Union do end up migrating and working together in cosmopolitan centres, including some centres, such as Istanbul, that were not part of Soviet-era mobilities, but are important trading centres linking the Middle East and post-Soviet Eurasia. The effects of Soviet-era cosmopolitanism thus shape post-Soviet economic ties and migration for work, but have resulted in fewer ongoing social ties.

Soviet-era cosmopolitanism has significant ties to mobility practices of the Russian Empire involving trade, education, and military expansion and governance. But Muslim Central Asia and the Caucasus were also linked internally and externally by cosmopolitan mobilities even before China and Russia conquered the regions. Many cities were important for trade, while some, such as Bukhara and Turkistan, were also important centres of Islamic education and pilgrimage. Education, political ties, and trade motivated travel and resettlement to and from the Ottoman Empire, China, Russia, and British India.

Looking further into the past, we find several millennia of important translocal mobilities in Central Asia: prominent examples are the conquests of Alexander the Great, the arrival of Greek settlers in Greco-Bactria (Holt 1989), and the Sogdian traders and literati moving among the Chinese, Sasanian, and Turkic Empires during the first millennium (de La Vaissière 2005, Rose 2016). In a different manner, nomadic pastoralists lived highly mobile lives that sometimes brought them into close contact with urban and settled society, but because their mobile economy offered greater wealth and flexibility, they generally maintained independent political and military practices that enabled both defence and occasional conquest. Nomads were willing participants in trade, but if they took up urban or cosmopolitan lifestyles most remained somewhat separate as conquerors or as soldiers serving those in power (Barfield 1993, di Cosmo 2002).

The Mongol conquest created some of the most important and long-lasting spatial networks for cosmopolitan formations connecting Central and Inner Asia, the Caucasus, Iran, and nearby regions. Merchants, officials, scholars, soldiers, and craftspeople moved great distances and distributed products and practices widely throughout the Mongol empire and its successor states. There is also a long history of Caucasian and Central Asian people moving as refugees and exiles due to conflicts, or because ruling groups have relocated them as settlers, farmers, and soldiers. This includes groups such as the Sibe and Taranchi, who were moved by Qing China's leaders to the Ili Region of Dzungaria in the eighteenth and nineteenth centuries. The so-called Volga Germans were recruited by Catherine the Great of Russia to help promote rural agricultural development in the eighteenth century, but many later moved, along with Russian agriculturalists, to Central Asia as settlers. Refugees fleeing conflicts include Kalmyks in the seventeenth century from Siberia and Dungans in the nineteenth from China. More recently, some of the largest movements involved the deportations of entire ethnic groups from Soviet border zones, particularly in the Caucasus and Korean border areas, to Central Asia under Stalin in the period around World War Two. Central Asians also repeatedly fled from conflict, collectivization, and hunger in both Russian and Chinese Central Asia, with significant groups of Kazakhs and Kyrgyz ending up as far abroad as Turkey, and Kalmyks in New Jersey in the United States. Each large-scale movement has resulted in continuing translocal mobility practices connecting these widespread communities.

Time

This sketch of movement and cosmopolitan identities across time in Central Asia is intended to direct attention to the final issue I wish to raise in this foreword. The capacity to move within and establish ongoing connections across space raises questions about how these relate to time, which plays an important role in movement but differs fundamentally as an experience, despite often being misleadingly described as a 'fourth dimension'. In the preceding paragraphs, I intentionally presented Central Asian history in a somewhat disjointed way to stimulate reflection upon more voluntary movements in time, through imagination, memory, and narrative.

Obviously, sequences of events or experiences in time, or even sequences of mental associations and perceptions, occur in contiguous moments of 'real' time. Nonetheless, memory, imagination, and social activities such as planning or narrative offer the power to reorganize events in time into meaningful associations that help make sense of experience. We can identify varieties of temporal translocality (transtemporality) that emerge both from sequences of experience in time, as well as from techniques that bring multiple moments together in consciousness. Transtemporality encompasses ways that people communicate with each other across time, carry out culturally meaningful life cycle rituals together, and invoke ideologically meaningful temporal formations around concepts such as civilization, economic development, or modernity. Movement through time is shaped and managed within social relations, and people rely on interactive social cognition to create futures and interpret pasts, to remember and plan. Communication, planning, and memory are in turn vital to organizing spatial mobility.

Communication media enable forms of co-presence that transcend distance in both time and space, although in profoundly different ways. Interactive dialogic communication has to take place synchronously, regardless of how far apart people are in space, while the converse, communication across time, is possible among people in the same or different places. In fact, both memory and technologies such as writing can be seen as ways a person communicates with him or herself. Writing, objects, public representations, and memories all help construct continuity among different moments of experience and thus help constitute individual and collective subjectivities.

One does not move voluntarily through time in the way that one can in space, but memory and imagination are tools for engaging with time and our passage through it. People have considerable control over physical movement in space, although they experience many constraints, while movement in 'real' time is continual, outside of people's control, and shared by all. Access to the past may differ depending upon memory capacity, or technologies for documenting, storing and retrieving, but people cannot shift in time to experience a different past or future. Everyone moves together in time. Although some people aim to recreate or reinhabit pasts or control movement into the future, they are simply creating a present that they believe is more like a desired past or future. Their ability to create such presents may reflect unequal access to resources and imaginaries in the present. Understanding the extent and expression of choice and agency in such situations is an important part of research into transtemporal practices.

Questions about spatial and temporal translocality and the relationships between them have only begun to be explored. The varied and rich chapters in this volume contribute to this effort. As Barak Kalir points out in his afterward, translocality helps overcome the kind of methodological regionalism reflected in the area studies paradigm, and reorients study towards the mobile subjects themselves. I would add that analysis of transtemporality can help overcome methodological contemporaneity and explore the complex ways people position themselves within time.

Most of the present chapters consider people's experiences and representations of temporal transformations as part of personal lived experience. However, those by Kamoludin Abdullaev, Henryk Alff, and Svetlana Jacquesson also investigate the ways people imagine and construct shared pasts and use them in social practices. Translocal and transtemporal perspectives study the ways people make lives amidst connections to different times, places, and people through movement, communication, and imagination. They reorient us from the imposition of institutional, legal, political, economic, or scholarly containers and boundaries that we use to purify our collections of objects and subjects, make our generalizations more accurate and our knowledge more stable. Analysis of mobile subjectivities draws us closer to people's experiences as they make sense of and move among different places and times.

References

'Armenian Americans', https://en.wikipedia.org/wiki/Armenian_Americans

Adey, Peter. *Mobility*. 2nd ed. London: Routledge, 2017.

Appadurai, Arjun. 'Disjuncture and Difference in the Global Cultural Economy'. *Theory, Culture & Society* 7.2 (1990): 295–310.

Anderson, B. *Imagined Communities: Reflections on the Origin and Spread of Nationalism*. London: Verso, 1983.

Anderson, Clare. *Subaltern Lives: Biographies of Colonialism in the Indian Ocean World, 1790–1920*. Cambridge: Cambridge University Press, 2012, https://doi.org/10.1017/cbo9781139057554

Arjomand, Saïd Amir. 'Axial Civilizations, Multiple Modernities, and Islam'. *Journal of Classical Sociology* 11.3 (2011): 327–35, https://doi.org/10.1177/1468795x11406032

Árnason, Jóhann P. *Civilizations in Dispute: Historical Questions and Theoretical Traditions*. Leiden: Brill, 2003.

Augé, Marc. *Non-Places: Introduction to an Anthropology of Supermodernity*. London: Verso, 1995.

Barfield, Thomas J. *The Nomadic Alternative*. Englewood Cliffs, NJ: Prentice Hall, 1993.

Bernal, Victoria. 'Diaspora, Cyberspace and Political Imagination: The Eritrean Diaspora Online'. *Global Networks* 6.2 (2006): 161–79, https://doi.org/10.1111/j.1471-0374.2006.00139.x

Casey, Edward S. *Imagining: A Phenomenological Study*. Bloomington: Indiana University Press, 1976.

Casey, Edward S. *Remembering: A Phenomenological Study*. Bloomington: Indiana University Press, 1987.

Casey, Edward S. *Getting Back Into Place: Toward a Renewed Understanding of the Place-World*. Bloomington: Indiana University Press, 1993.

Casey, Edward S. *The Fate of Place: A Philosophical History*. Berkeley: University of California Press, 1997.

Casey, Edward S. 'Between Geography and Philosophy: What Does It Mean to Be in the Place-World?' *Annals of the Association of American Geographers* 91.4 (2001): 683–93, https://doi.org/10.1111/0004-5608.00266

di Cosmo, Nicola. *Ancient China and its Enemies: The Rise of Nomadic Power in East Asian History*. Cambridge: Cambridge University Press, 2002, https://doi.org/10.1017/cbo9780511511967

Collins, James. 'Literacy and Literacies'. *Annual Review of Anthropology* 24.1 (1995): 75–93.

Cresswell, Tim. *On the Move: Mobility in the Modern Western World*. London: Routledge, 2006, https://doi.org/10.4324/9780203446713

de Certeau, Michel. *The Practice of Everyday Life*. Steven Rendall, trans. Berkeley: University of California Press, 1984.

Dale, Stephen Frederic. *Indian Merchants and Eurasian Trade, 1600–1750*. Cambridge: Cambridge University Press, 2002, https://doi.org/10.1017/CBO9780511523977

Deleuze, Gilles. *The Fold: Leibniz and the Baroque*. Tom Conley, trans. Minneapolis: University of Minnesota Press, 1993.

Deleuze, Gilles, and Félix Guattari. *A Thousand Plateaus: Capitalism and Schizophrenia*. Brian Massumi, trans. Minneapolis: University of Minnesota Press, 1987.

Edensor, Tim. 'Commuter: Mobility, Rhythm and Commuting'. In Tim Cresswell and Peter Merriman, eds. *Geographies of Mobilities: Practices, Spaces, Subjects*. Aldershot: Ashgate Publishing, 2011, pp. 189–204.

Eickelman, Dale F., and James Piscatori, eds. *Muslim Travellers: Pilgrimage, Migration and the Religious Imagination*. London: Routledge, 1990.

Eriksen, Thomas Hylland. *Overheating: An Anthropology of Accelerated Change*. London: Pluto Press, 2016, https://doi.org/10.2307/j.ctt1cc2mxj

Fabian, Johannes. *Time and the Other: How Anthropology Makes its Object*. New York: Columbia University Press, 1983.

Freitag, Ulrike. *Indian Ocean Migrants and State Formation in Hadhramaut: Reforming the Homeland*. Leiden: Brill, 2003.

Freitag, Ulrike, and Achim von Oppen. 'Introduction: "Translocality": An Approach to Connection and Transfer in Area Studies'. In Achim von Oppen and Ulrike Freitag, eds. *Translocality. The Study of Globalising Processes from a Southern Perspective*. Leiden: Brill, 2010, pp. 1–21, https://doi.org/10.1163/ej.9789004181168.i-452.8

Gelvin, James L., and Nile Green, eds. *Global Muslims in the Age of Steam and Print*. Berkeley: University of California Press, 2014.

Gilroy, Paul. *The Black Atlantic: Modernity and Double Consciousness*. Cambridge, MA: Harvard University Press, 1993.

Greenblatt, Stephen, 'Cultural Mobility: An Introduction'. In Greenblatt, *et al.*, eds. *Cultural Mobility: A Manifesto*. Cambridge: Cambridge University Press, 2009, pp. 1–23, https://doi.org/10.1017/cbo9780511804663.001

Harvey, David. *The Condition of Postmodernity: An Enquiry into the Origins of Social Change*. London: Blackwell, 1989.

Ho, Engseng. *The Graves of Tarim: Genealogy and Mobility Across the Indian Ocean*. Berkeley: University of California Press, 2006.

Hodgson, Marshall. *The Venture of Islam: Conscience and History in a World Civilization*. 3 vols. Chicago: University of Chicago Press, 1974. https://archive.org/details/TheVentureOfIslamClasicalAgeVol1MarshallHodgson (vol. 1) and https://archive.org/details/TheVentureOfIslamExpansionIn MiddleAgeVol2MarshallHodgson (vol. 2)

Holt, Frank L. *Alexander the Great and Bactria: The Formation of a Greek Frontier in Central Asia*. Leiden: Brill, 1989.

Humphrey, Caroline, and Vera Skvirskaja, eds. *Post-Cosmopolitan Cities: Explorations of Urban Coexistence*. Oxford: Berghahn Books, 2012.

Ingold, Tim. *Being Alive: Essays on Movement, Knowledge and Description*. New York: Routledge, 2011.

Kia, Mana. *The Persianate: Transregional Sensibilities of Belonging Before Nationalism*. Forthcoming.

Knauft, Bruce M., ed. *Critically Modern: Alternatives, Alterities, Anthropologies*. Bloomington: Indiana University Press, 2002.

de La Vaissière, Étienne. *Sogdian Traders: A History*. James Ward, trans. Leiden: Brill, 2005.

Leach, Edmund. *Political Systems of Highland Burma: A Study of Kachin Social Structure*. London: G. Bell & Sons, 1954.

Lefebvre, Henri. *Rhythmanalysis: Space, Time and Everyday Life*. Stuart Elden and Gerald Moore, trans. London: Continuum, 2004, https://doi.org/10.5040/9781472547385

Levi, Scott Cameron. *The Indian Diaspora in Central Asia and its Trade, 1550–1900*. Leiden: Brill, 2002.

Malkki, Liisa H. *Purity and Exile: Violence, Memory and National Cosmology Among Hutu Refugees in Tanzania*. Chicago: University of Chicago Press, 1995.

Manning, Patrick. 'Review Article. Africa and the African Diaspora: New Directions of Study'. *The Journal of African History* 44.3 (2003): 487–506, https://doi.org/10.1017/s0021853703008569

Marsden, Magnus. 'Muslim Cosmopolitans? Transnational Life in Northern Pakistan'. *The Journal of Asian Studies* 67.1 (2008): 213–47, https://doi.org/10.1017/s0021911808000077

Marsden, Magnus. *Trading Worlds: Afghan Merchants Across Modern Frontiers*. London: Hurst, 2016, https://doi.org/10.1093/acprof:oso/9780190247980.001.0001

Markovits, Claude. *The Global World of Indian Merchants, 1750–1947: Traders of Sind from Bukhara to Panama*. Cambridge: Cambridge University Press, 2000, https://doi.org/10.1017/cbo9780511497407

Meek, Ronald. *Social Science and the Ignoble Savage*. Cambridge: Cambridge University Press, 1976.

Merriman, Peter. *Driving Spaces: A Cultural-Historical Geography of England's M1 Motorway*. Oxford: Blackwell Publishing, 2007.

Mielke, Katja, and Anna-Katharina Hornidge. *Crossroads Studies: From Spatial Containers to Interactions in Differentiated Spatialities*. Bonn: Crossroads Asia Working Paper Series, No. 15, 2014, https://core.ac.uk/download/pdf/42111534.pdf

Miquel, André. *La géographie humaine du monde musulman jusqu'au milieu du XIème siècle*, 4 vols. Paris: Éditions de l'École des hautes études en sciences sociales, 1987.

Ong, Aihwa. *Flexible Citizenship: The Cultural Logics of Transnationality*. Durham, NC: Duke University Press, 1999.

Pollock, Sheldon. *The Language of the Gods in the World of Men: Sanskrit, Culture, and Power in Premodern India*. Berkeley: University of California Press, 2006.

Reeves, Madeleine. 'Politics, Cosmopolitics, and Preventive Development at the Kyrgyzstan-Uzbekistan Border'. In Nina Glick Schiller, and Andrew Irving, eds. *Whose Cosmopolitanism: Critical Perspectives, Relationalities, and Discontents*. Oxford: Berghahn Books, 2014, pp. 201–17.

Rose, Jenny. 'The Sogdians: Prime Movers between Boundaries'. *Comparative Studies of South Asia, Africa and the Middle East* 30.3 (2010): 410–19, https://doi.org/10.1215/1089201x-2010-024

Salazar, Noel. 'Towards an Anthropology of Cultural Mobilities'. *Crossings: Journal of Migration & Culture* 1.1 (2010): 53–68, https://doi.org/10.1386/cjmc.1.53_1

Salazar, Noel. 'Key Figures of Mobility: An Introduction'. *Social Anthropology* 25.1 (2017): 5–12, https://doi.org/10.1111/1469-8676.12393

Salazar, Noel B. and Nina Glick Schiller, eds. *Regimes of Mobility: Imaginaries and Relationalities of Power*. New York: Routledge, 2016.

Salazar, Noel B., Alice Elliot, and Roger Norum. 'Introduction. Studying Mobilities: Theoretical Notes and Methodological Queries'. In Elliot, Norum and Salazar, eds. *Methodologies of Mobility: Ethnography and Experiment*. New York: Berghahn, 2017, pp. 1–24.

Steinberg, Jonah. *Isma'ili Modern: Globalization and Identity in a Muslim Community*. Chapel Hill: University of North Carolina Press, 2011, https://doi.org/10.5149/9780807899458_steinberg

Street, Brian V., ed. *Cross-Cultural Approaches to Literacy*. Cambridge: Cambridge University Press, 1993.

Thornton, John. *Africa and Africans in the Making of the Atlantic World, 1400–1800.* Cambridge: Cambridge University Press, 1998.

Thum, Rian. *The Sacred Routes of Uyghur History.* Cambridge, MA: Harvard University Press, 2014, https://doi.org/10.4159/harvard.9780674736238

Urry, John. *Sociology Beyond Societies: Mobilities for the Twenty-First Century.* New York: Routledge, 2000.

Vertovec, Steven. 'Super-Diversity and its Implications'. *Ethnic and Racial Studies* 30.6 (2007): 1024–54, https://doi.org/10.1080/01419870701599465

Wennberg, Franz. *On the Edge: The Concept of Progress in Bukhara During the Rule of the Later Manghits.* Uppsala: Acta Universitatis Upsaliensis, 2014, http://www.diva-portal.org/smash/get/diva2:660812/FULLTEXT01.pdf

Werbner, Pnina. 'Global Pathways. Working Class Cosmopolitans and the Creation of Transnational Ethnic Worlds'. *Social Anthropology* 7.1 (1999): 17–35.

Werbner, Pnina. 'Vernacular Cosmopolitanism'. *Theory, Culture & Society* 23.2–3 (2006): 496–98, https://doi.org/10.1177/026327640602300291

Wilson, Samuel M., and Leighton C. Peterson. 'The Anthropology of Online Communities'. *Annual Review of Anthropology* 31.1 (2002): 449–67, https://doi.org/10.1146/annurev.anthro.31.040402.085436

Wolf, Eric R. *Europe and the People Without History.* Berkeley: University of California Press, 1982.

Introduction

Mobilities, Boundaries, and Travelling Ideas Beyond Central Asia and the Caucasus: A Translocal Perspective

Manja Stephan-Emmrich and Philipp Schröder

Translocality — a cross-cutting research perspective

Translocality, as Greiner and Sakdapolrak (2013) in their overview of the employment of the concept in the humanities have rightly pointed out, has come into vogue. Since Appadurai (1996) introduced the term in *Modernity at Large*, translocality has been widely used to depict the social and cultural representations of a globalizing world, which is shaped through the movement of people, goods, and ideas across borders. As an attempt to overcome methodological nationalism and to scrutinize the idea of culture as a closed entity, translocality has been used as a synonym for 'post-nationalism' and the 'deterritorialization' of social life. However, since then, the term has become a catchphrase in many disciplines such as geography, area studies, history, anthropology, and development studies and is used in various ways as a conceptual or descriptive tool to tackle the multiple social realities of mobility, migration, spatial connectedness, and cultural exchange across national borders. Although critical voices justifiably warn that

 https://doi.org/10.11647/OBP.0114.14

an inflationary and often unreflective use of translocality exposes the danger of turning 'trans-terminology' into 'empty signifiers' or 'catch-all phrases completely lacking any theoretical or analytical depth' (Bromber 2013:64), many studies have explored the potential of the concept to introduce new perspectives and epistemological parameters to established research traditions.

While, in migration studies, the term is often simply used as a synonym for transnationalism and thus promotes an understanding of 'trans-' processes merely as crossing nation state borders, human geographers use the term as a lens to trace how processes of migration and mobility feed into the formation of mobile, or translocal, subjectivities (Conradson and McKay 2007). Importantly, the concept emphasizes that such subjectivities emerge out of mobile actors' simultaneous situatedness both 'here' and 'there', which eventually leads to multiple belongings and different, yet changing notions of 'home' (Taylor 2013, Brickell 2011). Shifting from mobility and mobile subjectivity to practices and processes of emplacement, or placemaking, other studies have argued for a conceptualization of translocality that goes beyond merely geographical notions to include discussions about the social constructedness of place and space. Following Massey's idea of place as a setting for interaction (1993, 2006), in urban studies, for example, translocalities have been understood as places in which mobile subjects are locally grounded and where transnational ties are regulated and institutionalized. As such, urbanities are seen as significant 'stops' along people's many and diverse cross-border relations (Sinatti 2009:62–63).

Simultaneously, the translocality concept has influenced the methodological debate about mobile ethnography. Pointing to the importance of place-to-place relations, Hannerz (2013) develops an argument for a 'translocal' rather than 'multi-sited ethnography', because for him it is the conjunctions, interconnections, associations and juxtapositions among sites and places that matter most. Such an understanding of translocality has paved the way for an agency-oriented approach towards phenomena of mobility and connectedness, which helps to explore how mobile and immobile actors engage in translocal social fields, which are characterized by uneven power relations. Translocality thereby allows us to highlight the social experiences of mobile and immobile actors who negotiate and struggle over positions through the transformation of various forms of capital that are valued differently across different scales (Greiner and Sakdapolrak 2013:375), a phenomenon that has also been discussed as 'transnational habitus' (Kelly and Luis 2006).

The list of how translocality is used and conceptualized to explain cross-border mobility and other types of connectedness between places could go on. Most striking, however, is that many of these conceptualizations are discussed within the boundaries of academic disciplines instead of stimulating dialogue across them. Accordingly, most of the studies referred to so far exclusively address economic, political, or cultural processes; they discuss translocality as a matter related only to processes of twenty-first century globalization. In contrast, the groundbreaking volume *Translocality: An Approach to Connection and Transfer in Area Studies* by Freitag and von Oppen (2010) draws on sustained conversations between historians, anthropologists, linguists and area studies specialists to advocate an understanding of translocality as a cross-cutting field for researching spatial relationships from a 'Southern perspective'. With its focus on non-elitist mobile actors and the attempt to ground their movements and connections across borders in multi-scalar figurations of socio-historical entanglements in and beyond Asia, Africa, and the Middle East, their volume challenges the dominant Eurocentric historical narrative about post-/colonial modernity as a linear and monocentric process. Contributing a notion of 'alternate globalities' that predates twenty-first century globalization, the work of Freitag and von Oppen allows us to explore alternative epistemological avenues towards a new social history 'from below'. Following the idea of translocality as a cross-cutting perspective, the present volume assembles anthropological, historiographical, and sociological case studies as well as studies drawing from human geography and urban studies. Arranging them around the four main topics 'crossing boundaries', 'travelling ideas', 'economic and social movements' and finally 'pious endeavours', the volume aims to bring different disciplinary approaches into conversation with each other. The case studies employ translocality as a descriptive tool to capture practices of mobility and movement, exchange and transfer across Central Asia, the Caucasus, Eurasia, China, and the Middle East, as they have been shaped under the conditions of Soviet colonialism, post-Soviet transformations, global capitalism and cultural globalization in the region. Furthermore, the authors make use of translocality as an analytical perspective to discuss their empirical data in light of historical and ongoing processes of local and global transformation that connect concrete localities shaped by complex historical configurations, and by a wide range of social-spatial relations that non-elite actors engage in. Linking translocality with a wide range of current themes in academic writing on Central Asia and the Caucasus such as identity, ethnicity, Islam, the state, and the informal economy, this volume seeks to understand the dynamic, often competing, meanings and lived realities of these concepts beyond the epistemological normativity of spatial containers such as nation-state or area. Moreover, this volume approaches locality as a relational concept rather than a geographic or territorially bounded unit. From that angle, the contributions examine how localities are constructed and produced by social as well as spatial practices and relations; thereby addressing aspects of temporality, virtuality, materiality, and emotionality.

Although the empirical case studies assembled here speak to each other in very different ways, some more explicitly than others, this introduction highlights those findings that most strikingly reveal the benefits of a translocal perspective for studying movements, transfers, and exchanges beyond Central Asia and the Caucasus. We continue to elaborate on this in the following paragraphs, beginning with the suggestion that understanding *translocality as lived experience* can help to explore both the existential dimension of spatial movement and the uneven ways that processes of globalization are grounded in and beyond the regions under study here. With *alternative spatialisations* we critically address the pitfalls of methodological nationalism and regionalism and instead argue for alternative readings of socio-spatial configurations *beyond* Central Asia and the Caucasus. With *translocal livelihoods* we further elaborate a concept we have introduced elsewhere, and that draws on material and immaterial aspects that facilitate the processes of institutionalizing mobility (Schröder and Stephan-Emmrich 2014).

Furthermore, we invite the reader to follow the socio-spatial relations of student travellers, mobile traders, and businesspeople from Tajikistan to the Arab Emirates and Kyrgyzstan to China in order to address the epistemic limitations that arise when the lives of people from Central

Asia or the Caucasus are perceived only within a framework of post-Socialism or Soviet colonialism. Elaborating the term *transtemporalities*, we then argue that translocality as both a condition and a lived reality is always bound to both space *and* time. This volume's focus is merely on mobility in the Soviet and post-Soviet era, and that of post-Cold-War globalization. However, we are fully aware that many of the socio-spatial relations discussed herein built upon travel trajectories and spatial relations that date back to early or pre-Soviet time, and that have formed spaces of interaction and exchange across and beyond the borders of what we nowadays refer to as 'Central Asia' and 'the Caucasus' (see Nathan Light's foreword to this volume). Finally, many contributions in this book point to the *ambivalences around state borders and state policies* by tracing how transgressions of national borders and other boundaries are accompanied by processes of *translation*, during which the practitioners of translation undergo change, as do the particular localities where such translation occurs. With these clusters of themes, this volume expands the growing body of works dealing with the politics and lived realities of mobility, connectedness, and exchange in and beyond Central Asia and the Caucasus (Mostowlansky 2017, Marsden 2016, Alff and Benz 2014, Darieva 2013, among others).

Translocality as lived experience

Each of the contributions in this volume tackles translocality as a social reality, thereby illustrating different ways in which translocal practices and experiences are tied to physical or imagined localities. These grounded social realities include, for example, spiritual encounters in a Tablighi Jamaat mosque in Bishkek, informal trade practices in Georgia's borderlands, economic and cultural exchanges across the Kazakh-Chinese border, and the production of a 'new Kyrgyz history' from the desk of a private home in Kyrgyzstan. This confirms our previous observations that translocal contexts emerge from the practices and relations that mobile as well as non-mobile subjects engage in, as part of which they absorb, (re-)interpret and pass on new social, cultural, political, and religious contexts through time and space (Schröder and Stephan-Emmrich 2014). Accordingly, Mirzoev and Stephan-Emmrich in Chapter Two of this volume address the social networks of Tajik migrants in the Arab Emirates in order to show how translocality as a social reality is institutionalized, while Alff depicts in Chapter Five how circulating notions of Chinese modernity as a model of development is translated into local contexts in Kazakhstan.

In migration and mobility studies related to Central Asia and beyond, the movements of people and ideas are usually among the core topics of interest. To complement this research agenda, some contributions in the present volume explicitly consider the handling of material objects, which we here understand in a wider material and metaphorical sense (see Appadurai 1988). This includes the daily relevance of smartphones as devices to store and trigger spatial religious experiences; sacred genealogies within the wider Central Asian region, which have been preserved and transmitted orally or in writing, and nowadays are recreated and presented via the internet; printed texts on the management of water distribution systems that 'travel' from 'the West' to rural Uzbekistan; or the production and consumption of literature that contributes to new methods of Kyrgyz history-making extending as far as the United States. Beginning from such an examination of the 'social life of things' (Appadurai 1988), some chapters illustrate how translocality, as a lived experience, is articulated, represented and mediated materially, while at the same time material objects may become agents that facilitate or constrain people's spatial movement and social mobility (Svašek 2012). From such a perspective, this volume scrutinizes a wide range of themes such as the impact of nation states, transnational Muslim movements, and new media technology on mobile trajectories and identity formations, formal or informal economic activities in a post-Socialist capitalist environment, and, finally, the reproduction of social inequality through bureaucratic regimes.

Simultaneously, understanding translocality as a social reality provides insights into how actors from Central Asia and the Caucasus engage in 'multiple modernities' and various processes of globalization. With its focus on the lived experiences 'on the ground', this volume follows Ferguson (2006:23), who argues that scholars should focus discussions about the global less 'on transnational flows and images of unfettered connection than on the social relations that selectively constitute global society' (see also Jackson 2013:193). This enables the provision of 'experience-near accounts [...] of the existential aspects of migration' (Jackson 2013:194, Graw and Schielke 2013:16). At the same time, putting more emphasis on the 'everyday' allows us to follow the stratified, multi-scalar, and non-linear ways in which globalization is experienced in the regions under examination, which are somewhat obscured by the prominent notions of 'flows' or 'scapes'. Therefore, approaching translocality as an everyday experience also helps to capture the concise meanings and the particular situatedness of those political, economic, and other macro-dynamics, which have been framed as the globalization of Central Asia (Laruelle and Peyrouse 2013). The authors of this volume do so by associating local change in Central Asia and the Caucasus with larger scale phenomena such as labour migration, cross-border trade, the globalization of scholarship, and the circulation of concepts such as 'modernity', 'development' and 'Islam'. Thus, our volume picks up what Africa historian Frederic Cooper has identified as the shortcomings of globalization theory: the limits of interconnection as well the specificity of the structures that are necessary to make spatial relationships work (Cooper 2001:189–90). When tracing how movements and connections that transgress conventional borders and boundaries link to individual agency *and* the institutionalization or consolidation of cultural, political, and social structures, we respond to Freitag and von Oppen's pledge to develop a historical perspective that goes far beyond the era of the nation state and thus may embrace both transnationalism, globalization, and historical entanglements.

'Alternative spatialisations' and new epistemological avenues

The different ways in which the authors in this volume employ translocality either as a research perspective or object of research itself opens up a wide range of epistemological avenues that may challenge received methodologies or ontological assumptions about the anthropology, history, and sociology of Central Asia and the Caucasus. In Chapter Four, Elena Kim uses translocality as a lens to capture how the livelihoods of poor female landowners in rural Uzbekistan are shaped by the country's involvement in the global cotton trade. Drawing from micro-level observations of everyday negotiations, the author illustrates how poor rural households are systematically excluded from a system of community-based water management, which officially subscribes to international standards for improving social equality in Uzbekistan. For the institutional ethnographer, Kim argues, the translocality concept helps to unmask existing technologies of uneven power relations that inform institutional processes of water governance but remain mostly covert.

Svetlana Jacquesson argues that in modern historiography a translocality perspective ensures a better analytical grasp of non-elite actors who are involved in the production of a new, evidence-based ancient history of the Kyrgyz people. Tackling the intellectual endeavour of non-professional historians in Kyrgyzstan as a translocal field, Jacquesson's chapter (Chapter Six) shows that globalization can also be understood as the individual capacity to consider oneself as part of larger entities through being connected with other, previously separated places in the world and their respective histories. Thus, the author illustrates how Kyrgyz amateur historians voice their claims for agency in a world history that is still largely Eurocentric. Even more, such unexpected research outcomes may contradict the commonsensical expectations of what globalization should bring, as it invites a reflexive engagement with the researchers' sources, methods, and the ways in which academic knowledge is produced.

Obviously, a translocal perspective may help to reveal alternative spatialisations, which emerge from mobile actors' social relations and practices in and between very concrete places, and which transcend predominant academic notions of Central Asia and the Caucasus as fixed geographic or nation-/empire-bound territories. In that way, we aim to situate this volume in the field of new area studies, i.e., as a project that seeks to replace the container term 'area' with 'flexible definitions of spatial figurations, allowing for permeability and movement' without abandoning the notion of area entirely (Houben 2017:204). Similarly, van Schendel's work on *Geographies of Knowing and Ignorance* (2002:658) argues for a move away from 'trait' to 'process geography', which again opens up a new understanding of areas not as pre-given, 'static, timeless containers of historicity', but as socially constructed. In Central Asia Studies, several attempts have been made to match these claims. Canfield's (1992) idea of 'Greater Central Asia' as an extended, cross-border region or single zone, which covers the political, economic, and cultural interconnections among the population of Central Asia, China's westernmost province Xinjiang and its neighbors Afghanistan, Iran, and Pakistan, is in line with these thoughts, but still remains limited to the newly emerged geopolitical formations in the post-Cold-War era. In a more recent attempt, the inter-university Competence Network *Crossroads Asia*, which is based in Germany, has elaborated a new, promising understanding of 'area'. Accordingly, the concept of *Crossroads Asia* seeks to transcend geographic and geopolitical definitions and instead understands the region, which stretches from eastern Iran to the western parts of China and from northern Kazakhstan to the northern parts of India, as a 'multiply interconnected space'. This space emerges out of interactions, movements, and flows that cross and transcend spatial, social, and cultural boundaries (Crossroads Asia Working Group Migration 2012/2014: 1). The succeeding remarkable bulk of transdisciplinary works has initiated a wide range of new conceptual, theoretical, and epistemological perspectives that stress the importance of the local, intimate, contextual, and material forms of connectivity and the lived geographies these are entwined with (Alff and Benz 2014, Kreutzmann and Watanabe 2016). With an emphasis on the institutionalization and historical depth of cross-border relations, *Crossroads Asia*'s argument for a dynamic and permeable socio-spatial and historical configuration of exchange and connectedness takes into account the complex ways in which mobility is related to people's identities, and to political and economic situations (Marsden 2011:1–2).

Following the contributions to this volume, we can identify a wide range of such complex socio-spatial configurations, which result from cross-border networks and the related circulations of people, things and ideas, and challenge, for example, the colonial narrative of territorial boundedness. Among these configurations, for example, is the spatial Muslim concept of *dar ul-Islam*; i.e., the idea of a Muslim territory that transcends the political borders of the Southern region of the early Soviet empire and Afghanistan, and that becomes the very concrete emplacement for the rather abstract notion of the supranational community of Muslim believers, the *umma*. Exploring how religious doctrines have triggered a well-defined cross-border movement out of the Soviet empire (*hijra*), and giving colonized Muslim subjects a voice to explain their migration trajectories, Kamoludin Abdullaev's contribution to this volume presents a counter-narrative to Soviet and Western historiographies. Replacing the dominant lens of methodological Soviet nationalism with that of translocality, the author shows how colonial policies have turned cross-border mobilities of Central Asian Muslims into 'transnational migration' and thus constructed emigration from the Soviet territory as political action directed against a colonial regime. Using translocality as a descriptive tool, Abdullaev unmasks the common simplification of a complex phenomenon. Speaking implicitly to other chapters in this volume, his study helps to identify how old colonial resentments against the mobile tradition of Islam in the region continue in the negative evaluation and stigmatization of Muslim travellers in the political and public sphere in both postcolonial Uzbekistan and Tajikistan (see also Malikov and Stephan-Emmrich in Chapters Two and Nine of this volume).

Another example of how socio-spatial ties across national borders link historic and contemporary communal belonging is presented in regard to Dungan identity. Henryk Alff traces in Chapter Five how this ethnic group's positioning has been newly articulated in reference to the Eurasian land bridge between Central Asia and China, but how it is also based on the historical roots that this Chinese-speaking ethnic minority of Kazakhstan traces back to China. Examining how Dungan economic leaders successfully engage in local development through their translocal networks, Alff discusses alternative socio-spatial relations that may help to overcome established territorial notions (such as 'methodological nationalism'); binary conceptualizations of space (such as 'urban-rural' or 'centre-periphery'); and finally, perspectives that are restricted to the local 'boundedness' of resources and people.

Other authors in this volume show how spaces of cultural proximity evolve from the Soviet experience that Kyrgyz traders in Novosibirsk share with the Russian majority there (Schröder, Chapter Eight), or from the shared Persian culture that enables Tajik entrepreneurs in Dubai to integrate into established Sunni-Iranian and Afghan business networks in the Arab Emirates (Mirzoev and Stephan-Emmrich, Chapter Two). The spatial dimension of cultural proximity reminds us that encountering difference or engaging with realities of globalization in urban settings does not occur unfiltered but takes place in 'nested' contexts (see Kirmse 2011). These may consist of shared cultural or religious experiences, which allow the articulation of multiple belongings outside national frameworks (Stephan-Emmrich, and Alff, Chapter Nine and Chapter Five, respectively). But such contexts can also refer to new claims of agency, such as when rewriting world history from the Kyrgyz vantage point draws on the 'nested' framework of postcolonial nationalism (Jacquesson, Chapter Six).

At the same time, alternative spatialisations are practiced in virtual relations associated with the way mobile actors use the internet, social media, and new media technologies. Thus, carving out translocality as an intermediary concept, some contributions in this volume address how virtual spaces facilitate the articulation of multiple belongings, the emotional attachment to particular places, or an elusive homing instinct towards an ancestral home place. Working towards a translocal ethnography, Schröder asks in his 'epistemographic' notes what, in fact, research on highly mobile economic actors such as his Kyrgyz interlocutors in China and Russia 'can know'. Reflecting on his own fluid positionality as a researcher in regard to the complex situatedness of his interlocutors in different localities in Eurasia, he identifies various social and other boundaries, called 'house-rules' of fieldwork, which shape the very contours of producing anthropological knowledge in highly mobile field sites. Like Stephan-Emmrich in Chapter Nine, he argues for a stronger turn in Central Asian and Caucasus Studies towards virtual lifeworlds, in order to explore how translocality can be the result of, and part of, reality, while moving in(-between) virtual fields of economic transaction, identity and cultural consumption, belonging and home (see Ibold 2010, Kirmse 2013).

Another form of alternative spatialization is addressed in Emil Nasritdinov's anthropological study of the spiritual transformation of middle-aged Kyrgyz men, who after the chaos of the post-independence era in the 1990s became followers of the global Muslim Tablighi Jamaat movement. Discussing *hijra* as a spiritual, inner journey without spatial movement, the author links the 'trans' in translocality to a person's individual transformation towards becoming 'a better person': someone who is embedded in a complex environment of flows, folds and obstacles of space, time and society, and thus eventually changes his own notion of a very physical place, i.e., in Nasritdinov's case study, an urban neighborhood in Bishkek, Kyrgyzstan's capital city, where his main interlocutors dwell. With this focus on what Setha Low (2009) has described as 'embodied spaces', Nasritdinov offers an interesting alternative perspective on post-Soviet transition and urban change in contemporary Kyrgyzstan.

The complex realities of 'translocal livelihoods'

With our particular emphasis on how emotions, memories, and belongings produce alternative spatialisations, we have argued elsewhere for a broader understanding of livelihood as a concept that embraces both material (i.e., economic) and immaterial (i.e., social, cultural, and spiritual) concerns in order to understand how mobility and connectedness may be institutionalized (see Schröder and Stephan-Emmrich 2014:5). With such a widened focus, eventually, translocality can be apprehended and portrayed in its full complexity. A broader notion of 'translocal livelihood', for example, allows for a more open and flexible approach towards 'mobile' people's social experience and thus scrutinizes narrower understandings of migration as simply an economic practice and a relocation to 'where the money is'. Tracing how 'place', or a certain idea of it, is constructed when people (and their multiple belongings) move through space and time, some authors in this volume detect the entwinement and overlap of different modes of mobility, revealing the multifaceted reality of Muslim travel as a social and moral action (see Eickelman and Piscatori 1990) that may simultaneously encompass knowledge travel, labour migration, emigration, and pilgrimage. In this way, Stephan-Emmrich locates the emotional geographies of Tajik migrants in Dubai in the religious imagination of their ambitious piety projects. The positive or negative evaluation of the places where the migrants dwell or have dwelt before as 'good' or 'bad Muslim places' is associated with emotions, and with aspirations for accumulating new religious or other capital. Thus, both the emotional geography and religious makeup of these mobile agents trigger new forms of movement such as migration for work, pilgrimage (*hajj*) or Muslim emigration (*hijra*). Stephan-Emmrich shows, similarly to Abdullaev in Chapter One, how piety can mobilize people to migrate and provide a resource to make spatial movement and geographic place and space meaningful at the same time (see also Conermann and Smolarz 2015, Silvey 2007).

While many other contributions in this volume point to the positive effects of spatial mobility, which eventually may lead to economic, spiritual, or social success, Susanne Fehlings in her study on female petty traders in Chapter Seven emphasizes its negative effects. The socio-economic crisis in post-Soviet Georgia has produced 'marginal mobilities' that do not facilitate stories of personal achievement but became markers for poverty and lack of access to resources. Unfolding a gendered perspective on translocality, she shows how mobility can become a poor woman's way of life, and as such is indicative of stasis rather than movement and development. Furthermore, her chapter illustrates that success in trade tends to limit the women's involvement in mobile livelihoods and instead leads to immobility as a choice. Moreover, the economic success of these petty traders can replace spatial movement with a 'virtual mobility', i.e. engagement in internet-based trade.

Most of the contributions, however, make clear that translocal livelihoods facilitate both positive and negative experiences of spatial movement. Translocality thus also serves as an analytical tool with which to trace how the dialectic process of mobility and emplacement produces a wider range of ambivalences and contradictions (see also Barak Kalir's Afterword).

Finally, for some authors in this volume, translocality serves as an analytical instrument for scrutinizing the limits of the core academic concepts they work with. Fehlings argues that the mobile practices of female petty traders in Tbilisi are never clearly 'formal' or 'informal'. Tackling the 'everyday' of those mobile women for whom crossing the Georgian border is a core economic strategy, the author clarifies that petty trade practices and places are simultaneously 'formal' and 'informal', and that transgressions of the 'formal' as defined by others, i.e., the state, are gradual. Moreover, in her chapter she points out that Georgian women's trading practices and their support networks can, if institutionalized, create new structures beyond national horizons that weaken the role of the nation state and its regulation regimes. This notwithstanding, Fehlings argues that national borders and institutions still are relevant and that the petty traders have to deal with them creatively.

Ambivalent state borders

The complex social experience of translocal livelihoods becomes most obvious when the authors in this volume address the permeability or durability of social, economic, ethnic, religious, and political boundaries. Obviously, state borders and border regimes are of major concern. The state is extremely relevant to the understanding of both the dialectic process of movement and emplacement and the related spatial configurations and new identities in, beyond, and across Central Asia and the Caucasus. But we neither want to favour the practice of privileging state borders, nor do we attempt to use the nation state as a natural lens to study identity, ethnicity, or religion, as many studies on Central Asia and the Caucasus do. Our aim is thus to avoid the trap of what Kalir (2013:312) has termed a 'pervasive methodological nationalism', which would have meant approaching our research locations, interlocutors, and questions from 'stagnant paradigms' that we would have carried with us even when 'travelling with' the mobile subjects of our studies. Instead, we stress in this introduction that a translocal perspective may help us to look at political systems of mobility through the eyes of those directly involved in them. In other words, it may encourage us to consider how non-elite mobile actors perceive, assess, and experience the role of states, and cause us to scrutinize the contexts in which national belonging becomes an important matter. This accords with Reeves' recent argument for a spatial-relational approach to state borders, which puts emphasis on how the state, through situated practices of border work, is temporarily and contextually done, undone, invoked or ignored (2014:12–13). Tracing how borders in the Kyrgyzstani part of the Ferghana Valley appear, disappear, and materialize at certain times, Reeves unmasks academic representations of the state as a static, empty container or elusive agent. The author thus takes the approach of other recent anthropological studies that consider 'the state' as constructed by discourses and everyday practices in unruly and contradictory ways (Sökefeld 2016). Moreover, she scrutinizes the impact of the colonial or post-colonial state on mobility and spatial relations in its full complexity as dynamic and relational. Accordingly, some contributions to this volume reveal a striking ambivalence in the effects of Soviet or post-Soviet border policies in Central Asia and the Caucasus. On the one hand, state actors and policies continue to have a strong impact in regulating and hampering cross-border mobility. On the other hand, these policies trigger mobility, and they are involved in shaping mobile experiences and new identities outside state-led definitions to a striking extent. In early Soviet Central Asia, colonial border policies created obvious interruptions in the everyday mobility of people in the region. But simultaneously, as Abdullaev illustrates in Chapter One, they have triggered new forms of movement such as Muslim emigration (*hijra*). Moreover, looking through the lens of translocality, the author shows that spatial movement was only one response to Russian colonialization. In contrast, the emerging Basmachi movement mobilized religion-based resistance among those Muslims who stayed in the Soviet empire's territory. Accordingly, the Russian colonialization of Central Asia is presented by Abdullaev as a project that triggered diverse cross-border movements (Dagyeli 2014, Abdullaev 2009).

Alff develops a similar argument in Chapter Five. But he suggests that the Soviet Union's breakdown has created an ambivalent context for both the mobility and immobility of borderland communities such as the Dungans, whose settlements criss-cross the Kazakh-Chinese border. Kazakhstan's post-Socialist nationalism accelerated the reconsolidation of the then-permeable national border in the early years after independence. The resulting disconnectedness and limited mobility of Dungans and other Central Asians in the region fulfilled a core undertaking of Soviet political control and consequently hampered cross-border trade with neighboring Central Asian countries (see also Kosmarski 2011). Simultaneously, the relaxation of travel and foreign trade regulations opened up new avenues of mobility for Dungans in Kazakhstan, in particular to China. Dungans recognized this early on and became pioneers of an innovative cross-border business that in the meantime has facilitated the exchange of construction technology and agricultural innovation with China, as well as innovations in ethnic tourism and international education, thereby paving the way for the further entangling of cultural-economic ties between these two countries.

The virtual articulation of belonging that is addressed in certain contributions to this volume can be identified as a highly ambivalent practice as well. Often, the internet serves as a new translocal identity space, which may help to overcome state restrictions (Ibold 2010, Mcglinchey and Johnson 2007). However, Philipp Schröder clarifies in Chapter Eight that the ethno-national orientation of the younger generation of Kyrgyz in Novosibirsk is expressed through a virtual homing instinct, which connects youth to an ancestral homeland and thus essentializes features such as shame to be 'typically Kyrgyz' while interlocutors are far from their ancestral homeland.

The ambivalence of nation-state projects in the post-Soviet area and beyond reveals that state borders and other boundaries may be temporary as well as permeable. This elucidates how the transgression and penetration of state territory, or of other social or cultural spaces, happens according to different degrees. It is essential to scrutinize how, when and why state borders and boundaries matter to our interlocutors' mobile and spatial experiences, and scaling turns out to be a helpful methodological instrument in order to make visible the various existing boundaries within the flows, circulations, and cross-border movements of people, things, and ideas. This allows for a restructuring and rescaling of spatial arrangements to further an understanding, for example, of how local transformations speak to global processes. Translocality as a research perspective underlines that our global world is not borderless, but that territories, pathways, and places still matter since they are both constituted by, and result from, very concrete social processes. Following anthropologist and geographer Neil Smith (2010:31), scaling provides 'a metric for drawing social, political and economic boundaries in the landscape' (cited in Houben 2017:199–200). This becomes strikingly obvious in Elena Kim's analysis of the powerful technologies of state bureaucracy, which materialize in the need to possess a stamp in order to be granted access to regulation patterns of water flowing through the plough land of dispossessed rural Uzbek households.

Scrutinizing how state regimes may mobilize or restrict people's movement and mobility, a translocality approach may also help to illuminate how the state itself is embedded in, and formed by global assemblages, or how globalization occurs *through* the state (Heathershaw 2011:148, Adams 2010).

Transtemporalities

As result of the mobilities paradigm and the spatial turn, an increasing body of literature in the humanities deals with aspects of mobility and cross-border connectivity. In this way, the humanities have shifted from producing modernist narratives of linearity and history to investigating how the complex realities of social relations and practices in a globalized world are related to space and spatial figurations. Many of this volume's contributions, while addressing the negotiations of socio-spatial practices between and within places as they are subject to the agency of certain actors' strategies and choices, demonstrate that peoples' lives are highly relational and contextual in regard to their situatedness in both space *and* time. While the concept of translocality is overwhelmingly used to depict processes of circulation or transfer as well as spatial configurations across borders, time is often neglected as a crucial category for observation. Many of the contributions in this volume instead illustrate in various ways how time matters. More precisely, they show how the translocal spaces, identities and transformations of the people and places under study are embedded in distinct time-to-time relations and temporalities. Accordingly, this volume argues for an understanding of time as an integral part of translocality. For example, the sacred genealogies preserved by *khoja* families during the Soviet era (Malikov, Chapter Three), or the photographs that Muslim travellers store in their smartphones (Stephan-Emmrich, Chapter Nine), freeze time and fixate 'transtemporalities', i.e., movements that cross and connect times on different, yet 'jumping scales'. Insofar as the translocal realities of the mobile and immobile actors described in the contributions to this volume cut across mythical or ancient times, the period of Soviet colonialism, and the post-Soviet transformation period, they also embrace subjective times of memory, dream, and illusion. The nationalist attitude of new Kyrgyz historians, as discussed by Jacquesson (Chapter Six), relies heavily on a 'transtemporal' imagination that stretches from the very local to the very global arena. This imagination implies the capacity to relate to abstract ancestors far distant in time, of whom no or few material traces remain. This includes multi-scalar references to ancient empires, historical events, and places in Europe, America, and China. Therefore, by claiming that Kyrgyz warriors reached as far as Europe and have left their imprint there, such as in the architectural symbolism of Berlin's Brandenburger Tor, these non-elite knowledge brokers make sense of Kyrgyz identity in world history and advocate for their nation's core role in shaping it.

Other chapters in the volume, by contrast, approach transtemporality through memory and a nostalgic attachment to geographic sites, and examine them as constitutive markers of translocal connectivity and multiple belongings. The memories, as well as possible future lives associated with 'far off, ideal Muslim places', which the Tajik student migrants in Stephan-Emmrich's chapter imagine or dream of, constitute a major resource for articulating emotional geographies that span places of previous residence in Tajikistan and the Middle East, across political, social, and cultural boundaries. Stephan-Emmrich reveals that the conditions of the post-Socialist transformation in Tajikistan produce very individual temporal narratives of progress and development. This is in line with Jackson's observation that everyday lives 'do not unfold in straight lines and that there are many temporalities in history and subject times such as the reverie of dream, memory or crisis' (Jackson 2013:198). These subject times are often obscured by cause-and-effect models of linearity and history, but they can, as we argue here, be rediscovered through the lens of a translocality-cum-transtemporality approach.

While the Tajik student travellers through their nostalgic renderings of the past preserve a sense of locality and thus articulate their desire for 'belonging somewhere else', young members of the Kyrgyz diaspora in Novosibirsk base their transtemporal imagination on notions of an ancestral 'homeland' (Schröder, Chapter Eight). Representing a 'home away from home' (Smith 2011:195), the internet serves these youths as a virtual vehicle to mobilize an elusive 'homing desire' (Brah 1996) towards an ethno-national territory rarely visited in person. Schröder's contribution thus shows that such a form of nostalgic attachment is not merely an expression of regret for the passing of a joyful or glorious past. In contrast, he locates the agency of the second generation of young Kyrgyz in Novosibirsk in making sense of their families' mobile (trader) biographies. Kyrgyz youth in Novosibirsk thus translate the nostalgia of their parents' generation into new translocal identities, which embrace both a rather essentialized notion of 'Kyrgyzness' and a claim to belong to Russia.

Such a patriotic commitment is quite in line with the 'globalizing ethno-nationalism' of Jacquessons's Kyrgyz amateur historians. Connecting Kyrgyz history with places and people outside Kyrgyzstan, the writings of these alternative historians can be seen as the result of an intellectual practice of 'placemaking in the world', which feeds a nostalgia that enables the readership to connect to their ancestors and claim the Kyrgyz people's participation in ancient civilizations and powerful past empires.

Following another reading of 'transtemporality', some chapters in this volume demonstrate that translocality and its related transformations are possible without spatial movement at all, but with movement through time. Emil Nasritdinov, in Chapter Ten, traces the biography of a place. Providing an ethnography of the actual transformations of an urban neighborhood's spatial properties and its associated meanings, Nasritdinov, by adopting Deleuze's concept of the fold, argues for a new approach towards socio-spatial relations that enables the depiction of the ongoing, complex, and multi-directional becoming of a post-Soviet urban place through different time periods. He therefore shows that locality is not only a spatial but also temporal category (Freitag and von Oppen 2010:10). The religious transformation of members of the *Botanika* neighborhood in Bishkek reflects very local politics of 'placemaking'. These local politics materialize through the construction of a mosque, which becomes the social and religious centre of the newly established local branch of the global Tablighi Jamaat community. This religious appropriation of urban spaces transforms the identity of a particular place from a Soviet youth and post-Soviet adult space into a new, translocal space of religious belonging that serves the spiritual demands of the now grown-up residents, and also allows for individual readings of modernity, progress, and development. However, and going beyond Nasritdinov's ethnographic case study, the new religious identity of some *Botanika* residents may at the same time create a sense of local displacement among those who remained in the neighborhood after its transformation (Smith 2011:195), but did not become pious members of that novel mosque community.

Both Stephan-Emmrich's and Nasritdinov's contributions can be read as two different examples of a spatial biography, which evidences how the transformation of place, or at least the transforming notion of a place and its spatial properties, can coincide with the personal transformation of residents through time; i.e., during an individual life-course. Tracing the religious becoming of both mobile Tajik students and a single urban neighborhood in Kyrgyzstan's capital through 'spatial narratives', both chapters also unfold how the personal memories of both the ethnographer and his or her research partners are embedded in and bonded to place (Casey 1987). Simultaneously, such spatial narratives are comprehensible as both border-transgressing and border-generating spaces of Muslim encounter, experience, and identification.

Besides biography, a transgenerational perspective might help to trace the transformation of a particular place through time. Comparing the relatively short-term development of the Tajik Dubai business since the early 2000s with that of a Kyrgyz (traders') diaspora in Novosibirsk, which was established in the early 1990s and covers a number of trading generations (Schröder, Chapter Eight), a transtemporal approach may clarify that transformations of people and places happen at different speeds and with different scales of volatility or sustainability. While well-established Kyrgyz trader networks led to the institutionalization of cross-border mobility between Kyrgyzstan and Russia, and finally the establishment of a 'vibrant' ethnic community abroad, the more recent history of the Tajik Dubai business has not yet established a similarly sustainable socio-cultural environment away from home. In contrast, precarious working conditions in Dubai have increased with the new generation of migrant workers, stimulating the search for new destinations.

Translocality and translation

Mobility across space and time induces various forms and processes of translation. Dealing with a wide range of boundaries (political, linguistic, cultural, religious, ethnic), some of the translocal actors examined in this volume take the roles of translators who quite literally 'carry across' embodied and materialized meanings, values, skills, and ideas from one context into another. In these ways, they introduce 'newness' into the localities to which they come to dwell while usually staying connected to their 'original homes'. Drawing on the etymological meaning of the Latin term translation as 'movement', 'disruption', or 'displacement', the term is used here to capture the cultural practices of transfer that occur in the various translocal contexts explored in this volume. We thereby follow an anthropological reading of translation as a process of transporting specific understandings of reality across boundaries of time, place, and culture (Tambiah 1985). So far, this reading is in line with how translation is depicted in area studies, i.e. as a process that involves practices of 'shifting into a different system of meaning' (Houben 2017:206). Translation in these terms becomes apparent for example in the writings of Kyrgyz amateur historians that transgress a wide range of boundaries: linguistically through the translation of core texts into or from English, as well as metaphorically in the sense that a non-academic work is based on scholarly methods of handling sources to produce alternative readings of a 'global ethnogenesis' of the Kyrgyz nation. Thus, Kyrgyz historians transfer and translate different knowledge repertoires from one context into another, i.e., from academic to lay readership, and from Western to (post-)Soviet epistemologies.

According to the chapters by Abdullaev, Schröder, Mirzoev, and Stephan-Emmrich, which address experiences of labour migration and forced mobility within and beyond places and regions in Central Asia and the Caucasus, processes of translation are best understood as the repositioning of 'a foreign interpretative horizon into a new locale' that causes various interactions resulting from encounters between different interpretative horizons (Conway 2012:270). This observation agrees with that of Longinovic (2002:6–7), that mobile people come to understand their identities through their displacement and the experience of being different. Mobile experiences therefore open up a horizon for a new performance of cultural or other identities, while translation can make a journey or a mobile livelihood project seem meaningful and stimulate processes of reworking national, religious, and other identities (Schlehe and Lücking 2016). At the same time, agents who translate can operate outside of prevailing cultural and political logic, as Homi Bhabha (1994) has suggested with his concept of a *third space*. Such a reading, for example, invites consideration of the material, and in particular visual, displays of a flexible and new Muslim identity among Tajiks in Dubai as a means of political intervention that interrupts hegemonic narratives of national identity (Buden and Novotny 2009). Also, Tajiks' heightened mobility within competing religious traditions can be understood as a challenge to the narrow state-led official version of a homegrown and national Tajik Islam, which excludes and stigmatizes the new Muslim piety of student travellers as 'foreign', 'imported' and therefore 'dangerous' (Stephan 2006).

With an emphasis on the agency of translocal actors who rework identities and belongings, the practice of translation also involves the individual's capacity to deal with change, difference, strangeness, and the ambivalent experience of coping with the prevalent distinctions between 'here' and 'there'. This can simultaneously produce openings and closures, possibilities and constraints, joys and sorrows, as some of the chapters in this volume show. However, cultural translations are above all a prerequisite for successful translocal livelihoods. As some chapters reveal, migrants transfer knowledge, ideas, language skills, and forms of multiple belonging into various translocal economic strategies, which are elsewhere described as integral aspects of a migrant's 'transnational habitus' (Kelly and Lusis 2006). Schröder in Chapter Eight, for example, illustrates how border transgressions happen via internet-based business practices in China. According to Azamat, an interlocutor of Schroeder, Mandarin language skills and knowledge of local search engines are key resources for the first generation of Kyrgyz businessmen to navigate China's state-censored virtual landscapes. By definition, in his profession as a middleman who facilitates business-deals between Chinese manufacturers and his various Russian-speaking clients from Central Asia, the Caucasus or Russia, Azamat's primary task and skill is translating. This translation work, if successful, bridges multiple gaps between borders, languages, and forms of knowledge.

The role of language as a crucial resource for translation is also stressed in Mirzoev and Stephan-Emmrich's study on the Tajik Dubai business. By way of their 'polyglotism', Tajiks in Dubai are able to attach themselves to multiple business networks and translate their cultural, symbolic, and spatial capital into different economic contexts. In their capacities as middlemen they engage with other Muslims across cultural differences (Arabs, Iranians, Afghans), different business sectors (trade, tourism), and different markets at 'home' and among their counterparts in the Middle East and Eurasia.

Translation abilities also form a crucial part of the Dungans' cross-border group identity. According to Alff in Chapter Five, Dungans in Kazakhstan position themselves as intermediaries between Kazakhstan and China as part of the transfer of models of economic development, and they thus make sense of their cross-border group existence in between these two countries. The Dungans' particular socio-spatial situatedness as middlemen entails their translating knowledge, skills, and ideas of social change. At the same time, their role as brokers informs and is produced by the Dungan sense of multiple belonging and cultural embeddedness in both the Chinese and Kazakh contexts. Ultimately, the mediating role of Dungans is articulated in their self-representations, which are performed in relation to state-led official discourses, which both in China and Kazakhstan have been focusing on building a 'modern Silk Road' or 'Eurasian land bridge'.

Processes of translation are also closely entwined with practices of placemaking. Carrying across language skills, cultural knowledge, religious values and patterns of identification, the Tajiks and Uzbeks who were forced by the Soviet colonizers to leave their places of origin have appropriated distant places in neighboring Afghanistan (Abdullaev, Chapter One). Appropriating these destinations as their new home, Muslim migrants from Central Asia became agents of change, while at the same time they underwent change themselves when they became Afghan citizens.

With a focus, for example, on the introduction of new agricultural technologies to the Tajiks' and Uzbeks' places of resettlement in Afghanistan, on the successful transcultural business of Tajik migrant workers in Dubai, or on young and dynamic Kyrgyz entrepreneurs in China, particular chapters of this volume emphasize the positive outcomes of translocal mobility. Translation thus may turn out to be the capability to cope with uncertainty, difference, and diversity in places far away from home. Accordingly, migration opens up opportunities to accumulate and transform different forms of capital and thus translate skills, meanings, values, and other mobile properties into economic, spiritual, or social progress. In this regard, the digital conversations that Stephan-Emmrich (Chapter Nine) had with Tajik student travellers in the Arab Emirates illustrate how her research partners mediate their spiritual progress (a heightened mobility across divergent Islamic traditions) through the publicly performed usage of smartphone apps and digital photo albums, i.e., through prestigious consumer goods that simultaneously demonstrate the economic success of their translocal livelihoods. Obviously, the benefit of the translation concept for the volume is that it serves as a suitable prism to enable us to bring into focus the agency of people who act or think translocally and discuss how these people find room to manoeuvre and address those issues they consider most salient (Kathiravelu 2016:97).

However, the mobile agents examined here are also constrained in their ability to transfer knowledge, ideas and meanings from one context into another. Depending on a variety of social, political, and historical circumstances, they thus 'operate within a bounded horizon of possible choices' (Conway 2012:277, see also Vertovec 2010:9). Relying on a 'shared Sunni-Persian tradition', the careers of male Tajiks in Dubai depend upon good relations with Afghan traders and businessmen from Baluchistan. Whilst this facilitates translocal spaces of cultural and religious proximity within which the Tajiks of Dubai easily move and pursue their economic projects, access to Emirati citizens, Arab residents, and members of the long-established Iranian diaspora in Dubai seems almost impossible. Consequently, their business networks create an 'institutional coziness' (Finke 2014) that enables and filters but also limits the ways in which Tajiks in Dubai experience what they describe as belonging to the 'global' *umma*. But can border-transgressing movements occur without translation? Following the spatial movements of petty traders and various border regions in Georgia, Susanne Fehlings (Chapter Seven) points out that although the women's precarious mobile livelihoods are embedded in multi-scalar and spatial connectivities and flows between the Caucasus region and places in Turkey, Russia, and China, their translocal experiences are nevertheless limited to specific, and often small-scale, spaces of interaction. Being confined to the realms of household or local market might not, then, foster economic success and may prove detrimental for individual social mobility. The marginal mobility of her research partners therefore does not entail processes and practices of significant cross-context translation and in consequence does not facilitate the emergence of new translocal identities.

Even more, Elena Kim's chapter (Chapter Four) impressively shows what may happen when translation processes fail or become interrupted by powerful state interventions. Tracing the everyday governance of water resources in rural Uzbekistan through water union associations (WUA), her contribution depicts how well-intended local managerial work, which aims at implementing the global and efficient technologies of corporate capitalism, ultimately becomes counterproductive and instead entrenches social injustice and produces highly precarious rural livelihoods that depend on the labour migration of male family members. Receiving a stamp to signal legal WUA membership turns into an unachievable prerequisite for many poor farmers as the state limits far-reaching access to scarce water resources in order to purse its own monoculture cotton-cultivation projects. A legacy from the Soviet era, cotton cultivation is among the few ways the Uzbek state can gain a foothold in the global economy. Translation, therefore, turns out to be the process of 'localizing' globalized ideas of equality, democracy, and development into the specific framework of Uzbekistan's agrarian sector. Using translocality as an analytical lens, Kim uncovers the state's weakness or unwillingness to mediate between institutionalized forms of equality and development management 'from outside' and the internal needs of farmers. Although the latter were the intended beneficiaries of the water management programs, the farmers are hampered by bureaucratic obstacles to participation in the state-led project of cotton cultivation.

Finally, this introduction and the contributions assembled in this volume allow us to understand translation as an observable practice through which mobile and immobile actors can deal with the permeability of state borders and other boundaries; they can negotiate the uncertainties, limitations, and opportunities of their 'translocal livelihoods', which are structured by various mobility regimes, and they can connect and give meaning to different places through time and space as part of emergent 'alternative spatialisations' or 'transtemporalities' beyond conventional academic and other containers. The examination of the processes of cultural translation thus may help us to break down abstract concepts, such as translocality itself, into observable patterns and contextualize these empirically within specific local-to-local relations (see Ferguson 2011). Accordingly, and as the following contributions will exemplify, translocality is a condition as much as a process, which simultaneously gives shape to and is shaped by the lived experiences of migrants, refugees, mobile traders, Muslim travellers, and amateur historians. At the same time, the complex ways mobility, movement, connectedness, and transfer are negotiated by people from Central Asia and the Caucasus requires us to consider both the opportunities and restraints that promote or hamper cultural translations. This reveals the relational character of translocality and should allow us to avoid 'the teleological trap' of 'using the concept as a normative category' (Bromber 2013:65) that emphasizes either the positive outcomes *or* the political and other constraints of migration, cross-border trade, global scholarship, and student travel.

References

Abdullaev, Kamoludin. *Ot Sintsyanya do Khorasana. Iz istorii sredneaziatskoy emmigratsii 20 veka* [From Xinjiang to Khurasan. From the History of the Twentieth-Century Central Asian Emigration]. Dushanbe: Irfon, 2009.

Adams, Laura. *The Spectacular State. Culture and National Identity in Uzbekistan.* Durham, N.C.: Duke University Press, 2010, https://doi.org/10.1215/9780822392538

Alff, Henryk, and Andreas Benz, eds. *Tracing Connections: Explorations of Spaces and Places in Asian Contexts.* Berlin: Wissenschaftlicher Verlag, 2014.

Appadurai, Arjun. *Modernity at Large: Cultural Dimensions of Globalization.* Minneapolis: University of Minnesota, 1996.

Appadurai, Arjun, ed. *The Social Life of Things: Commodities in Cultural Perspective.* Cambridge: Cambridge University Press, 1988.

Benz, Andreas. 'Positionality at the Crossroads. Gendered Lifeworlds, Social Situatedness and the Relational Production of Place in the Context of Student Migration to Gilgit, Pakistan'. 4th Crossroads Asia Conference, 'Crossroads Studies: Mobilities, Immobilities and the Issue of Positionality for Rethinking Area Studies', University of Bonn, 28 November 2014.

Bhabha, Homi. *The Location of Culture.* New York: Routledge, 1994.

Brah, Avtar. *Cartographies of Diaspora: Contesting Identities.* London: Routledge, 1996.

Brickell, Katherine. 'Translocal Geographies of "Home" in Siem Reap, Cambodia'. In Katherine Brickell and Ayona Datta, eds. *Translocal Geographies: Spaces, Places, Connections.* Burlington: Ashgate, 2011, pp. 28–38.

Bromber, Katrin. 'Working With "Translocality": Conceptual Implications and Analytical Consequences'. In Steffen Wippel, ed. *Regionalizing Oman: Political, Economic and Social Dynamics.* Dordrecht: Springer, 2013, pp. 63–72, https://doi.org/10.1007/978-94-007-6821-5_4

Buden, Boris, and Stefan Novotny. 'Cultural Translation: An Introduction to the Problem'. *Translation Studies* 2.2 (2009): 196–208, https://doi.org/10.1080/14781700902937730

Canfield, Robert. 'Restructuring in Greater Central Asia: Changing Political Configurations'. *Asian Survey* 32.10 (1992): 875–87, https://doi.org/10.2307/2645046

Casey, Edward. *Remembering. A Phenomenological Study.* Bloomington: Indiana University Press, 1987.

Conermann, Stephan, and Elena Smolarz. *Mobilizing Religion: Networks and Mobility.* Bonner Asienstudien 12. Berlin: ebv-Verlag, 2015.

Conradson, David, and Deirdre McKay. 'Translocal Subjectivities: Mobility, Connection, Emotion'. *Mobilities* 2.2 (2007), 167–74, https://doi.org/10.1080/17450100701381524

Conway, Kyle. 'A Conceptual and Empirical Approach to Cultural Translation'. *Translation Studies* 5.3 (2012), 264–79, https://doi.org/10.1080/14781700.2012.701938

Cooper, Frederick. 'What is the Concept of Globalization Good For? An African Historian's Perspective'. *African Affairs* 100.399 (2001): 189–213, https://doi.org/10.1093/afraf/100.399.189

Crossroads Asia Working Group Migration (2012/2014), 'Crossroads Asia Through the Lens of Mobility and Migration: A Conceptual Approach (with Postscript)'. Crossroads Asia Concept Paper Series, No. 3, Bonn.

Dagyeli, Jeanine. 'Shifting Grounds: Trans-Border Migration and East Bukharan Local Identity in the Secondary City of Kulob'. Crossroads Asia Workshop, 'Transregional Crossroads of Social Interaction', Leibniz-Zentrum Moderner Orient, 21 March 2014.

Darieva, Tsypylma. 'Homeland Tourism, Long-Distance Nationalism and Production of a New Diasporic Identity (Armenian Case)'. *Journal of Intercultural Research Center*, Kobe University Press, 2013, 36–53, http://web.cla.kobe-u.ac.jp/group/IReC/pdf/2012_darieva.pdf

Eickelman, Dale, and James Piscatori. *Muslim Travellers: Pilgrimage, Migration, and the Religious Imagination*. Berkeley: University of California Press, 1990.

Ferguson, James. 'Novelty and Method. Reflections on Global Fieldwork'. In Simon Coleman and Pauline von Hellermann, eds. *Multi-Sited Ethnography. Problems and Possibilities in the Translocation of Research Methods*. New York: Routledge, 2011, pp. 197–207.

Ferguson, James. *Global Shadows: Africa in the Neoliberal World Order*. Durham: Duke University Press, 2006.

Finke, Peter. 'Historical Homelands and Transnational Ties: The Case of the Mongolian Kazaks'. *Zeitschrift für Ethnologie* 138.2 (2013): 175–94.

Freitag, Ulrike, and Achim von Oppen. 'Introduction: "Translocality": An Approach to Connection and Transfer in Area Studies'. In Ulrike Freitag and Achim von Oppen, eds. *Translocality: The Study of Globalising Processes from a Southern Perspective*. Leiden: Brill, 2010, pp. 1–24, https://doi.org/10.1163/ej.9789004181168.i-452.8

Graw, Knut, and Samuli Schielke. 'Introduction: Reflections on Migratory Expectations in Africa and Beyond'. In Knut Graw and Samuli Schielke, eds. *The Global Horizon: Expectations of Migration in Africa and the Middle East*. Leuven: Leuven University Press, 2012, pp. 7–22.

Greiner, Clemens, and Patrick Sakdapolrak. 'Translocality: Concepts, Applications and Emerging Research Perspectives'. *Geography Compass* 7.5 (2013): 373–84, https://doi.org/10.1111/gec3.12048

Hannerz, Ulf. 'Being There… and There… and There! Reflections on Multi-Site Ethnography'. In Antonius Robben and Jeffrey Sluka, eds. *Ethnographic Fieldwork. An Anthropological Reader*. Malden: Wiley-Blackwell, 2012, pp. 399–408.

Heathershaw, John. 'Tajikistan Amidst Globalization: State Failure or State Transformation?' *Central Asian Survey* 30.1 (2011): 147–68, https://doi.org/10.1080/02634937.2011.554070

Houben, Vincent. 'New Area Studies, Translation and Mid-Range Concepts'. In Katja Mielke and Anna-Katharina Hornidge, eds. *Area Studies at the Crossroads. Knowledge Production after the Mobility Turn*. Basingstoke: Palgrave Macmillan, 2017, pp. 195–211, https://doi.org/10.1057/978-1-137-59834-9_11

Houben, Vincent. 'The New Area Studies and Southeast Asian History'. DORISEA Working Papers No. 4 (2013): 1–10.

Ibold, Hans. 'Disjuncture 2.0: Youth, Internet Use and Cultural Identity in Bishkek'. *Central Asian Survey* 29.4 Special Issue Stefan Kirmse, ed. Youth in the Former Soviet South: Everyday Lives Between Experimentation and Regulation (2010): 521–35, https://doi.org/10.1080/02634937.2010.537135

Jackson, Michael. 'Afterword'. In Knut Graw and Samuli Schielke, eds. *The Global Horizon: Expectations of Migration in Africa and the Middle East*. Leuven: Leuven University Press, 2012, pp. 193–99.

Kalir, Barak. 'Moving Subjects, Stagnant Paradigms: Can the "Mobilities Paradigm" Transcend Methodological Nationalism?' *Journal of Ethnic and Migration Studies* 39.2 (2012): 311–27, https://doi.org/10.1080/1369183X.2013.723260

Kathiravelu, Laavanya. *Migrant Dubai. Low Wage Workers and the Construction of a Global City*. Basingstoke: Palgrave Macmillan, 2016, https://doi.org/10.1057/9781137450180

Kelly, Philip, and Tom Lusis. 'Migration and the Transnational Habitus: Evidence from Canada and the Philippines'. *Environment and Planning A: Economy and Space* 38.5 (2006): 831–47, https://doi.org/10.1068/a37214

Kirmse, Stefan. *Youth and Globalization in Central Asia. Everyday Life between Religion, Media, and International Donors*. Frankfurt: Campus Verlag, 2013.

Kirmse, Stefan. '"Nested Globalization" in Osh, Kyrgyzstan: Urban Youth Culture in a "Southern" City'. In Tsypylma Darieva, Wolfgang Kaschuba and Melanie Krebs, eds. *Urban Spaces after Socialism. Ethnographies of Public Places in Eurasian Cities*. Frankfurt: Campus Verlag, 2012, pp. 283–306.

Kosmarski, Artem. 'Grandeur and Decay of the "Soviet Byzantium": Spaces, Peoples and Memories of Tashkent, Uzbekistan'. In Tsypylma Darieva, Wolfgang Kaschuba and Melanie Krebs, eds. *Urban Spaces after Socialism. Ethnographies of Public Places in Eurasian Cities.* Frankfurt: Campus Verlag, 2012, pp. 33–56.

Kreutzmann, Hermann, and Teiji Watanabe. *Mapping Transition in the Pamirs. Changing Human-Environmental Landscapes.* Springer, 2016, https://doi. org/10.1007/978-3-319-23198-3

Laruelle, Marlène, and Sébastien Peyrouse. *Globalizing Central Asia. Geopolitics and Changing Economic Development.* Armonk: M. E. Sharpe, 2013.

Longinovic, Tomislav. 'Fearful Asymmetries: A Manifesto of Cultural Translation'. *Journal of the Midwest Modern Language Association* 35.2 (2002): 5–12, https://doi.org/10.2307/1315162

Low, Setha. 'Towards an Anthropological Theory of Space and Place'. *Semiotica* 2009.175 (2009): 21–37, https://doi.org/10.1515/semi.2009.041

Marsden, Magnus. *Trading Worlds. Afghan Merchants Across Modern Frontiers.* London: Hurst & Co. Publishers, 2016, https://doi.org/10.1093/acprof:o so/9780190247980.001.0001

Marsden, Magnus. 'Mobile Lives on the Frontiers of Crossroads Asia'. *Crossroads Asia Working Paper Series* 1 (2011): 1–13.

Massey, Doreen. 'A Global Sense of Place'. *Marxism Today* 38 (1991): 24–29.

Massey, Doreen. 'Power-Geometry and a Progressive Sense of Place'. In John Bird, Barry Curtis, Tim Putnam, George Robertson, and Lisa Tickner, eds. *Mapping the Futures: Local Cultures, Global Change.* London: Routledge, 1993, pp. 59–69.

Massey, Doreen. 'The Geographical Mind'. In David Balderstone, eds. *The Secondary Geography Handbook.* Sheffield: Geographical Association, 2006, pp. 46–51.

McGlinchey, Eric, and Erica Johnson. 'Aiding the Internet in Central Asia'. *Democratization* 14.2 (2007): 273–88, https://doi.org/10.1080/ 13510340701245785

Mostowlansky, Till. *Azan on the Moon. Entangling Modernity along Tajikistan's Pamir Highway.* University of Pittsburgh Press, 2017, https://doi.org/10.2307/j. ctt1pk85xv

Reeves, Madeleine. *Border Work. Spatial Lives of the State in Rural Central Asia.* Ithaca: Cornell University Press, 2014.

Schlehe, Judith, and Mirjam Lücking. 'Academic and Religious Pilgrimages from Indonesia to the Middle East'. Paper presented at the 'Trans-L-Encounters, Religious Education and Islamic Popular Culture in Asia and the Middle East', Conference, Philipps-Universität Marburg, 26–28 May 2016.

Schröder, Philipp, and Manja Stephan-Emmrich. 'The Institutionalization of Mobility: Wellbeing and Social Hierarchies in Central Asian Translocal Livelihoods'. *Mobilities* 11.3 (2014): 1–24, https://doi.org/10.1080/17450101.2014.984939

Silvey, Rachel. 'Mobilizing Piety: Gendered Morality and Indonesian-Saudi Transnational Migration'. *Mobilities* 2.2 (2007): 219–29, https://doi.org/10.1080/17450100701381565

Sinatti, Guilia. 'The Making of Urban Translocalities: Senegalese Migrants in Dakar and Zingonia'. In Michael Smith and John Eade, eds. *Transnational Ties. Cities, Migration and Identities*. New Brunswick: Transaction Publishers, 2008, pp. 61–76.

Smith, Michael. 'Translocality: A Critical Reflection'. In Katherine Brickell and Ayona Datta, eds. *Translocal Geographies: Spaces, Places, Connections*. Burlington: Ashgate, 2011, pp. 181–89.

Smith, Neil. 'Remapping Area Knowledge. Beyond Glocal/Local'. In Terence Wesley-Smith and Jon Gross, eds. *Remaking Area Studies: Teaching and Learning Across Asia and the Pacific*. Honolulu: University of Hawai'i Press, 2010, pp. 24–40, https://doi.org/10.21313/hawaii/9780824833213.003.0002

Sökefeld, Martin. 'Crossroads Studies and the State: Anthropological Perspectives'. In Evelin Dürr, Frank Heidemann, Thomas Reinhardt, and Martin Sökefeld, eds. Working Papers in Social and Cultural Anthropology Vol. 20. Munich: Ludwig-Maximilians-Universität München, 2016, pp. 1–16.

Svašek, Maruška. 'Introduction. Affective Moves: Transit, Transition and Transformations'. In Maruška Svašek (ed.) *Moving Subjects, Moving Objects. Transnationalism, Cultural Production and Emotions*. New York: Berghahn, 2012, pp. 1–40.

Tambiah, Stanley. *Culture, Thought and Social Action. An Anthropological Perspective*. Cambridge: Harvard University Press, 1985.

Taylor, Steve. '"Home is Never Fully Achieved… Even When We Are In it": Migration, Belonging and Social Exclusion within Punjabi Transnational Mobility'. *Mobilities* 10.2 (2013): 1–18, https://doi.org/10.1080/17450101.2013.848606

van Schendel, Willem. 'Geographies of Knowing, Geographies of Ignorance: Jumping Scale in Southeast Asia'. *Environment and Planning D* 20.6 (2002): 647–68, https://doi.org/10.1068/d16s

Vertovec, Steven. 'Cosmopolitanism'. In Kim Knott and Sean McLoughlin, eds. *Diasporas: Concepts, Intersections, Identities*. London: Zed Books, 2010, pp. 63–68.

PART 1

CROSSING BOUNDARIES:
MOBILITIES THEN AND NOW

1. Emigration Within, Across, and Beyond Central Asia in the Early Soviet Period from a Perspective of Translocality

Kamoludin Abdullaev

Any consideration of the movement or migration of people triggers a number of fundamental questions: who migrated and how did they migrate, where from, where to, and why? How many migrated? What impact does mass exodus have on the environment, demography, and, most importantly, the socio-political life of society? What are the effects on the people who are left behind, on those who are living at the migrants' destination, and beyond? Despite the importance of these questions, however, Soviet historiographers avoided them. In the Soviet Union, historians were tasked with constructing an image of the new territorial-cultural region called 'Soviet Central Asia', which was quite separate from the neighboring regions that were known as 'Muslim', 'Turkic', 'Iranian', etc. This artificial construct was aided by an impenetrable political border erected along the Amu Darya River and across the Turkmen steppe, and by the establishment of a scientific framework with its associated institutes and set of academic concepts. The study of outmigration from Soviet Central Asia was less a subject of scholarly investigation than a form of political history in which those who migrated from the USSR were identified as opponents of the Soviet regime — counter-revolutionaries whose influence needed to be eradicated (Zevelev 1981).

Since the collapse of the USSR in 1991, the paradigm of 'class struggle' has been replaced by one of ethnic determinism. Newly independent Central Asian nations realized that most of the political borders drawn during the Anglo-Russian delimitation in the late nineteenth century

 https://doi.org/10.11647/OBP.0114.01

and the national delimitation of Central Asia in 1924–1936 were an artificial construct and were not ethnologically grounded. After the fall of the 'iron curtain' this realization brought with it a romantic interest in 'compatriots abroad' in all Central Asian states, which set in motion an independent state-building process from the ruins of the Soviet empire. All presidents of independent Central Asian states were declared leaders of 'co-ethnics (Kazakhs, Tajiks, Kyrgyz) of the world', but this unity was short-lived and very soon an ethnic- and state-based nationalism emerged. As a result, there are only a few scholars in Central Asia today who are writing a history of the region as a whole. Rather, official historiographies focus on 'national histories', i.e. on separate 'nationalities' with distinct ethnogenesis, cultures, languages and territory (see Jacquesson in Chapter Six).

Despite the predominance of national histories, theories of transnationalism have started to emerge, inspired by the realization that the study of Central Asia must transcend national borders and challenge existing concepts of nationhood. Those who study the region have started to consider this issue more carefully and to undertake diaspora studies (Abdullaev 2009; Mendikulova 1997). Similarly, by taking a transnational approach as a starting point for further exploration, this chapter attempts to overcome the limitations of long-established approaches to the study of Central Asian emigration dating back to the early Soviet period. Transnational research is defined here as comparative research between populations of two or more countries.

The study of emigration within, across, and beyond Central Asia is spatially expansive. It covers the history shared by Central Asia and the neighboring areas of Afghanistan, Western China, and part of Iranian Khorasan. This common past connects Central Asia with the destinations of its outmigrants, which include Afghanistan, China, Iran, and India. Later, in the years between the First and Second World Wars, many exiled Central Asians also took refuge in Turkey, Saudi Arabia, Poland, Germany, and other states, including the Americas and the Far East (Balci 2009). The arrival of Central Asians during the 1920s and 1930s had an important impact on the history of those countries.

The study of the migration of almost one million Central Asians, exiles of Bolshevism, has generally focussed on general political trends, the movement of peoples and on the elites who led these outmigrations.

These leaders include charismatic tribal insurgents (or Basmachis) such as Ibrahimbek Loqay (Fraser 1987a-b; Abdullaev 2009); the toppled emir of Bukhara Alim Khan and his entourage; the leaders of secular Turkestani nationalists; and the pan-Turkic general Enver Pasha (Yamauchi 1991; Andican 2007; Abdullaev 2009). Those who didn't belong to the political elite either remained marginalized or were disadvantaged and therefore invisible. This contribution tries to fill these gaps.

Another way to explore translocal connections in the region is to consider the significance of religion. The exodus of Central Asians during the first and second decades of the twentieth century can be viewed as a characteristically Muslim form of travel known as *hijra*. For exiled Central Asians, religion served as an important source of support to cope with the ostracism they experienced in their host country, as well as a means to depart from the strictly local, in territorial and cultural terms, and embrace more extraterritorial and translocal world views and imaginations.

Fig. 1.1 Group of Basmachis of Eastern Bukhara in the mid-1920s. State Archive of Film and Photograph Documents of the Republic of Tajikistan. Public domain

Fig. 1.2 Ibrahimbek Laqai, arrested in 1931. State Archive of Film and
Photograph Documents of the Republic of Tajikistan. Public domain

Mapping Central Asia

Living at the crossroads of East-West and North-South trading routes,
Central Asian peoples moved freely within their tribal and ethno-cultural
areas for centuries. After the Anglo-Russian delimitation, however,
boundaries became barriers to such movements. In the nineteenth
century, the area turned into a sphere of rivalry between three empires:
Russia, Britain and, to a much lesser extent, China. This political contest,
often referred to as the 'Great Game', pitted against each other three
powers that, at first glance, had dissimilar interests.

The British, who were primarily concerned with India, arrived
in Central Asia indirectly through their control of Afghanistan. Their
sphere of influence, however, was limited to the plains north of the
Hindu Kush Mountains in Afghanistan, both because of a political and
diplomatic backlash from Russia, and fierce Afghan resistance. The
three bloody Anglo-Afghan wars dampened Britain's colonial zeal.
These circumstances were fateful for the peoples of Movarounnahr (first
and foremost for Tajiks and Uzbeks), who were involuntarily absorbed
into the Russian orbit.

Russians invaded Central Asia in the nineteenth century. After
defeating the Kazakhs, incorporating the steppe and occupying
Tashkent, the Russians moved south, where they occupied the right
bank of the Amu Darya. The Emir of Bukhara became a Russian vassal

in 1869. Russia also conquered the Central Asian states of Khiva and Kokand (Khuqand) and incorporated them into Turkistan General-Gubernatorial, with the capital at Tashkent.

Strictly-marked borders that divided two states and were drawn along indisputable lines were a constant preoccupation for colonial European powers in the nineteenth century. The major mapmakers were Russia and Great Britain. London sought to restrain the Russian advancement toward Britain's Indian frontiers. The 'Afghan buffer' and its northern edge, the Amu Darya's[1] course from Lake Victoria (Zor Kul) in the Eastern Pamirs, served as a natural line of defense between the empires. At that particular time, the Amu Darya, a clear demarcation, was more useful than mountain ranges to decide who controlled what. From a 'scientific' or historical point of view, mountain ranges were more appropriate boundaries, but the Europeans found these were difficult to map accurately. Many Britons of the 'scientific frontier' school saw the Hindu Kush as the natural defensive boundary of India, though British authorities disagreed (see Dacosta 1891). Had the British divided the territories along the Hindu Kush, the region of Eurasia would perhaps look completely different.

Negotiations for the division of the Russian and British spheres of influence concluded with the Russian-British Agreement of January 1873 and the consequent Demarcation of 1895. According to these agreements, Russia could not claim any territories south of the Amu Darya. Clarity of demarcation took precedence over any local concerns. As a result, the new frontiers were artificial and not grounded in the ethnological realities of the region.

Through this process of drawing borders, Central Asia was alienated from its own cultural, historical, and economic traditions to serve the interests of distant powers playing a 'Great Game'. Local rulers, emirs of Afghanistan and Bukhara, not to mention the peoples of the region, played only a passive role. The interests of Bukhara were 'promoted' by Moscow, while London provided support for Kabul. In search of new territories, the Afghan feudal lords turned their gaze to their northern neighbors — the khanates of Southern Turkestan, parts of which were under the nominal rule of the Bukharan Amir. In the 1850s and 1860s,

---

1   The Amu Darya, from its upper stream in the Pamir Mountains to its confluence with the Vakhsh River, is called the Panj River.

Afghans, with the active support of the British, conquered the bordering khanates of Balkh, Shibirgan, and Herat. In 1883, the independent Pamir governorates of Rushan, Shughnan and Wakhan, situated along both coasts of the Amu River, became part of Afghanistan with the help of the British. The Russian government strongly objected, pointing out that the transfer violated the Anglo-Russian agreement of 1873. Following drawn-out diplomatic negotiations, military expeditions and skirmishes, the khanates of Rushan, Shugnan, and Wakhan located on the right bank of the river were definitively transferred to Russia (and then to Bukhara). In other words, Britain and Russia drew up the Afghan-Bukhara borders along the Amu Darya according to the 1873 agreement.

The Amu Darya became the dividing line between Russia proper and Afghanistan and no bridges were built across it. Up until the early twentieth century, the river served as the main artery of the region. Steamship lines were only developed in the lower stream between Termez and Chardjui.[2] The Afghan conquest of South Turkestan and their enslavement of local populations led to an economic crisis. The cities on the left (Afghan) bank of the Amu Darya gradually became deserted. After Afghans settled in Tashkurgan, which once had twelve thousand inhabitants, only about seven thousand remained. The rest fled to Bukhara.

As far as Chinese border policy in Central Asia is concerned, the Chinese never intended to rule this region directly, unlike the Russians, who regarded Central Asia as Russia's trophy. The Chinese maintained a clear distinction between tributary areas and China proper. Chinese control over its northwestern frontiers was established by the Qing dynasty (1644–1912), which gradually extended Chinese influence westward into the area of what is now the Xinjiang-Uighur Autonomous Region, also known by its historical name, Eastern (or Chinese) Turkistan. China at the end of the nineteenth century was too weak to compete as an equal rival with Russia and England in Central Asia. Until the end of the nineteenth century, the border between China and the territory of today's Tajikistan and Afghanistan was not clearly delineated. The Russian and British foreign ministers did not draw the

---

2   Today in Termez, the Soviet-built Friendship Bridge crosses the river to connect Uzbekistan to Khairatan in Afghanistan.

line eastward to meet the Chinese boundary in mountainous Wakhan, which borders not only China, but also the northwestern outermost tip of British India. The sides finally decided that their frontiers should not converge, providing Afghans with access to China. Wakhan formed a narrow wedge (a panhandle, fifteen kilometers wide in certain areas) separating Russian territories in Pamir from the northwestern borders of India (Hunza, Chitral, and Gilgit). As one of the senior British diplomats noticed, the Afghan Wakhan became 'the long, attenuated arm of Afghanistan reaching out to touch China with the tips of its fingers' (Habberton 1937:67). On the outermost eastern tip of the Wakhan corridor lie the Little Pamirs — an uninhabited alpine region — where the Hindu Kush, Pamirs, Karakoram, and Himalayas, as well as three empires, those of Britain, Russia, and China, met. Today the Wakhan corridor is an Afghan territory sparsely inhabited by traditional Tajik and Kyrgyz pastoralists that separates Tajikistan's southern border from Pakistan's north.

The borders established in the late nineteenth century are still maintained, although the states themselves have changed. The various Russian-British demarcations in 1895 created a Russian-Afghan frontier with a total length of 2,330 kilometers. With the establishment of the Soviet Union in 1924–1929, this boundary was transformed into the Afghan-Turkmen (802 km), the Afghan-Uzbek (140 km) and the Afghan-Tajik (1,334 km) borders. The Peking Treaty of 1860, which demarcated a line between the Russian Pamirs and Chinese Xinjiang, created the Russian-Chinese border. With the fall of the Soviet Union, this line was recognized as the legal boundary between China and Tajikistan (430 km).

By the end of nineteenth century the region was relatively peaceful, at least until the early years of the twentieth century, when the escalation of British-German and Russian-German disagreements led to increasingly tolerant relations between London and Moscow. The British-Russian agreement of 1907 was the second step on the way to completing the separation of spheres of influence. It laid the foundations for the creation of a military-political bloc between Russia, France, and Great Britain — the Entente.

While the compromise among the empires proved to be satisfactory in terms of preserving international security, the outcome for the local peoples who inhabited the territories was more problematic. First of all, the compromise was designed to maintain the stability of the three colonial empires established by China, Russia, and Britain. Each part of Central Asia was expected to develop peacefully within its own imperial sphere. Naturally, none of the leaders who struck these agreements considered the possibility that changes might bring about the demise of their respective empires, and all were opposed to any developments that would allow independence and the creation of national ethnic states in Central Asia.

Until the 'Bukharan revolution' in September 1920, which resulted in the establishment of Soviet power in the region, the Afghans and Bukharans maintained close relationships. Until the arrival of the Bolsheviks in late 1920 Afghan subjects — merchants, laborers, and others — lived in Bukhara and Turkestan. Afghan labour migration to 'Russian' Central Asia at the beginning of the twentieth century was linked to the revival there of trade and economic growth as a result of Russian capital flow into Turkestan and Bukhara. However, the Soviet invasion and military strife forced these Afghans to return to Afghanistan.[3] The central government of the Soviet Union established a firm monopoly on foreign affairs and no Central Asians were allowed to have contact with their Afghan brethren.

Constructing Central Asia

Translocality focuses on 'place' as the setting for movement. There has never been a fixed understanding of Central Asia as a place. Western and Russian explorers introduced the term 'Central Asia' to political and geographical terminology in the mid-nineteenth century. According to Yuri Bregel, in cultural and historical terms, Central Asia is the western, Turko-Iranian part of the Inner Asian[4] heartland,

---

3   However, some Afghans remained in Tajikistan, contributing to its development. One of them was Nisar Muhammedov, a Peshavar-born Pashtun-Yusufzay, who was People's Commissar (minister) of Education of the Tajik Soviet Republic from 1926–1930 and professor of the Central Asian State University in Tashkent in the 1930s. He was arrested on 8 October 1937 and died (or was killed) during interrogation on 22 October 1937. One of the streets of Dushanbe bears his name.

4   Inner Asia consists of vast territories situated between the heartland of China and Russia stretching from Manchuria in the east to Mongolia, to the Ural mountains,

the indigenous population of which consisted of various Iranian peoples. The majority of this population has been Turkified, while the growing Turkic population has, to various degrees, assimilated into the region's indigenous Iranian culture. In geographical terms, Central Asia stretches from the Caspian Sea in the west to the Altai Mountains (Russia) and Turfan oasis (China) in the east, and from the limits of the Kazakh steppes and Southern Siberia in the north to the Hindu-Kush range (Afghanistan) in the south (Bregel 1995:viii).

During the Cold War, Central Asia was mostly associated with the five Soviet Central Asian republics of Kazakhstan, Uzbekistan, Tajikistan, Kyrgyzstan, and Turkmenistan. In more recent studies of the region, some experts have also included Eastern Iran, Northern Afghanistan, and the Xinjiang-Uighur Autonomous province of China as parts of Central Asia.

Historical narratives often refer to Central Asia as *Turkistan* (i.e., 'Land of Turks'). This is something of a misnomer, considering the local population spoke mostly Iranian languages in medieval times. In the ninth and tenth centuries, Arab writers applied the term *Turkistan* only to the area north-east of the Syr Darya (modern-day Kazakhstan). Afterwards, however, the number and influence of Turkic tribes in the region increased. They formed powerful ruling dynasties, most notably the empire established by Tamerlane in the fifteenth century.

In the nineteenth century, the British and Russians adopted the expression *Turkistan* (or 'Turkestan') as a geographic term to indicate their assets in Central Asia. This was further subdivided into 'Western' or 'Russian' Turkistan (which is post-Soviet Central Asia), 'Southern' or 'Afghan' Turkistan (northern Afghanistan) and 'Eastern' or 'Chinese' Turkistan (the southern part of Xinjiang-Uighur Autonomous Region of China).

In recent times, a new term, 'Greater Central Asia', has been introduced to identify the region under study. This is more a policy-oriented rather than a geographic term and was proposed by American scholars (Canfield 1992). At its core is the idea of the US-led creation of a new region that integrates post-Soviet Central Asia with South Asia

---

to the Tibetan plateau, to Xinjiang, and finally to Central Asia including northern Afghanistan and Eastern Iran. Inner Asia was originally populated by non-Russians and non-Chinese.

via Afghanistan. The '*Greater Central Asia Partnership for Afghanistan and its Neighbors*' project, run by the Central Asia Caucasus Institute and Silk Road Studies Program, proposes the transformation of Afghanistan and the entire region into a zone of protected sovereignties that share practical market economies, secular and open systems of governance with respect to civil rights, and positive relations with the US (Starr 2005). However, most Central Asian and, especially, Russian politicians and the expert community at large were sceptical about the Greater Central Asia project, pointing out to the differences in cultural identity and lack of cooperation between the Central Asians and the people of South Asia in the past.

The Cold-War definition of Central Asia as five Muslim-populated Soviet Republics east of the Caspian Sea is no longer valid due to the end of the Soviet order. Prior to the imposed Soviet borders, the people of 'Central Asia' had significant freedom of movement within and across the various Emirates and Khanates that made up the political units of the region. In the post-Soviet period, the region has been defined as five post-Soviet 'stans' plus northeastern Iran, northern Afghanistan, the northernmost part of trans-Pamirian Indo-Pakistan and the northwestern part of China. This definition is almost identical to the one Russian and British authorities introduced more than one hundred years ago. It is the right moment to bring it back to the international vocabulary.

The end of a 'stateless' Central Asia

Colonization put an end to the stateless 'free ride' in Central Asia in the nineteenth century. Urban and oasis dwellers mostly accepted the establishment of the Russian administration, while rural, tribal segments of Central Asian society showed fierce resistance.[5] One might argue that rural resistance was Islamic in nature: it was local *jihad* by tribes for whom Islam has always been intertwined with tribal networks. Others argue that these tribal elements would have resisted any form of government — native or foreign. Both arguments — culturalist and constructivist — are valid. The establishment of effective state control

---

5   For example, the uprising in Ferghana led by Madali, or Ishani Dukchi in 1898.

in the vast Central Asian territories was a prerequisite for the new European-dominated world order, which required the formation of nation states with clearly-defined and rigid borders in order to protect national sovereignty and reinforce national symbols and values. In the early twentieth century this Westphalian[6] legal and political framework for modern inter-state relations did not apply to Muslim-populated territories, as colonizers did not see a 'basis on which principles of national self-determination can [be] buil[t]'[7] in those territories. For the first time in history, Central Asian Muslims were subject to the jurisdiction of non-Muslims, who imposed a secular vision that contradicted a Muslim sense of being in the world. This governance undermined the customary way of life, erecting political borders and putting restrictions on migration.

At the same time, the establishment of Russian rule in the region launched the consolidation of disparate tribal, local, and ethnic identities into larger identity groups that later formed the backbone of modern nation states. Most Central Asians became citizens of the Russian Empire. Because they were non-Slavs and non-Christians, the Tsarist government discriminated against them by labelling them as unorthodox (*inorodets*). They shared this status with other minority peoples in the Russian Empire, such as the Kalmyks (the indigenous peoples of Siberia), Jews, and other non-Slavic peoples. This status limited their access to educational institutions, military or state service, and places of residence. However, the Tsarist regime attempted to win over the tribal and patrimonial leaders or local aristocracy by granting them special privileges. This gradual incorporation of ungoverned tribes into proto-national units played an important role in nation-building in Central Asia.

Dividing Central Asia into three spheres was an afterthought of colonial expansion and it just happened to succeed. Because these areas were primarily buffer zones, there was no direct collision between Great Britain, Russia, and China in Central Asia during their two centuries of rivalry. In other words, the participants of the Great Game in Central Asia played peacefully and according to the rules they established by

---

6   The Westphalian system of sovereign states was established in 1648 as part of the Peace of Westphalia.
7   India Office Library (IOL)/P&S/11/142.

themselves and for themselves. Conflicts rarely amounted to anything more than short-term military expeditions.

By the beginning of the twentieth century, the vast strategic buffer zone between the empires encompassing Manchuria, Mongolia, Xinjiang, Afghanistan, and Central Asia was formed. Russian Central Asia (Turkestan, Bukhara, Semirechie, Khiva, Turkmenia) proved too rich in human and natural resources for the Tsarist colonial regime to develop fully. Moscow was unable to transform the culture of large populations with their own historically established identities. As a result, the incorporation of Central Asia into the Russian Empire was weak, both politically and economically. Russian cultural influence in Central Asia was not as pronounced as it was in the Caucasus, where close cultural ties between the colony- and parent-state had begun to take shape by the nineteenth century. In Central Asia, Russians limited themselves mainly to the establishment of structural means of control in the region, such as building railways and other infrastructure projects. Only a small group of the local elite (mainly Kazakhs, Russia's closest neighbors) adopted the Russian culture. Major urban centres remained divided into two unrelated parts: Russian-dominated centres and native 'old cities'.

These artificial boundaries served colonial powers by preventing ethnic and religious unity and the mobilization of peoples with common interests. Some argue that the main Muslim response to colonialism in Central Asia was a military one: a call to clash with the enemy, the West (see for example Alimova 2000:167, Ziyoev 1998). Others argue that there was an internal crisis in Islamic society that was only exacerbated by the encounter with colonial Europe (see Ayni 1987, Fitrat 1988). The colonization of Muslim states was not therefore a treacherous Christian incursion, but a rational response by the emerging empires to weakening neighbors and former adversaries. According to this view, the main reasons for colonization were situation- and network-dependent; they did not stem from ideology or deep-seated animosity between religions.

However, this is not to say that the concept of a 'clash of civilizations' (Huntington 2000) is not applicable to interrelationships between the empires in Central Asia. The Russians and British invaded these territories with a Eurocentric project of 'modernization'. According to this simplistic model, the southern borders of Central Asia were considered the frontier between a capitalist Russia, as the eastern stronghold of the Christian West, against a feudal Muslim world. This confrontation had its roots in the West's historical memory of the nomads of Central Asia as aggressive 'barbarians' bent on the destruction of urban civilization and the image of the 'fanatic Muslim' as an enemy.[8] The imagined threat of what was later called 'Islamic fundamentalism' was created and fanned by the empires that took part in the Great Game. In light of this 'clash of civilizations', Russia appeared to be the defender of the West from the 'wild' East, even though in other contexts Russia itself was often condemned as a bulwark of 'eastern' autocracy and despotism.

The inhabitants of the region paid the price for peace between the empires. Imperial policies resulted in the fragmentation of historic, political, national, and social relationships that accelerated the decline of Central Asia. Thus, at the end of the nineteenth century, the region became politically and economically dependent on the West, and the seeds were planted for future conflicts, social shocks, and population movements that would create complex socio-spatial dynamics to transcend these externally imposed boundaries.

Central Asia's first international migration

The Russian revolution, the invasion of the Red Army in 1917–1920, and the collapse of the state, followed by a violent conflict and political pressures, triggered various movements of the Central Asian population that were undertaken for a variety of motivations, over a range of distances, and over different periods. These movements created complex interactions between the social and spatial flows of people and things that deeply changed the environment and society in this part of the world.

Central Asia saw two waves of emigration during the two decades following the Russian Revolution of 1917. The first phase of flight started

---

8   In the aftermath of World War One the British did not believe that Bolshevism as a political doctrine could be installed in the region. 'A more serious danger lies in the possibility of a general Muslim uprising against Bolshevik excesses, and the attempt to create a series of independent Muslim States out of the ruins', stated the British officials in Delhi in a memorandum to the Paris World Conference held in 1919. Finally, in 1918 the British decided to leave the region of Central Asia under Russian/Bolshevik control. See The British Library, India Office Records and Private Papers, IOR: L/P&S/ll/142.

with the establishment of Bolshevik rule in Tashkent in November 1917 and continued with the downfall of the nationalist Kokand government in February 1918, the defeat of Kolchak's[9] White Armies in Siberia, and, finally, the fall of Bukhara in 1920. For Bukharans, the day the Emir Said Alim Khan ran away from Bukhara is remembered as a separation day (*ruzi firoq*) that was preceded by what is described as 'a small end of the world' (*qiemati asghar*) (Baljuvoni 1994:61). This first wave of emigration ended with the arguable elimination of Basmachism[10] in Tajikistan in mid-1926 when Ibrahimbek Chakobai Ughli, Tajikistan's Basmachi leader in 1921–1932, crossed the Soviet-Afghan border. He was a descendant of the Uzbek Laqai tribe, a son of the tribal chief in the Ishon Khoja family.[11]

The first outflow of Central Asian Muslims was caused directly by the Red Army invasion of the Bukharan Emirate and mainly affected the population of frontier regions, mostly nomadic and semi-nomadic Uzbek and Turkmen tribes. Together with the Emir of Bukhara, they escaped the military advancement of the Bolshevik forces. The Tajiks composed the third largest number of émigrés after the Turkmen and Uzbeks. According to the Red Army investigations, Tajiks were the dominant ethnic group in Eastern Bukhara (today: central and southern Tajikistan and southeastern Uzbekistan), composing 60 percent of the whole population, while the Uzbeks accounted for 30 percent. The national composition of Eastern Bukharan Basmachi groups, however, shows the reverse: Uzbeks made up 60 percent and Tajiks 30 percent.[12] Similarly, there were a greater number of Uzbeks in exile. It seems this was due to differences in social and political status between the two

---

9   Alexander Vasilyevich Kolchak (1874–1920), a commander in the Imperial Russian Navy, established an anti-communist government in Siberia during the Russian Civil War. He was recognized as the 'Supreme Ruler' by the other leaders of the White movement. Kolchak was captured and executed by the Bolsheviks in 1920.

10   Basmachis: Muslim guerrillas who fought against Soviet power in Central Asia during the early Soviet period.

11   Laqai is an Uzbek-language ethnic group in Tajikistan. Laqais are descendants of semi-nomadic Turkified Mongols from the Kazakh steppes who migrated to Bukhara in the 16th century. The Laqai population fell drastically after the Bukharan Revolution of 1920, as most Laqais sided with the Basmachi and fought Soviet rule under the command of Ibrahimbek. Consequently, many Laqais were killed or exiled to Afghanistan. In 1924, about 25,000 Laqais were registered in Tajikistan, mostly in Hisor and Baljuvon (Kulob). In the 1990s, the Laqais enjoyed a cultural revival and created a cultural center in Tajikistan. The 2000 census recorded 51,000 Laqais in Tajikistan.

12   Archive of the Communist Party of Tajikistan (ACPT), fond.1, opis.1, delo.63, list. 39.

population groups. The Uzbek minority occupied a high social position and historically the Uzbeks had used their power to politically dominate the less militarized Tajik majority. As a result the Tajiks were more likely to look favorably on the new power that had dismantled the existing Uzbek tribal-feudal supremacy.[13] Besides, Tajiks led a settled way of life (they were peasants and urban dwellers), while many of Eastern Bukhara's Uzbeks and Turkmen were nomadic and semi-nomadic stockbreeders. Tajik peasants owned only the land that they cultivated and this could not be taken along when emigrating, but livestock was relatively easy to move from one place to another.

Nonetheless, after the establishment of Soviet rule in Bukhara, during first wave of emigration, some Tajiks did flee, not only to Afghanistan but also to the remote Tajik-populated mountainous regions of Qarategin (Gharm), and Darvoz. The Soviets moved into these areas in the summer of 1923 with a large-scale military attack by the Red Army. In total according to the information given by the government of the Tajik Autonomous Soviet Socialist Republic (TASSR), 44,000 families, or 206,800 people[14] had abandoned Eastern Bukhara by the end of 1926. This constituted 25 percent of the general population, and 33 percent of all families in Tajikistan. The overwhelming majority of émigrés were Uzbeks and Tajiks from Qurghonteppa, Kulob, and Hisor provinces (*veloyats*). Only half of the total population was left in the Qurghonteppa region. Forty-nine villages (*qyshloqs*) that had been completely abandoned were found in Qurghonteppa *veloyat* by the governmental commission. Fields, gardens, and melon fields were overgrown. Homes and other structures were destroyed and ruined; *duvals* (fences made of clay) were levelled to the ground (Abdullaev 1995:20). The Tajiks did not only flee the territory of Tajikistan, they also abandoned the region of Surkhan-Darya in Uzbekistan. In the early 1920s, 40,000 Tajiks and Uzbeks moved from Surkhan-Darya to Afghanistan. These included

---

13   This did not mean that Tajiks supported the strife against the Uzbeks and Turkmens. The unity of the peoples of Central Asia was strengthened by their affinity to Sunni Islam, to the Hanafi School of law and to traditions of long-lasting and peaceful coexistence, all of which deterred national rivalry. In general, Tajiks often served as ideological leaders of the resistance. The majority of Bukharan clergy were Tajiks and many of them migrated to Afghanistan. In an interview conducted in Dushanbe on 24 August 2006, Bashir Baghlani told me that among these Tajik clergymen was Ishani Bulbul (Dovud) Kulobi, the mulla-imam (confessor) of Ibraghimbek. Ishani Dovud died in the 1970s in Afghan Badakhshan.

14   The average number of people in a family is calculated as 4.7 persons.

Kyrgyz emigrants, with 1,300 families from Qarategin and the Vakhsh valley, and over 1,000 Kyrgyz people from eastern Pamir passing over the border to Afghan Badakhshan and Qataghan in the first half of the 1920s (Abdullaev 1995;20).[15]

The flight of almost 20,000 Russian Cossacks and about 50,000 Russian peasant colonists from Semirechie (today's southeastern Kazakhstan and northern Kyrgyzstan) to Xinjiang in 1920 was not directly connected to *jihad* and the exodus of Muslims; it was also a political phenomenon caused by the victorious Bolshevik advance and defeat of the White Russians.[16]

The second wave of outmigration began immediately after the first during the second part of the 1920s. It reached its peak between 1929 and 1932, during far-reaching economic, social, political, and cultural changes that included collectivization, cruel anti-Islamic policies, 'cultural revolution', and forcible female emancipation aimed at the demolition of traditional society in Central Asia. A new wave of refugees fled from the restrictions, severe enforcement practices, and suppression of dissent that characterized Soviet rule. During the second phase of migration, people of different origins from all parts of the region, including the neighboring mountainous Bukharan territories, moved abroad. These migrants were known as *muhajeers* that is, those who performed *hijrat*, or escaped in order to protect, to preserve, and to further develop their religious identity.

In the first half of the 1920s, hundreds of thousands of Central Asian emigrants rushed to Afghanistan settling along the northern border from Badakhshan in the east to Herat in the west. In fact, modern Central Asia experienced its first refugee crisis during the second decade of the twentieth century. At the end of this crisis in 1932, there were roughly one million Central Asian refugees, mostly in northern Afghanistan and Western China but also in India, Iran, and Turkey. One in four inhabitants of Tajikistan in 1925, for example, became a refugee (Abdullaev 2009). The actual number of emigrants is probably rather

---

15 *Tsentralnyi Gosudarstennyi arkhiv Uzbekistana* (TsGA Uz), f. 8–17, op. 3, d. 19, l. 105–08.
16 The Russians of Xinjiang lived mainly in Ili, and partly in Kashgar, Kucheng, Tarbagatai and Altai regions. The Kazakhs, the Kyrgyz, the Dungans, the Uzbeks, the Tatars and other former Russian citizens, in addition to Russians themselves, migrated to China (Abdullaev, 2009).

higher than noted. Small emigrant settlements were also established in Kabul, Peshawar (India), Mashhad (Persia) and in some other towns of Afghanistan, India and Iran. Statistical research done by the Soviets in Central Asia in 1922, 1924, and 1926 concludes: 'Depopulation as the result of emigration characterizes the whole region. But the greatest emigration was from Tajikistan's pre-frontier territory'.[17]

Mass migration was not the only response to the Russian Revolution. Why did the majority of Central Asians choose not to migrate? A negative approach to the Soviet past that portrays Russian rule as despotic is widespread in Western, as well as modern Central-Asian historiography, but this interpretation cannot adequately describe the raw force of the Revolution of 1917; therefore, it cannot explain how Soviet power survived this early period. Was it only because of the weakness of Basmachism, which derived from fragmentation, mismanagement, and its limited social base of resistance? Or did the reason lie in the failure of the West, Turkey, Iran, and Afghanistan to aid Basmachis? In fact, several aspects helped the Bolsheviks to strengthen their position in the region and weaken the fierce Basmachi resistance, particularly:

1. In the 'Reds versus Whites' Russian dispute that was at the core of the revolution and the civil war, most Central Asians took the part of the former, as they promised land, freedom, and peace for all people irrespective of nation and religion.

2. By the end of the 1920s, the Soviets had established themselves as the only real, effective — if unjust — government. Emirs, Khans, and the Russian provisional government had failed and discredited themselves in the eyes of the majority of the population. Long-lasting civil strife and disorder was responsible for a tradition of political resignation and submission among Central Asians.

3. The Bolsheviks defined themselves as anti-imperialistic and not exclusively pro-Russian, and neighboring Eastern countries regarded them as allies in their struggle for independence. The Bolsheviks reestablished Russian rule in Central Asia in part because Turkey and Afghanistan saw them as a bulwark against

---

17   *Tsentralnyi Gosudarstvennyi arkhiv Tadzhikistana* (TsGA Tadj), f. 21, op. 7, d. 2, l. 66.

Western imperialism. Neither Afghan Emir Amanullah, nor the first president of Turkey, Mustafa Kemal Ataturk, provided significant support to the Basmachis. The international isolation of the anti-Soviet resistance strengthened the position of the new authorities among Central Asians.

These factors contributed to greater calm in the region and weakened outmigration from Central Asia.

The story of these 'exiles of Bolshevism' ended in the middle of the 1930s, by which time the USSR had consolidated its power in the region and established secure, closed borders with Afghanistan and other southern neighbors. The decline of the *muhajeer* and *mujahed* (*jihad* fighter) in the second half of the 1930s coincided with the transformation of Central Asian politics. In Afghanistan, the influence of the universal (supranational) religiosity of the non-governmental *ulama* and of traditional Islamic forces on the one side, and of the idealistic secularist reformism of Amanullah-like leaders on the other, had waned, clearing the way for more stable *modus vivendi* between the state and tribal or local powers.

In Soviet Central Asia the national delimitation of 1924, the growth in economic development, the successes of mass secular education, state provision of health care, and the emancipation of women had also changed the situation. This inevitably involved the separation of religion from the political sphere and the separation of the Qur'an-based *muhajeer* and *mujahed* concepts from the emerging Central Asian *realpolitik*, which resulted in an era of relative stability, in which the Muslim community moved in the direction of political quietism and submission to political authority (despite the latter's non-Islamic practices). The creation of centralized 'stans' in Central Asia and the stabilization of Afghanistan in the beginning of the 1930s was accompanied by a gradual rise of nationalism, the emergence of official state-sponsored religious institutions, and the co-option of the religious class into state structures.

These years of 'muted Islamic politics' (Brown 2000:111) were followed by the reanimation of the 'Islamic factor' in identity formation, which began with the Soviet invasion of Afghanistan in 1979, putting an end to a period of relative stability and leading to another phase of politically-defined mass international migration in Central and Southern Asia.

Fig. 1.3 A group of Soviet activists in Hisor (Tajikistan) in the mid-1920s. State Archive of Film and Photograph Documents of the Republic of Tajikistan. Public domain

Religious identity formation that transcends boundaries

When studying Central Asian emigration, the question of why the majority of exiles moved to economically underdeveloped Afghanistan is key. There are several answers: its geographic location, an open frontier free of troops, and shared historical and ethnic identities. The strongest pull, however, was a shared religion.

Most of the exiled Central Asians were Muslims. Their exodus fits within categories of Muslim travel. These movements include the Hajj pilgrimage (*hajj*), travel for learning and other purposes (*rihla*), visits to shrines (*ziyara*), and emigration (*hijra*). These were not just physical actions, but involved spiritual practices as well. Qur'anic *hijra* (which means 'to abandon', 'to break linkages with someone', or 'to migrate' in Arabic) began with the migration of the Prophet Muhammad and his followers from Mecca to Medina in 622 AD. Later, *hijra*, the obligation to migrate from lands where the practice of Islam is constrained to those lands where, in principle, no such constraints exist, became one of the fundamental precepts of Muslim doctrine.

When the Bolsheviks captured Bukhara during the 1920s, Muslim preachers advised Central Asians, 'the *hijra* is a holy obligation now' (*'Hijrat fard va vojib ast'*).[18] Muslims accept that if the political environment is not conducive to the exercise and propagation of Islam, then one must declare his country an enemy territory (*dar ul-harb*) and wage a holy war (*jihad*) against it until it is restored as an Islamic state (*dar ul-Islam*). If not, one should migrate (perform *hijra*) and leave the country altogether (Masud 1990:29).

Ideally *hijra* is the transition of the mind from a state of dishonesty to one of purity (see Emil Nasritdinov in Chapter Ten). The crucial impetus behind *hijra* is to maintain one's religious and cultural identity; pragmatic motivations must be secondary to this desire. Ideally, the exiles or *muhajeers* should migrate to the holy cities of Mecca and Medina. In the first half of the twentieth century, the religious elite of Central Asia, the Caucasus, and Afghanistan often found shelter near Muslim shrines in these holy cities (See Balci 2009). Doctrine and practice do not always precisely coincide, and the exercise and significance of the Islamic faith in any given historical setting cannot readily be predicted from first principles of dogma or belief (Masud 1990:18). Dale Eickelman proposes the idea of flexible Islam, arguing that 'the motives for action in general, as for (Muslim) travel in particular, are inevitably mixed — a combination of holy reason and social, economic, and political concern' (Eickelman and Piscatori 1990:5). In this context, *hijra* is a 'normal' migratory process and social action operating in an Islamically-determined cultural context.

Most Central Asian migrants fled to Afghanistan. After the fall of the Ottoman Empire in 1918–1923, many considered independent Afghanistan to be the only legitimate Islamic state in the region. In the 1920s the country served as a place of refuge for the Muslims of

---

18   This information was recorded in Dushanbe, Tajikistan, in February 1991 during my interview with Bashir Baghlani. His father Kasir, being the head of the one of the first Soviet collective farms (*kolkhoz*) in Kulob, migrated to Afghanistan in 1929. Bashir Baglani was born in 1931 and in the 1980s headed the Ministry of Justice of Afghanistan. He returned to Dushanbe in 1989, after the Soviets withdrew their troops from Afghanistan, and later migrated to Germany.

Central Asia, as well as for some 20,000 co-religionists from British India, who constituted the Hijrat movement (Minault 1982). The poor Afghan country could not offer *muhajeers* any economic benefits, only the restoration (real or false) of a spiritual balance violated by external oppression.

In other words, it was a religiously imagined 'journey of the mind' across geographical and political lines, an escape from reality, a reflection of the deeply cherished popular utopia of *dar-ul Islam*,[19] the imagined 'golden village', an ideal home for Muslims. In exile, between *muhajeers* and *ansars* (hosts, in this case the Afghan Muslims) a new bond of unity (*mu'akhat*) was established.

This universal, supranational religious identity that transcends political borders has survived in spite of colonial divides and the introduction of the secular concepts of the nation state and nationalism. Relatedly, it is worth mentioning that doctrinally *hijra* is at odds with a secular understanding of emigration and diaspora formation, as it rejects the concept of the nationalism of a particular ethnic group, and that of the homeland as a territory where the group resides and to which it is culturally bound. Ideally, *hijra* would encourage Muslims to separate from those who rejected migration from *dar ul-harb*. Religious doctrine would unite *muhajeers* with a new state on a supranational, i.e., religious, basis. Meanwhile (secular) diasporas cherish the memory of the state of origin. Diasporas never completely abandon the idea of returning to a historical homeland. In contrast to *muhajeeri* groups, diasporas are inclined to identify themselves more with the abandoned mother country than with a new host state.

While in exile, the *muhajeers* faced many difficulties, including differences in language, culture, race, and nationality that inevitably existed inside the Islamic community or *umma*. They had to accept the fact that every state, including an Islamic state, cannot be absolutely protected from wars, revolutions, rebellions, and other violent conflicts.

---

19 In fact, this utopia has pre-Islamic roots. It is worth mentioning the imagined country, 'Chambuli Maston', taken from the Tajik-Turkic epic 'Gur Ughli', which gave shelter to the weak and defeated and provided them with justice and happiness. In Soviet times a Tajik popular poet, Mirsaid Mirshakar (1912–1993), created a powerful image of the Soviet state as a 'Qyshloqi Tilloi', that is, a 'Golden Village'.

In spite of this, Central Asian *muhajeers* and exiled *mujaheeds* saw their religion as a source of agency and emancipation, as it helped them to find a safe haven in Afghanistan and facilitated common ground with local Pashtuns, Tajiks, Uzbeks, and other Afghan groups. Muslim faith and piety, as symbolic capital, strengthened *muhajeers'* social status and self-confidence. Local Afghans treated them simultaneously as exiled co-religionists and as foreign people, known as 'beyond the river' (*poridarya*). Belonging to the imagined Muslim brotherhood (*umma*), that rejects political, geographical, and ethno-national borders as well as to a temporal, Uzbek-Tajik (Bukharan or Ferghanan) community ensured material wellbeing, cultural continuity, and emotional balance among refugees and émigrés. In this light, the region under study emerges as a place where new forms of identity are formed, which do not fit the customary understanding of nationality and ethnicity.

Members of Central Asian diasporas and irredentists constitute a very large part of the Afghan population today. The appearance of half a million Central Asians during the 1920s and 1930s had an important impact on the history of Afghanistan. In spite of their ethnic multiplicity, these 'minorities' have always been to a certain extent aware of their group identity as different from the Pashtun majority of Afghanistan and related to abandoned compatriots 'beyond the river'. This connectedness is emerging with increasing intensity. Islamic and ethnic solidarity in Central Asia, where frontiers are not ethnographically grounded, has been a significant cause of political destabilization, weakening centralized power and loosening international control on both sides of the Amu Darya. It has always been a crucial prerequisite for Central Asian insurgency that Afghanistan is available as a potential place of escape, since it is loosely controlled by central government and populated by fellow Muslims of similar ethnicity. Such a situation existed in the USSR in the early 1920s, in Afghanistan at the end of that decade and the beginning of the 1930s, and in the recent past: in the beginning of the 1990s, government authority collapsed once again and civil wars began in Tajikistan and Afghanistan simultaneously. The frontier between these two countries again became a maelstrom of regional instability, with the arrival of a great number of migrants seeking a chimerical 'state of purity'.

Translocality and the emergence of multidirectional networks

Islamist ideologies that have recently shaken the entire world were not created in a vacuum. The appearance of hundreds of thousands of Muslim refugees in the Central Asian region in the 1920s created a loss of confidence and sense of frustration with both the West and with weak, corrupt indigenous governments. At the same time, it gave a strong impetus to an Islamic reawakening. Central Asian *mujaheds* and *muhajeers* served as a symbol of sacredness, and of submission to Muslim ideals, which became associated with the Afghan resistance against the Soviet invaders. During the Soviet-Afghan war in the 1980s, forums for *mujaheed* groups were created and books and magazines were published by the Afghan *jihadi* parties in Pakistan that presented their resistance to the Soviets as a continuation of the Basmachi course (see Moruvat 1983). Later, the second Chechen war (1999–2009) was interpreted as part of the *jihad* that started in Central Asia in the 1920s by ideologues who championed anti-Russian resistance.

In the 1980s, some Central Asian *muhajeer* communities took an active part in the fight against the Soviet army. For example, Azad Bek, one of the leaders of the Islamic Union of the Northern Provinces of Afghanistan, was a great grandson of Nasriddin, the last Khan of the Khanate of Kokand (who ruled from 1875–1876). Azad Bek did succeed in enlisting the support of some Uzbek, Tajik, and even Turkmen field commanders, notably Uzbek *muhajeers* from Soviet Central Asia, such Khaluddin of Kunduz and Ait Murad from Barqa (Baghlan province). According to the Indian scholar K. Warikoo, this grouping of Afghan *mujaheds* was backed by the Pakistani government and aimed to '[bring] together all the Turks of Afghanistan and then to liberate Soviet Turkestan' (Roy 80). Warikoo stressed that it was not a mere coincidence that Pakistan's aggressive policy in Afghanistan and Central Asia at that time was pursued by Mirza Aslam Bek, the former Chief of Pakistan's army, who was a descendant of a Central Asian *muhajeer* and was also related to Azad Bek (Warikoo 1995, Andican 2007).

These kinds of speculations portray Central Asia and Afghanistan as a dangerous hotspot, permanently fomenting the 'Islamic threat' and representing a danger to 'infidels'. There is no doubt that today Central Asia's Islamism emerged partly within a tradition rooted in the 1920s. However, it would be a mistake to equate Basmachis and modern *mujaheds*, or *jihadis*. The Central Asian resistance movement against the Bolsheviks was unique. More recent *mujaheds*, as byproducts of the Cold War, were mostly clients of outside forces (Pakistan, Iran, Russia, the US, etc.). Basmachism was one of the last purely Muslim movements with few influences from outside the Muslim community.

Translocality and transformations of the physical and natural environment in Central Asia

The translocality perspective elaborated in this volume helps us to understand the role of mobility in connecting and transforming places, as well as in circulating practices, skills, and competencies across the region (see in particular Henryk Alff in Chapter Five).

Immigrants of Central Asian origin were able to make notable contributions to the development of the economies, cultures, and environments of their host countries. The exiled Bukharan elite, mostly the Jadids, supported King Amanulla Khan in his efforts to modernize Afghanistan. Some of them, including the Ferghanan *qurbashi* (commander) Shermuhammad (Kurshermat) even defended Amanulla from the attacks of insurgents in 1928–1929. The exiled Basmachis of Bukharan origin under the leadership of Ibrahimbek, however, supported the opposite side, that of the new Amir of Afghanistan, Habibulla Bacha-i Saqqao. More traditional Persian-speaking (Tajik) Bukharans chose Afghanistan, while Turkestani Turks (mostly Uzbeks) opted for Turkey as their host country. The second generation of exiled Bukharans had ensured Afghanistan's cultural progress in the 1960s having founded the practice of journalism, modern pedagogy, and the study of the history of Persian literature in Afghanistan (Abdullaev 2009:451–70). In Turkey, the Turkestani émigrés took an active part in the foundation of Ankara University, especially its agricultural department.

Many Central Asians with extensive Russian contacts, especially those from the second wave of emigration of 1926–1934, were more educated than the local Afghans and Xinjiangies, and took a more modern approach to life. These migrants fostered the cultivation of corn and beets, introduced silk-making, enlarged the herds of the famous Hisor lambs, and developed carpet weaving in Afghanistan (Abdullaev 2009:451–70, 510–12). Soon after the Soviets began cotton production in Southern Tajikistan and Uzbekistan, the young Afghani Abdul Aziz Londoni, realizing that Qataghan had similar natural conditions to the best cotton producers in Central Asia, bought up lands populated by émigrés in the Qunduz area and later established a company called Spin Zar (White Gold, in Pashto) giving a big boost to cotton production in Afghanistan (Shalinsky 1993:27–29). These emigrant activities changed the societal, economic, cultural, and natural environment of Afghanistan. At the same time, the development of Northern Afghanistan eased the introduction of Central Asians to life in exile and transformed their mentality towards modernization within the framework of a Muslim state, and towards becoming Afghan citizens, thus widening the gap between them and their former compatriots from the Soviet part of Central Asia.

The international migration of the early Soviet period contributed to important changes in demography, ethnic composition and, subsequently, the political landscape of the entire region of Central and Southern Asia. The majority of those who escaped from Central Asia were Uzbek semi-nomads from the pre-frontier zone of Tajikistan, and Uzbeks from other provinces of Soviet Central Asia who emigrated during the 1920s and the first half of the 1930s. In Afghanistan, they joined the local Uzbeks (in particular the Qataghani tribe), who were subjugated by Pashtuns during the 1860s. Together, Afghan Uzbeks formed the third-largest ethnic community and one of the strongest political and military forces during the Soviet-Afghan war and the Taliban period.

Simultaneously, on the other side of the border, in the Tajik south, the flight of semi-nomadic Uzbeks, whose tribal chiefs, before the arrival of Red Russians in the 1920s, used to control and even to oppress local Tajik sedentary peasants, allowed the movement of land-hungry Tajiks from Hisor and other internal provinces to this area. Not surprisingly, they were sympathetic to Soviet rule, as they saw the Soviets as liberators and and viewed their arrival as an opportunity for economic gain. The liquidation of Basmachism by the mid-1930s put an end to the Uzbek control of Tajik-populated Eastern Bukhara and allowed for the irrigation of the Vakhsh Valley and the cultivation of a much-needed thin fibre (grey) cotton to secure the strategically vital 'cotton independence' of the Soviet Union.

Summing up, the large-scale Muslim migration processes from Bukhara, Russia and the USSR in the early Soviet period had a crucial impact on the reconfiguration of Muslim society and culture in what we know as 'modern South Asia' and 'the Middle East'. The migration of the 'exiles of Bolshevism' was caused by the invasion of the Red Army and subsequent military conflict and it brought suffering and deprivation to the region. However, from a translocal research perspective, this migration emerges as a complex phenomenon that challenges the state-based static vision of history that is commonly accepted in Central Asia, which relates identity to a distinct, unique, and fixed culture, ethnicity and territory. This migration provided major actors with more social power and more options, and enhanced their ability to realize various life schemes and societal goals; it did not leave them as helpless refugees and defeated insurgents. People, ideas, symbols, and skills were able to transgress conservative political, 'civilizational', national, regional, technical, and other boundaries.

References

Abdullaev, Kamoludin. 'Central Asian Émigrés in Afghanistan: First Wave (1918–1932)'. In *Central Asia Monitor*, 4 and 5 (1994): 28–32; 16–27.

Abdullaev, Kamoludin. *Ot Sintsiana do Khorasana. iz Istorii Sredneaziatskoi Emigratsii 20 veka*. Dushanbe: Irfon, 2009.

Alimova, D. A., ed. *Turkestan v nachale XX veka: K istorii istokov natsional'noy nezavisimosti*. Tashkent: Sharq, 2000.

Andican, A. Ahat. *Turkestan Struggle Abroad: From Jadidism to Independence*. Istanbul: SOTA Publications, 2007.

Ayni, S. *Ta'rihi Inqilobi Bukhoro*. Dushanbe: Adib, 1987.

Balci, Bayram. 'Central Asian Refugees in Saudi Arabia: Religious Evolution and Contributing to the Reislamization of Their Motherland'. *Refugee Survey Quarterly* 26.2 (2009), https://doi.org/10.1093/rsq/hdi0223

Baljuvoni, Muhammad Ali. *Ta'rikh-iNofe'-i*. Dushanbe: Irfon, 1994.

Bregel, Yuri, ed. *Bibliography of Islamic Central Asia*. Bloomington: Research Institute for Inner Asian Studies, 1995.

Brown, Carl. *Religion and State. The Muslim Approach to Politics*. New York: Columbia University Press, 2000.

Canfield, Robert L. 'Restructuring in Greater Central Asia'. *Asian Survey* 32.10 (1992): 875–87.

Dacosta, John. *A Scientific Frontier, or, The Danger of a Russian Invasion of India*. London: W. H. Allen, 1891.

Eickelman, Dale, and James Piscatori. 'Social Theory in the Study of Muslim Societies'. In Dale Eickelman and James Piscatori, eds. *Muslim Travellers: Pilgrimage, Migration, and the Religious Imagination*. Berkley: University of California Press, 1990, pp. 3–28.

Fitrat, Abdurauf. *Bayonoti sayyohi hindi*. Dushanbe: Sadoi Sharq, 1988.

Fraser, Glenda. 'Basmachi — I'. *Central Asian Survey* 6.1 (1987a): 1–73, https://doi.org/10.1080/02634938708400571

Fraser, Glenda. 'Basmachi — II'. *Central Asian Survey* 6.2 (1987b): 7–42, https://doi.org/10.1080/02634938708400582

Habberton, William. *Anglo-Russian Relations Concerning Afghanistan 1937–1907*. Champaign: University of Illinois at Urbana-Champaign, 1937.

Huntington, Samuel P. 'The Clash of Civilizations?' In Frank J. Lecher and John Boli, eds. *The Globalization Reader*. Malden, MS: Blackwell Publishers, 2000, pp. 27–34, https://doi.org/10.2307/j.ctt2005tk7.6

Masud, Muhammad K. 'The Obligation to Migrate: The Doctrine of *hijra* in Islamic Law'. In Dale Eickelman and James Piscatori, eds. *Muslim Travellers: Pilgrimage, Migration, and the Religious Imagination.* Berkley: University of California Press, 1990, pp. 29–49.

McLoughlin, Sean. 'Muslim Travellers: Home, the Ummah and British Pakistanis'. In Kim Knott and Sean McLoughlin, eds. *Diasporas: Concepts, Intersections, Identities.* London: Zed Books, 2010, pp. 223–29.

Mendikulova, Gulnara. *Istoricheskie Sud'by Kazakhskoy Diaspory. Proiskhozhdenie i Razvitie.* Almaty: Gylym, 1997.

Minault, Gail. *The Khilafat Movement: Religious Symbolism and Political Mobilization in India.* New York: Columbia University Press, 1982.

Moruvat, Fazl al-Rahimkhan. *Dar Muqobili Kommunizmi Rus.* Peshawar, 1983.

Roy, Oliver. 'Ethnic Identity and Political Expression in Northern Afghanistan'. In Jo-Ann Gross, ed. *Muslims in Central Asia: Expressions of Identity and Change.* Durham, NC, and London: Duke University Press, 1992.

Shalinsky, Audrey C. *Long Years of Exile: Central Asian Refugees in Afghanistan and Pakistan.* Lanham: University Press of America, 1993.

Starr, Frederick. 'A Partnership for Central Asia'. *Foreign Affairs* July/August (2005), http://www.foreignaffairs.com/articles/60833/s-frederick-starr/a-partnership-for-central-asia

Warikoo, K. 'Cockpit of Central Asia: Afghanistan Factor in Tajikistan's Crisis'. In K. Warikoo, ed. *Central Asia: Emerging New Order.* Delhi: Har-anand Publications, 1995, pp. 193–225, http://ikashmir.net/afghanistan/warikoo.html

Yamauchi, Masayuki. *The Green Crescent Under the Red Star: Enver Pasha in Soviet Russia 1919–1922.* Tokyo: University of Foreign Studies, 1991.

Zevelev A. I., I. A. Poliakov, and A. I. Chugunov. *Basmachestvo: vozniknovenie, sushnost', krakh.* Moscow: Nauka, 1981.

2. Crossing Economic and Cultural Boundaries: Tajik Middlemen in the Translocal Dubai Business Sector

Abdullah Mirzoev and Manja Stephan-Emmrich

Introduction

Thirty-seven-year-old Firuz visited Dubai for the first time in December 2007. He came to celebrate the New Year with many other tourists in front of the Burj Khalifa tower. Firuz worked for a construction company in Moscow, but after his Dubai trip he left Russia to join a friend who was running a business exporting second-hand cars from the United Arab Emirates to Tajikistan. In Dubai, Firuz had quickly come to appreciate the better living conditions and business-friendly environment that would allow him to earn money in culturally familiar surroundings, able to move around the city and live his life free from the migrant deportation regime in Russia. After his vacation, Firuz bought a Japanese-made car from Dubai and thus became involved in his friend's export business:

> 'From the first time, when I came to Dubai, I found this environment much better than Moscow. People everywhere were speaking Persian (*farsi*) and Russian and the main clients of Tajiks in Dubai are Russian tourists here [...] many shop owners and vendors are Iranians or Afghans, who speak in a language I do understand. Here in Dubai, a big number of Tajik migrants collaborate closely with our Afghan and Iranian fellow brothers. And everyone is friendly. Being a tourist and

 https://doi.org/10.11647/OBP.0114.02

working in a small business, I am walking in the streets, beaches and near hotels, offering various stuff to tourists to get a commission. This is not hard work and I am not worrying about being stopped by the police like in Moscow. I am free (*ozod*). I am not dependent on anyone and my monthly income now is much higher than in Moscow' (Dubai, 2012).

Like Firuz, many Tajiks try to get a foothold in Dubai's vibrant economy. When Dubai's growing popularity reached Tajikistan's markets and households in the late 1990s-early 2000s, many Tajiks were attracted by the United Arab Emirates' brand of 'autocratic Islamic governance combined with neoliberal economics', which suggested a post-Western form of modernization (Kathiravelu 2016:39). They longed for Dubai as an alternative and ideal place abroad that promised to help them overcome the precarious conditions of Tajikistan's and Russia's economic sectors.

Based on the results of our long-term, multi-sited ethnographic and fieldwork in Tajikistan and the United Arab Emirates between 2010 and 2014, this chapter explores how Tajiks capitalize on their university degrees in economics, international relations, agriculture, and engineering, as well as on their language skills and social connections (*svyazi, aloqa*) in both Tajikistan and Russia, to integrate into Dubai's booming global tourism and transregional trading sector.[1] Both areas are dominated by established Iranian companies, Iranian entrepreneurs, and Afghan traders and businessmen, most of whom quickly came to appreciate the cultural skills and business connections of Tajiks, who provide ways to communicate with Russians and can move flexibly in and across different cultural settings.

As a result, and as the ethnographic case study of Dilshod and Rustam in this chapter will illustrate, Tajiks working in Dubai's informal economy turn into middlemen who connect different economic actors in

---

1   This chapter is the outcome of collaborative fieldwork in Dubai in winter 2012/13. Although both authors pursued their individual research projects within the framework of the overarching 'Translocal Goods' project, they share an interest in the religious dimension of the Tajik Dubai business, and the related translocal religio-economic transfers and interactions between Tajikistan and the Arab Emirates.

different business sectors and effectively mediate among their Tajikistan, Russia, and Dubai-based business networks. They thereby create a translocal space of connectedness and belonging, which transgresses cultural and economic boundaries, crosses different regions, and links Russia's growing middle-class tourism and post-Soviet history as a migration destination with the different trading traditions and business cultures of Afghans and Iranians. These translocal spaces, socio-spatial religions and economic practices form what we call the translocal 'Tajik Dubai business', by analogy with the Kyrgyz 'China Business' Philipp Schröder describes in Chapter Eight. Although articulated by our interlocutors as an alternative or exit option, we argue that the Tajik Dubai business does not create ruptures with previous economic activities and environments in Tajikistan and Russia. In fact, Dubai, with its vibrant economic sector, becomes a pivotal spatial knot of a larger socio-spatial configuration, which creates a 'cultural nestedness' or 'cosiness' (Finke 2003) that enables Tajiks to involve themselves successfully in, as well as shape, new fields of economic activity. In this capacity, Tajik middlemen enrich the interregional history of the emirate's merchant cosmopolitanism (Osella and Osella 2012, Ahmed 2012). Furthermore, since they can draw on their cultural familiarity with Afghans, with Sunni-Hanafi Iranians mostly from Baluchistan, and with Russian (or Russian-speaking) tourists, Tajik middlemen in Dubai have become creative and innovative agents of globalization as the case studies of Rustam and Dilshod will illustrate.

Studies on migration from Tajikistan focus more broadly on labour migration to Russia (Olimova 2013, Khusenova 2013, Roche 2014, among others). Therefore, they obscure the fact that each of the post-Soviet states (CIS), including post-Soviet Tajikistan, has connected with the global scene in very different ways, and that the global trading business and tourism sectors in the vibrant urban centres of the Gulf have made an important contribution to this phenomenon; not least as a promising 'Muslim' alternative to Russia's exploitative and Central Asia's limited and unstable labour market (Stephan-Emmrich 2017). In this chapter we want to complement our previous focus on how Muslims in Tajikistan have become involved in the global market of Islamic lifestyle consumption (Stephan-Emmrich and

Mirzoev 2016) by shifting our anthropological gaze from Tajikistan to Dubai's vibrant mercantile and migration economy, as well as to the urban places where translocal economic actions, connections, and relations take on a spatialized form, i.e., the migrant guesthouses in the neighborhood of Dubai Deira. Thus, we are driven by our interest in how Tajiks actively shape the complex, dynamic, and multifaceted nature of Dubai's informal economy.

By conceptualizing Tajiks working in Dubai not as one-dimensional 'migrants' but showing how they act as 'middlemen' (*posrednik, kamak*)[2] we also want to point to the shortcomings of the United Arab Emirates' hegemonic discourse about 'foreign migrant workers' that frames Tajiks, like other foreigners in the Gulf, solely in regard to the labour they do and the economic outcomes they estimate from it, and thus reduces them to *homo economicus* only (Ahmad 2012). Moreover, understanding Tajiks' position in Dubai's informal economy as that of middlemen and mediators, we emphasize their capacity to capitalize on their cultural and social skills and resources in order to pursue successful livelihoods, thus making sense of their precarious life conditions and the mobility regimes they have to deal with. Furthermore, the concept of middlemen opens up new epistemological avenues for understanding 'livelihood' not merely in economic terms but, more broadly, as a concept that links economic strategies with forms of longing and belonging and the assessment of wellbeing (Schröder and Stephan-Emmrich 2014). This includes, as Firuz described above, the experience of economic freedom and safety when moving in public, as well as the possibility of a transnational lifestyle that enables the combination of living in an attractive tourist site with pursuing a successful business, while staying connected with 'home' (Pelican 2014). Finally, as we will show, the 'middlemen' concept highlights the capacity of Tajiks to leave the centre of their own networks, to cross various boundaries, and to deal with difference, thereby translating different cultural and economic contexts.

---

2   Although the Tajik Dubai business is not solely a male issue and also involves businesswomen, female traders and employees, this chapter presents male perspectives only. Accordingly, the term 'middlemen' refers to male actors.

Avenues into the translocal 'Dubai business'

Tajikistan's integration into Dubai's economy began with the first official visit of President Rahmon to the United Arab Emirates in December 1995. Since that time, the Tajikistan-Dubai business relationship has developed, and now covers different forms of state and non-state collaborations in the fields of trading, technology, investment, and tourism. A striking interrelationship between tourism and trade existed from the very beginning. Although economic avenues into the Gulf were initiated first by the government and economic elites, the Tajikistan-Dubai business relationship is to a large extent sustained, developed, and expanded by traders as well as small and middle-scale entrepreneurs and middlemen, whose business relations, cooperation, and activities can be situated in the grey zone between formality and informality (see also Fehlings in Chapter Seven).

In the early 1990s, Tajikistan's then political elite discovered Dubai as an exclusive tourist destination and simultaneously established a cargo business trading luxury cars. Later, small-scale traders and entrepreneurs discovered Dubai's and Abu Dhabi's markets for their businesses. They began to import luxury clothing, home decorations, fashionable fabrics and clothing, and mobile phones to Tajikistan. Such consumer goods became especially desirable because they were branded as *dubaiskiy*; i.e., made in or imported from Dubai and thus considered high-quality and prestigious lifestyle products. Others, like Firuz and his friend Rustam, started to import second-hand cars from the United Arab Emirates to Tajikistan. Increasing trade with Dubai goods also fuelled the travel aspirations of Tajikistan's upper and middle-class and, thus, caused tourist companies to expand their travel destinations into the Gulf region. In the early 2000s, Tajikistan's tourism sector experienced a Dubai boom, and many Tajikistani tourist companies started to maintain collaborations with Dubai-based Iranian tourist agencies. This trend accelerated when flydubai opened up a flight route to Tajikistan and enabled middle-class business travel, tourist trips and labour migrants' mobility at affordable prices. Furthermore, in the last decade, Dubai's famous city skyline has become a priority location for music video shoots among famous Tajik pop artists. These artists created links between Tajikistan's pop music industry and Dubai's spectacular image of post-Western modernity (Kathiravelu 2016), thereby contributing to the involvement of Tajikistan's Muslims into a growing global Islamic consumerism and simultaneously feeding the lifestyle aspirations of the new urban middle class (Pink 2009).

Dubai's appealing radiance as the city of possibility is further enhanced by Tajikistan's overall economic instability, the dominance of regimes of corruption, nepotism and arbitrariness, and the dearth of professional opportunities for well-educated and economically aspiring entrepreneurs. The specific combination of globally mediated economic opportunities in the Gulf and the political and economic constraints at home encouraged many Tajiks to establish or get involved in translocal businesses in the United Arab Emirates. Among them were well-educated young men such as the two middlemen Rustam and Dilshod who will be introduced later, and who left the country due to the lack of enticing employment opportunities. In the Arab Emirates, they were able to capitalize on their Russian, Persian, Arab, and English language skills, university degrees, travel experiences, and aura of urban sophistication and began successful economic careers as middlemen.

In the last five years, many entrepreneurs suffering from adverse conditions in the non-state economy have been attracted to Dubai's business-friendly environment. To run a successful business in Tajikistan, entrepreneurs must have informal 'access' (*kanal*), or 'connections' (*svyazi, aloqa*) to government officials. In recent years, these costly connections and the corruption linked to them, together with the overall economic crisis in the country, have caused difficulties for entrepreneurs struggling to cover their business expenses. In addition, the decline of migrants' remittances due to the financial crisis in Russia[3] critically affected Tajikistan's economy. As a consequence, the government increased taxes and thus jeopardized small- and middle-scale entrepreneurial and business enterprises (Mullodjanov 2016). The informal economy is additionally hampered by constant surveillance practices through local authorities and elite groups who seek to monopolize the trading and bazaar business. Fires in the central bazaars of both Dushanbe and Kulob destroyed many vendors' property.

---

3   The country depends heavily on remittance from migrants in Russia, which provides an equivalent of half of the country's GDP (Malyuchenko 2015).

These vendors were mainly uninsured, making them ineligible for compensation for their lost property.[4] It is important to note that the insurance system in Tajikistan is neither well-developed nor trusted. Many of the affected traders used bank loans to reopen their business. Banks in Tajikistan offer loans at extremely high interest rates[5] and overburden borrowers with a lot of confusing bureaucratic paperwork. Eventually, many vendors transferred their business to the United Arab Emirates in order to pursue their economic interests without the pressure to get involved in corruption, the need to pay bribes, or the high risk of being targeted by the government's arbitrary surveillance and regulation regime in the informal economy.[6]

Furthermore, the integration of Tajiks into Dubai's global trade and tourism business cannot be understood without considering the role of Russia and its changing migration policy, as well as the emergence of a new consumer-friendly and status-oriented urban middle class in Russia and the countries of Central Asia, such as Kazakhstan, that have been enjoying tourist trips to the Gulf since the early 2000s.

In recent decades, migration from Tajikistan has significantly increased due to the country's uncertain socio-economic situation. Of the total amount of Tajik migrants, about 90% go to Russia, while the rest migrate to Kazakhstan, the United Arab Emirates, Turkey, South Korea and some overseas countries (ILO 2010). Due to Russia's citizenship law, educated and highly qualified foreigners enjoy certain privileges, such as the right to acquire Russian citizenship after some years of work in Russia. Therefore, the emigration of Tajik intellectuals and entrepreneurs to Russia has significantly increased during the last ten years.[7] However, due to growing Russian nationalism, many Tajiks, like other migrants from Central Asia and other foreigners, are increasingly facing racism in their everyday life in Russia (Habeck and Schröder

---

4   See http://news.tj/en/news/tajikistan/incidents/20120314/damage-caused-qurghon-tepppa-s-central-bazaar-fire-estimated-312000-somoni,   http://www.rferl.org/a/kulob-bazaar-fire-market-sahovat-shops/25465601.html

5   In 2016, the bank rate was 29% to 32% for Somoni, and 22% to 35% for USD. See http://fmfb.com.tj/ru/legal/loans/

6   See   https://www.ukessays.com/essays/economics/barriers-to-entrepreneurship-development-in-tajikistan-economics-essay.php

7   For instance, Tajiks have been resettled in Russia's Tambov Region within the Russian voluntary resettlement program — including twenty high-qualified medical doctors and their families (Pastrova 2014).

2016:10f, 12f).[8] For example, many struggle with structural exploitation[9] in the workplace (Ryazantsev 2016:5–6). Violent xenophobia in Russian society has diminished their overall wellbeing, and when the economic crisis hit Russia, many Tajiks left for the Emirates, while others were deported back to Tajikistan and later followed their more successful relatives to Dubai.

Although Dubai is for many Tajiks an alternative migration destination to escape the precarious working and living conditions in Russia, in the Gulf they nevertheless retain links to Russia's socio-economic development, as well as to the shared Soviet past (see Philipp Schröder in Chapter Eight). On the one hand, they profit from the influx of Russian middle-class tourists to Dubai's tourism sector. On the other hand, many Tajiks who maintain and cultivate close relations with the Tajik migrant diaspora in Russia are able to expand their Dubai-based businesses into markets in Russia and wider Eurasia.

Fig. 2.1 'Mexa, shuba!': fur-coat shops for Russian tourists in Dubai Deira. Photo © Manja Stephan-Emmrich (2013), CC BY 4.0

---

8   See http://content.time.com/time/nation/article/0,8599,1304096,00.html
9   See for instance the widespread practice of non-payment of salaries or residency in poor living conditions (Olimova 2013, p. 72).

Al Nasr Square: Russian tourists, Iranian and Afghan business partners

The best way to meet Tajiks in Dubai is by walking around Al-Nasser Square, a public place nearby the Baniyas underground station in Dubai Deira. As a meeting place for both tourists and foreigners (Elsheshtawy 2008), Al Nasr Square forms the spatial centre of the Tajik Dubai business. Like other migrant workers from CIS countries, Tajiks jokingly refer to Al Nasr Square as mini *Cherkiz* bazaar.[10]

Deira, a vibrant urban district located in the heart of Dubai, offers plenty of shopping malls, market halls, hotels, and restaurants. Surrounding the Dubai Creek River with its city port, Deira is the main shopping district in Dubai's historic quarter. Russian and other tourists have access to a wide variety of popular fashion shops, brands, and restaurants, as well as the offices of numerous trading, cargo and shipping companies. Additionally, there is an extensive selection of electronic, cosmetic, jewelry, and toy stores, and the majority of Dubai's fur coat shops are located around Al Nasr Square.[11]

Historically, the Deira district, located between the Creek side and Al Nasr Square, was the commercial centre of Dubai. However, when revenues from the oil industry and tourist sectors soared over the last two decades, Dubai expanded from a mere two square kilometers in 1950 to 1,000 square kilometers in 2015, moving the centre of the city to Sheikh Zayed Road and the Business Bay districts with their high-rise commercial buildings. Nevertheless, Deira remains one of the main business centres, a popular destination for tourists, as well as a dwelling area for foreign migrant workers and residents from Asia and Africa who work in construction, hotels, the care sector or in one of the city's many malls and street markets. Deira is therefore also known as Dubai's 'migrant quarter'.

Due to the high density of hotels booked by tourists and businesspeople from Russia and other post-Soviet states in Eurasia, many Tajik workers,

---

10   *Cherkiz* bazaar was one of the biggest international bazaars in Moscow, were many Tajiks, Uzbeks, Kyrgyz and Azerbaijani migrants worked, until it was closed by the city administration in 2008.

11   Also known as Jamal Abd el-Nasr Square, close to the Dubai underground station Baniyas square.

businesspeople, and entrepreneurs locate their offices, work, and living places around Al Nasr Square. Above all, the area is the workplace of about 300 to 500 *kamak*,[12] street brokers who invite tourists from Russia and other CIS countries to visit the fur-coat shops they work for and later share the commission they get from the purchase. Tajik *kamak*, like those from other post-Soviet countries, have their own gathering points around Al Nasr Square, thereby following the spatial segregation of the local fur-coat business along ethnic and national lines. They wait in small groups in front of hotels, tourist shops, and restaurants, trying to find clients and offering them their shopping services. Like many other Tajiks in Dubai who work as vendors in souvenir, smartphone, or fur coat shops, as tourist guides or small-scale entrepreneurs and traders, they pursue their business interests in the grey zone between formality and informality. While only a minority of Tajiks, i.e., those working in shops or companies, have employment contracts that allow for long-term residence and family settlement in the United Arab Emirates, the majority are seasonal workers staying during the peak tourist season, from October until April. When the tourists leave, the workers return home to Tajikistan or Russia, where they wait until the new tourist season starts. Long-term residence is tied to an employment contract with a Dubai-based company, which requires connections (*wasta*) to informal networks around business elites and the Arab *kafala* system of sponsorship, which is the system by which foreign migration is managed and governed in the United Arab Emirates (see Gardner 2012, Vora 2009). Tajik *kamak*, while trying hard to become 'connected' to the business or social network around a *kafeel* (an Arab sponsor) through knowing the 'right' people and having the 'right' knowledge, work on the basis of tourist visas. The latter, however, allow for short-term residence but do not include a work permission. Tajiks are therefore often involved in illicit economic practices and street work activities.

---

12   Due to the undocumented status of *kamak*, work statistical data or official numbers do not exist. The number above reproduces our main Tajik interlocutors' estimation of Tajik *kamak* working around Al Nasr Square in Dubai Deira between 1010 and 2014. *Kamak* is a Greek word referring commissioners, i.e. people who introduce potential customers to a specific business and in return receive a commission of 10–15% of the total sale from the owner. However, since the fur coat business in Dubai depends on Greeks, the term *kamak* only refers to commissioners working in the fur coat trade.

Tajiks are newcomers in Dubai's economy. Nevertheless, many Tajiks successfully integrate into the emirate's global tourist and trading business simply because they are able to capitalize on their close cultural ties with Iranian and Afghan traders, entrepreneurs, and businessmen. Cultivating relations to the established Afghan or Iranian diaspora in the emirate, Afghan traders and Iranian businessmen have an influential position in the transregional trading business in the UAE and simultaneously invest in the real estate sector and Dubai's booming middle- and upper-class tourist sector (see Elshashtawy 2008, Parsa and Keivani 2002). For Tajiks, they are therefore potential doorkeepers to relations (*wasta*) around potential Arab sponsors (*kafeel*), and, as such, an important prerequisite to upgrade one's one status as 'foreign migrant worker' through moving from the informal to the formal economy; i.e., to gain formal employment with a Dubai-based company.

'We trade with whom we trust' is a core principle ruling not only the Tajik Dubai business. It first of all points to the importance of ethnicity- and kin-based business networks and the leading role family members play as ideal business partners because they 'would never cheat you'. However, the cultural proximity of Iranians from Baluchistan and Dari-speaking Afghans turn them into 'trusted familiars' instead of 'strangers' (Osella and Osella 2012:128). Belonging to the Sunni-Hanafi branch of Islam and sharing their rootedness in Persian culture, literature, and history, Tajiks perceive Afghans, Baluch, and other Sunni Iranians as 'brothers' (*barodar*) and claim to belong to 'one people' (*yak millat*) and share one historic-cultural identity. It is therefore no surprise that Tajiks consider Sunni Iranians and Dari-speaking Afghans as 'culturally closer' (*nazdik*) than Turkish speaking Central Asians or Uzbeks from Tajikistan. Another important factor, however, is the Sunni-Shia divide. Although a common claim among Tajiks we met in Dubai was that they do business 'with everyone as long as he is a Muslim', our interlocutors simultaneously emphasized that they 'would never share their accommodation with a Shiite!' Strikingly, religious and cultural belonging has a great impact on how Tajiks adapt to the city, integrate into Dubai business sectors and articulate unity, sameness, and difference (see also Landa, 2013:3).

We thus argue that Tajiks pursue their Dubai business projects in a flexible space of 'cultural nestedness'. This allows for leaving the centre of one's one ethnicity- and kin-based network, crossing over its natural boundaries. It also means involving oneself in the production of what Finke, in his study on the Kazakh minority in Mongolia, has called 'institutional cosiness'; i.e., the institutional production of ideas about appropriateness that include the longing for 'a geographical and social environment with which one is familiar, knows the rules of the game, and feels at home' (Finke 2003:178).

Figs. 2.2 and 2.3 Dubai Deira around Al Nasr Square: Commercial Center and 'Meeting Place'. Photos © Manja Stephan-Emmrich (2013), CC BY 4.0

Migrant guesthouses as a 'meeting place'

The main places where the 'cultural nestedness' or 'cosiness' of Tajik networks in Dubai become spatialized are the temporary migrant accommodations situated in and around Al Nasr Square. By residing in a migrant guesthouse or in one of the low-budget hotels around Al Nasr Square, Tajiks adapt to Dubai's urban everyday life, get involved into new economic sectors, and enlarge the scope of their businesses. Understanding migrants' accommodations as a place of 'entanglement, the meeting up of different histories many of them without previous connections to others' (Massey 2006:46–71), we argue that migrant guesthouses serve as pivotal urban meeting place, where Tajiks engage in different forms of temporary conviviality, migrant solidarity, and the exchange of business knowledge across cultural, national, and other boundaries. Furthermore, the vibrant and cross-cultural living spaces of migrant accommodations challenge Tajiks' capacity to deal with differences, to manoeuvre through different systems of meaning, and to utilize different cultural registers in order to be economically successful (Vertovec 2010). In a nutshell, Tajiks' career as middlemen in the Dubai trade and tourism business sector usually starts in the migrant guesthouses where they reside.

The area around Dubai Deira offers different categories of guesthouse. The low-budget, overcrowded, and poorly equipped guesthouses provide an affordable residence option for the majority of Tajik migrants working seasonally as *kamak* or vendors in tourist or smartphone shops. Job contracts and employment in a Dubai-based company allow for longer residency and enables Tajiks to eventually move to more expensive but better-equipped guesthouses, which offer more space and comfort. Only a minority of Tajiks manage, like Rustam, to buy an apartment in the neighboring emirates of Sharjah or Ajman, enabling them to bring their families in the United Arab Emirates and to reside in the country for longer periods. These economic actors stay closely connected with Tajikistan through regular visits or business trips home or by including family members in their translocal businesses.

The four guesthouses we[13] stayed in during our fieldwork are owned and managed by Afghans who rent three- or four-bedroom apartments in Deira's residential areas situated near the main business sectors, to traders, middlemen, and businesspeople from Afghanistan, Iran, and Tajikistan. A guesthouse's landlord is responsible for his tenants' safety; he supervises the maintenance of the house rules, and he sometimes also stores and manages the migrants' cash income. The guesthouses we stayed in were equipped with a separate safe where the tenants

---

13 For reasons of legibility, we continue using 'we' here, although it should be noted that migrant guesthouses in Dubai Deira are male-dominated, 'bachelor' spaces. Consequently, only the male co-author of this chapter had permanent access to the guesthouses Tajiks dwell in, while the female co-author visited migrant guesthouses only when invited for common lunch or dinner. Otherwise she stayed in hotels nearby or lived with the families of long-term-resident Tajiks in their apartments in the emirate of Sharjah.

kept their documents and the money they earned. Afghan landlords in Deira also employ a cook (often an Afghan as well) who is responsible for lunch and dinner, operates as room cleaner, facility manager and sometimes stores the migrants' earnings.

The guestrooms we stayed in were always overcrowded. Six or seven people lived in each room and new guests often had to sleep on the floor. Although there was a constant flow of people, the Tajiks we met had their fixed place in a single guesthouse, where they would stay during every trip to Dubai, often with other Afghan or Baluch tenants whom they have known for many years. Following their own business during the daytime, all residents meet daily in the guesthouse for common lunches and dinners. Eating and relaxing together, this time off from work creates a social space for debating politics, economics, and religion, exchanging business knowledge about trading conditions, prices, contacts and visa regulations, and sharing their latest family stories and the joys and sorrows of mobile life. Eventually, many of the after-lunch or dinner conversations result in new business ideas and relationships, thereby creating new spaces for articulating and imagining a Muslim business community that traverses national, ethnic, and other boundaries (Stephan-Emmrich 2017).

Tajiks' preference for Afghan-owned guesthouses are overwhelmingly articulated in religious and cultural terms. However, as demonstrated by our own experiences gaining access to guesthouses where our Tajik interlocutors resided, besides cultural closeness, trust plays a pivotal role. Placing an emphasis on social contacts, who may serve as middlemen and thus gatekeepers to favorable guesthouses, as well as access to financial resources and personal qualities such as reliability and a good social reputation, Tajiks are involved in a system of 'informal sponsorship' and the 'right connections' that institutionalizes the overlap between living and doing business in Dubai. In order to get permission to stay in the guesthouse of one of our key Tajik interlocutors, we had to find someone who trusted us and accepted the responsibility of paying the monthly rent on our behalf in case we were not able to pay for ourselves.

Ideally, the 'informal sponsor' runs a sustainable business on the basis of long-term residency and a work contract with a Dubai-based company. Alternatively, gatekeepers to a guesthouse-based residency in Deira are often close 'contacts' (business partners or relatives) of the guesthouse landlord, or of the owners of the tourist or phone shops that Tajiks typically work for. Our eventual gatekeeper and informal sponsor was a Tajik who, working as consultant for Russian and Arab tourists in an Iranian supermarket for many years, has cultivated long-term connections in the mobile Afghan trading community and had the necessary links to the Afghan owner of the guesthouse.[14]

Acting as middlemen in very different contexts, Tajiks in Dubai cross culturally varied spheres of living and working, and thus form networks among 'trusted familiars' who may even share their business profits and clients. This is exactly what Boissevain (1974:28) terms 'linkages between persons in a network', which 'may be examined in terms of their structural diversity, the goods and services exchanged, the direction in which these move, and finally the frequency of interaction'. Linking ethnicity- and kin-based business networks in the Emirates with those of Afghan and Iranian co-tenants, Tajiks actively create opportunities for the pursuit of a successful career as middleman, agent, vendor, or sales consultant far from their Tajik homes or Russia's precarious labour market regimes. Through their Afghan and Iranian business contacts, they enlarge the 'institutional cosiness' of their Tajik networks in Dubai and are thus able to move outside the restrictive social responsibilities and structures of their ethnicity- and kin-based networks. They are therefore able to take advantage of the economic freedom (*ozody*) Firuz pointed to earlier in his assessment of Dubai as a 'good' and business-friendly place.

Simultaneously, participating in everyday life in migrants' guesthouses, we gained insight into the hierarchies, dependencies, and constraints that Dubai's trade and tourist economy create and that Tajiks have to cope with. On the one hand, in their position as newcomers to the Dubai business realm, Tajiks are dependent on their better established and connected Afghan and Iranian business partners or roommates. Tajiks therefore tend to accept, yet are subordinate to, the often-claimed cultural superiority, economic competence, and leadership of Iranian business partners and roommates. Due to the rather flexible notion of 'Afghanness', Afghans consider themselves as having been part of

---

14 It should be mentioned here that the male co-author of this article worked for several years in the Dubai tourism business. Our access to Tajik migrant guesthouses therefore heavily relied on his previously-established business contacts with an Iranian supermarket in Dubai Deira.

the Soviet Union (see Marsden 2015) and thus claim a shared Soviet experience with their Tajik partners, while Iranians see Tajiks as 'little Soviet brothers', who, due to their isolation from the wider Muslim community during the Soviet period, have a profound lack of cultural and religious knowledge. Tajiks become therefore frequent targets of an aggressive religious and cultural proselytization. For example: one of our main interlocutors, a young man who spent some years studying Islamic subjects in Riyadh, left the room, when in one of the numerous after-lunch discussions his Iranian roommate boasted of the cultural sophistication of the Iranian people and their crucial role in shaping Islamic civilization. He later explained: 'Iranians always boost their culture. I don't like it. [...] I [also] don't share [his roommate's] religious conviction (Arab *aqīda*). What he says about women in Islam, for example, is not right. But he's the best friend of my employer. So, I keep quiet, or leave the room'.

Situating themselves in the social, cultural, and religious hierarchies of their business networks, Tajiks in Dubai face a wide range of limitations and constraints that they have to accept, cope with, and try to overcome. Therefore, as the following paragraphs illustrate, Tajiks successfully act as social mediators, economic middlemen, and cultural translators. In this regard, Iranian and Afghan business projects, enterprises, and companies obviously profit from their Tajik employees' social contacts and their capacity to connect, recruit, and expand their trading businesses into new economic fields, as well as new markets in Central Asia, Eurasia, Europe, and the United States.

Tajik middlemen in the 'Dubai business': connecting, expanding, translating

Working as *kamak*, shop vendors, or traders around Al Nasr Square, many Tajiks, including our respondents Firuz, Dilshod, and Rustam, additionally operate as economic middlemen (*posrednik*). Speaking the Russian language and being familiar with the habits of Russians and their culture they also share common cultural, linguistic, and religious traditions with Sunni-Hanafi Iranians and Afghans. Equipped with these cultural capacities, Tajiks serve as a bridge between Afghan and Iranian business activities and the Russian tourist market. They therefore often switch between undocumented and legal work. Moving in and across culturally and ethnically different local settings, Tajiks as middlemen are able to combine economic success with an assessment of wellbeing that is grounded in the experience of being independent from the political constraints and structural exploitation prevalent in Tajikistan and Russia. At the same time, their economic brokerage position empowers Tajiks to situationally bypass the social obligations and structural constraints institutionalized in their ethnicity- and kin-related network and thereby become creative and innovative economic agents.

Dilshod and the tourist business

Dilshod has worked as a tour guide for an Iranian tourist company based in Dubai since 2011. Prior to moving to Dubai, he was employed as a sales consultant in an Afghani shop in Moscow's *Cherkiz* bazaar. When the bazaar was closed in 2008, the Afghan shop owner recommended Dilshod to a business partner in Dubai. Due to Dilshod's Russian, English, and Dari language proficiency and his university degree in economics, he was hired quickly to work in a phone shop at Al Nasr Square, where he worked as sales specialist for Russian-speaking customers. Capitalizing on the idea of a 'shared Persian culture', Dilshod successfully integrated into the Afghan business community in Dubai. He shared apartments with his Afghan colleagues and became the best seller in the phone shop. However, his career was also advanced by his piety and the depth and soundness of his religious knowledge. Praying five times a day and speaking excellent Dari, Dilshod easily conveys his fine character and priorities, which led to an excellent reputation within the Afghan business community in Dubai. While working for the Afghani phone shop, in the course of two years, Dilshod was able to invest in new business connections and managed to get a job offer from an Iranian tourist company. As a tour guide, he utilized his contacts with Russian and Russian-speaking tourists and was thus able to explore new business contacts in Almaty, Novosibirsk, Kazan, Moscow, and Dushanbe. Eventually, he helped his company to expand their tourist business into Central Asia, the Caucasus, and Eurasia. Due to his successful networking, Dilshod became a respected and trusted staff member, but simultaneously maintained his old connections to the Afghan business community. When we met him in winter 2013, he worked both as a tourist guide and as a sales consultant and had started to connect Russian clients interested in mobile phones with the Afghan phone shop he used to work for. As an economic broker, he also expanded his own business activities in different directions and also opened up new avenues for his Iranian tourist company into Dubai's Russian tourist market. While the company used to focus merely on Iranian and Indian tourists, with the business Dilshod brought in, they were able to raise their profits during the tourist season by nearly fifteen percent.

By connecting different trade and tourist sectors through his business ties, Dilshod simultaneously increased his own material and immaterial profits. Drawing on his connections with other Tajik middlemen in Dubai, Dilshod started to organize informal shopping tours for his clients to shopping malls and markets where his partners were employed, allowing them to benefit from this deal through commissions. Dilshod was also able to invest in the social ties that link him with his family at home: he brought his cousin from Tajikistan and managed to find a job for him in Dilshod's former workplace, i.e., the Afghan phone shop.

Fig. 2.4 Loading cars and other commodities: Iranian companies and the car cargo shipment at Dubai Creek. Photo © Manja Stephan-Emmrich (2014), CC BY 4.0

Rustam and the UAE car market

Rustam's story shows that Tajiks are also active as middlemen in the United Arab Emirates' booming new and second-hand car market, a business sector in which many Afghan traders and dealers and Iranian cargo companies invest and are active (Paterson 2005:16ff.). Profiting from the established free-trade zones, the United Arab Emirates' car business stretches from the regions' port cities via the Hormuz corridor to Iranian port cities such as Bandar Abbas, and from there further afield to markets in Europe, Asia, and the US (Ali and Keivani 2002). Due to their multiple middlemen competencies, Tajiks act as intermediaries between Iranian cargo companies and Afghan dealers in the Arab Emirates and clients, dealers, and sellers in Central Asia and other parts of Asia, Russia, the Caucasus, wider Europe, and the United States. As Rustam's case study illustrates, the booming car trade facilitates successful entrepreneurial projects that allow Tajiks in Dubai to engage in translocal lifestyles and to pursue a livelihood based on living simultaneously 'here' and 'there', benefiting from both ethnicity- and kin-based business ties at home, in Russia, and in the United Arab Emirates. Building on trust and a good reputation, Tajik middlemen increase their social status both at home and in the business community in Dubai.

Rustam is a middle-scale entrepreneur in the car cargo business, who shifted his business base from Dushanbe to Dubai in 2009. Before that, he undertook several business trips to the Gulf in order to establish ties with Afghan and Iranian entrepreneurs and to become involved with their business networks. When his efforts began to pay off, he moved to Dubai and opened a car showroom there and a small spare-parts shop in the neighboring emirate, Sharjah. He also bought a two-bedroom apartment in the Ajman emirate and eventually brought his family to the United Arab Emirates. Within five years, he was able to expand his business ties further to South Korea and the US and link them to his existing business networks in Tajikistan, Russia, and the Emirates. He currently imports new and used cars from the US and spare car parts from South Korea and ships them as cargo via Dubai Deira and Bandar Abbas to his business partners in Tajikistan, Russia, and elsewhere.

'I have been involved in the car trade business since 1997. Until 2002, I brought Russian-made cars from Russian markets, mainly from Samara and Tolyatti, to Dushanbe. When the demand for Japanese cars increased in the Tajikistani market, we started to specialize in Japanese cars and invested in contacts in the UAE car market. In the beginning, we just exported cars from Dubai, and by 2009 I had done several shipments of new and used Japanese cars to Tajikistan. In 2009, we expanded our business through a good connection (*kanal*) to the USA and South Korea. For this purpose, I moved to Dubai and opened up a local office in order to manage the retransmission of cars and spare parts (via Dubai) to Tajikistan. Why Dubai? For example, if we send one container of car spare parts from South Korea to Tajikistan, we have to pay 15,000 USD, plus we have to up- and download the cargo several times and therefore sometimes loose goods. Besides, it takes a long time to deliver the commodities. If we transmit the same container via Dubai we don't lose a lot of time for delivery and we are able to reduce our expenses by 35–40%' (Dubai, 2012).

While Rustam has been very successful in expanding his transregional and crosscultural business networks into new markets in Russia, the CIS, Iran, and Afghanistan, he simultaneously 'invests' in the Tajik migrant community in Dubai. For example, he has good relations with Tajik *kamak*. Acting as 'business marketers without payments', *kamak* advertise Rustam's goods among their own tourist clients. In return, they use Rustam as a bank, i.e., he stores and manages their cash earnings and sends cash to Tajikistan via his business contacts in Dushanbe. This is obviously a profitable deal for both sides, again built on trust: both sides avoid paperwork and save remittance fees, and Rustam can work with their money while it travels to Dushanbe. For example, he uses it in Dubai to purchase goods for his shop in Dushanbe while that amount is later replaced by the relatives working in Rustam's shop in Dushanbe. Supporting *kamak*, Rustam at the same time accumulates social prestige in the Tajik community in Dubai, which he re-capitalizes into further business networks.

Rustam's car business also involves Tajik friends and relatives. Firuz, whom we introduced above, works as a middleman for Rustam. He systematically acquires new clients for Rustam's car showroom and the spare-parts shop and gets a commission from their purchases. Rustam also employs family members. He organized a visa for his younger brother who is now managing his shop in Dubai, and he also transferred the responsibility for his spare-parts shop in Dushanbe to another brother. Thus, Rustam keeps close ties to his relatives and with their help has managed to maintain Dushanbe as second base for his cargo business. Like many other Tajiks, Rustam utilizes his relatives as a local channel to expand the repertoire of his Dubai export goods to include clothing, computer technology, and other prestigious lifestyle commodities advertised as *dubaijsky*, and thus enables these relatives to integrate into the global Dubai trade business 'from home'.

By moving in, as well as creating, culturally familiar spaces of economic activity, as economic middlemen Tajiks like Rustam or Dilshod can combine entrepreneurial activities with professional and educational careers (see also Pelican 2014:299). They thereby amass a kind of 'freedom' (*ozody*) and independence that forms an integral part of their self-understanding as 'businessmen' or 'entrepreneurs'. This is in line with Pelican's observation that the lack of flexibility and the structurally exploitative work and salary conditions in the United Arab Emirates has motivated Cameroonian migrants to switch from formal employment to the cargo business, or to combine formal employment with informal activities (Pelican 2014:280).

Challenges, changes, constraints

While both Rustam and Dilshod have built successful careers as middlemen in the Dubai business community, we do not want to one-dimensionally celebrate the opportunities that result from Tajiks' involvement in the Dubai business. The flexibility Tajik middlemen show while pursuing their entrepreneurial strategies and finding their niche in the vibrant Dubai business scene is subject to the precarious and uncertain conditions set by rapidly shifting global markets and changing (trans-)national migration regimes. Stressing the 'translocal' dimension of the Tajik Dubai business, in this chapter we explicitly want to point to the complex interplay of opportunities and limitations that shape the livelihoods of Tajik middlemen in the Dubai business community (Bromber 2013, Freitag and von Oppen 2010). In this context, migration studies have extensively discussed transnationalism and translocality as a lived reality shaped by the migrant's multiple situatedness or connectedness in, or with, 'here' and 'there' (Smith 2011). This may lead eventually to the individual's engagement in transnational lifestyles, or 'habitus' (Kelly and Lusis 2006). This gives Tajiks the opportunity to move flexibly in and across the United Arab Emirates and Tajikistan, to link family with business partners, and thereby enables them to '[try] to make the best of their stay in Dubai, while focusing on investments back home and expanding their business networks' (Pelican 2014:294–95).

Tajiks also respond directly to their precarious status in Dubai as 'foreign migrants'. As mentioned above, this status is structurally promoted by the *kafala* sponsorship system and an immigration regime that excludes non-Emiratis from access to citizenship and defines all foreigners in relation to 'labour' only (Ahmad 2012). Tajiks are therefore only 'temporary visitors' in Dubai, whose long-term residence is tied up with access to formal employment (Vora 2009, Gardner 2012). Consequently, the Dubai business is a highly volatile field. After it was announced that Dubai will host the next World Expo in 2020, the police intensified their street raids around Al-Nasser Square to clear street workers (*kamak*) without a working licence from the area in order to make it more tourist-friendly. This action led to a rapid increase of deportations of Tajiks and other Central Asians in the winter of 2013–2014 and fuelled the fear of deportation for Tajiks working in Dubai. At the same time, the current economic crisis in Russia has led to a striking slump in the number of Russian tourists and thus forced many Tajiks working in the tourist sector to look for new job opportunities outside the Emirates.

Struggling with these problems, Tajiks in Dubai simultaneously have to cope with a new wave of migrants from Tajikistan and Russia, who stimulate the 'homegrown' urban fear of 'ruralization' through the arrival of migrants from remote areas to the urban setting of Dubai. Due to the economic crisis in both Tajikistan and Russia, many unskilled and badly educated young men from rural areas try to become successful in running a business in Dubai. While some of the young men use their family connections, others utilize their social networks (*odnoklasnik*) and move directly from Russia to the Emirates. Still others come to Dubai after having been deported from Russia. Badly skilled, inexperienced, and without the necessary language proficiency, they face difficulties in gaining a foothold in the established Dubai business world and overwhelmingly become involved in undocumented street work as *kamak*. The Russian tourist sector, therefore, has become a highly competitive field. Many established middlemen complained to us about the youngsters' crude and ill-mannered behavior, as these relative newcomers hang around in large groups in front of hotels and shops and lack the work ethic of the Tajik community that operates in Al Nasr Square. Thus, they fear that the newcomers could frighten away the tourists and jeopardize the good reputation Tajik middlemen have among Afghans and Iranians in the Emirates, or, as a concerned middleman working as *kamak* and tourist guide at Al Nasr Square has put it:

> 'We Tajiks are everywhere! But everywhere our reputation (*obrū*) is very low (*past*). In Russia, they call us *churky* (wooden stump). Many of us come from rural areas. We are (a) poor (nation). Many (Tajiks) came to Dubai also in the hope to get respected [...] as Muslims, because Dubai is an Islamic country. [...] we worked hard to gain standing here. We are educated, have good manners (*odob*), we are urbanites (*shahry*). That's why Afghans, Iranians, and even Arab migrants (*migranty*) show us respect. They trust us and do business with us. But now they (the newly arrived Tajik youngsters) come directly from the villages. They've never lived in a city, they aren't educated, they speak with loud voices and shout, are dressed like farmers (*dehqonho*), and they violate our rules [...]. They will destroy our businesses and tarnish our reputation' (Dubai, 2013).

As a consequence, many Tajik middlemen seek to leave the *kamak* business and instead increase their investment in Afghan or Iranian business connections. In this context, the perceived shame of Tajik identity is increasingly detrimental to Tajiks' self-perception as economic middlemen in the Dubai business world and eventually led to a heightened identification as 'Muslim', rather than 'Tajik'.

On translocality

This chapter has explored the translocal livelihoods of well-educated, mobile Tajiks working in the United Arab Emirates ever since the Dubai boom that reached Tajikistan in the late 1990s and connected local markets and households with the global flows of wholesale and retail trade, as well with the thriving Gulf tourism industry. Tracing how our interlocutors operate as economic middlemen and mediators, this chapter has depicted the economic mobility of Dubai's Tajiks between their 'homes' in Tajikistan, the migrant community in Russia, and various formal and informal business sectors in the Gulf. As the three selected ethnographic case studies have illustrated, Dubai is a key site of economic linkages spanning national and cultural boundaries, and it offers a wide range of work availabilities for Tajiks, particularly in the tourist and trading sectors. Pushed by Russia's recent attempts to restrict residency status for Tajik and other Central Asian migrants who are not citizens of a member-state of the Eurasian Economic Union, Dubai has become an alternative destination for many skilled and unskilled Tajiks. As we have shown, Tajiks invest their cultural and social capital in multiple ways and they successfully integrate into various economic sectors. As they are familiar with the Russian language and culture, they connect Afghan and Iranian entrepreneurs with the booming Russian-speaking tourist market in the United Arab Emirates. Crossing cultural boundaries through their language proficiency, translocal business networks, and religious identity as Sunni-Hanafi Muslims, many Tajiks connect people, places, and markets at 'home' with those in the Middle East and Eurasia. In their brokerage position, they create as well as move in translocal spaces which can facilitate economic success, social mobility, and the amassing of wellbeing and belonging. This creates a setting in which Tajiks creatively and innovatively involve themselves in processes of globalization (see also Henry Alff in Chapter Five).

However, local migration regimes such as the United Arab Emirates' limited residency permits for 'foreign migrant workers', as well the fragile economic situation at 'home', push many Tajiks in Dubai into the status of undocumented workers facing uncertainty and vulnerability. We therefore argue that the livelihoods of Tajik middlemen in Dubai are characterized by complex processes of negotiation between multiple opportunities and constraints. Thus, translocality is a possibility, i.e., an urban setting that facilitates the pursuit of a livelihood outside the limitations created by economic, migration, and deportation systems. But the Dubai business is at the same time a highly volatile field that creates new, uncertain, and precarious working conditions for Tajik migrants. Translocality is therefore both produced and experienced by our Tajik interlocutors as a social reality that is formed by the creative and flexible combination of economic strategies, mobile experiences, and cultural competencies by which Tajiks in the Gulf try to ensure the sustainability and success of their mobile livelihoods shaped by incomplete post-Soviet nation-building projects and the precarious outcomes of the global economy.

Conceptualizing 'translocality' as a research perspective also allows us to critically scrutinize hegemonic theories of migration and globalization. As a consequence, this chapter has put emphasis on how translocal connections and transfers between Central Asia, Russia, and the Gulf are socially constructed by non-elite and non-state actors, who in the academic literature are often one-dimensionally portrayed as peripheral actors moving in marginal urban spaces (see Smith 2011). Emphasizing their capacity to connect, mediate, and expand, we have explored how Tajiks in Dubai play a pivotal role in shaping the circulation and transfer of consumer goods, people, knowledge, and ideas. Obviously, Tajiks' involvement in the global trading and tourist business is not a unidirectional transfer process from the Gulf to Tajikistan. The Tajik Dubai business covers multidirectional transfer processes, in which Tajik middlemen substantially contribute to the transcultural and transnational urbanism and cosmopolitanism of Dubai's city spaces and business sectors. Hence translocality as a research perspective opens up new epistemological avenues into understanding globalization not merely by focusing on macro- or meso-level processes termed as 'Gulfization' or 'Dubaization' in the fields of the economy and urbanization (Wippel *et al.* 2014). With its focus on Tajik middlemen, this chapter has instead argued for a 'social history' of the Tajik Dubai business 'from below' (Freitag and von Oppen 2010:5) written from the perspective of actors who are not integral parts of the Gulf's interregional economic and social past (Osella and Osella 2012, Vora 2013), but who, through their cultural and business ties, actively connect to it. Furthermore, by becoming involved in and expanding the Russian tourist business, Tajik middlemen become influential actors in shaping translocal relations in Dubai's informal economy. This leads us to support Neha Vora's critical response to dominant academic representation of the Gulf as 'exclusively Middle Eastern' (Vora 2013:3).

Finally, we have argued that the Tajik Dubai business is 'translocal' because the economic activities Tajik middlemen are involved in are embedded, yet also 'emplaced' in a complex configuration of spatial relations between people, places, and markets in Central Asia, Eurasia, and the Gulf. These configurations also include Tajiks' spatial experiences tied to these places. We thus associate being a middleman with the capacity, and the awareness of the capacity, to cope with uncertainty and volatility in geographic settings far from 'home'. Showing a cultural competence, or 'a built-up skill in manoeuvring more or less expertly with a particular system of meanings and meaningful forms' (Hannerz 1990:239), Tajik middleman open up new economic paths into the vibrant Dubai business. In the process, they connect, mediate, transfer, and translate their academic and business knowledge into culturally and economically different local contexts.

References

Ahmad, Attiya. 'Beyond Labor: Foreign Residents in the Persian Gulf States'. In Mehran Kamrava and Zahra Babar, eds. *Migrant Labor in the Persian Gulf.* London: Hurst & Co., 2012, pp. 21–40.

Boissevain, Jeremy. *Friends of Friends: Networks, Manipulators and Coalitions.* Oxford: Basil Blackwell, 1974.

Bromber, Katrin. 'Working With "Translocality": Conceptual Implications and Analytical Consequences'. In Steffen Wippel, ed. *Regionalizing Oman: Political, Economic and Social Dynamics.* Dordrecht: Springer, 2013, pp. 63–72, https://doi.org/10.1007/978-94-007-6821-5_4

Elsheshtawy, Yasser. 'Transitory Sites: Mapping Dubai's "Forgotten" Urban Spaces'. *International Journal of Urban and Regional Research* 32.4 (2008): 968–88, https://doi.org/10.1111/j.1468-2427.2008.00819.x

Finke, Peter. 'Historical Homelands and Transnational Ties: The Case of the Mongolian Kazaks'. *Zeitschrift für Ethnologie* 138 (2014): 175–94.

Freitag, Ulrike, and Achim von Oppen, eds. *Translocality. The Study of Globalising Processes from a Southern Perspective.* Leiden: Brill, 2010, https://doi.org/10.1163/ej.9789004181168.i-452

Gardner, Andrew. 'Why do they keep coming? Labor Migrants in the Gulf States'. In Mehran Kamrava and Zahra Babar, eds. *Migrant Labor in the Persian Gulf.* London: Hurst & Co., 2012, pp. 41–58.

Habeck, Joachim Otto, and Philipp Schröder, eds. 'From Siberia with Love or Angst in the City?' *Ethnoscripts* 18.1 (2016): 5–24.

Hannerz, Ulf. 'Cosmopolitans and Locals in World Culture'. In Mike Featherstone, ed. *Global Culture: Nationalism, Globalization, and Modernity.* London: Sage, 1990, pp. 237–51.

Hannerz, Ulf. *Exploring the City. Inquiries towards an Urban Anthropology.* New York: Columbia University Press, 1980.

ILO. *Migration and Development in Tajikistan-Emigration, Return and Diaspora* Moscow: International Labour Organization, 2010.

Kathiravelu, Laavanya. *Migrant Dubai. Low Wage Workers and the Construction of a Global City.* Basingstoke: Palgrave Macmillan, 2016, https://doi.org/10.1057/9781137450180

Kelly, Philip, and Tom Lusis. 'Migration and the Transnational Habitus: Evidence from Canada and the Philippines'. *Environment and Planning A: Economy and Space* 38.5 (2006): 831–47, https://doi.org/10.1068/a37214

Khusenova, Nafisa. 'The Feminization of Tajik Labor Migration to Russia'. In Marlene Laruelle, ed. *Migration and Social Upheaval as the Face of Globalization in Central Asia*. Leiden and Boston: Brill, 2013, pp. 355–75, https://doi.org/10.1163/9789004249509_022

Landa, Janet. 'Economic Success of Ethnically Homogeneous Middleman Diasporas in the Provision of Club Goods: The Role of Culture, Religion, Ethnic Identity, and Ethnic Boundaries'. In Waltraut Kokot, Mijal Gandelsman-Trier and Christian Giordano, eds. *Diaspora as a Resource. Comparative Studies in Strategies, Networks and Urban Space*. Zurich: LIT-Verlag, 2003, pp. 41–66.

Marsden, Magnus. 'From Kabul to Kiev: Afghan Trading Networks Across the Former Soviet Union'. *Modern Asian Studies* 49.4 (2015): 1010–48, https://doi.org/10.1017/S0026749X14000584

Massey, Doreen. 'The Geographical Mind'. In David Balderstone, ed. *The Secondary Geography Handbook*. Sheffield: Geographical Association, 2006, pp. 46–51.

Mullodjanov, Parviz. 'Tajikistan in 2016: Challenges, Risks, Trends'. *CABAR — Central Asian Bureau for Analytical Reporting* (14/3/2016), http://cabar.asia/en/2094-2/

Olimova, Saodat. 'To Stay or Not to Stay: The Global Economic Crisis and Return Migration to Tajikistan'. In Marlene Laruelle, ed. *Migration and Social Upheaval as the Face of Globalization in Central Asia*. Leiden and Bosten: Brill, 2013, pp. 65–85, https://doi.org/10.1163/9789004249509_007

Osella, Caroline, and Filippo Osella. 'Migration, Networks and Connectedness Across the Indian Ocean'. In Mehran Kamrava and Zahra Babar, eds. *Migrant Labor in the Persian Gulf*. London: Hurst & Co., 2012, pp. 105–36.

Parsa, Ali, and Ramin Keivani. 'The Hormuz Corridor: Building and Cross-Border Region between Iran and the UAE'. In Saskia Sassen, ed. *Global Networks, Linked Cities*. New York: Routledge, 2002, pp. 183–207.

Pastrova, Ekaterina. 'National Information Agency of Tajikistan'. NIAT 'Khovar' (2014), http://khovar.tj

Paterson, Anna. 'Understanding Markets in Afghanistan. A Study of the Market of Second-Hand Cars'. *Afghanistan Research Evaluation Unit* (2005): 1–32, https://doi.org/10.2458/azu_acku_pamphlet_hf3770_6_p384_2005

Pelican, Michaela. 'Urban Lifeworlds of Cameroonian Migrants in Dubai'. *Urban Anthropology and Studies of Cultural Systems and World Economic Development* 43.1–3 (2014): 255–309.

Pink, Johanna, ed. *Muslim Societies in the Age of Mass Consumption: Politics, Culture and Identity Between the Local and the Global*. Cambridge: Cambridge Scholars Publication, 2009.

Roche, Sophie. 'The Role of Islam in the Lives of Central Asian Migrants in Moscow'. *CERIA Brief: Central Asia Program* 2 (2014): 2–5.

Ryazantsev, Sergej. 'Labor Migration from Central Asia to Russia in the Context of the Economic Crisis'. *Russia in Global Affairs* (08/03/2016), http://eng.globalaffairs.ru/valday/Labour-Migration-from-Central-Asia-to-Russia-in-the-Context-of-the-Economic-Crisis-18334

Schröder, Philipp, and Manja Stephan-Emmrich. 'The Institutionalization of Mobility: Wellbeing and Social Hierarchies in Central Asian Translocal Livelihoods'. *Mobilities* 11.3 (2014): 1–24, https://doi.org/10.1080/17450101.2014.984939

Smith, Michael Peter. 'Translocality: A Critical Reflection'. In Katherine Brickell and Ayona Datta, eds. *Translocal Geographies: Spaces, Places and Connections*. Burlington, VT: Ashgate, 2011, pp. 181–98.

Stephan-Emmrich, Manja. 'Playing Cosmopolitan: Muslim Self-Fashioning, Migration, and (Be-)Longing in the Tajik Dubai Business Sector'. *Central Asian Affairs* 4.3 (2017): 270–91, https://doi.org/10.1163/9789004357242_010

Stephan-Emmrich, Manja. 'Studying Islam Abroad: Pious Enterprises and Educational Aspirations of Young Tajik Muslims'. In Pauline Jones Luong, ed. *Islam, Society, and Politics in Central Asia*. Pittsburgh: University of Pittsburgh Press, 2017, pp. 263–324, https://doi.org/10.2307/j.ctt1r6b097.15

Vora, Neha. *Impossible Citizens: Dubai's Indian Diaspora*. Durham and London: Duke University Press, 2013, https://doi.org/10.1215/9780822397533

Wippel, Steffen, Katrin Bromber, Christian Steiner, and Birgit Krawietz, eds. *Under Construction: Logics of Urbanism in the Gulf Region*. Burlington, VT: Ashgate, 2014, https://doi.org/10.4324/9781315549323

PART 2

TRAVELLING IDEAS:
SACRED AND SECULAR

3. Sacred Lineages in Central Asia: Translocality and Identity

Azim Malikov

Introduction

One of the striking aspects of Central Asia is its cultural and ethnic diversity from ancient times until today. In the pre-Soviet period, group identities including tribal, clan, local, and family identities were more important for the Central Asian population in determining loyalties than ethnic origin (Baldauf 1992:5). A complex of multiple identities was intimately intertwined with the social and economic conditions of the region. Social identity is therefore conceived of as open, flexible, multiple and contextual in place and time.

While ethnic groups have been the main focus of study among ethnologists interested in Central Asian social identity, I contend that the examination of lower-level social units such as clans and lineages is also important to understand identity-formation processes. For example, the same clan can often be found in more than one ethnic group (Schlee 1994).

Out of many different social, tribal, and regional groups in Central Asia, so-called 'holy groups',[1] or sacred lineages,[2] whose identity was

---

1   By 'sacred lineage' or 'holy group' I mean privileged groups that have high social status and claim to be descendants of the Prophet Muhammad, his companions, the first caliphs and Sufi saints.
2   A lineage is usually taken to be a group of people who trace descent unilineally from a common ancestor through a series of traceable links (Holý 1996:74–75).

          https://doi.org/10.11647/OBP.0114.03

transformed during the twentieth century, are the focus of this chapter. At present, due to different models of nation-building and social and cultural shifts in countries of the region, new changes in their identity are taking place.

The Kazakhs, Karakalpaks, Tajiks, Turkmens, Uyghurs and Uzbeks in Central Asia share some distinct 'holy groups' including the Khoja,[3] Sayyids,[4] and Ishon.[5] Some of these lineages feature among two or more of these ethno-regional groups. The ways these ethnic groups conceptulize membership of the Khoja or Sayyid lineages provides an excellent case study of the translocal dimension of these groups' links and relations.

The term translocality refers to a complex and multi-faceted phenomenon. Tenhunen (2011:416) defines translocality as relations that 'extend beyond the village community'. Other scholars use translocality as a descriptive tool that refers to the 'sum of phenomena which result from a multitude of circulations and transfers' (Freitag and von Oppen 2010:5). One aspect of translocality is the visualisation and imagining of linkages between places, what Brickell and Datta (2011:18) refer to as 'translocal imagination'. Translocal approaches are applied to enhance the understanding of various phenomena, covering such issues as identity formation, media usage, and knowledge transfer.

Understanding processes of identification requires familiarity with the contexts in which they occur. 'Such contexts include particular geographical and infrastructural conditions, the actors who live under such conditions, a wide variety of institutions, different kinds of social relations, material resources, and also the kinds of symbolic and discursive resources that we call collective identities' (Donahoe et al. 2009:10). Various identities become applicable in various situations. Collective identities are articulated with reference to different

---

3   The terms *Khoja, Khwaja, Khodja, Qozha* which mean 'master' in Persian have been taken to imply, variously, descent from 'Arabs', descent from the Prophet or Ali, descent from the first caliphs, or descent from Islamizing saints (DeWeese, 1999). There is also the term *Ahl Al-bayt* ('People of the House', meaning the household of Prophet Muhammad).
4   The Sayyids are a group of people who claim direct patrilineal descent from the Prophet Muhammad through his daughter Fatima.
5   Ishon was a title or a name given to respected religious figures — the heads of Sufi brotherhoods of various levels and their descendants.

dimensions (nationality, ethnicity, kinship, language, religion, local or regional origins, etc.). In some situations we want to note distinction, and in others we look for something in common or a general affiliation. Groups in certain conditions can keep their clan identity after an ethnic reaffiliation (Schlee 1994:234). The history of Central Asian 'holy groups', their genealogy and identification has been studied by O. Sukhareva (1960), B. Karmysheva (1976), A. Muminov (1996, 1998, 2011), D. DeWeese (1995, 1999, 2008), B. Privratsky (2001, 2004), S. Abashin (2001a, 2001b, 2005, 2006), Z. Ibadullaeva (2001), B. Babajanov (2006), Yayoi Kawahara (2012), Morimoto Kazuo (2014), K. Abdullaev (2008:373–80), and K. Kalonov (2005) and others. A significant proportion of these studies, however, deal with local societies.

Abashin studied the sacred lineages of the Ferghana Valley, the relationships between them, and what he considers the area's 'holy groups' as part of the larger group of 'the descendants of the saints' in Central Asia (Abashin 2005:70). Kazakh researcher Ibadullaeva studied the Khoja in southern Kazakhstan. She also analyzed the oral history of this holy group and their kinship networks in some provinces of Uzbekistan (Ibadullaeva 2001). According to Finke, in the southern part of Karakalpakstan and Khorezm 'a few interlocutors assigned Khoja the status of an ethnic group, but this has not been officially recognized. Most people in above mentioned regions would probably disagree with such a claim. This second interpretation unites Khoja across different ethnic groups, in particular Karakalpaks, Kazaks and Uzbeks' (Finke 2014:122).

Some 'holy groups' fulfilled eminent religious and social duties in pre-Soviet Central Asian society and were held in very high esteem by everyone (Sukhareva 1960:66–68). Members of these lineages performed religious services at ritual celebrations, acted as healers, and helped settle disputes. Some were also the caretakers of Sufi shrines (DeWeese 1999). During the Soviet period, state policies on restructuring society and local identities in Central Asia led to the transformation of sacred lineages. Khojas lost their previous religious status as mediators between local communities, because the Soviet authorities denied their legal and economic privileges, persecuted, and repressed them (see Abdullaev in Chapter One).

My previous research on the Khoja of Central Asia[6] has established criteria for the study of the translocal communications of 'holy groups'. I examine how members of these 'holy groups' create, discursively perform and renegotiate the boundaries of their own group on various scales (local and translocal), and how they thereby refer to very different symbols and markers of identity. Acknowledging the heterogeneity that exists across Central Asia, my examples are based on two regions, namely the Turkistan region of Kazakhstan and Tashkent city of Uzbekistan.

My goal is to study the transformation of the translocal links between, and the identities of, the 'holy groups' over the past 110 years, including the following periods: the Russian Empire (1867–1917), the Soviet period (1917–1991), and the post-Soviet period. Each interval had its own peculiarities and a different degree of influence on 'holy groups' and their identification. The largest transformations of society took place during the Soviet period. Nowadays, the influence of ideological development on post-Soviet countries as well as the broadening effects of globalization are more tangible.

This chapter marks, to my knowledge, the first application of the concept of translocality to the study of 'holy groups'. Some of these groups can be called 'translocal communities', because they relate 'to a group of (translocal) households, whose members live in diverse locations, which are connected through functional interdependencies' (Lohnert and Steinbrink 2005:98). These 'holy groups' demonstrate multiple identities, one of which is translocal in nature, i.e., it goes beyond a single village, region, country, or social group. I studied Khoja and Sayyid groups in Tashkent, a context that, prior to this, has not been studied specifically, and I examined 'holy groups' in two regions, and within different social and cultural contexts. The data I shall present was collected during multiple short-term field-research trips between 2010 and 2015, mainly to Tashkent city in Uzbekistan, as well as to the Turkistan region of Kazakhstan.[7]

---

6   For more detailed analysis of the history of Khoja lineages in the Turkistan region
    see Malikov and Khoji (2014) and Malikov (2013a).

7   Most of my data from the Turkistan region was collected with financial and scientific
    support from the Max-Planck Institute for Social Anthropology during my field
    trips in 2010 and 2011; additional data from the Tashkent province of Uzbekistan

In this chapter I employ a conceptual framework based on the notion of 'translocality', and a methodological framework based on the combination of multi-sited ethnography with an oral history approach. I trace the flow of ideas and imagined translocal links between 'holy groups' and investigate differences in the practical meaning and uses of Khoja, Sayyid, and other identities in the above-mentioned communities. I examine the translocal relationships between sacred lineages that have different language and regional affiliations. Thus, my research covers two Central Asian countries with different models of nation-building, ideology, etc.

My choice of Tashkent province and the Turkistan region as my objects of study is far from random. Tashkent is known as a city where representatives of 'holy groups' had high status in the past and created their own state at the end of the eighteenth century. The Turkistan region of Kazakhstan is the biggest religious centre in the country. There, many Khoja and Sayyids of various lineages and ethnic affiliations are concentrated. These localities are meaningful for my analysis because of their sacred value as historically relevant junctions of transregional pilgrimage, and within scholarly and other networks. As such, they are relevant for the formation of certain social and religious identities. In the past, translocal communications took place between particular sacred lineages who lived in different regions, driven by several mutually overlapping reasons: family ties, leadership or membership in Sufi brotherhoods, visiting shrines such as the graves of ancestors, etc.

I argue that the Soviet policy to modernize and homogenize society in Central Asia and to create national identities did not eliminate ancestral identities in the region. Despite the Soviet nationalities policy, some families belonging to 'holy groups' preserved a kind of 'hidden identity'. I observed a wide array of ways to identify members of sacred lineages in Central Asia depending on geographic, social and

---

was collected with financial support from the Volkswagen Foundation's project 'Translocal Goods — Education, Work, and Commodities between Tajikistan, Kyrgyzstan, Russia, China, and the Arab Emirates' in 2015. I would like to express my gratitude to Manja Stephan-Emmrich, Philipp Schröder, Nathan Light, Jeanine Dagyeli, Tricia Ryan and anonymous reviewers for comments and suggestions on this chapter.

cultural contexts. In the pre-Soviet period, the criteria used to recognize different groups of Khoja and Sayyid were genealogy and the name of an ancestor who was a Sufi figure; now, from our point of view, it is advisable to use criteria such as linguistic affiliation to better understand how changes occurred, especially after seventy years of Soviet rule and the development of national republics, national ideologies, and national histories.

This chapter consists of six parts: the introduction above, an overview of the theoretical framework, a historical review, descriptions of research in the Turkistan region of Kazakhstan and in Tashkent in the Republic of Uzbekistan, and my conclusions.

Theoretical approach

A translocal perspective captures the diverse and contradictory effects of interconnectedness between places, institutions, and actors (Freitag and von Oppen 2010:1, Greiner and Sakdapolrak 2013:3–4). The study of borders between locality and translocality from the points of view of geography, time, and social groupings is also important. It is necessary to take into consideration the factors that change social relations and local places due to the arrival of electronic media and the consequent breakdown of barriers around space, place, and culture (Gupta and Ferguson 1992).

This chapter conceptualizes identity and belonging through the lens of translocality and we should therefore examine this concept in several aspects: 1) translocality is clearly understood as interrelation and connectedness between different geographic places; 2) translocality is also applied to study the use of media and the circulation of knowledge and ideas in globally operating networks; 3) the concept of translocality also refers to symbolic flows such as movements of ideas, images, and symbols (Greiner and Sakdapolrak 2013:5); 4) I use the term 'translocal' to explore the overlapping relational identities that emerge within, and the multi-directional dynamics of, 'holy groups'. Accordingly, translocality is understood as an imaginary bridge between the past and the present, and as the circulation of ideas between different chronological periods and geographical locations. Translocal imagination is a kind of place perception, linking locality to a broader set of processes.

The concept of translocality allows us to better understand three aspects of the relationships between 'holy groups' in Central Asia: interregional connections, links between different timescales, and relationships between the 'holy groups' located in different cultural and political environments. The collected empirical material allows us to make a contribution to the discussion about the concept of translocality given the complexity of social, cultural, and genealogical relationships between the groups of sacred lineages, as well as the transformation of identities through different historical periods. Comparative analysis between the two above-mentioned regions allows the application of the translocality concept to four contexts: rural, urban, interregional and interstate. The translocations in these two latter contexts are intertwined.

Historical review

The 'holy groups' (Sayyid, Khoja, Ishon etc.) had a particular position in the social hierarchy of Muslim communities in Central Asia. As in many other Muslim societies, they have long enjoyed a privileged status. Scholars have come to the conclusion that the Sayyids or Alids emerged as one of the local elites in Central Asia in the late ninth century (Bernheimer 2005:44).

The terms *Khoja* or *Khwaja* (which mean 'master' in Persian) were first mentioned in written sources in the tenth century; they were applied to some government officials (Rezvan 1991:280). Apparently, the use of Khoja as the name of a group of religious descent started in the fourteenth and fifteenth centuries. Different groups of Khoja use various explanations for their origin. Some Khoja groups are believed to be the descendants of the first caliphs Abu Bakr, Umar, Uthman, and Ali (excluding his descendants from the daughter of Prophet Muhammad, Fatima) (Rezvan 1991:280), whereas some other groups claim to be descendants of the Prophet Muhammad. It is worth mentioning that in some areas the term *Khoja* has various meanings today; for example, a teacher, a mullah, a title of honour, etc.

In Central Asia, the so-called 'holy groups' also differ in their names: Khoja, Qoja, Ovlat, Sayyid, Khan, Mir, Mahdum-zada, Shaykh, Ishon, Tura, etc. According to Muminov, the descendants of Ali ibn Abi Talib from the Prophet's daughter Fatima (Sayyid, Sharif) in some Central Asian societies have equal status with the Khoja groups, and sometimes are less revered than these families (Muminov 2011:26). According to my observations, in some regions of Central Asia the term *Sayyid* is a synonym of *Ishon*, which means 'they' in Persian, while in some areas Sayyids and Ishons are perceived as different groups. The designations given to 'holy families' are very diverse; for example, some of them refer to the titles of rulers (*Shah, Khan, Amir*), others refer to the upper class of society (*Tura, Ishon, Mahdum, Khwaja, Sayyid*); 'the descendants of the saint' (*aulad, Mahdum-zoda, Ishon-zoda*), etc. Researchers call them by the generic term 'descendants of saints' (*aulad-i awliya*) (Muminov 2011:26).

Before 1917, Uzbek and Kazakh societies were divided into two hereditary social groups, named *Oqsuyak* or *Aksuyek* (White Bone) which included 'holy groups' (Sayyid, Khoja, Ishon etc.) and *Qorasuyak* or *Qarasuyek* (*Qoracha*, Black Bone), the term used to denote commoners. In different regions there are smaller gradations of 'holy groups' and there were various criteria that determined the position of certain 'holy lineages'. According to Abashin, in the Fergana Valley, the first rank of nobility took Tura, the second Eshon (Ishon), the third Khoja, and the last Makhsum (Abashin 2006:269–71). The degree of nobility of 'holy groups' depended on marriages with political leaders and the sanctity of those families. One man could have several or even all of the above titles. He could be a Khoja, and in some cases at the same time he could be a Sayyid, i.e., the Prophet's descendant. He could have a right to the titles of Ishon and Sheykh as well (Abashin 2001a).

In general, the 'holy groups' follow the cultural traditions of the majority of the population among whom they live. However, they have some traits that mark them out from the rest of population. Frequently, the members of these families add the titles of Khoja, Sayyid and Khon to their names (Muminov 2011:27). According to written sources, in the nineteenth century Sayyids were included in the composition of the Khoja; nevertheless, the Kazakhs gave them higher status than other 'holy groups' (Beysenbayuli 1994:95). Among experts in genealogy, there are different versions of the classification of lineages of the

Kazakh-speaking Khoja (see Muminov 2011). According to one version, just seventeen clans (*ru*) of the Kazakh Khoja are specified as equal in status (Muminov 2011:26).[8]

The name and authority of the holy Sufi leader Khoja Ahmad Yassavi is used in different ways at the consecration of the alliances of different Khoja families. For example, among the Kazakh-speaking Khojas of *Alty shaykh balalari*, the succession continues only by patrilineage through Ahmad Yassavi's brother, Sadr-khoja, and among the contemporary Uzbek-speaking Khoja of Turkistan, through the line of his daughters (his biological daughter, Gaukhar Shakhnaz, and foster daughter Djamila-bibi). Their descendants are the following groups of Khoja: Shaykh al-Islam, Nakib, Shaykh-'azlar (DeWeese 1999:514).

In other regions of Central Asia, one can find other classifications of 'holy groups'. For example, Sadriddin Aini (1878–1954), who was one of the Bukharian reformist intellectuals (*jadids*), gave a panoramic overview of rural life in Bukhara during the nineteenth century in his unfinished *Reminiscences*. He considered the Khoja as a distinct regional group and gave the classification of Khoja to his village, Soktare, which was near the town of Ghijduvan in the modern Bukhara province of Uzbekistan. Khojas of this village constituted four clans: Mirakoni, Sayyid Atoi, Ghijduvoni, and Soktaregi (Aini 1998:31–32).

Gellner (1995:160) mentions that in northern Africa the distinction between religious orders and holy lineages is a loose one. Religious orders are led by holy lineages, and in turn successful holy lineages may expand their following into *tariqa*, an order (Gellner 1995:160). One can say the same thing about the Central Asian Khojas or Shaykhs, who became leaders of the Naqshbandi and Yassavi Sufi orders in the region (DeWeese 1999). Not all Khojas were mullahs even in pre-Soviet times. Many Khojas were simply peasants, some nomadized with the Kazakhs, and others, as in Tashkent, were successful merchants. Also, not all members of the Khoja or Sayyid groups were socially equal; some families were very rich, others not. For the male non-Khoja and non-Sayyid it was not possible to become a member of a Sayyid or Khoja group that had hereditary rights (Sukhareva 1960:66–67).

---

8   Among others, these include Akorgandik, Akkoja, Baksayis, Khorasan, Duana, Seyit, Qilishti, Sabult, Qilavuz.

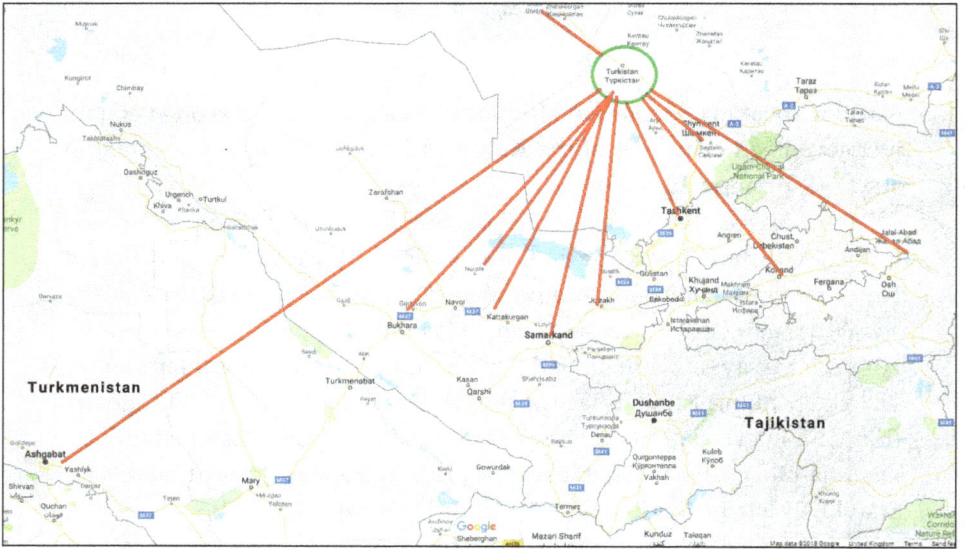

Fig. 3.1 Genealogical links of the descendants of Khoja Ahmad Yassavi.
Map data © Google (2018), all rights reserved

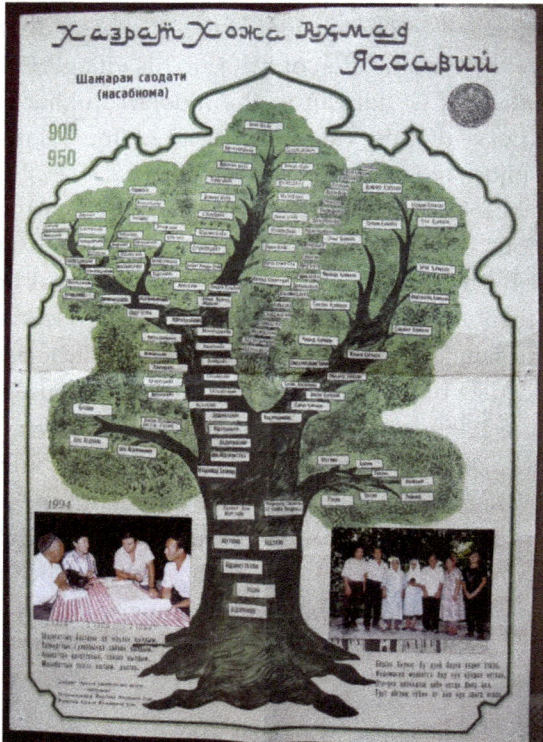

Fig. 3.2 Family tree of the descendants of Khoja Ahmad Yassavi.
Photo © Azim Malikov (2010), CC BY 4.0

In the pre-Soviet period, the Khoja (*Qoja*) title was widespread among the sacred lineages of Kazakhs and Uzbeks in the Turkistan region. Kazakh-speaking Khoja groups are comprised of lineages operating as components of complex, segmented societies. Most ethnic Kazakhs belonged to one of three 'hordes' (*djuz*). While these Kazakh tribal confederations were regarded as the 'Black Bone' (*qara süyek*), the Khoja (as well as the *Tore*, the offspring of Genghis Khan) were considered honour groups belonging to the 'White Bone' (*aq süyek*). Accordingly, the Khoja and *Tore* groups are not included in numerous Kazakh genealogies (*Qazaq shezhiresi*) (Privratsky 2004:167).

In the nineteenth and early twentieth centuries the most famous and noble lineages of Khoja in the Turkistan region of Kazakhstan consisted of many groups: Sayyid Ata, Qilishti khoja, descendants of the third son of Caliph Ali, Muhammad Khanafiya, descendants of Khoja Ahmad Yassavi etc. (Sukhareva 1960:66–67). Before 1917, genealogy had several purposes. It was the main legal and symbolic record of sacred lineages and it granted these groups certain rights; in some cases it was confirmation of the special status of the lineage. According to Sukhareva's research, particularly 'noble' Khoja lineages maintained written genealogical records (*shajara*) (Sukhareva 1960:67–68).

When studying the Khoja in Kazakh society, it is necessary to distinguish those groups that formed independently in the Kazakh steppes from groups of representatives of famous Khoja lineages already known and politically influential in the Central Asian states. For example, Mahdumi Azam[9] (1461–1542), an outstanding theologian and Sufi leader of the sixteenth century, had thirteen sons, each of whom became progenitors of Khoja lineages among Uzbeks, Tajiks, Kazakhs, and the Uyghur. Kazakh sultans and *biys* invited Khoja to control religious rituals and customs such as wedding ceremonies, funeral ceremonies, circumcisions, etc.

Similar to the ideas of Donahoe and Schlee about how trans-ethnic groups emerged in Eastern Africa and Siberia (2003:79–80), translocal Sayyid identity in Central Asia was formed in two different ways. Firstly, Sayyid predates the emergence of the ethnic identities Kazakh and Uzbek. Secondly, after the boundaries between modern ethnic groups had started to come into being, individuals or groups crossed

---

9   Shaykh Aḥmad ibn Mawlānā Jalāl al-Dīn Khwājagī Kāsānī 'Mahdūm-i Aʻẓam'.

them and affiliated themselves with another ethnic group. In the cases
in which they started to follow a nomadic lifestyle, they did not give up
their original affiliation. These collective adoptions did not supersede
the older clan relationships by descent or putative descent, particularly
in urban areas and adjacent territories.

According to Abashin, each family of the 'descendants of saints'
was fixed to a particular territory, a particular group of the population,
of which they have been trans-generational spiritual leaders (*pirs*). In
Tashkent, the *pirs* of local rulers were descendants of Shaykh Hovand-i
Tokhur, who lived in the fourteenth century (Abashin 2001b:127). Some
Khoja and Sayyid lineages have links with local shrines, which constitute
an important symbolic resource for them. A shrine for a Khoja is first
of all a place of memory, i.e., the memory of an ancestor's historical
activity. These major shrines act as symbols for the imaginary translocal
communities of Khoja. Thus, the role of shrines as a geographic place or
locality, and also as a sacred site, can be conceptualized with reference
to 'translocality'.

In the pre-Soviet and early Soviet period (the 1920s), Sufi shrines
in Central Asia played a strong role as concrete physical or material
'places' within the more geographical places of the oases or regions; i.e.,
they served as 'mediators' or 'communicators' of ideas and practices,
or as nodes in the connections between the different geographic places.
In the pre-Soviet period, cemeteries, shrines and tombstones of some
outstanding Khojas with a *tugh* (top of a banner which was attached to
the grave of famous saint, i.e., a *wali*) (Babajanov, Nekrasova, 2006:384–
85) were among the symbols of Uzbek-speaking Khoja. In general, Sufi
actors, groups, and networks have had a big impact on the history of
Islam in Muslim Central Asia (Sukhareva 1960).

The main shrines of Central Asia were located in Samarkand
(the shrine of Qusam ibn Abbos and the shrine of Mahdumi Azam
in Daghbit, Samarkand province), Tashkent (the shrine of Shaykh
Hovandi Tokhur), Turkistan (the shrine of Khoja Ahmad Yassavi), and
Bukhara (the shrine of Bahauddin Naqshband). Thousands of pilgrims
from the different parts of Central Asia visit these shrines annually. The
graves of the ancestors of some groups of Kazakh-speaking Khoja are in
Samarkand (Mahdumi Azam, his sons), and some shrines of the Uzbek-
speaking Khoja are located in the Turkistan region.

Some Khoja and Sayyid studied in the Bukhara's and Samarkand's famous Islamic schools (*madrasa*). Besides their religious activities, members of sacred lineages migrated from one region to another due to economic reasons. Those involved in Sufi practice often had thousands of disciples in different parts of Central Asia. Moreover, Uzbek-speaking Khoja and Ishons usually had disciples among Kazakhs in border territories.

The following elements united the Khoja and Sayyid of Central Asia into one translocal group and formed a sense of 'translocal imagination': the shared idea of an origin from the Prophet, the first caliphs, or a Sufi saint; shrines; a shared sacred genealogy; and commoners' perceptions of the group as sacred. The stories about holy ancestors were spread through oral narratives passed on from one generation to another as well as through religious books. Later, Soviet national identity policies played an important role in destroying these translocal communications. According to Barth, the state is 'a specifiable third player in the processes of boundary construction between groups, rather than confound the regime, and its powers and interests, with the more nebulous concepts of state and nation' (1994:19). In 1924, the existing political-administrative organization was broken up by the national delimitation of Central Asia and replaced by ethnically defined Soviet republics. This national delimitation was seen as the implementation of the people's right to self-determination. Language was viewed as the central criteria for affiliation to an ethnic group (Fedtke 2007:21–24). The formation of Soviet republics laid the structural foundations for a reformulation of the parameters of identity in modern Central Asia (Akiner 1998:12–13).

Accordingly, Soviet state policy also had a great deal of influence on the identity of 'sacred lineages' and it had dramatic consequences for many Khojas in Central Asia. Khoja communities lost their property and their sources of income. In the 1920s and 1930s, a significant proportion of Central Asian Khoja intellectuals were arrested and killed, especially if they were mullahs and teachers of Islam (Privratsky 2001). Nevertheless, according to Schoeberlein-Engel: 'Later, during the 1960–1980s in some areas descendants of religious elite groups were well-represented in the local KGB, police force, and positions of authority controlled by the Communist party. Members of this group were maximizing their benefit from structures of significance that contribute to the construction of legitimate elite status' (Schoeberlein-Engel 1994:259).

In Central Asia, 'the descendants of the saints — despite the strength of both nationalism and fundamentalism — has not dissolved into modernized society, but on the contrary, has preserved its position to a great extent' (Abashin 2005:70). This is despite the fact that some Tashkent Khoja families sacrificed their religious identity in order to announce themselves 'bearers of national consciousness' and 'the intellectual elite' (Abashin 2005:78). There were also changes to marriage traditions in the Soviet period, meaning that more Khoja families formed marriage alliances with the non-Khoja elite (Abashin 2005). Additionally, a transformation of identity and the loss of the social and economic status of the holy families occurred during the Soviet period. Pilgrimages to shrines were prohibited, and pilgrims were prosecuted by the authorities (Muminov 1996:366). Many sacred places were destroyed, abandoned or turned into museums on the orders of the Soviet state. Any transfer of ideas of sainthood through books and manuscripts was rigorously prosecuted.

During the first years of the post-Soviet period, a new interest in local history was supported by a revival of sacred places and the publication of books on the history of sacred lineages. Since the breakdown of the Soviet Union and the independence of the Central Asian republics in 1991, the Khojas, particularly in Kazakhstan, have recovered some of their former prestige. The Soviet policy of societal homogenization in Central Asia and the creation of national identities could not eliminate some specific groups in the region. Despite the strictures put in place by Soviet ideology, some Khoja families kept alive their memory of the past and maintained the symbolic capital of shrines and genealogies during the 1980 and 1990s.

The scale of the translocal relations (or even translocal imagination) of sacred lineages differed. I distinguish several levels: between villages, between rural and urban areas, across regions, and between states. It should be noted that not all groups of the sacred lineages of the pre-Soviet period can be called 'translocal societies'. It was common for a few Khoja families to live in one village, and they had to seek marriage partners belonging to their 'sacred group' in other villages.

Turkistan region

The Turkistan region lies on the frontier of the settled oasis culture of Transoxiana to the south, and the world of the former steppe nomads to the north. It is the homeland of the holy Sufi leader Khoja Ahmad Yassavi, who lived here during the twelfth century and is buried in the town. In 1930, more than 200 families in the city of Turkistan considered themselves the descendants of Khoja Ahmad Yassavi (Masson 1930:19).

Turkistan is a part of the South Kazakhstan province of the Republic of Kazakhstan, which borders Uzbekistan's Tashkent province. The population of Turkistan city is more than 152,000.[10] In 2016, almost 73% of the population of South Kazakhstan province were Kazakhs; the second largest population were Uzbeks, comprising 16.8%. In terms of population, the South Kazakhstan region is the largest in Kazakhstan, being 2,841,000.[11]

Turkistan is inhabited by various 'holy groups', including Khojas (Privratsky 2001). Traditionally Kazakhs belong to the Sunni branch of Islam, which is influenced by Sufism. South Kazakhstan traditions differ in some respects from the central parts of Central Asia, mainly related to the localization and interpretation of certain Qur'anic subjects (Muminov 1996:356).

After independence in 1991, the political elite of Kazakhstan started elaborating a new national ideology to create patriotic feelings towards the new state. The search for balance between the multiethnic and multiconfessional nature of the population and the development of the Kazakh nation began. This double process encompassed both nationalization in favour of representatives of the titular nation ('Kazakhization') and promotion of a civic Kazakhstan identity ('Kazakhstanization') (Davenel 2012:19). Scholars believe that this process influenced all spheres of social life, which, to some degree, is a continuation of the policy of 'rooting' (*korenizatsia*) that occurred in the Kazakh Soviet Socialistic Republic in the 1960s (Davenel, 2012:19–20). From some researchers' point of view, although Kazakhstan is

---

10   http://meta.kz/novosti/kazakhstan/777107-samymi-bystrorastuschimi-gorodami-v-rk-za-poslednie-10-let-stali-turkestan-zhanaozen-i-kaskelen.html

11   http://www.stat.gov.kz/faces/wcnav_externalId/publBullS14-2016

a multiconfessional state, the elite use Islam to encourage citizens to identify with state support of religious institutions (Cummings, 2005:88). The state ideology propagandizes Khoja Ahmad Yassavi and his shrine as the national spiritual and religious centre. Indeed, this policy is aimed at building the nation and forming a national ideology.

One can observe a reconstitution of lineage-based identities, in large part due to local initiatives. 'The *ru* and *zhuz*-based genealogies experienced a revival as traits that distinguished ethnic Kazakhs from the non-titular citizens of independent Kazakhstan' (Schatz 2000). The existence of so-called lineage-based identity, which favours the preservation of the local and translocal identities of separate groups of Khoja in South Kazakhstan, is significant to social processes. The stories of local saints emphasize the presence of the Khoja throughout Kazakhstan's history. Graves of saints, local and translocal, are important for the authentication of this past. These places bear evidence of days gone by and are important mediators between past and present. Local traditions are preserved by the descendants of sacred lineages in the form of the revival of shrines, the publication of the literature on saints and shrines, and the organization of festivals at the shrines (Sattarov 2010).

Sacred lineages of the Turkistan region consist of two linguistic groups: Uzbek-speaking and Kazakh-speaking. Uzbek-speaking Khojas claim to be descendants of Khoja Ahmad Yassavi or his relatives and disciples, including Gaukhar ana, Ali Khoja, Sadr ata etc. According to other legends, they are descendants of the people serving at the shrine of Khoja Ahmad Yassavi. Among Uzbeks in Kazakhstan, internal differentiation has traditionally been organized according to regional origin, i.e., Turkistonlik, Qarnoqlik, etc. Regional identities still play a more important role than ethnic identities (Malikov 2017:80). According to oral traditions, some Khojas came from Bukhara in the nineteenth century.[12]

Until the 1950s, the Uzbek-speaking Khojas in Turkistan strictly followed endogamous marriage practices. They never allowed daughters to marry *qoracha* — commoners. In some cases, they intermarried with Kazakh-speaking Khojas.[13] The latter differ from Uzbek-speaking

---

12   Interview with Uzbek-speaking Khoja, native of Turkistan, 55 years old, 2010.
13   *Ibid.*

Khojas due to their specific lineage names. Some examples of these include Khorasan[14] Khoja or descendants of Khorasan Ata (Abdujalil Bab), Duvana Khoja, Qilishti Khoja, etc.

In my case studies, one can differentiate identities on various levels, including ethnic identities (e.g., Kazakh, Uzbek, Arab), civic identities (e.g., Kazakhstani), regional identities, tribal and clan identities or Khoja lineages and sub-lineages, particularly among Kazakh-speaking Khojas. Locality, as well as other aspects, can be a significant factor in forming identities.

During my interviews, some Khoja were often confused about ethnic categories. Some respondents doubted that Kazakhs have Khoja groups, and vice versa; some Kazakh-speaking Khoja did not understand questions about Uzbek Khojas. Turkistan Khojas had close relationships and marriages with Samarkand and Tashkent Khojas in the past. In the 1930s, many of them left Turkestan for Samarkand and Tashkent. As one of my interlocutors mentioned, 'There are no Kazakh or Uzbek Khojas, all of them belong to a single Khoja group. So-called 'Uzbek' and 'Kazakh' Khojas are a result of the Soviet nationalities policy' (Malikov 2013a:105). In elaborating specific Kazakh-Khoja qualities, some Khoja very often seek to distinguish themselves from Uzbek Khojas, as the following statement by an interlocutor exemplifies: 'The Kazakh-Khojas know their seven ancestors; they have higher moral values and sincerity. The "Uzbek Khojas" are completely different people' (Malikov 2013a: 105). Aside from the purely genetic explanation for the specific Khoja qualities, some Khojas also mention their particular history and their religious values.

In Kazakh and Uzbek societies, some existing groups of Khoja interpret the shrines as their symbolic capital. There are Khojas today who retain traditional roles as caretakers (*shiraqshi*) of the mausoleums of their ancestors, for instance the shrine of Khorasan-ata in Uzgend, Kazakhstan. For Khojas, a shrine is first of all a place of memory: the memory of an ancestor's activity in history. According to my observations, for some Khoja groups living in different regions

---

14   Khorasan comes from the name of a historical region in Southern Central Asia and Northern Iran. Perhaps the ancestors of Khorasan Khoja arrived in the territory of modern Kazakhstan from this historical region. Currently, Khorasan Khojas speak the Kazakh language, and in some areas they know Uzbek and Russian languages.

and even countries, particular shrines are the main symbols of their past and culture. For example, the shrine of Khoja Ahmad Yassavi in Turkistan (Kazakhstan) is the general place of worship for some families of Khojas from Kazakhstan and Uzbekistan, who suppose themselves to be descendants of Khoja Ahmad Yassavi. Some families speak only in Uzbek and other families of Khojas speak native Kazakh. Therefore, in some cases the shared reverence for a holy man as their ancestor unites these groups. Translocality exists in the intersection of national, ethnic, and even geographic borders. Most Khoja know at least the rough outlines of their genealogy from the oral tradition of their kinship network. Among Kazakh-speaking Khojas the idea that each person should know his or her lineage for seven generations (*jetty ata*) is widespread.

Some Khoja groups in Kazakhstan had links with sacred lineages in Tashkent city and province before 1917. In the 1990s, the Kazakh-speaking Khoja of southern Kazakhstan tried to establish connections with related Khoja groups in the Samarkand and Tashkent regions. They invited related Khojas from Uzbekistan to festivals to Turkistan. Kazakh-speaking Khojas and Uzbek-speaking Khojas visited the shrines and mausoleums of their ancestors together. In the 1990s, a particular Kazakh-speaking Khoja family invited craftsmen from Samarkand province to construct Khoja shrines in southern Kazakhstan.[15]

During our interview, one of the Kazakh-speaking Khojas repeatedly stressed his respect for such cities as Samarkand and Bukhara. These cities were considered traditional centres of Islamic education and of magnificent Islamic architecture, where the sacred lineages lived and live. This articulated a cultural translocality, which was not simply expressed verbally but also in material terms. In the 1990s, craftsmen from Samarkand were invited to construct a shrine for one of the Khojas, and they used their local architectural style. But why did they invite craftsmen from Samarkand, and not from Turkistan, Shymkent, or Tashkent, which are closer to their shrine? Perhaps because one of the major figures of this Khoja family was buried in Samarkand, making it a holy city. Unfortunately, I could not talk with the Khojas who organized the construction of the shrine to find out their motivation for engaging

---

15   Interview with a Kazakh-speaking Khoja, native of Turkistan, 65 years old, 2010.

Samarkand craftsmen for construction. Based on my observations, this case is not typical in Kazakhstan.

Translocality can also be also applied to study the use of media and the circulation of knowledge and ideas in global networks. The post-industrial, information-based world we live in today is dominated by computer-linked technology and exists in an age of globalization, which is characterized by increasingly interconnected societies, according to Macionis and Plummer (2008:42). The internet is an instrument to create and shape relations across time and space, and it enables and facilitates translocal links between sacred lineages in different parts of Central Asia, especially in Kazakhstan. The internet, the influence of which is particularly tangible in Kazakhstan, became a powerful way to spread the history of holy lineages and their symbols. The flow of information, ideas, and opinions through the internet, and its influence on identity formation, shows how young Khojas in Kazakhstan use online forums to construct and negotiate their identities as Khojas alongside their identities as Kazakhs. The role of the internet in producing 'translocal relations and imageries' is also present in Kazakhstan. For example, certain Khoja groups from different parts of Kazakhstan use websites such as kazakh.ru,[16] which are devoted to Khoja history and are used to organize various events. The internet thus provides a new virtual technology that facilitates changing patterns of translocal communication among 'holy groups' in Central Asia in the modern globalized world.

Tashkent City

Tashkent, the capital city, is the largest city of Uzbekistan with a population of approximately 2.4 million as of 2016 (Demograficheskiy, 2016:25). Tashkent is a megalopolis, where representatives of different nationalities and regional groups live. In this context, sacred lineages belonging to the city exist in an environment surrounded by representatives of different regional and ethnic groups that influence their identity and status.

In the city and the area around Tashkent, an important centre of interaction between nomadic and settled cultures, the phenomenon of

---

16 http://www.kazakh.ru

sacred lineages manifested in a specific way. Each of the four blocks (*daha*) of the city was dominated by members of certain lineages: the descendants of Qara-Khan, the descendants of Shihab al-din al-Suhrawardi, the descendants of the Shaykh Hovand-i Tokhur, descendants of Yuvash Bab, his brother Ishaq Bab, and the successors of the line of Muhammad ibn al-Hanafiya. A total of seventy-three Khoja clans lived and operated in Tashkent in Soviet times, and some leaders of these families played a prominent role in public and cultural life (Muminov 2011:57).[17]

During my research in Tashkent, I interviewed members of the sacred lineages of different ages and occupations, both Uzbek-speaking and Kazakh-speaking. Thus, I was able to observe the diverse nature of Khojas' emic identification depending on the geographic, social, and cultural specifics of the region. There is some kind of hierarchy in the minds of Uzbek-speaking Khoja intellectuals. Strikingly, knowledge of most of the saints who were members of other groups (Khoja, Sayyid, Mir, Ishon) in Tashkent is very limited. My respondents tend to be able to name only their own relatives and those with whom they communicate, such as neighbors, colleagues, and friends.

The next criterion for the categorization of 'holy groups' is their lineage affiliation established through genealogy, linking them with the Prophet or the first caliphs. In Tashkent, elderly and middle-age Khojas differentiate Shayhontokhur Khojas, descendants of the famous Sufi leader Ahmad Yassavi, and Kazakh-speaking Khojas. Here, 'holy groups' consist of two linguistic categories: Kazakh-speaking and Uzbek-speaking groups, which in the past were closely connected with the Ferghana Valley and the Turkistan region. Nowadays these links are considerably weakened and expressed through the visiting of shrines. There is insufficient data on the relationships between the sacred lineages of Tashkent and Turkistan after the Russian conquest in 1865, i.e., the time when they began to deteriorate. During the Stalinist repressions, a considerable number of Khojas from Turkistan escaped, mainly to the Tashkent oasis, in order to survive.[18]

---

17   For example, Ziauddin mufti Babakhanov (1908–1982) the head of the Spiritual Administration of the Muslims of Central Asia and Kazakhstan (SADUM), 1957–1982.
18   Interview with Kazakh-speaking Khoja, native of Turkistan, 65 years old, 2010.

The descendants of different sacred lineages of Tashkent live dispersed in different quarters of the city. I found one significant feature: some representatives of the older generation possess relatively deep knowledge of the history of the sacred lineages, names of groups, and their cultures. In the Soviet period, an attempt was made by the government to create a new translocal imagined society — the Soviet people (*homo sovieticus*). However, according to my observations, this idea did not become popular among sacred lineages in Central Asia.

The younger generation (aged between 18–35) know only what they observe in life and what they read in post-1991 publications. When I talked with young people, I found out that by participating in traditional festivities such as weddings, wakes, etc., they became acquainted with other representatives of the sacred lineages of such cities as Tashkent and Turkistan.[19] Thus, public events, to a certain extent, contributed to an expansion of their views of sacred lineages in such cities as Tashkent and Turkistan. But in many cases, it was 'not the origin but the social status and personal relationships of people [that] are more important'.[20]

It is important to note that the representatives of the sacred lineages, once they had migrated from Turkistan to Tashkent, were divided by Tashkent's inhabitants into two groups: the first group, the Turkistanis, were former Tashkentis, who moved from Tashkent to Turkistan 130–150 years ago, and then returned. The second group, the so-called indigenous people of Turkistan, included the Khoja and non-elite groups.[21]

Representatives of the Kazakh-speaking Khoja from southern Kazakhstan often take wives from the Kazakh-speaking Khoja of the Tashkent oasis because 'they believe that their families more strongly follow traditional values and were less westernized than the population of southern Kazakhstan'.[22] Meanwhile, representatives of sacred lineages from more northern regions, such as the Kyzyl-orda province of Kazakhstan, claimed that the 'Kazakh-speaking Khoja of the Tashkent oasis are more 'Uzbekized' and have lost some original Kazakh values.

---

19 Interview with Uzbek-speaking Khoja, native of Tashkent, 32 years old, 2015.
20 *Ibid.*
21 *Ibid.*
22 Interview with a Kazakh scholar, native of Tashkent, 48 years old, 2015.

For example, they do not follow exogamous marriage rules'.[23] Thus, in this case, one can observe manifestations of locality and the influence of official ideology applied to the formation of an image of the nation with certain features and values. It can be assumed that certain cultural and social features of the Kazakh-speaking Khoja in Tashkent have changed as a result of acculturation among the Uzbek population.

In the 1990s, an overall process of cultural restoration, including the restoration of sacred lineages, was initiated by local activists, and attempts to establish lines of communication between enthusiasts of the sacred lineages of Uzbekistan and Kazakhstan were made. The crucial evidence is the organization of joint meals as though these were meetings of the representatives of one group, members of which lived in different regions and even countries. 'These meetings aimed to acquaint relatives with each other and to circulate books telling their history. In some cases, richer relatives furnished financial assistance to indigent members of their group'.[24] However, according to my observations, since 2000, this process is not as active as it was before, probably due to the strengthening of the state policy against transnational so-called 'radical' religious groups.

An interlocutor from Tashkent province supposed that in the past, Khojas were descendants of *sakhoba* — missionaries of Islam and the local aristocracy in the region. Also, marriages were endogamous, many of them were blood marriages, but there were some marriages with '*qoracha*' (Black Bone). He did not know his ancestry seven generations back, as opposed to the Kazakhs. In pre-Soviet and Soviet times, the main occupations of my interlocutor's own ancestors were agriculture and construction. Up until the 1950s, some members of his family were doctors or worked as imams[25] among the local Kazakhs.[26] According to a popular legend among the Khojas of his village, his folks were descendants of Khoja Ahmad Yassavi. However, his family did not have formal genealogical records. He supposed that such records were kept only among the intelligentsia and clergy, and these documents meant

---

23   Interview with a Kazakh-speaking Khoja, native of Turkistan, 65 years old, 2010.
24   *Ibid.*
25   Imam is the title of a worship leader of a mosque and Muslim community.
26   Interview with Uzbek-speaking Khoja, native of Tashkent province, 60 years old, 2015.

nothing for craftsmen, or that they were lost during migration. In his perception, the society of Khojas appeared as follows: 'the Tajik-speaking Khojas are the closest due to similar cultures, customs (*urf-odat*) and mentality, although the language is different. Previously close ties with such regions as Turkistan in Kazakhstan and the Fergana Valley existed'. According to him, Khojas from Turkistan claimed descent from Khoja Ahmad Yassavi.[27]

In the post-Soviet period, the Khojas of Tashkent have published a series of books on their origin and genealogy (Iskandarov 2004, Nusratov 2010). One of them describes their family history and explains the concept of Khoja:

> Khojas are a well-educated, cultured and highly esteemed people notable for honesty, firmness and decency. Traditions of Khoja at that time were not to espouse and to marry off children out of their kin. Every Khoja was proud to have the right to add the word 'Khoja' or 'khon' to their names like the French 'de' and the German 'von'. The majority of them inhabited the centre of Tashkent in quarters of 'Sheikhan-Taur', 'Mergancha' and 'Koryogdi'. The Uzbek 'mixed' with the Arab — descendants of the first two just caliphs Abu Bakr and Umar ibn al-Hattab were named Khoja. Both of them were the Prophet's father-in-law and inherently Khoja was the Prophet's remote kinsman. (Nusratov 2010:22)

The author of another book on Khoja family history asserts that the goal of the book is to fulfil the 'duty of a descendant to an ancestor', to revive the genealogical roots of his family of Khoja so that relatives can discover each other and their ancestors back seven generations (Iskandarov 2004:3–6). The author collected materials about his relatives for twenty-five years, starting in the late Soviet period (1979), and he started his genealogy from his forefather Uzbekkhon Khoja, whose descendants were gunsmiths. The author did not mention the direct links with the family of the Prophet Muhammad or the first caliphs. He found out that there were three brothers, whose offspring live in three regions: Tashkent, Khodjent (Northern Tajikistan), and Qurama (Tashkent province) (Iskandarov 2004:3–6). According to the author, representatives of Khoja families are distinguished by their integrity, spiritual purity, and high morals. According to his point of view, this

---

27 *Ibid.*

was the basis for endogamous marriages (*ibid.*). Analyzing the author's ancestors' names, one can assume that they were likely Sufi, because their names had the prefix *Ishon*. However, the author himself avoided this issue and the religious aspect of the history of Khoja in general. Thus, in this case, the history of sacred lineages is represented by the author as having translocal lines, in that they all originated in various regions, but the author does not link these groups with more global parallels (with other groups of Khoja, Sayyid, and the Islamic world). Translocal communications remain at the level of marriage between some 'holy groups' of Uzbekistan and Kazakhstan, especially in border territories.[28] Here, 'translocality' is clearly understood as the interrelation and connectedness between different geographical places.

Conclusion

Based on multi-sited fieldwork in Kazakhstan and Uzbekistan, and combining classical historical research with anthropological methods, this chapter has examined the complex ways in which 'sacred groups' in Central Asia have been negotiating, articulating and reconfiguring group identity and multiple group belongings through history. A 'translocal' approach has helped me to develop a cross-cutting research perspective on 'holy' or 'sacred groups' that critically scrutinizes 'methodological nationalism' in scholarship on Central Asia, according to which religious identities are viewed as naturally embedded within and fixed by the boundaries of the Soviet and post-Soviet nation state. This chapter has taken a contrasting approach, paying attention to a wide range of non-hierarchic interactions, configurations and institutions, and exploring how these interactions and configurations facilitate translocal knowledge transfer and the circulation of religious ideas and symbols among 'holy groups'. Obviously, knowledge transfer, identity formation and media usage among 'sacred groups' in Central Asia traverses places, regions, social groups, generations, language barriers and nation-states, as well as connecting and crossing different periods in history.

---

28   Interview with Uzbek-speaking Khoja, native of Tashkent province, 60 years old, 2015.

Until now, 'translocal communication' and 'imagination' among dispersed 'sacred groups' revealed itself through such practices as worshipping at the graves of ancestors, which have been perceived as sacred places. The preservation of written genealogies, linked with local saints or Sufi figures, the Prophet Muhammad, or the first caliphs, is also common in the regions discussed. There are regional differences, however. In Kazakhstan, digital communication via the internet is used more widely than in Uzbekistan to connect members of holy families, who increasingly use this medium to gather information about their past or to organize regular meetings among youth who share a saintly ancestor. In addition, young people of both sexes and from different parts of the country take part in online forums. These processes reinforce translocal ideas about a common history, a common past, and a common Khoja culture, regardless of the place of residence of representatives of different Khoja groups in the vast territories of Kazakhstan and Central Asia. Accordingly, investigating how sacred groups 'go online' opens up a new research field to analyze how sacred groups' translocal identities are reconfigured and renegotiated in a globalized world.

References

Abashin, S. N. 'The Logic of Islamic Practice: A Religious Conflict in Central Asia'. *Central Asian Survey* 25.3 (2006): 267–86, https://doi.org/10.1080/02634930601022542

Abashin, S. N. 'Gellner, the "Saints" and Central Asia: Between Islam and Nationalism'. *Inner Asia* 7.1 (2005): 65–86, https://doi.org/10.1163/146481705793647017

Abashin, S. N. 'Potomki svyatykh v sovremennoi Srednei Azii'. *Etnograficheskoye obozreniye* 4 (2001a): 62–83.

Abashin S. N. 'Sufism v Srednei Azii: tochka zrenia etnografa'. *Vestnik Evrazii* 4 (2001b): 117–41.

Abdullaev, Kamoludin. *Ot Sintsyanya do Khorasana. Iz istorii sredneaziatskoy emmigratsii 20 veka.* Dushanbe: Irfon, 2009.

Aini, Sadriddin. *The Sands of Oxus. Boyhood Reminiscences of Sadriddin Aini.* Translated from Tajik Persian with an introduction by John R. Perry and Rachel Lehr. Costa Mesa, CA: Mazda Publishers, 1998.

Akiner, Shirin. 'Social and Political Reorganization in Central Asia: Transition from Pre-Colonial to Post-Colonial Society'. In Touraj Atabaki and John O'Kane, eds. *Post-Soviet Central Asia.* London: I. B. Tauris, 1998, pp. 1–34.

Babajanov, B. 'Mahdumi A'zam'. In S. M. Prozorov, ed. *Islam na territorii bivshei Rossiyskoi imperii. Entsiklopedicheskiy slovar.* Moscow: Vostochnaya literatura, 2006, pp. 262–63.

Babajanov B., and E. Nekrasova. 'Tugh'. In S. M. Prozorov, ed. *Islam na territorii bivshei Rossiyskoi imperii. Entsiklopedicheskiy slovar.* Moscow: Vostochnaya literatura, 2006, pp. 384–85.

Baldauf, Ingeborg. *'Kraevedenie' and Uzbek National Consciousness.* Papers on Inner Asia: Central Asia, Issue 20. Bloomington: Indiana University, Research Institute for Inner Asian Studies, 1992, pp. 1–29.

Barth, Frederik. 'Enduring and Emerging Issues in the Analysis of Ethnicity'. In Hans Vermeulen and Cora Govers, eds. *The Anthropology of Ethnicity. Beyond 'Ethnic Groups and Boundaries'.* Amsterdam: Het Spinhuis, 1994, pp. 11–32.

Bernheimer, Teresa. 'The Rise of Sayyids and Sadat: The Al Zubara and Other Alids in Ninth- to Eleventh-Century Nishapur'. *Studia Islamica* 100.1 (2005): 43–69.

Beysenbayuli, Jarilkap. *Kazakh shejiresi.* Almaty: Atamura, 1994.

Brickell, Katherine, and Ayona Datta. 'Introduction: Translocal Geographies'. In Katherine Brickell and Ayona Datta, eds. *Translocal Geographies, Spaces, Places, Connections.* Burlington: Ashgate, 2011, pp. 3–22.

Cummings, Sally N. *Kazakhstan: Power and the Elite*. London: I. B. Tauris, 2005.

Davenel, Yves-Marie. 'Cultural Mobilization in Post-Soviet Kazakhstan: Views from the State and from Non-Titular Nationalities Compared'. *Central Asian Survey* 31.1 (2012): 17–29, https://doi.org/10.1080/02634937.2012.649583

Demograficheskiy ezhegodnik Uzbekistana. Tashkent: Gosudarstvenniy statisticheskiy komitet Respubliki Uzbekistan, 2016.

DeWeese, Devin. 'The Descendants of Sayyid Ata and the Rank of Naqib in Central Asia'. *Journal of the American Oriental Society* 115 (1995): 612–34.

DeWeese, Devin. 'The Politics of Sacred Lineages in Nineteenth-Century Central Asia: Descent Groups Linked to Khwaja Ahmad Yasavi in Shrine Documents and Genealogical Charters'. *International Journal of Middle Eastern Studies* 31.4 (1999): 507–30, https://doi.org/10.1017/S002074380005707X

DeWeese, Devin. 'Foreword'. In Ashirbek Muminov, Anke von Kügelgen, Devin DeWeese, and Michael Kemper, eds. *Islamization and Sacred Lineages in Central Asia. The Legacy of Ishaq Bab in Narrative and Genealogical Traditions, vol. 2: Genealogical Charters and Sacred Families: Nasab-namas and Khoja Groups Linked to the Ishaq Bab Narrative, 19th-21st Centuries*. Almaty: Daik Press, 2008, pp. 6–33.

Donahoe, Brian, and Günther Schlee. 'Interethnic Clan Relationships in Asia and Africa'. *Max Planck Institute for Social Anthropology Report 2002–2003* (2003): 79–88, https://www.eth.mpg.de/3026204/mpi-report-2002-2003.pdf

Donahoe, Brian, John Eidson, Dereje Feyissa, Veronika Fuest, Markus V. Hoehne, Boris Nieswand, Günther Schlee, and Olaf Zenker. 'The Formation and Mobilization of Collective Identities in Situations of Conflict and Integration'. *Max Planck Institute for Social Anthropology Working Paper* 116 (2009), http://www.eth.mpg.de/pubs/wps/pdf/mpi-eth-working-paper-0116.pdf

Fedtke, Gero. 'How Bukharans Turned into Uzbeks and Tajiks: Soviet Nationalities Policy in the Light of a Personal Rivalry'. In Paolo Sartori and Tommaso Trevisani, eds. *Patterns of Transformation in and Around Uzbekistan*. Reggio Emilia: Diabasis, 2007, pp. 19–50.

Finke, Peter. *Variations on Uzbek Identity: Strategic Choices, Cognitive Schemas and Political Constraints in Identification Processes*. London and New York: Bergahn, 2014.

Freitag, U., and A. von Oppen. 'Introduction: Translocality, An Approach to Connection and Transfer in Area Studies'. In U. Freitag and A. von Oppen, eds. *Translocality: The Study of Globalising Processes from a Southern Perspective*. Leiden: Brill, 2010, pp. 1–24, https://doi.org/10.1163/ej.9789004181168.i-452.8

Gellner, Ernest. *Muslim Society*. Cambridge: Cambridge University Press, 1995.

Greiner, Clemens, and Patrick Sakdapolrak. 'Translocality: Concepts, Applications and Emerging Research Perspectives'. *Geography Compass* 7.5 (2013): 373–84, https://doi.org/10.1111/gec3.12048

Gupta, Akhil, and James Ferguson. 'Beyond "Culture": Space, Identity, and the Politics of Difference'. *Cultural Anthropology* 7.1 (1992): 6–23, https://doi.org/10.1525/can.1992.7.1.02a00020

Holý, Ladislav. *Anthropological Perspectives on Kinship*. London: Pluto Press, 1996.

Ibadullaeva, Z. O. *Qazaq khalkynyn kuramyndagy kozhalar (tarikhi-etnografik zertteu). Tarikh gilimdarinin kandidati derejesin alu ushin dayindalghan dissertatsiyanin avtoreferati*. Doctoral thesis, University of Almaty, 2001.

Iskandarov, T. *Mening Khuja ajdodlarim va avlodlarim shajarasi*. Tashkent, 2004.

Kalanov Komil. *Markaziy Osie xududidagi ijtimoij-diniy tabaqalar (diniy-ekologik va sotsioantropologik taxlil)*. Rabochie dokumenti — Document de travail de 1'IFEAC [IFEAC Working Paper], 16 (May 2006) Tashkent, 2006, pp. 5–8.

Karmisheva, B. Kh. *Ocherki etnicheskoy istorii yunikh rayonov Uzbekistana i Tajikistana*. Moscow: Nauka, 1976, https://archive.nyu.edu/handle/2451/39969

Kawahara Yayoi, *Private Archives on a Makhdumzada Family in Marghilan*. TIAS Central Eurasian research series No. 7. Tokyo: Tokyo Press, 2012.

Lohnert, B., and M. Steinbrink. 'Rural and Urban Livelihoods: A Translocal Perspective in a South African Context'. *South African Geographical Journal* 87.2 (2005): 95–103, https://doi.org/10.1080/03736245.2005.9713832

Macionis, John J., and Ken Plummer. *Sociology. A Global Introduction*. Harlow: Pearson Education Ltd., 2008.

Malikov, Azim. Khoji dolini Nijnego Zerafshana in Religioznaya jizn narodov Tsentralnoi Evrazii. Otvetstvenniy redaktor V. I. Kharitonova. Moskva: Institut etnologii i antropologii Rossiyskoi Akademii nauk, 2012:176–80.

Malikov, Azim. 'Khoja in Kazakhstan: Identity Transformations'. In Peter Finke and Günther Schlee eds. *Framing the Research, Initial Projects*. Max Planck Institute for Social Anthropology Department 'Integration and Conflict' Field Notes and research Projects VI (Halle/Saale, 2013a), pp. 101–07, https://www.eth.mpg.de/3374775/FN_Vol06_CASCA_web.pdf

Malikov Azim, 'Collective Memory, History and Identity in the Bukharan Oasis in the Post-Soviet Period'. *Warsaw East European Review* 3 (2013b): 213–28.

Malikov, Azim, Khoji Yujnogo, 'Kazakhstana: istoriya i identichnost". *Ethnograficheskoe obozrenie* 4 (2014): 35–45.

Malikov, Azim, 'Kinship Systems of Xoja Groups in South Kazakhstan' *Anthropology of the Middle East* 12. 2 (Winter 2017):78–91, https://doi.org/10.3167/ame.2017.120206

Morimoto, Kazuo. 'Keeping the Prophet's Family Alive: Profile of a Genealogical Discipline'. In Sarah Bowen Savant and Helena de Felipe (eds.), *Genealogy and Knowledge in Muslim Societies: Understanding the Past*. Edinburgh: Edinburgh University Press, 2014, pp. 11–23, https://doi.org/10.3366/edinburgh/9780748644971.003.0002

Masson M. E. *Mavzoley Khoja Akhmeta Yasevi*. Tashkent: Sir-Dariinskoe otdelenie Obshestva izucheniya Kazakstana, 1930.

Muminov, Ashirbek. 'Veneration of Holy Sites of the Mid-Sirdarya Valley: Continuity and Transformation'. In Michael Kemper, Anke von Kügelgen, and Dimitriy Yermakov, eds. *Muslim Culture in Russia and Central Asia from the 18th to the Early 20th Centuries*. Berlin: Klaus Schwarz Verlag, 1996, pp. 355–67.

Muminov, Ashirbek. 'Die Qožas. Arabische Genealogien in Kasachstan'. In Anke von Kuegelgen, Michael Kemper, and Allen J. Frank, eds. *Muslim Culture in Russia and Central Asia from the 18th to the Early 20th Centuries*. Vol. 2: Inter-Regional and Inter-Ethnic Relations. Islamkundliche Untersuchungen. Band 216. Berlin: Klaus Schwarz Verlag, 1998, pp. 193–209.

Muminov, Ashirbek, with A. Sh. Nurmanovaia and S. Sattarov. *Rodoslovnoe drevo Mukhtara Auzzova*. Almaty: Jibek joli, 2011.

Nusratov T. *Sokhib name: Nusratov Sakhib Nusratovich. Esse sinya*. Tashkent, 2010.

Privratsky, Bruce. '"Turkistan Belongs to the Qojas": Local Knowledge of a Muslim Tradition'. In Stéphane A. Dudoignon, ed. *Devout Societies vs. Impious States? Transmitting Islamic Learning in Russia, Central Asia and China, Through the Twentieth Century*. Proceedings of an International Colloquium held in the Carré des Sciences, French Ministry of Research, Paris, November 12–13, 2001. Islamkundliche Untersuchungen, Band 258. Berlin: Klaus Schwarz Verlag, 2004, pp. 161–212.

Privratsky, Bruce. *Muslim Turkistan. Kazak Religion and Collective Memory*. Richmond, Surrey: Curzon, 2001, https://doi.org/10.4324/9781315028293

Rezvan E. *Khoja in Islam. Entsiklopedicheskiy slovar*. Moscow: Nauka, 1991.

Sattarov, Seyitomar. *Mukhtar Auezotin atategi*. Almaty: Jibek joli baspa uji, 2010.

Schatz, Edward, 'The Politics of Multiple Identities: Lineage and Ethnicity in Kazakhstan', *Europe-Asia Studies* 52.3 (2000): 489–506, https://doi.org/10.1080/713663070

Schlee, Günther, *Identities on the Move: Clanship and Pastoralism in Northern Kenya* (Nairobi: Gideon S. Were Press, 1994).

Schoeberlein-Engel, John. *Identity in Central Asia: Construction and Contention in the Conceptions of 'Ozbek', 'Tajik', 'Muslim', 'Samarqandi' and Other Groups*. Doctoral thesis, Harvard University, 1994.

Schröder, Philipp, and Manja Stephan-Emmrich, 'The Institutionalization of Mobility: Wellbeing and Social Hierarchies in Central Asian Translocal Livelihoods' *Mobilities* 11.3 (2014): 420–43, https://doi.org/10.1080/17450101.2014.984939

Statisticeskiy ezhegodnik regionov Respubliki Uzbekistana. Tashkent: Gosudarstvennyi statistischeskii komitet Uzbekistana, 2016.

Sukhareva O. A. *Islam v Uzbekistane*. Tashkent: Izdatelstvo Akademii nauk Uzbekskoi SSR, 1960.

Tenhunen, Sirpa. 'Culture, Conflict, and Translocal Communication: Mobile Technology and Politics in Rural West Bengal, India'. *Etnos* 76.3 (2011): 398–420, https://doi.org/10.1080/00141844.2011.580356

4. Explicating Translocal Organization of Everyday Life: Stories from Rural Uzbekistan

Elena Kim

Introduction

In this chapter I adopt Dorothy Smith's theoretical framework of the 'social organization of knowledge' (Smith 2005:10) and a related method of inquiry, institutional ethnography (*ibid.*:14), to illustrate how the everyday existence of people living in the poorest areas of rural Uzbekistan is shaped by invisible but powerful processes, which I call translocal ruling relations. Institutional ethnography tells us that no local activity in the contemporary world takes place in isolation from larger social and institutional arrangements, but is always coordinated from outside the local space (Smith 1987:1–30). This investigation produces empirical insights that develop our understanding of 'translocal' as an analytical and a methodological concept.

I focus on the events taking place in a village located in the northwestern part of Uzbekistan, where, similar to many other places in Central Asia, most Uzbek families have experienced profound change as a result of the large-scale migration of the male population in search of paid work. Female-headed households live in precarious conditions, as the remittances from their male partners are unreliable and often insufficient. These women's own sources of livelihood, which come primarily from small-scale agriculture, are made precarious by

 https://doi.org/10.11647/OBP.0114.04

reduced irrigation resources and the difficulty of accessing them. Using my chosen methodological framework, I begin from these people's stories and identify traces of the powerful forces that have shaped their lives. I ask: why were these men were forced to leave their homes? How do these rural women organize their lives and negotiate their material and immaterial resources? What influences their experiences, choices, and coping strategies? I seek to answer these questions by focusing on implicit but identifiable mechanisms and technologies in which translocal institutions, ideologies, and discourses infiltrate local settings. Hence this chapter offers a concrete illustration, in a specific place in Uzbekistan, of the operation of translocal power, expressed in institutional discourses and ideological practices that shape these people's experiences.

By mapping translocal relations in my research, I find that the operation of local community-based irrigation management is aligned with the interests of the state agricultural export industry and, as such, fails to recognize certain categories (mostly, smallholder households) of land- and water-users as legitimate recipients of state-supported irrigation. Eligibility for agricultural support and services from the state is established based on a specific understanding of efficient agricultural management. Institutional eligibility is indicated by documents and other text-based practices produced by professionals at the many levels of the state management of agricultural export. As a result, many poor households are deprived of opportunities to secure agricultural inputs such as irrigation services and, subsequently, suffer lower production, which impacts on their quality of life. Ultimately, men are forced to seek alternative sources of income outside the agricultural sector and outside their villages. These men often find themselves in insecure and risky work conditions with unreliable and/or insufficient income (Zanca 2011:45). Women, as is customary, are left at home to engage in the everyday struggle to support their families (Kim 2014:106–20).

An institutional ethnographic framework can and has been used by scholars to study migration-related topics as well as a variety of other research questions, including those related to environmental policy, education and health reforms, international development, economic reorganization, etc. To provide just a few examples, Naples (2009:14–20) explored the migration of Mexican citizens to rural North America and described how socially constructed problems of migration, immigration and economic restructuring impacted community-based practices and contributed to an exclusionary regulation of citizenship. Ng's (1996:81–89) institutional ethnography of Canadian immigration policies demonstrated that state discourses about 'immigrant women' from the global South framed them as 'dependents' and thus informed working practices that reproduced gender and race inequalities. The research of Kim and Campbell (2013:195–201) on non-governmental organizations in Kyrgyzstan showed how global peace-building initiatives shaped the everyday work of local women's groups and affected the quality of services these could offer to their beneficiaries.

However, this chapter does not focus on the mobility of people per se. Rather, it expands on existing and highly regarded scholarship on connectivity across research sites, albeit on a different conceptual basis. Specifically, I concentrate on the mobility of ideas, discourses, texts, and practices and their influence on the everyday reality of largely immobile people. Indeed, female smallholders live within a traditional gender hierarchy that fixes their place within the private spheres of their homes: they have limited access to public space in their villages and their migration abroad is nearly impossible. However, this chapter, like many other institutional ethnographies, demonstrates that, notwithstanding this lack of mobility, in today's globalized world even the most immobile subjects can be seriously impacted by processes, people, institutions, and ideologies located outside their own environment.

The concept of translocal ruling relations helps us to understand how this impact is achieved and maintained. Smith understands translocal ruling relations to be 'expansive, historically specific apparat[i] of management and control that arose with the development of corporate capitalism and support[s] its operation' (Devault 2006:259). The concept of the translocal is derived from the understanding that no activity, regardless of its location in the contemporary world, takes place in isolation from larger social and institutional arrangements, but is always coordinated from outside of the local space, i.e., translocally (Smith 1999:80–92). Institutional ethnographies focus on discovering the exact processes by which such coordination is accomplished, paying attention to the consequences resulting from the ruling relations (Campbell 2006:94). Empirical observations demonstrate that translocal power, seen in technologies of social control, is increasingly textual and discursive (Smith 1999:80–92). In an organizational setting, texts such as charts, strategic plans, monitoring sheets, reporting matrices and the like are the mechanisms that coordinate and connect work processes. These connections are called 'social relations' and people doing their everyday work are drawn into them, aligning their activities with the institutional interests expressed in these texts but not necessarily with their own, personal, interests. People are often ruled by the assumed power of texts and discourses. This chapter aims to look at a specific setting in rural Uzbekistan in order to identify, describe, and analyze the processes involved in making this rule possible. This undertaking has important social implications in helping us to detect how and where well-intended managerial work becomes counter-productive.

Also deserving of attention is the larger political and historical context in which the research took place. Today, Uzbekistan is the largest and most populous nation state in Central Asia, with a population of nearly thirty million people (World Bank 2015). In 2014, the estimated gross domestic product (GDP) per capita was 5,600 USD. The unemployment rate stood at 4.9 percent in 2014. Uzbekistan has abundant natural resources such as large deposits of gold, silver, zinc, uranium, lead, copper, and molybdenum. The country's energy resources include natural gas and deposits of coal and oil. About sixty-five percent of the population are rural settlers. Nearly twenty-six percent of the labour force work in the agricultural sector, which accounts for more than eighteen percent of GDP (*ibid.*).

During the Soviet era, Moscow forced Uzbekistan to produce cotton as a monoculture. This crop was unsuitable for the area, mostly due to the fact that seventy percent of the country's territory was desert and only eleven percent of its area was arable land (Herbst *et al.* 2006:306). Excessive use of water from the Syr Darya and Amu Darya rivers, which feed the Aral Sea, led to drastic social and environmental consequences. The depletion of the Aral Sea led to widespread salinization of the soil throughout the already arid region. Additionally, the use of pesticides and fertilizers in the agricultural sector raised soil and water toxicity. Since independence, the government has made little progress toward mitigating environmental degradation (World Bank 2015). Today, pressing concerns include untreated wastewater, lack of clean drinking water, and air pollution from heavy industry. However, even though some progress toward agricultural diversification has been made, the country remains one of the largest exporters of cotton in the world (The National Cotton Council: 1) and continues to rely heavily on imported food.

According to the 1991 constitution, Uzbekistan is a secular, democratic republic. Political power is vested in a president who can serve multiple five-year terms and is elected by direct vote. In reality, political power has been maintained through state-backed violence and elections, none of which have been deemed free or fair by the international community (CIA World Factbook:1). The ruling party believes in enacting harsh measures as a means of avoiding civil wars and other conflicts (*ibid.*). The country is often classified as a hard authoritarian regime with limited civil rights (United States Department of State 2013:1–5) in which violations of virtually all basic human rights are widespread (International Helsinki Federation for Human Rights 2004).

In terms of territorial administration, Uzbekistan is comprised of twelve provinces. Among them, the Khorezm region has been the worst hit by the Aral Sea crisis. Khorezm is surrounded by two deserts, the Qaraqum in the south and west, and the Qyzylqum in the north and east (Kehl-Bodrogi 2006:235–37). The inhabitants of the province are predominantly Uzbek along with a small number of Turkmen ethnic groups, and its Uzbek residents speak a dialect not widely understood outside the region. Nearly eighty percent of the population lives in the countryside, making a living from irrigation-based agriculture (*ibid.*). Its disadvantageous position, 400 kilometers south of the Aral Sea alongside the lower course of the Amu Darya River, the major source of irrigation, creates a number of serious problems for agriculture (Kehl-Bodrogi 2006:235–37). In addition to this, grave ecological issues caused by a high water table and soil salinization hinder smooth agricultural production (Herbst *et al.* 2006:306). A large proportion of the population is economically disadvantaged and lacks social security (Kehl-Bodrogi 2006:235–37).

My institutional ethnographic research took place in one of the villages in the Khorezm region, recognized as one of the poorest in the area (Abdullaev and Mollinga 2010:89–96) and located at the furthest tip of the Amu Darya river. Irrigated agriculture is the predominant means of employment for its population of about eleven thousand people. Due to its unfortunate location, this village (henceforth given the pseudonym 'Hayat'[1]) suffers from a markedly insufficient and unreliable water supply, especially during the frequent periods of water scarcity (Veldwisch and Bock 2011:581–84).

Two types of farmers operate in Hayat: private farmers and smallholders. These two categories emerged during a series of national land reforms in 2006, 2008, and 2010 (Djanivekov *et al.* 2012:1106–20). These reforms, intended to restructure a cumbersome agricultural administration in response to new political and economic conditions, nonetheless maintained many features of the old system. To provide a brief historical overview: four years after Uzbekistan became part of the Soviet Union in 1924, it actively enforced the agrarian policy of 'collectivization' (Kandiyoti 2002). This policy required the consolidation of individually owned land into communal farms, i.e. collective farms and state farms, with the expectation that this would lead to increases in agricultural exports, supplies of raw materials for industry, and food provision for the urban population. As a result, by 1932, nearly 80% of all rural households had been incorporated into 9,734 collective farms and 94 state farms (*ibid.*).

Collective farms were typically organized by merging small individual farms into a cooperative structure, whereas state farms were created by the state on the land confiscated from former large estates. The workers on state farms were recruited from among landless rural residents. The work within collective and state farms was internally divided among working groups, known as 'brigades' and headed by a brigade's leader or 'brigadier' (Veldwisch and Bock 2011:581–84). The workers on collective and state farms used to receive a small piece of 'private' land for their own food production (about 0.25 ha) as part of their payment and in order to keep the workers bound to the collective farm (*ibid.*).

After the dissolution of the Soviet Union in 1991, the Uzbek government, wishing to transition to a market economy, introduced a reverse process of 'de-collectivization' within which agricultural land

---

1   In order to protect my interlocutors' integrity the real name of the village has been replaced by this pseudonym.

was privatized and redistributed (Djanivekov *et al.* 2012:1106–20). De-collectivization led to the establishment of a new agrarian category of 'private farms'. Local administrations selected leaders of the former communal farms (*ibid.*) to become private farmers; they were leased land for cultivation. Private farmers were expected to hire the rest of the rural population, yet in practice they employed only a small number of workers, thus leaving many families jobless. Scholars recognize that this agricultural reform was largely unsuccessful (Abdullaev *et al.* 2005:115) and its social impact was extremely harmful. When unemployment and poverty became widespread among the rest of the former workers of the communal farms and food security was at risk, the government granted additional small plots of land (0.12 ha) to each smallholder household. Formally, this land policy created a new category of 'smallholding peasants' (here, referred to as 'smallholders').

Agrarian land reforms were followed by changes to irrigation management policy. Regional water resources were depleted due to decades of intensive cotton production as well as inadequate water management institutions and outdated water allocation mechanisms (*ibid.*). To tackle these problems, policy makers introduced Water User Associations (WUAs), to form a democratic and community-based water management organization that would not only practice efficient and fair distribution of water for irrigation, but would provide 'social assistance to the most vulnerable groups' (Asian Development Bank 2011:11) through improved agricultural activities. Globally, WUAs are recognized as grassroots initiatives led by water users, and organized on the principles of equity and efficiency in the distribution of water and the use of irrigation and drainage systems (Zavgorodnaya 2006). Since 2005, hundreds of WUAs have been established in Uzbekistan, many in accordance with the so-called 'Uzbek' model, whereby government departments (mostly within the Ministry of Agriculture and Water Resources of the Republic of Uzbekistan) designed and set up WUAs with little involvement from water users, who were supposed to be the initiators of these processes. The WUA leaders and their technical employees were appointed under the close supervision of local authorities and regional departments of the ministry (Zavgorodnaya 2006).

At the time of my fieldwork, the village had already undergone these reforms and 29 private farmers were appointed as farm leaders from among the former collective. Additionally, more than 2,000 households had attained the status of smallholder farms (Zavgorodnaya 2006). All of the 29 private farms produced cotton and were headed by men. In the majority of smallholders' families, life was rather fragmented. The men were absent for long periods of time working as migrant laborers in Russia, Kazakhstan, and urban areas of Uzbekistan. Women became the heads of the households and assumed all of the farming work in addition to their traditional domestic chores (Kim 2014:106–20). Maintaining agricultural production became one of their main responsibilities. In the vast number of these emerging female-headed households, their main source of livelihood, small-scale agriculture, was continuously endangered by reduced irrigation resources and the difficulty of accessing them (*ibid.*). All this took place in the presence of a local WUA, which consisted of a chairman, an accountant, and five water engineers. The WUA took responsibility for all matters related to irrigation within the village, and their role became more prominent during the years in which water was scarce, because regional water regulation forced villages to queue for water. The village received water once every 2 weeks for about 2 to 3 days (and nights).

As a point of entry into my study I researched the experiences of smallholders, investigating why, even after the state's policy to counteract unemployment and hunger, these men were forced to leave their homes. Furthermore, why did rural women who were left behind continue to experience challenges in securing water to sustain their families even with the existence of a WUA? Questions such as these, which arise from listening to local people and shape the course of the ongoing inquiry, are called 'the problematic' in institutional ethnography (Smith 2005:68–80). My problematic emerged from ethnographic data revealing that water scarcity presented persistent challenges to the entire village population. I sought to understand how it was possible that, after having received additional agricultural land and in the presence of the WUA, smallholder families continued to endure insecure livelihoods and are forced to send family members abroad for income. This chapter seeks to provide answers these questions by rigorously applying an institutional ethnographic approach.

The organization of village life is not only a matter of personal choice, or ineptitude, but is impacted by people and institutions situated outside the local context, whose actions are not directed at that particular village. By investigating the workings of these institutions, their operation and activities, and the connections between them, this chapter uncovers the translocal coordinating power of national policies of foreign agricultural trade and commerce and their impact on an individual village. By examining the implicit but identifiable mechanisms and technologies through which translocal institutions, ideologies, and discourses infiltrate local settings, I argue that rural Uzbek people's realities, which are characterized by uncertainty and increasing economic insecurity that is exacerbated by deteriorating environmental conditions, are not 'just happening' but result from national agricultural trade policies. I reveal the various material connections and interactions between the state and the individual smallholders, and the consequences of these dynamics.

Conceptual framework

The term 'translocality' has come into vogue over the past two or three decades (Greiner and Sakdapolrak 2013:373–76). It is used by scholars from different disciplinary fields such as geography, history, area studies, cultural studies, anthropology, and development studies. In 1996, Arjun Appadurai argued that this concept could be used to understand what he termed the reproduction of the local in the context of transnational mobility (1995:216). He argued that migrants actively reproduced their own localities outside their home countries in the sites of their new residences and such 'production and reproduction of locality, in which ties of marriage, work, business and leisure weave together various circulating kinds of "locals" are increasingly complex' (*ibid.*). Challenging the accepted notion of transnationalism with its focus on national borders, he argued that translocality is a contemporary feature of globalization that offers a different perspective on the relations between apparently insular locales (Greiner and Sakdapolrak 2013:373–76). Increasingly, the notion of translocality has been theoretically and methodologically helpful to scholars who seek to capture much more nuanced local connections across national boundaries (Appadurai 1995:216–22).

A review of the existing literature on the concept of translocality reveals the wide use of the term. Translocality involves mobility, space, connectedness, and associated knowledge. In discussing the analytic use of translocality, this chapter does not focus on the stories of mobile subjects, but on the interactions between global ideas, discourses, ideologies, and local experiences. In doing so, I follow Stephan-Emmrich (Chapter Nine) and concur with Hage's understanding of translocality as an analytic 'double gaze' to argue that local environments and global dynamics are inherently interrelated (2005:464–70). Like her, I argue that, in today's world, in which social realities are shaped by globalization, the 'double gaze' needs to be able to capture lived experiences and the forces that structure them. In agreement with Burawoy's theory of a 'global ethnography of space' (Burawoy *et al.* 2000:35–42), this chapter suggests that local experiences can connect to wider geographical processes and spaces and that certain methodologies, like his 'extended case method', help researchers to explore how to reach out from micro processes to macro forces and thus link the local to the global. One important aspect of institutional ethnography is its commitment to an empirical method of tracing and mapping the multiple connections between local lives and global powers. All of these connections, or 'social relations', are material and discoverable rather than dialectic or theoretical, especially when it comes to explanations of the global modality of the local (Smith 2005:68–80).

The term 'social relations' does not refer to interpersonal relationships but to how various connections between different sites of experience are made. These sites are not necessarily connected by people who know each other and exchange something, as they do in social networks. In fact, institutional ethnographers argue that in many cases different sites are connected by people who do not know about each other's existence but are connected through the use of the same ideas, work sequences, routine responsibilities, etc. In contemporary institutions, defined as complexes of activities organized around a distinctive function such as migration policy, international trade, etc., activities are initiated and designed as a means to fulfil institutional functions (*ibid.*). People located in different positions in an institution carry out these activities following guidance and instructions developed elsewhere, usually in texts, within the institutional structure (*ibid.*). Through such textually circulated instructions, organizational rules, forms, standardized procedures, etc., people participate and contribute to the maintenance of institutions and to institutional knowledge, resources and purposes (*ibid.*). People's everyday lives play out within such social relations, called 'social organization', which integrate their local experiences into wider institutional regimes (*ibid.*). I will show later in my analysis how the everyday work of the rural water managers in Uzbekistan is socially organized, through texts and rules, to facilitate state-led agricultural export. Resource management experts have recognized some aspects of this system as good governance. It involves both private farmers and smallholders, but it envisages different purposes for each and impacts them differently.

Returning to the theoretical framework of institutional ethnography, translocal social relations are defined by Smith as 'coordinated chains of action that connect embodied experiences, which occur at a specific local site, to work that is performed at other sites' (*ibid.*:38), a statement that emphasizes the extent to which social relations within an institution can shape and direct people's work. Smith refers to translocal 'ruling social relations' which 'reach beyond and coordinate what a particular person is experiencing locally' (*ibid.*:34). Further research is needed to fully explain the work practices that connect people who have no direct knowledge of each other and who live in different locations. These connections are material and not theoretical, because institutionally designed and implemented activities affect the actions of people in local settings. Therefore, in any institutional ethnographic project 'translocal forms of coordinating people's work are explored as they are to be found in the actual ways in which coordination is locally accomplished' (*ibid.*:38).

Institutional ethnographic analysis shows that people are typically unaware that their everyday lives are organized across space, time, and institutions, which connect them to a range of people, texts, and work practices. Invisible, translocal relations can nevertheless be uncovered by researchers who can describe and track them from local to extra-local sites. In other words, these relations are identifiable in people's socially-organized work activities because they are objectively present. Here, in agreement with Alff (in Chapter Five), I argue that contextual factors influence the agency of actors and the outcomes of their strategies.

Institutional ethnographers put forward a more radical argument, claiming that the strategies and choices, including resistance, in which individual people engage are shaped, often invisibly, by translocal ruling relations.

This is not to say that people's activities are not of interest to institutional ethnographers. On the contrary, people as actors always remain central to research, and the analysis of what people do every day to put their lives together allows institutional ethnographers to identify, track, and explain how particular translocal relations work in specific settings. An investigation typically begins by exploring the experiences of those involved in an institutional setting; the analytical goal is to discover and map linkages between everyday life, organizations, and translocal processes of power (Devault and McCoy 2006:18). The researcher gets to know what happens in a setting, learning from the people themselves and identifying a research problematic — usually concerned with dislocations between ruling ideas and local people's experiences and knowledge. But how does this work in practice? The researcher's analytical framework provides a sense of socially organized knowledge guiding local actions; a belief that nothing 'just happens' but rather is made to happen.

In institutional ethnography the analysis of institutional texts is important. 'Texts' can be documents or any form of representation that has a 'relatively fixed and replicable character' (Deveau 2008:9) and that people routinely use in the conduct of their work. These include organizational charts, work manuals, reporting guidelines, monitoring sheets, logical frameworks, etc. Institutional texts travel in various forms and are passed from one set of users to another, where they are read as instructions and written as records. Smith uses the metaphor of DNA to illustrate how socially organized knowledge produced in one location becomes packaged in texts and then replicated either electronically or in hard-copy format in multiple locations, becoming a blueprint to regulate local activities and organize social relations among people (*ibid.*:4). It is precisely in these texts that traces of ruling relations can become visible. Texts operate as material carriers of ruling relations because the latter 'rely on textually based realities to produce, reproduce and stabilize institutions, because texts have the capacity to preserve meaning in the absence of local context' (Smith 2005:103).

However, not all documentary materials and texts form part of institutional ethnographic research, only 'active' texts. In other words, the texts are treated as 'data' if people use or 'activate' them in their everyday work and if their engagement with these texts coordinates their actions (Campbell and Gregor 2002:82–90). Ethnographers ask who uses which texts, how the texts are used, what is focused on and what is ignored, and how people align their work with texts. In this way researchers can identify the text's capacity to orient people's activities in the directions that are institutionally relevant. Smith calls human engagement with texts a 'text-reader conversation' in which the reader 'responds to, interprets, and acts from it [the text]' (Smith 2005:105) and in doing so becomes an agent of this text. Language coordinates the reader's consciousness and exerts control over her response. Such textual mediation becomes the practical or material form through which ruling relations enter the local setting and order its routines (*ibid.*). Understanding how this happens in any particular case is an essential part of institutional ethnographic research projects.

Methodology

Institutional ethnography is both a theoretical framework, deeply concerned with the political and economic processes in which everyday lives are lived, and also a methodological approach to research (Eastwood and Devault 2001). Institutional ethnographers use a variety of research methods, such as in-depth and semi-structured interviews, focus groups, participant observation, and textual analysis to examine social relations (Campbell 2006). In my research project, data collection involved unstructured and semi-structured interviews, direct and participant observations, and text analysis.

Exact empirical processes in institutional ethnography cannot be predicted beforehand because researchers 'know what they want to explain, but only step by step can they discover who they need to interview and what texts or discourses they need to examine' (Slade 2008:83). The data collection process is iterative and can be divided into three stages, beginning with entry into the research site. My research project began with an inquiry into the everyday lives of smallholder households through participant observations and in-depth interviews;

I visited participants' homes and also lived with a local family, which helped me to formulate questions about their experiences. Adopting their standpoint, I then formulated a narrative about their everyday lives, work, worries, challenges, etc., and identified gaps in my understanding to be pursued further. These missing pieces of information indicated possible explanations for the difficult experiences of smallholders. The main aim of this first stage was to formulate the problematic of my study — the question of how the smallholders' everyday lives, with their struggles and increased workloads, were socially organized.

In the second stage, using this data I mapped connections between the institutions of water management and agricultural administration. I also conducted semi-structured interviews with relevant institutional actors and directly observed their work. In institutional ethnography, data collection and analysis are not completely distinct phases; in my research the initial extensive interviews were used both to identify the translocal social linkages that existed in people's everyday lives and to direct my ethnographic gaze toward the next steps of data collection. During the interview process I paid extremely close attention to whether my interviewees mentioned specific names, people, institutions, government agencies, etc., as I tried to understand what linked these people or institutions to the respondent's experiences.

These newly-identified interlocutors included private farmers, members of local committees, employees of the local WUA, etc., whom I subsequently interviewed. When interviewing them, I paid careful attention to any textual documents they used and, through interviews and direct observation, I inquired into exactly how they engaged with these texts during their work. These new data allowed me to further refine my research goals. The core idea at this stage of research is that what the interlocutors do, know, and tell is coordinated by the ruling relations of the institution. The task is then to extend the interlocutors' own knowledge by uncovering the local coordination that is structured by the ruling relations. This takes place in the third stage of the research, which involves analyzing the institutional texts that were revealed in the previous stage. Here, I focused on identifying the origins of the working texts, which, I discovered, coordinated the work of local institutional actors. This process involved mapping out different documents and the connections between them and, finally, uncovering the social organization of ruling relations governing the work of agricultural management.

The pool of data used for this analysis consisted of forty in-depth and semi-structured interviews. I began with a conversation with a water engineer who used a specific document to plan and sequence irrigation in the village. I learned that this document was part of a body of texts that facilitated the implementation of the same national policy, itself a component of Uzbekistan's national cotton export programme. In what follows, I describe this institutional map.

Discovering translocal connections between local experiences and global trade

As mentioned earlier, Uzbekistan remains one of the world's largest cotton producers. This is the result of the prioritization of cotton cultivation ordered by the central Soviet administration throughout its period of governance (Abdullaev *et al.* 2005:113). The Soviet administration wanted to make the USSR self-sufficient and forced some of its republics to become highly specialized producers of certain commodities for consumption both within the internal and export markets (*ibid.*). Thus Uzbekistan became a territory of intensive cotton cultivation, producing seventy percent of the entire Soviet supply (*ibid.*). This industry employed about forty percent of the republic's total labour force and accounted for more than sixty percent of its total economic input (*ibid.*:115). By the early 1980s, the USSR had become one of the major exporters of cotton, accounting for more than a fifth of world's production and only lagging behind China (*ibid.*).

In contemporary Uzbekistan, the Soviet legacy has been preserved in both the cotton monoculture and the high level of state control of the industry. The production and international trading of cotton is strictly regulated by the government (Rudenko 2009:285) with cotton's contribution accounting for twenty-five percent of Uzbekistan's gross domestic product (Muradov and Ilkhamov 2014:11) and total agricultural exports accounting for more than forty percent of total exports (World Food Programme 2008). State control in the post-Soviet era operates through imposing quotas on 'output and area, a state purchase system and price, quantity of production, and controls on farm outputs' (Abdullaev *et al.* 2005:115). Directly after independence in 1991, all agricultural produce, except that grown in kitchen gardens, were required to be sold to the state. Five years later, state quotas were removed for some agricultural crops but not for cotton (Abdullaev *et al.* 2005:115). After a series of agrarian land reforms, described at the beginning of this chapter, private farmers (or 'fermers' in the local language) became the sole suppliers of cotton, although cotton farms remain state property. Today, private farmers are mandated to plant cotton and they must sow a certain area of land with the plant, else they are penalized (Abdullaev *et al.* 2005:115). Furthermore, private farmers are obligated to supply all of the cotton they grow (with a quota on the minimum required) to the state at a pre-determined rate. Needless to say, the internal purchasing price for cotton is almost half the international market price (Rudenko 2009:285–60). In return for their cotton, farmers are entitled to free land tenure and receive support from government-sponsored agencies in the form of seeds, fertilizers, machinery and irrigation. In legal terms, becoming a private farmer meant that an individual selected or appointed by the local administration was registered as such and signed a contract with the Ministry of Agriculture and Water Resources of Uzbekistan where all the described quotas and government-sponsored services were laid out.

In contrast, smallholders (or *dehkans* in the local language) came into existence very differently, in response to the breakdown of the centralized Soviet system when millions of rural people lost their livelihoods due to decreases in production, shortfalls of basic food products, and lack of previously-provided social infrastructure (Kandiyoti 2002, Abdullaev *et al.* 2005:115). In 1994, to increase food security and respond to growing poverty, the government withdrew some land from collective farms and distributed it among the rural population, formally describing these owners as *dehkans* who were granted permanent and inheritable rights to the land (Zayforodnaya 2006).

There are thus two distinct sets of goals and expectations for private farmers and for smallholders: to provide the state with a crop required to maintain the national export industry; and to respond to the apparently inefficient agricultural governance with a quick and effective solution to an unexpected side-effect of the agrarian reforms. In both cases, however, the availability of irrigation, a controversial issue in Uzbekistan, is key.

WUAs were established to address the problem of irrigation scarcity and distribute water equally and democratically. However, as my findings show, the reality fails to live up to this promise. I argue that WUAs are an integral part of the policy that supports the large-scale production of cotton by private farmers and exists to help these farmers increase their productivity, rather than to assist the most vulnerable groups.

The vulnerability of smallholders was evident from the outset of the research. I soon learned that agricultural produce from their gardens and small plots of land are absolutely essential for food and for animal breeding. In most cases these families do not have any other source of income, except anything that male family members who have left the village can send back. The majority of families have been broken up by labour migration, and the remittances sent home by these men provide the only source of meaningful cash income. 'There is no job for our men here in the village', a female smallholder told me. This puzzled me because the cultivation of 0.13 ha of land, breeding animals, and selling crops and livestock appeared to provide enough work for entire family. However, as I later discovered, generating hard cash revenue from their plot is so labour-intensive that going abroad as a migrant worker becomes a much more attractive option financially, despite the costly price these men have to pay on a personal level. As a result, I observed highly feminized smallhold agriculture characterized by the increasing difficulty of securing the necessary support for agricultural production, chiefly irrigation. At the same time, my interviews with the male private farmers indicated that they suffered no limitations in terms of the provision of water and services (Kim 2014:68–80). Neither did their family structure seem to have been affected by outmigration. This brought me back to my research problematic and my consideration of the different impacts a social organization can have on different constituencies, i.e., the smallholders versus the private farmers.

As I looked more closely at the everyday work of the irrigators in the local WUA, I realized that giving precedence to the irrigation needs of the private farmers over those of the smallholders was not something that these professional irrigators 'just did'. On the contrary, their work was socially organized and coordinated by institutional texts such as irrigation schedules, monitoring, and report forms. Water engineers did their jobs professionally and responsibly by using these forms in their everyday work. Below (in Figure 4.1) I provide an example of a monitoring sheet used by all water engineers in the WUA called '*kontur*'.

#	Kontur-related information		Irrigation-related information								
			Amount of irrigation water delivered			Total irrigated area		Type of crop			
1	Size of the field, ha	Number of kontur	As indicated in the contract	Actual amount of water	Difference between the two	Planned	Actual	Cotton	Wheat	Potatoes	Fodder
	5	218									
	3.7	220									
	3.9	224									
	0.9	225–226									
Signature											
DWRD											
Land surveyor											
WUA											
Farmer											

Fig. 4.1 *Kontur* (monitoring sheet) translated by the author.
Image © Elena Kim (2014), CC BY 4.0

In the words of water engineer Ikram,[2] he 'controls the number of the watered hectares [and] looks at the *kontur*. They have numbers that correspond to the *fermers'* land. [He] marks which land has been watered and informs the WUA'.

If we attend to the column in the *kontur* called '*Kontur* Number' we see different numbers each corresponding to a specific piece of land in the village. Once a piece of land is numbered by the land surveyor, it is marked as a *kontur*. From Ikram, we learned that these *konturs* mark only the land cultivated by private farmers. In my second interview with him the WUA chairperson supported this observation, as he stated that '*myrabs* [water engineers] use the *konturs* of the farmer's land only'.

This is an example in which a text directed the attention of the WUA to a particular category of water user. Using the *kontur*, water engineers ensured that efficient provision of water was only provided to the

---

2   Here and hereafter pseudonyms are used.

selected areas. I tracked the use of *konturs* in the WUA and discovered that the information they provided fed into a standardized reporting form, which itself contained the sub-heading *'Fermer*'s land'. I learned that the standardized reporting form and the *kontur* were, in fact, appendices to the WUA's Charter. The Charter itself states that its main areas of activity are the delivery and distribution of water among its members. Membership is acquired by signing an agreement with the WUA. As the WUA chairperson told me, the 'agreement is the most important; if there is an agreement, there is water; no agreement means "no water"'.

However, he also indicated that not everybody is eligible to sign. As WUA staff explained:

> An agreement with smallholders cannot be signed because they do not have a stamp, while farmers have the contract with the State. They have cotton and wheat […], while they (smallholders) do not have a stamp.

All the private farmers were in a position to sign such an agreement with the WUA because they were already legal entities who had a contract with the state to provide cotton. For this reason they were equipped with their own stamps, without which they could not be private farmers at all. The situation of smallholders was entirely different in this respect. Their existence as a category of agricultural producers was the result of a forced measure and an *ad hoc* decision rather than a strategic choice; their crops provided subsistence rather than contributing to state commerce. Since smallholders did not have to supply the state with their crops and did not have to enter into contracts with the state, they were not recognized as legal entities and were not granted stamps. The WUA was organized to operate as a 'closed club' with membership limited to private farmers, thus failing to address the needs of the poorer smallholders. As an institutional ethnographer, I understood that the exclusionary practices of the WUA developed not because of deliberate efforts by individuals but because they were translocally incentivized: the WUA Charter and its rules on membership and eligibility, which directed the work of its employees, was part of a larger institutional system. It was therefore important to focus my analysis on the institutional origins of the WUA Charter. I found out that what was happening locally was linked, through a number of translocal, textual and discursive connections, to Uzbekistan's global cotton trade. The policy of the WUA establishment in Uzbekistan formed an inherent part of the state's agricultural reforms that aimed to increase agricultural productivity. This policy was put into practice in an appendix document regulating the set up of private farming entities throughout Uzbekistan. This appendix, which included the definition and roles of WUAs, was accompanied by the documentation needed to set up this type of organization, such as blueprints for the Charter, agreements, reporting forms, *konturs*, etc. This package was circulated throughout Uzbekistan, and the village I studied also relied on it for its everyday operations. Thus the activities of individual water engineers in the village were directed by a sequence of texts that were coordinated by the state with the aim of maximizing produce for international trade. Their everyday work, with its unintended negative impact on smallholders, was thus translocally coordinated.

Translocal organization of water management and its unjust consequences

Uzbekistan participates in the global cotton trade to sustain its economy and its regional and international influence. The government have initiated a number of policy efforts, which they claimed were intended to mitigate the negative social effects of monoculture production on the poorest groups. These included the 1994 land reform and the promise of democratic water management through the introduction of WUAs. However, in practice, these apparently benevolent policies supported commercial interests, which affected individual farms in a systematic way. The need to sustain the trade in cotton resulted in land reforms that were intended to increase agricultural production, as well as methods of irrigation management that supported this. WUAs were (and still are) part of the state's regulation of agriculture and, through texts such as *konturs*, established the regime's priorities and neglected those who did not directly contribute to cotton production, i.e., smallholders, who became institutionally invisible. Smallholders were not listed among the beneficiaries of the improved water distribution by the WUA when its policies were drawn up, and therefore they could not appear in the WUA's statutory, regulatory and operational texts as legitimate water users. Their absence from the *kontur* restricted water engineers from providing them with irrigation services and as a result smallholders cannot easily access water to irrigate their plots.

Smallholders 'will find water by themselves', the water masters told me when I asked them how peasant households were expected to receive irrigation services. Having been trained to use WUA texts in their work, their attention is routinely directed away from smallholders' needs. Smallholders do indeed 'find water by themselves' to maintain their farms and feed their family members, but they do so at the considerable expense of their time, health, and labor. For male smallholders, for whom working in the fields used to be a full-time job, inefficient agricultural practices were compounded by the unreliable water supply and this created a powerful incentive to travel to Russia for work. These men often live precarious lives full of uncertainty, anxiety, unreliable sources of income, and even violence, in pitiable living conditions. They lack social security and suffer the constant fear of deportation (Khajimukhamedov 2008).

For female smallholders, the exclusion from irrigation systems often means a tremendous increase in their workloads. In my previous work I described in detail the devastatingly difficult living conditions of the female smallholders who remain in the village while their male partners are working abroad (Kim 2014, Kim *et al.* forthcoming). These women are expected to do the work of three people in order to sustain their families and households: domestic work, their own farming activities, and, now, the agricultural labour of their husbands. In addition to their traditional tasks of maintaining the house, working in the field, rearing children, and taking care of elderly family members, they have assumed new responsibilities such as soil fertilization, planting, irrigating and harvesting, and they are forced to manage their time to accomplish this intensified workload. My ethnographic observation notes from just one day living with a smallholder family record: 'that day, talking to Norida was almost impossible because of her all-consuming work, the shouting of the children around her'. Without even basic house and garden equipment, time-consuming and physically complex work becomes even more so. For instance, breadmaking is done from scratch using a mud stove heated by brushwood that the women must gather, and the preparation of food for canning is accomplished manually by following a dozen carefully sequenced procedures.

Fig. 4.2 A peasant woman working in her field.
Photo © Elena Kim (2014), CC BY 4.0

I discovered that these women had to undertake even more work to ensure sufficient access to water, which was taking up more time than they could afford. Since water only arrived in the canals once or twice per month for two or three days, women had to engage in time-consuming labour to find out if it was available so that they could open their canals and irrigate their fields. Many physically traveled to the canal, which might be a journey ranging from fifty meters to more than several kilometers of unpaved roads. My ethnographic notes describe what it means for many women to monitor water availability:

> Nargiza takes two hours by her donkey-harnessed cart to reach her field and look at the canal. If the water is not flowing, this long journey is undertaken in vain. If the water is there, she queues with other smallholders and waits until she can open her ditch and let the water flow into her plot of land. Depending on the water pressure, irrigating one plot takes from forty minutes to five hours. This adds up to long hours of work, added to the additional hours of the journey back and forth to the village. Norida walks or uses her bicycle to go to the canal. By bicycle it takes her twenty minutes to reach the place and she has to do this once every two or three days during the vegetation season.

These smallholders often failed to irrigate their land because they did not have timely information, or they were absent when the water arrived, or else it was already used up. All of this threatens their basic livelihood and wellbeing, because smallholder families must subsist almost entirely on what they grow in their fields while the remittances from their male partners can be unreliable and insufficient. The lack of recognition of smallholders families in the WUA is thus especially problematic. Although WUAs were inspired by inclusive and democratic principles (Abdullaev and Mollinga 2010:85–100), my analysis of the translocal organization of water management shows that even the most well-intended social and managerial policy can routinely produce unexpectedly harmful consequences.

The translocal organization of smallholder families' livelihoods in Uzbekistan is invisible to them, yet it systematically affects their lives. Regardless of the individual choices these families make every day, their experiences are shaped externally by forces that are not immediately obvious to them, preventing them from fully understanding the challenges they face. Translocal power is coordinated by, and operates materially and discursively through, institutional texts and the institutional actors who use them. This is how translocal institutions shape the day-to-day realities of those on whose behalf they claim to function. Water governance then, as a routine work process, is based on exclusionary practices that lead to increased vulnerability, uncertainty and profound social inequality among smallholders.

References

Abdullaev, Iskender, and Peter Mollinga. 'The Socio-Technical Aspects of Water Management: Emerging Trends at Grass Roots Level in Uzbekistan'. *Water* 2 (2010): 85–100, https://doi.org/10.3390/w2010085

Abdullaev, Iskender, Mark Giordano, and Aziz Rasulov. 'Cotton in Uzbekistan: Water and Welfare', paper presented at the Conference on 'Cotton Sector in Central Asia: Economic Policy and Development Challenges', School of Oriental and African Studies, University of London, 3–4 November 2005:1–19, https://www.zef.de/uploads/tx_zefportal/Publications/83a8_Abdullaev%20100807.pdf

Asian Development Bank. 'Uzbekistan: Ak Altin Agricultural Development Project'. *Completion Report* (2011): 10–30, http://www.adb.org/documents/uzbekistan-ak-altin-agricultural-development-project

Appadurai, Arjun. 'Production of Locality'. In Richard Fardon, ed. *Counterwork: Managing the Diversity of Knowledge*. London: Routledge, 1995, pp. 208–29.

Burawoy, Michael, Joseph Blum, Sheba George, Zsuzsa Gille, and Millie Thayer. *Global Ethnography. Forces, Connections, and Imaginations in a Post-Modern World*. Los Angeles: University of California Press, 2000.

Campbell, Marie, and Frances Gregor. *Mapping Social Relations. A Primer in Doing Institutional Ethnography*. Aurora, Ontario: Garamond Press, 2002.

Campbell, Marie. 'Institutional Ethnography and Experience as Data'. In Dorothy Smith ed. *Institutional Ethnography as Practice*. Lanham: Rowman & Littlefield Publishers, Inc., 2006, pp. 91–109.

Central Intelligence Agency (CIA). 'Uzbekistan'. *The World Factbook*, p. 1, https://www.cia.gov/library/publications/the-world-factbook/geos/uz.html

Devault, Marjorie L. 'Introduction: What is Institutional Ethnography?' *Social Problems* 53 (2006): 294–98, https://doi.org/10.1525/sp.2006.53.3.294

Devault, Marjorie L., and Liza McCoy. 'Institutional Ethnography: Using Interviews to Investigate Ruling Relations'. In Dorothy Smith, ed. *Institutional Ethnography as Practice*. Lanham: Rowman & Littlefield Publishers, Inc., 2006, pp. 15–45.

Deveau, Jean L. 'Examining the Institutional Ethnographer's Toolkit'. *Socialist Studies* 4 (2008): 1–19, https://doi.org/10.18740/S4F60Z

Djanivekov, Nodir, Kristof Van Assche, Ihtiyor Bobojonov, and John Lamers. 'Farm Restructuring and Land Consolidation in Uzbekistan: New Farms with Old Barriers'. *Europe-Asia Studies* 64.6 (2012): 1101–26, https://doi.org/10.1080/09668136.2012.691720

Greiner, Clemens, and Patrick Sakdapolrak. 'Translocality: Concepts, Applications and Emerging Research Perspectives'. *Geography Compass* 7.5 (2013): 373–84, https://doi.org/10.1111/gec3.12048

Hage, Ghassan. 'A Not So Multi-Sited Ethnography of a Not So Imagined Community'. *Anthropological Theory* 5.4 (2005): 463–75, https://doi.org/10.1177/1463499605059232

Herbst, Susanne, Dilorom Fayzieva, and Thomas Kistemann. 'Risk Factor Analysis of Diarrhoeal Diseases in the Aral Sea Area (Khorezm, Uzbekistan)'. *International Journal of Environmental Health Research* 18.5 (2006): 305–21, https://doi.org/10.1080/09603120701834507

International Helsinki Federation for Human Rights. 'Human Rights in OSCE Region: Europe, Central Asia and North America — Uzbekistan' (2004), https://web.archive.org/web/20100129175624/http://www.ihf-hr.org/documents/doc_summary.php?sec_id=3&d_id=3860 [as archived on 29/01/2010].

Kandiyoti, Deniz. 'Agrarian Reform, Gender and Land Rights in Uzbekistan'. *Social Policy and Development Programme Paper* (2002): 22–60, http://www.unrisd.org/80256B3C005BCCF9/search/C2919AC1CD7B5379C1256CCA00369D07

Kehl-Bodrogi, Krisztina. 'Who Owns the Shrine? Competing Meanings and Authorities at a Pilgrimage Site in Khorezm'. *Central Asian Survey* 25.3 (2006): 235–50, https://doi.org/10.1080/02634930601022526

Khajimukhamedov, Marat. 'External Labor Migration'. In Evgeniy Abdullaev, ed. *Labour Migration in Uzbekistan: Social, Legal And Gender Aspects*. Tashkent: UNDP Country Office in Uzbekistan, 2008, pp. 130–83.

Kim, Elena, and Marie Campbell. 'Violence Against Women and Peace Building: Tracking Ruling Relations in Women's Development NGO in Kyrgyzstan'. In Aziz Choudry and D. Kapoor, eds. *NGO-ization: Complicity, Contradictions and Prospects*. London: Zed Books, 2013, pp. 185–206.

Kim, Elena. 'International Development and Research in Central Asia: Exploring the Knowledge-Based Social Organization of Gender'. Doctoral thesis, Bonn University, 2014.

Kim, Elena, Anna-Katharina Hornidge, and Conrad Schetter. 'Uzbekistani Agrarian Policy Reforms and their Gendered Effects on Women's Water-Management Practices'. In Laura Bisaillon, ed. *Impact of Public Policy on Everyday Life: The Policy Stories That People Tell*. Springer, forthcoming.

Muradov, Bakhodyr, and Alisher Ilkhamov 2014. *Uzbekistan's Cotton Sector: Financial Flows and Distribution of Resources*. New York: Open Society Foundations, Working Paper, https://www.opensocietyfoundations.org/sites/default/files/uzbekistans-cotton-sector-20141021.pdf

Naples, Nancy. 'Crossing Borders: Community Activism, Globalization, and Social Justice'. *Social Problems* 56.1 (2009): 2–20.

Ng, Roxana. *The Politics of Community Services: Immigrant Women, Class and the State*. Halifax: Fernwood, 1996.

Rudenko, Irina. 'Can Uzbek Farmers Get More for their Cotton?' *European Journal of Development Research* 21 (2009): 283–96, https://doi.org/10.1057/ejdr.2009.3

Smith, Dorothy E. *The Everyday World as Problematic: A Feminist Sociology*. Toronto: University of Toronto Press, 1987.

Smith, Dorothy E. *Writing the Social. Critique, Theory and Investigation*. Toronto: University of Toronto Press, 1999.

Smith, Dorothy E. *Institutional Ethnography: A Sociology for People*. Lanham, MD: AltaMira Press/Rowman and Littlefield, 2005.

The National Cotton Council of America. 'Ranking'. http://www.cotton.org/econ/cropinfo/cropdata/rankings.cfm

United States Department of State. 'Uzbekistan 2013 Human Rights Report' (2013), http://www.state.gov/documents/organization/220622.pdf

Veldwisch, Gert J., and Bettina B. Bock. 'Dehkans, Diversification and Dependencies: Rural Transformation in Post-Soviet Uzbekistan'. *Journal of Agrarian Change* 11.4 (2011): 581–97, https://doi.org/10.1111/j.1471-0366.2011.00327.x

World Bank. 'Uzbekistan'. *World Bank Group* (2015), http://www.worldbank.org/en/country/uzbekistan

World Food Programme. 'Poverty and Food Insecurity in Uzbekistan' (2008), http://documents.wfp.org/stellent/groups/public/documents/ena/wfp179011.pdf

Zanca, Russel. *Life in a Muslim Uzbek Village: Cotton Farming After Communism*. Belmont, CA: Wadsworth, Cengage Learning, 2011.

Zavgorodnaya, Dariya. 'Water Users Association in the Republic of Uzbekistan: Theory and Practice'. Doctoral thesis, Bonn University, 2006.

5. A Sense of Multiple Belonging: Translocal Relations and Narratives of Change Within a Dungan Community[1]

Henryk Alff

Introduction

The so-called 'Forum for Culture and Science' organized by the Assembly of People of Kazakhstan, a major legislative body nominally chaired by President of State Nursultan Nazarbaev was attended by numerous leaders of the country's 'diasporas'. Held in September 2011 in one of Almaty's most prestigious restaurants, its entertainment program consisted of 'traditional' dance performances accompanied by various signature dishes belonging to the different groups that are part of multi-ethnic Kazakhstan, alongside national delicacies. However, Husey Daurov, a successful businessman and head of Kazakhstan's

1   The research for this chapter was funded by the German Federal Ministry for Education and Research (BMBF) in the framework of the competence network 'Crossroads Asia'. I would like to thank both BMBF and Crossroads Asia for their generous support during the research process. Furthermore, I am grateful for the open discussion of an earlier version of this chapter at a workshop of the Volkswagen-Foundation-funded project 'Translocal Goods' of Humboldt-Universität zu Berlin, held in Bishkek, Kyrgyzstan, in April 2015. I especially want to thank Philipp Schröder and Manja Stephan-Emmrich as well as Barak Kalir, Nathan Light and the two anonymous reviewers of the volume for their valuable input, which helped to improve the argument.

https://doi.org/10.11647/OBP.0114.05

Association of Dungans, a group of Chinese-speaking Muslims, used the event as a venue for negotiating business deals rather than celebrating culture and science. Trade entrepreneurs seeking support, as well as phone calls to and from China, constantly interrupted my interview with Daurov, an interview that took place on the sidelines of the larger meeting. As Daurov clarified, excusing himself for the frequent interruptions, Dungan connections built over the past three decades between Central Asia and China far exceed the level of mere commerce. They include a range of exchanges regarding education and innovation that facilitate the Dungans' role as political and socio-economic mediators across what is presented from the state perspective in both Kazakhstan and China as a newly emerging 'Silk Road'.

Originating predominantly from the Chinese provinces of Shaanxi and Gansu, Dungans in Central Asia are descendants of refugees who were forced to leave the late Qing Empire in the course of what has become known as the Hui revolts (1862–1877). Following these events they established themselves in the Russian Empire and later in Soviet Central Asia in the late nineteenth and early twentieth centuries. In the second half of the twentieth century, Dungans were negatively affected by the Sino-Soviet divide that, in 1963, led to the closing of the border between the two Communist powers. However, starting with the Sino-Soviet rapprochement and increasingly so since the breakup of the Soviet Union, many of Kazakhstan's Dungans have managed to establish relations with Huizu[2] and Han Chinese business networks and position themselves favorably in cross-border exchanges between coastal China, Xinjiang, and post-Soviet Central Asia. Dungans value the position of socio-spatial liminality they occupy, and they often attribute particular meaning to the places their practices connect. It is therefore worthwhile to investigate the relational and translocal production of place and the sense of multiple belongings that occur as a result. Notably, during interviews in Russian, my Dungan interlocutors referred not only to themselves but also to their perceived co-ethnics in China, as Dungan, even though Hueitsu is in widespread use as a common emic label or ethnic self-denomination in the 'Dungan language'.

---

2   The Huizu are an ethnic group; the word is used in the People's Republic of China (PRC) collectively for Chinese Muslims. They are one of the fifty-six officially recognized ethnic groups in the PRC.

This chapter explores the relations and practices among the people of coastal China, Almaty, and south-eastern Kazakhstan and the impact they have on notions of belonging and social change within a Dungan community. It takes an ethnographic approach to examine how the socio-economic and socio-cultural changes in interrelated places are perceived, represented, and narrated and how they both shape and are shaped by the actors' social practices. The focus of this inquiry, therefore, is on issues of human interaction and translocal flows of ideas and how they influence the production of a particular sense of place. I argue that because of their discursive positioning between 'rising' China and post-Soviet Kazakhstan, the Dungans perceive themselves as belonging to multiple groups. I will then investigate how the translocal socio-spatial positioning of a group impacts on the exchange of goods and people, as well as the appropriation or translation of particular ideas of social change between interconnected places.

Field research for this study was conducted between September 2011 and May 2014[3] in the large village of Shortobe, about 200 kilometers from Almaty, and in the *Barakholka* bazaar agglomeration in Almaty. My ethnographic methods included semi-structured interviews with residents and participant observation.

My initial engagement with the Dungan community of Kazakhstan was facilitated by Husey Daurov, the most prominent community leader and businessman in Almaty. Since travelling to the People's Republic of China in search of family links for the first time during the 1980s, Daurov has remained the main facilitator of Dungan cultural and political exchanges between Central Asia and China. As one interview partner said: 'Husey Shimarovich [Daurov] has done a lot for the Dungans, in particular for those here in Shortobe. In fact, all of the people doing business with Chinese partners have received contacts and built their business through him'. Daurov therefore served as a crucial resource for my inquiries into Dungan history. He was also a key point of entry into the Dungan community, helping me to identify other interlocutors, including students and entrepreneurs in Shortobe and Guangzhou. The twenty respondents I selected were predominantly entrepreneurs, running their own trade businesses in Almaty, but the

---

3   These periods of field research were complemented by a short stay in Guangzhou in December 2014.

group also included local representatives of the Association of Dungans, several high-school teachers, and college students in Shortobe and the neighboring Dungan-populated village of Masanchi. In addition to these more formal interviews, I enjoyed many informal conversations with Dungans in Kyrgyzstan, as well as three interviews with Dungan students in Guangzhou, Southeast China.

This method of acquiring contacts enabled translocal research. However, my reliance on Husey Daurov as a gatekeeper resulted in interlocutors who were close to the community leaders. Facilitated by this 'snowball system', but also due to the self-proclaimed pious Muslim identity of the Dungans, my interlocutors belonged exclusively to the well-connected and highly mobile male Dungan community. This introduces a certain amount of gender and (im-)mobility bias to the current study,which reflects the fact that the vast majority of Dungan women do not take part in either trade operations or educational exchanges with China.

This chapter comprises six parts in total: a brief section on the socio-cultural and historical background of Kazakhstan's Dungans, followed by an outline of the theoretical background of this research. The remainder of the chapter explores Shortobe's Dungans and their relations, socio-spatial boundaries and narratives of multiple belongings, ending with some concluding remarks on my analysis.

Historical and socio-cultural background

Kazakhstan's Dungans, a group of Chinese-speaking Muslims about 56,000 strong, predominantly live in a cluster of compact settlements in the Zhambyl *oblast* in the southeast of the country (Agenstvo po statistike 2012). They also form one of the largest minority groups in the Chuy and Issyk Köl *oblast* of neighboring Kyrgyzstan. Yet, while Dungans in the Central Asian republic (and in China, where they are subsumed under the ethnic category of Huizu)[4] are widely considered to be a more or less coherent ethnic group, those originating from the Shaanxi and Gansu provinces of China speak different dialects of

---

4   See the extensive work by Dru Gladney (1991, 1996, 2004) for thorough ethnographic research on the Huizu in China.

Mandarin[5] and often inhabit distinct settlements (Jimenez Tovar 2013). In Kyrgyzstan, those claiming their origins in Gansu province dominate among the 60,000 Dungans and form the intellectual elite.[6]

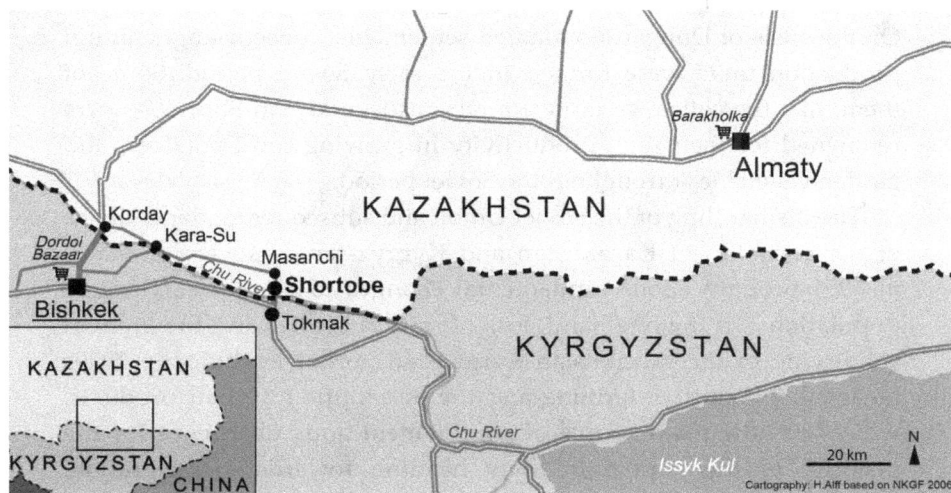

Fig. 5.1 Shortobe and the Dungan-populated villages in South Eastern Kazakhstan. Map © Henryk Alff (2014), CC BY 4.0

The 20,000 Dungan inhabitants of Shortobe, as well as those forming the overwhelming majority of the populous nearby villages of Masanchi, Bular Batyr, and Aukhatty, are almost exclusively descendants of refugees hailing from the Chinese province of Shaanxi. During the late 1870s, they left Qing China under the guidance of Muhammad Ayub Biyanhu, one of the military leaders of the Hui Revolts (Vansvanova 2000). Having escaped annihilation in the Qing Empire, the Dungan refugee groups were settled by Tsarist authorities a few kilometers north of the garrison of Tokmak (Shushanlo 1967), now a regional centre

---

5   In Dungan studies, as well as by the Dungans themselves, their language, however, is regarded not as a form of Chinese, but as a language proper, see for example Svetlana Rimsky-Korsakoff Dyer, 'Soviet Dungan Nationalism: A Few Comments on Their Origin and Language', *Monumenta Serica*, 33 (1978): 363–78.

6   The chair of Dungan Studies (*dunganovedenie* in Russian) at the Kyrgyz Academy of Sciences is the only scholarly institution in the former Soviet Union dedicated to the study of the Dungan language, history, and culture. It is also responsible for the editing of Dungan school textbooks, which are based on the Gansu dialect of the Dungan language.

across the border in Kyrgyzstan with a sizable Dungan community. Along the fertile valley of the Chu River, the Dungan refugees cultivated former pasture land and established irrigated farms, making use of their advanced agricultural skills and the seeds they brought from China.[7] On the basis of Dungan-dominated settlements, collective agricultural production units were formed in the early Soviet period. Some of them, like the collective farm 'Kommunisticheskiy' in Shortobe, were renowned for their high productivity in growing corn, potatoes, and garden vegetables throughout the Soviet period.

The dismantling of the Soviet Union and subsequent independence of the republics of Kazakhstan and Kyrgyzstan as sovereign states in 1991 brought about fundamental changes to Shortobe's Dungan population. On the one hand, loss of state subsidies and the gradual solidifying of the Kazakhstan-Kyrgyzstan border in the early 1990s meant that collective farming and the distribution of their products, which was the main source of employment and subsistence for the majority of the population, was heading towards disintegration. On the other hand, Shortobe's Dungans were among the first rural dwellers in Kazakhstan to gain from the relaxation of travel and foreign trade regulations across the newly opened Sino-Soviet border. Drawing on their ethno-linguistic (and religious) affiliation with Huizu and Han Chinese, Dungan community leaders from Shortobe started to form close interpersonal relations with partners across mainland China (Laruelle and Peyrouse 2012:123) and even as far as Malaysia. Unlike adjacent, mostly Kazakh-populated villages, Shortobe continues to expand and thrive thanks to intensive high-yield agriculture, catering for the markets and for Dungan restaurants in the major cities of Kazakhstan. Trans-Eurasian trade and transport, linking manufacturing centres in China's seaboard, Xinjiang, with the post-Soviet states, is the community's second source of income. Furthermore, dozens of Dungan students now study at the universities or are employed in Xi'an and Lanzhou and in the manufacturing centres of coastal China.

---

7   See Kamol Abdullaev's discussion in Chapter One about Tajik refugees in
     Afghanistan for an example of the 'flow of agricultural innovation' in the early
     Soviet period.

The end of the Soviet Union, however, has also brought about a religious revival and an exchange of ideas about Islam among the Dungan population of Shortobe. Over the past two decades, eighteen mosques were constructed there and in the neighboring Dungan-populated villages, with at least one in what is locally called the 'Chinese style', referring to the curved gable construction of the roof. Shortobe's Dungans consider themselves pious Muslims and usually follow their religious obligations more strictly than their Kazakh co-villagers. In interviews Dungans often described themselves as following the strict rules of Islam, in contrast to their neighbors. Thus, one of my interlocutors in Shortobe joked that Kazakhs consider themselves Muslims only three times in their entire life: when they are born, when they marry, and when they die. For Dungans, on the contrary, Islam is fundamental to their lives and religious duties are to be discharged on an everyday basis.[8] Dungans in Shortobe regularly engage in the prescribed five-times daily prayer; travel for *hajj* at least once (but often twice);[9] and abstain from alcohol and tobacco, substances that have been banned from sale in local shops by the community's elders.

Islam plays an important role in Dungans' self-identification and has certainly contributed to the expansion of Hui-Dungan business relations, as a strict self-definition as pious Muslims among both Dungan and Hui has generated mutual trust based on a shared belief in their mutual honesty.[10] However, this is accompanied by a general tightening of state control, particularly in China, but also in Kazakhstan, over what some government leaders perceive as religious extremism and the establishment of suspicious religious networks. However, given the sensitivity of this topic, the religious aspects have not been studied in great detail in the present study.

---

8   Interview, 20 May 2014, Shortobe.
9   Hundreds of Dungans from Kazakhstan leave for *hajj* every year on charter flights, taking up a considerable proportion of the government quota for these journeys.
10 Cross-border Muslim solidarity among Dungan groups plays out, for example, in the organization of *hajj* tours. During an interview on 4 April 2012, a female director of a Bishkek-based Dungan travel agency explained how she arranged journeys predominantly for Dungans from Xinjiang, making use of the comparatively relaxed religious policies in Kyrgyzstan and bypassing the limited annual state quota for *hajj* travel in China.

The relational thinking of place
and the concept of translocality

In this section, I outline how places are constituted through complex sets of human interactions, negotiations of socio-spatial relations, and flows of ideas and meaning, or 'alternative spatialities'. This approach stems from the paradigmatic changes throughout the social sciences since the 1980s, in particular the 'spatial turn', i.e., the recognition of the constructivist, multidimensional character of spatial production. In particular, I shall refer to Doreen Massey's oft-cited conceptualization of relational placemaking (1991, 1998, 2004) and Zoomers and van Westen's concept of translocal development (2011).

Massey argues that people's identities have a decisive impact on the production of particular places and vice versa. This insight implies that the specific meanings, feelings and values that people associate with a location invoke what John Agnew has called 'a sense of place' (Agnew 2008). We must therefore go beyond physical qualities to consider the imagined values and symbolic attachments that places can possess (for additional discussion of this symbolic meaning, see Manja Stephan-Emmrich in Chapter Nine). Yet, while these qualities appear to be properties of a specific place, they may instead result from, and possibly be expressed because of, human connections to other locations (Castree 2008). Local identities may be based in particular places, but they are rarely bound to them (*ibid.*). Thus, Massey argues rightly that it is 'routes rather than roots', the flows of meaning, that matter for the production of a sense of place (Massey 1998), and these routes also characterise distinct feelings of belonging in the Dungan case, as I shall suggest.

Massey also argues that places should not be conceptualized as static, predetermined (essentialized), and bounded (territorialized) spatial entities, but rather considered according to their ongoing production, or what Gilles Deleuze has termed the process of 'becoming' (Deleuze 1995) (see also Emil Nasritdinov in Chapter Ten). Thus places are constructed through their entanglements with other places, and these interrelations are created by human interactions, processes of exchange, and mobility (Massey 2004). This understanding of places as 'nodes in networks' or as 'meeting places' implies a certain degree of unevenness and inequality, or what Massey has called 'power geometries'. Scalar thinking in the social sciences often results in the suggestion that 'local inequalities are *caused* by global interlinkages' (Castree 2008:165–66), thus assuming a nested hierarchy. However, the negotiation of socio-spatial relations between and within places is, to a considerable degree, subject to the agency of actors and their strategic choices and practices. Individual relationships are always situated in time and space and are, therefore, highly contextual.

Recently, the concept of translocality has gained considerable prominence in socio-spatial theory,[11] both as an object of enquiry and as a research perspective. Freitag and von Oppen define translocality in a descriptive sense as 'the sum of phenomena which result from a multitude of circulations and transfers. It designates the outcome of concrete movements of people, goods, ideas and symbols which span spatial distances and cross boundaries, be they geographical, cultural or political' (Freitag and von Oppen 2010:5). Similar to other theoretical contributions on translocality, Freitag and von Oppen describe and explain the multiple and heterogeneous 'interactions and connections between places, institutions and concepts' using the concept of networks (*ibid.*). They consider interactions to be the central constitutive element of connections, and interactions can be broadly summarized as intense processes of movement, communication, and exchange between particular places and/or situated actors (Alff and Benz 2014:9).

It must be noted that the movement of people, goods, and ideas from one place to another (and from one context to another), which is inherent to the process of interaction, is a central feature of translocality, further contributing to its relational character. The notion of translation, especially regarding the movement of ideas, identities, and meanings between places, implies a moment of transformation or innovation during a process of reconfiguration (De Lima Costa and Alvarez 2014:557). At the same time, paradoxically the 'trans-' in translation and translocality suggests a particularity to locality that contributes to the maintenance of distinctive dynamics or orders. Consequently, Freitag and von Oppen point out that translocality 'focuses neither exclusively on movement, broadly conceived, nor on a particular order, real or imagined. Rather, it investigates the tensions between movement and order' and thus 'attempts to cope with transgression *and* with the need for localizing some kind of order' (Freitag and von Oppen 2010:8, emphasis theirs).

---

11   For the extensive literature in the social sciences on translocality see Freitag and von Oppen (2010), Brickell and Datta (2011), Zoomers and van Westen (2011). For ethnographic accounts of translocality in China see Oakes and Schein (2006).

As an important extension to the general translocality concept, Zoomers and van Westen (2011) have suggested the notion of 'translocal development', which contributes to my analysis of the Dungan case. This concept highlights the impact that local-to-local relations and flows of capital, goods, people, and information can have on transformations that occur in interconnected places (*ibid.*:377). Conceptualizations of 'translocal development' thus seek to overcome established territorializations ('methodological nationalism, regionalism, localism'), binary spatial dichotomies (rural-urban, central-peripheral) and an analytical assessment that is restricted to the local 'boundedness' of resources and people in separate places (*ibid.*).They allow 'alternative spatialisations', which challenge the significance of topographical distance and of borders, thereby contributing to an understanding of the place- and actor-based production of space that occurs daily. Zoomers and van Westen rightly argue that globalization is 'connecting people and places that are distant in space but linked in such ways that what happens in one place has direct bearing on the other' (*ibid.*:379). This focus on translocal connections that are established through mobilities and exchanges is not intended to downplay or ignore the importance of local dynamics or place-based historical formations in processes of change. Nevertheless, 'the translocal links might generate additional perspectives for "local" development' (*ibid.*:380).

The following two sections reflect upon the ways in which interpersonal relationships across space and translocal flows of meaning between different places contribute to socio-spatial transformations in Shortobe, and how this affects the sense of belonging felt by the Dungan population.

Negotiations of socio-spatial relations and flows of people, goods, and meaning

In Kazakhstani society during the late Soviet era, Dungans were considered a distinct and tight-knit ethnic community[12] of successful

---

12   The inward-looking nature of the Dungan community, revealed in their conversations with trade entrepreneurs in Almaty, was often linked to their short-lived demands in the early post-Soviet period for political autonomy in the Korday district.

and particularly hard-working agriculturalists (Hong 2005:138). Some of the most productive irrigated vegetable farms in the south of the Kazakh Soviet Socialist Republic (SSR) were the collective farms located in predominantly Dungan-populated rural settlements such as Dunganovka (on the outskirts of the city of Taraz) and the cluster of villages around Shortobe (in the Korday District of Zhambyl *oblast*). They acquired in-depth knowledge of, and access to, distribution networks by providing agricultural produce to formal state organizations, and they supplied the surplus goods to informal farmers' markets in large cities in Soviet Central Asia and Siberia. These relationships were key to their status as one of the central groups in the private trade sector after the dissolution of the Soviet Union. At the beginning of the 1990s, state-controlled provision schemes were replaced by private wholesale and retail bazaars, such as the *Dordoi* bazaar in Bishkek and the *Barakholka* agglomeration in Almaty. Dungan entrepreneurs from rural places, led by Husey Daurov, actively facilitated this process by strategically extending and rebuilding business relations with China.

Fig. 5.2 Dungan vegetable farming in Shortobe.
Photo © Henryk Alff (2014), CC BY 4.0

The Dungans of Shortobe consider themselves ancestors of a group of refugees that left the Qing Empire in 1877. While some households still retain pieces of cloth, jewelry, and even walking sticks[13] from their ancestors' flight, passing them down from generation to generation, ancestral links to China have gradually deteriorated over the past 140 years. Rimsky-Korsakoff Dyer (1978:356) notes that during the Soviet period there was almost no contact between Dungan groups in Soviet Central Asia and Huizu groups in the People's Republic, a fact she does not connect to the conflict between the leaders of the Soviet Union and the PRC during that time, but rather to almost a century of separation between Dungans and their kin in China. With the Sino-Soviet rapprochement in the late 1980s, communication with and travel to China became less restricted. Husey Daurov, a former history teacher in Shortobe's secondary school and then the secretary of Shortobe's collective farm 'Kommunisticheskiy' was the first to build up new ties with Huizu and Han political and economic circles, first in Xi'an, the capital of Shaanxi province, and later in other places across China. Daurov thereby became a pioneer and retains great influence over the extensive social networks that currently link Shortobe with China, as one of my interlocutors in Shortobe stated:

> 'Husey Shimarovich [Daurov] has done a lot for the Dungans, in particular for those here in Shortobe. In fact, all of the people running business with Chinese partners have received contacts and built their business through him. He is the moral authority of our people' (2014, Shortobe).

A sense of cross-border solidarity and loyalty, based on ethnic and linguistic affiliation, exists between Dungans and their Han Chinese business partners, which has contributed to the establishment of enduring, trusting, and often exclusive commercial and political alliances. These were stronger than the ties between their Kazakh, Kyrgyz, and Uyghur competitors and the evolving Chinese business sector (Laruelle and Peyrouse 2012:123). Dungan groups in Kazakhstan are being appropriated by the Chinese state as an 'overseas Chinese ethnic minority' (*shao shu min zu hua qiao hua ren* in Chinese), which gives them particularly favorable access to social benefits offered by the Chinese authorities, e.g., to cultural and educational exchange programmes and university grants (Jiménez Tovar 2013, 2016).

---

13   Interview with Husey Daurov, 12 May 2014, Almaty.

Fig. 5.3 Translocal connections between Central Asia and China forged
by Shortobe's Dungans. Map © Henryk Alff (2015), CC BY 4.0

The export of scrap metal and Soviet-era industrial installations to China in the 1900s was the first economic activity that arose from these connections between Dungan and Han entrepreneurs. The outflow of labourers from Shortobe and the neighboring villages to Bishkek and Almaty was facilitated by the organization of transport schemes between coastal China, Kyrgyzstan, Kazakhstan, and Russia and by the highly profitable wholesale import of Chinese-made consumer goods such as textiles, shoes, and household items to Kazakhstan, which flourished in the second half of the decade. Today, in up to eighty percent of Shortobe's households, one or more members are reported to be self-employed in the urban trade sector,[14] especially in wholesale and larger retail trade based at Almaty's *Barakholka* bazaar agglomeration, complementing the agricultural economic orientation of the village. Those people running

---

14   Fieldnotes based on a conversation with a local Dungan businessman, 18 May 2014, Shortobe.

the trade business travel to China for supplies — either to Urumqi or directly to the manufacturing centres on China's eastern seaboard — on a regular basis. Yet, many of them return to Shortobe during the weekly day off at Almaty's *Barakholka*, from Sunday evening to Tuesday morning. During a taxi ride with Dungan retail traders from Shortobe to Almaty's *Baisat* bazaar in October 2012, one of them explained the evolution of his business:

> 'I moved from Shortobe to help out my elder brother with his business back in 2002. Bazaar trade became a highly profitable way of making a living, as Kazakhstan recovered from the 1998 financial crisis. I soon could buy a sales container on my own and started to travel to Urumqi almost every two months for supplies of household appliances using the contacts my brother had established. Sales went well, nowadays they have slowed, but still I was able to buy a new house in Shortobe a year ago, although retail prices in Shortobe have reached the level of Almaty.'[15]

The connections to China fostered the increasing mobility of Dungan trade entrepreneurs and the circulation of goods and capital, but also the exchange of innovative ideas that often accompanies these translocal flows. In the mid-1990s Husey Daurov, then the head of the privatised farm 'Shaanxi' in Shortobe, imported agricultural innovations from Xi'an, such as basic greenhouse and mushroom-growing technology, to generate income for the village in the late autumn and early spring months. These technologies later spread to other parts of southern Kazakhstan. Rapid housing construction triggered the constant expansion of Shortobe[16] and its neighboring villages, and small-scale brick and paint production facilities were built in the neighboring villages of Bular Batyr and Aukhatty using Chinese technology and expertise[17] to satisfy local demand. During a visit to the paint factory in May 2014, a Dungan foreman emphasized that the half-mechanized production is the only industrial facility in the Korday district. The

---

15   Fieldnotes, 8 October 2012.
16   One of my interlocutors in Shortobe named these extensive new quarters on the fringes of Shortobe 'micro-districts' (*microrayon* in Russian), pointing to their increasingly urbanized character.
17   The small-scale paint factory in Aukhatty is currently run by a Han Chinese manager from Fujian province, employing around thirty workers from surrounding villages.

products are currently sold across Kazakhstan and are always in high demand due to the lack of serious domestic competition.[18]

Fig. 5.4 Paint production facility in Aukhatty.
Photo © Henryk Alff (2014), CC BY 4.0

As a way to 'develop' Shortobe, Daurov proposed a project of 'community-based tourism as seen in many parts of China nowadays' to attract larger numbers of Chinese visitors, who seek to experience a highly folklorized version of 'traditional Hui culture' that has vanished in China after the Cultural Revolution.[19] According to Daurov's vision, inviting Chinese people to stay in Dungan homes and participate in 'traditional Dungan wedding ceremonies', as well as constructing an ethnographic village with 'ancient Dungan-style houses and Kazakh yurts', promote Chinese-Dungan dialogue and interaction and provide new modes of income (*ibid.*, see also Laruelle and Peyrouse 2012:121–23).

---

18   Fieldnotes, 19 May 2014.
19   Interview, 9 October 2012, Almaty.

A Dungan tendency towards history-making and self-mythologization is evident in such ethno-tourism, as they explain their contemporary existence as a Chinese-speaking group in Kazakhstan with reference to a reimagined (folklorized) past (see also Svetlana Jacquesson in Chapter Six). Several of my interlocutors in Shortobe outlined that not only have Chinese tourists arrived in increasing numbers in search of what they imagine as their lost selves, but journalists, film crews, and social anthropologists from mainland China have also visited Shortobe for investigation or field research. This strategy of historicizing present, everyday reality in Dungan settlements apparently serves to attract attention from China and tap new sources of income for the rural Dungan population. It is part of a project that exploits (and appropriates) images from the past to build a prosperous future.

Social change in Shortobe and other Dungan settlements during the past two decades was entangled with state-led modernisation across China. This is particularly true with respect to agricultural innovation in Shortobe and the simultaneous increase in more urbanized economic activities such as international trade, tourism, and manufacturing, which all contribute to what is perceived as modern society. The influx of ideas for development together with these new entrepreneurial activities is vividly expressed by my Dungan interlocutors' descriptions of particular elements of China's modernisation ideology. A member of Shortobe's local branch of Kazakhstan's Association of Dungans on one occasion said:

> 'In China, the advancement of people and society is given highest priority. The Chinese government supports unity, equity, and dialogue in society though various measures, because this comes as a pledge for societal improvement and wellbeing. As Dungans in Kazakhstan's society, we also retain a high degree of respect for our compatriots' (2011, Shortobe).

The importance of dialogue, harmony, and equity in society as a precondition for positive change and, at the same time, a major goal thereof, seems to be influenced by the notion of 'social harmony' (*hexie shehui* in Chinese), which is prominent in the Chinese modernisation discourse (Brox and Bellér-Hann 2014). However, the reference to 'social harmony' is not the only aspect of 'Chinese modernity' brought up during conversation by Dungans in Shortobe. The ability to flexibly and pragmatically react to changing socio-economic conditions, e.g., to adapt their supplies to the demand for products or services, or to adjust cross-border trade and transport networks to navigate changing modes of regulation and to trade effectively, are considered quintessential entrepreneurial qualities.

Thus, among my Dungan interlocutors there is a positive sense of symbolic connectedness to the flow of ideas and forces of development in China, on the one hand, and their impact on modernisation in Shortobe, on the other. In fact, Shortobe's Dungan population has a certain fascination with development in China. As I have stated elsewhere in more detail, it appears that by promoting particular ideas about development across borders, Chinese state elites will eventually be able to use the Dungan population for their own purposes by inspiring translocal developments that are favourable to China and are forged by key actors and communities within the Dungan population (Alff 2014, Jiménez Tovar 2016).

Fig. 5.5 Miniature version of Astana's Baiterek Tower in a Dungan village. Photo © Henryk Alff (2014), CC BY 4.0

While this policy has elicited predominantly positive feedback among my interlocutors, who often agree with Chinese ideas about modernity, they have also tended to assert their 'Kazakhstaniness' and therefore their position in the post-Soviet societal order. Many of my respondents explicitly emphasized that Dungans belong to Kazakhstan's multi-ethnic population, a claim that is reinforced by the extensive use, even by Central Asian standards, of Kazakhstani state symbols in Shortobe's public spaces, for example the erection of miniature versions of Astana's Baiterek Tower in schoolyards and central junctions of Dungan-populated villages (see fig. 5.5 and also Koch 2010).[20] Dungan elites, at the same time, have offered themselves as go-betweens to the Kazakhstani government, which has allowed them to rebut the impression that they have been co-opted by China and to enhance their own influence in commercial exchanges. Thus, Dungan business people often quite literally act as translators for government delegations to China, while gaining from lucrative business deals. In the following section I shall examine how these interconnections between China and Kazakhstan foster translocal development and a sense of multiple belongings.

Translocal development and multiple belongings

As has been outlined above, the dynamic transformation of place occurs in human interactions that shape and are shaped by socio-spatial relations as well as flows of people, goods, and ideas. Such exchanges position the village of Shortobe as a 'node in networks' rather than a strictly-bounded entity in space. In the Dungan case, this is nowhere more apparent than in the socio-spatial effects of educational migration.

Over the past couple of years, several hundred Dungan students[21] in Kazakhstan, predominantly from Shortobe and the surrounding villages, have left to attend long-term Chinese language courses or to gain higher education in universities across China. These universities

---

20   Another example is the Dungan gold medal winners at the London 2012 Olympic Games, Zulfiya Chinshanlo and Maya Maneza (recently deprived of their medals due to alleged use of doping) who were widely praised in Shortobe as Kazakhstani idols, despite having been trained in China. See also Jiménez Tovar (2013:1).

21   According to a local member of the Association of Dungans, 200 students were sent in 2013 alone for one-year language courses and undergraduate studies (my fieldnotes, 18 May 2014, Shortobe).

provide stipends[22] to Dungans who are officially deemed 'Overseas Chinese ethnic minorities'; thus higher education in Xi'an, Lanzhou, Beijing, Shanghai, and Guangzhou, has become accessible to the rural Dungan population. This spatial mobility for educational purposes fosters a certain degree of social mobility, but in a selective way. The prospect of a career in business thanks to the relationship between Kazakhstan and China, and in particular thanks to the investment of Chinese state corporations in Kazakhstan's economy, has increased the popular demand for these scholarships among the Dungan population.[23] It has also driven initiatives that provide *Putonghua*, or Chinese-standard language training, in Shortobe and neighboring villages at the secondary school level. A major outcome of improved Chinese language training in, and increasing educational migration from, Shortobe is a stronger awareness of the potential of the Dungans' cultural-historical and socio-economic links to China, particularly among the younger generation (Allés 2005).

During a research stay in the thriving southern Chinese metropolis of Guangzhou in December 2014, I met two Dungan undergraduate students from Shortobe who, having transferred from Shaanxi Normal University to the prestigious Sun Yatsen University in Guangzhou, praised the socio-economic opportunities that China's major commercial centre has to offer. During a dinner in one of Guangzhou's numerous Huizu-owned restaurants one of them said:

> 'I first studied in Xi'an. I then came to Guangzhou to continue my studies about a year ago. As Guangzhou is continuously expanding and booming, naturally there are many more opportunities here than in Shortobe or even in Xi'an for earning extra income. There was not much to do [in Xi'an]; when we came home from school, we went to have a nap. Here, when a trade fair is coming up or a business delegation from Kazakhstan is due to arrive, we get a call from Husey Shimarovich [Daurov] and are hired as interpreters' (2014, Guangzhou).

The two students outlined the seemingly endless possibilities that China's rapid development offered to them as Dungans, especially in places like Guangzhou. They pointed out that their origins in a Dungan village

---

22 These stipends are allocated by Kazakhstan's Association of Dungans.
23 The allocation of grants is allegedly not always carried out in an entirely transparent way, leading to complaints by some applicants, which I once witnessed.

in Kazakhstan and their lengthy stays in Xi'an and Guangzhou were particularly beneficial in allowing them to make use of the opportunities offered by China's rapid development. In common with several of those returning from China, whom I interviewed in Shortobe and Almaty, they emphasized their Dungan, Russian, Kazakh, and Chinese language skills and their in-depth knowledge of local conditions in both places as crucial for their daily life as well as for future plans.[24] They highlighted their desire to contribute to the prosperity of their families back home in Shortobe, as they expected to become employed in well-paid positions in branches of Chinese corporations in Kazakhstan upon their return.

The interviews in Guangzhou revealed, moreover, that it is not only Dungan students' knowledge of several languages, local customs, and business culture that has contributed to their favorable position as intermediaries, but also their embeddedness in Kazakhstani Dungan-Chinese political networks. The students had direct connections to the leaders of the Association of Dungans and its regional offices in China. This resulted in relatively tight social control from above regarding their academic achievements and their housing, but it also provided direct access to influential business circles and even to official government delegations for 'our Dungan students', as Husey Daurov called them.

What becomes clear from the students' case, first and foremost, is the impact of cross-border (educational) mobility and local-to-local relations between geographically distant, yet socio-spatially interconnected places. The changes occurring in one place are therefore understood to a considerable degree through translocal human interaction, as in the case of Dungan educational migration between Shortobe and Chinese university cities. Through the allocation of Chinese-funded stipends to Dungan students in villages in Kazakhstan and the continued interest of Kazakhstani business circles in benefitting from the know-how and embeddedness of Dungans in Guangzhou or other manufacturing centres, these local-to-local connections become visible and relevant for analysis. Secondly, the intermediary socio-spatial or brokering position of the Dungans between China and Central Asia has become evident. As Husey Daurov, during one of our meetings, emphasized:

---

24 For another example of the valorization of the use of language as cultural capital see Abdullah Mirzoev and Manja Stephan-Emmrich's contribution on the socio-economic strategies of Tajik migrants in Dubai in Chapter Three.

'China with accelerated velocity draws closer to the US [...]. Dungans, who know the local mentality and realities, speak both Russian and Kazakh, share commonalities in culture and language with the Chinese, should use the historical chances China's rapid development has to offer in any way they can' (2012, Shortobe).

According Daurov, Dungans are expected to occupy an intermediate position in what he calls China's path towards development and global leadership (see also Gladney 1996:454–58). Described as 'relational alterity' by Gladney (1996:454), the Dungans' strategic practice of positioning themselves as intermediaries between China and Kazakhstan highlights the way in which they make sense of their group's existence. The pronounced socio-spatial situatedness of Dungans as middlemen entails the translation of knowledge, skills, and particular ideas of social change, as has been outlined above, and as has also been referred to by Philipp Schröder in his study of Kyrgyz traders and by Abdullah Mirzoev and Manja Stephan-Emmrich in their chapter on Tajik migrants in Dubai (Chapters Eight and Three, respectively). Their role as brokers, moreover, both informs and is produced by what could be called a Dungan sense of multiple (translocal) belongings and embeddedness within the different socio-spatial contexts of China and post-Soviet Kazakhstan. Interestingly, Dungans of different social backgrounds have pointed this out during my interviews and conversations.

In fact, numerous conversations with interlocutors in Shortobe revealed that the city of Xi'an in Shaanxi province was commonly referred to as the historical homeland (*istoricheskaya rodina* in Russian) of the Dungans. This calls to mind the concept of 'native place' (*guxiang* in Chinese), which derives its significance not from its 'localization', but rather from historic and ongoing processes of identification (Oakes and Schein 2006:19). The crucial symbolic position of Xi'an in Dungan discourses of belonging has been strengthened over the last few years by the multi-purpose links forged with this city through cross-border cultural and educational exchanges as well as the circulation of innovative ideas. These links were institutionalized by the establishment of an official partnership between Zhambyl *oblast* and Shaanxi province, which was initiated by Husey Daurov using his connections to both the Kazakhstani state elite and to regional authorities in Xi'an.

The cluster of villages around Shortobe, on the other hand, was often posited as the nucleus of the Dungan population in Kazakhstan. The unique nature of this cluster, which is rapidly developing and much more prosperous than surrounding Kazakh-inhabited settlements, was often proudly highlighted. Furthermore, several interlocutors emphasized Dungans' strong social attachment to the places where they settle. While the demand for building plots remains high, with real estate prices in Shortobe approaching those in Kazakhstan's largest cities, much private investment is dedicated to the maintenance and improvement of local infrastructure.

Along with these claims of multiple belongings (see also Jiménez Tovar 2016) the emphasis on the Dungans' role as brokers has been expressed by widespread self-representations of their existence as a product of exchanges (both of people and religious values) along the historic 'Silk Road'.[25] This claim finds its contemporary extension in the position of Dungan entrepreneurs within the state-led political discourse in China and Kazakhstan, as they discuss the creation of a modern 'Silk Road' or 'Eurasian land bridge'. Several of my interlocutors in Shortobe as Chinese Muslims traced their ancestry to the century-long flows of people and values along the 'Silk Road', thereby connecting their past ideas with their visions of ongoing social change. Husey Daurov explicitly references the powerful political ambition to rebuild a modern 'Silk Road' when he praises the contemporary and future opportunities that Dungans should grasp to promote their community's socio-economic advancement (Alff 2014).

Conclusion

This chapter has drawn attention to the particularities of the constitution of place(s) through the lens of socio-spatial connections rather than through the 'territorial trap' (Agnew 2008) in the case of the Dungan village of Shortobe in southeastern Kazakhstan. Dungans, previously exclusively regarded as a close-knit group of farmers in Soviet-era public discourse in Kazakhstan, have strategically expanded their connections to Hui and Han Chinese groups across China in the last two decades. By so doing, they have positioned themselves favorably as mediators in the trade between China and Kazakhstan, as well as in the processes of exchange along what is often conceived from a

---

25   Svetlana Jacquesson's study of popular historiographies in Kyrgyzstan in Chapter Six may be another good case in point for this process of the 'invention of history'.

state perspective as a newly emerging 'Silk Road'. At the same time, Shortobe's Dungan population has experienced a sense of multiple belongings thanks to the increasing level of translocal interaction for educational and business purposes between Shortobe, Almaty, and the booming cities of the Chinese seaboard. The Dungans' multiple belonging evolves from both top-down (appropriation) and bottom-up (self-definition) processes.

Analysis of the Dungan case reveals that it is largely through the mobility of people and the dynamically changing flows of goods, ideas, and meaning that Shortobe's transformation over the last two decades literally 'takes place'. Thus, it is not (or at least not alone) the rootedness or boundedness of distinct meaning in place, as Doreen Massey has rightly argued, but the intersecting flows of meaning through human interaction and exchanges between places that forge a particular 'sense of place' among actors. The construction of a 'sense of place' can be seen in the modernisation rhetoric that has followed the introduction of agricultural innovations in Shortobe and the promotion among its population of 'more modern' means of making a living. Thus I have argued, following Massey's concept of place as a 'node in networks', that the constitution of place needs to be explored relationally, rather than thinking of it as a bounded entity in space.

This approach to thinking about place through its connections may be further enriched by the concept of translocality, and more specifically with Zoomers and van Westen's (2011) notion of 'translocal development'. The central idea behind 'translocal development' is to scrutinize transformations in one place through its local-to-local relations with interconnected places, implying that changes in one place have a direct impact on the other. The case of Shortobe suggests that the relationships between interconnected places are far from even or balanced. The outcome of translocal development has been exemplified by the educational migration of Dungan students between Shortobe and university cities in eastern China. The increased yet still selective access to higher education abroad has increased the appreciation of the value of closer cultural-historical and socio-economic links to China, especially among the younger generation of Shortobe's Dungans. The experience of a rapidly developing China has fostered hopes among Dungan students that they might personally benefit from these changes and at the same time contribute to ongoing development in Shortobe.

References

Agenstvo po statistike. *Chislennost' naseleniya Respubliki Kazakhstan po otdel'nym etnosam na nachalo 2012 goda*. Astana: Agenstvo Respubliki Kazakhstan po statistike, 2012.

Agnew, John. *Place and Politics*. Boston: Allen & Unwin, 1987.

Agnew, John. 'Borders on the Mind: Re-Framing Border Thinking'. *Ethics & Global Politics* 1.4 (2008): 175–91, https://doi.org/10.3402/egp.v1i4.1892

Allés, Elisabeth. 'The Chinese-Speaking Muslims (Dungans) of Central Asia: A Case of Multiple Identities in a Changing Context'. *Asian Ethnicity* 6.2 (2005): 121–34, https://doi.org/10.1080/14631360500135716

Alff, Henryk. 'Embracing Chinese Modernity? Articulation and Positioning in China-Kazakhstan Trade and Exchange Processes'. *Crossroads Asia Working Paper Series* 21 (2014): 23, http://hdl.handle.net/20.500.11811/154

Alff, Henryk, and Andreas Benz, eds. *Tracing Connections: Explorations of Spaces and Places in Asian Contexts*. Berlin: Wissenschaftlicher Verlag Berlin, 2014.

Brickell, Katherine, and Ayona Datta, eds. *Translocal Geographies: Spaces, Places, Connections*. Farnham: Ashgate, 2011, https://doi.org/10.4324/9781315549910

Brox, Trine, and Ildikó Bellér-Hann, eds. *On the Fringes of the Harmonious Society: Tibetans and Uyghurs in Socialist China*. Copenhagen: NIAS Press, 2014.

Castree, Noel. 'Place: Connections and Boundaries in an Interdependent World'. In Nicholas Clifford, Sarah L. Holloway, Stephen P. Rice, and Gill Valentine, eds. *Key Concepts in Geography*. London: Sage, 2008, pp. 154–72.

Deleuze, Gilles. *Negotiations, 1972–1990*. New York: Columbia University Press, 1995.

De Lima Costa, Claudia, and Sonia A. Alvarez. 'Dislocating the Sign: Towards a Translocal Feminist Politics of Translation'. *Signs: Journal of Women in Culture and Society* 39.3 (2014): 557–63, https://doi.org/10.1086/674381

Freitag, Ulrike, and Achim von Oppen, eds. *Translocality. The Study of Globalising Processes from a Southern Perspective*. Leiden: Brill, 2011, https://doi.org/10.1163/ej.9789004181168.i-452

Freitag, Ulrike, and Achim von Oppen. 'Introduction. Translocality: An Approach to Connection and Transfer in Area Studies'. In Ulrike Freitag and Achim von Oppen, eds. *Translocality. The Study of Globalising Processes from a Southern Perspective*. Leiden: Brill, 2011, pp. 1–21, https://doi.org/10.1163/ej.9789004181168.i-452.8

Gladney, Dru. *Muslim Chinese: Ethnic Nationalism in the People's Republic*. Cambridge: Harvard University Press, 1991.

Gladney, Dru. 'Relational Alterity: Constructing Dungan (Hui), Uygur, and Kazakh Identities Across China, Central Asia, and Turkey'. *History and Anthropology* 9.4 (1996): 445–77, https://doi.org/10.1080/02757206.1996.9960 889

Gladney, Dru. *Dislocating China: Muslims, Minorities, and Other Subaltern Subjects.* Chicago: University of Chicago Press, 2004.

Hong, Ding. 'A Comparative Study on the Cultures of the Dungan and the Hui Peoples'. *Asian Ethnicity* 6.2 (2005): 135–40, https://doi. org/10.1080/14631360500135765

Jiménez Tovar, Soledad. 'Coming Back (to Which) Home? Kazakhstan Dungans' Migration to China'. Working paper, *Relocating Borders 13*. Berlin: EastBordNet, 2013.

Jiménez Tovar, Soledad. 'Limits of Diaspority in Central Asia: Contextualizing Dungan's Multiple Belongings'. *Central Asian Survey* 35.3 (2016): 387–404, https://doi.org/10.1080/02634937.2016.1151626

Koch, Natalie. 'The Monumental and the Miniature: Imagining "Modernity" in Astana'. *Social and Cultural Geography* 11.8 (2010): 769–87, https://doi.org/10. 1080/14649365.2010.521854

Laruelle, Marlène, and Sébastian Peyrouse. *The Chinese Question in Central Asia: Domestic Order, Social Change, and the Chinese Factor.* New York: Columbia University Press, 2012.

Massey, Doreen. 'A Global Sense of Place'. *Marxism Today* 38 (1991): 24–29.

Massey, Doreen. 'The Spatial Construction of Youth Cultures'. In Tracey Skelton, and Gill Valentine, eds. *Cool Places: Geographies of Youth Cultures.* London: Routledge, 1998, pp. 121–29.

Massey, Doreen. 'Geographies of Responsibility'. *Geografiska Annaler B* 86.1 (2004): 5–18, https://doi.org/10.1111/j.0435-3684.2004.00150.x

Oakes, Tim, and Louisa Schein. 'Translocal China: An Introduction'. In Tim Oakes and Louisa Schein, eds. *Translocal China: Linkages, Identities and the Reimagining of Space.* London: Routledge, 2006, pp. 1–35.

Rimsky-Korsakoff Dyer, Svetlana. 'Soviet Dungan Nationalism: A Few Comments on Their Origin and Language'. *Monumenta Serica* 33 (1978): 349–62.

Sushanlo, Muhamed. *Ocherki istorii sovetskikh dungan.* Frunze: Ilim, 1967.

Vansvanova, Mariya. *Dungane: Lyudi sud'by.* Almaty: Sözdik-Slovar, 2000.

Zoomers, Annelies, and Guus van Westen. 'Introduction: Translocal Development, Development Corridors and Development Chains'. *International Development Planning Review* 33.4 (2011): 377–88, https://doi.org/10.3828/idpr.2011.19

PART 3

MOVEMENTS FROM BELOW:
ECONOMIC AND SOCIAL

6. 'New History' as a Translocal Field

Svetlana Jacquesson

Introduction

My first field trips to Kyrgyzstan date back to the late 1990s. Much of the fieldwork I carried out at first followed well-established anthropological methods: participant observation, discussions, eavesdropping, interviews. Though I could interact quite freely with my interlocutors in the field, since I had clumsy but efficient Kyrgyz language skills and nearly fluent Russian, I was never fully satisfied with my field data alone. I was curious about what Kyrgyz people wrote, read, or discussed when they were not interacting with an outsider. I believed that publications in Kyrgyz could allow me at least a partial access to a 'cultural intimacy'[1] I could never attain otherwise, no matter how much time I spent in the field. I remember visiting every single bookshop and avidly buying any publication in Kyrgyz available at the time. In the late 1990s this was still possible: publications

---

1   By using 'cultural intimacy' here, I stretch the concept as it was coined by Michael Herzfeld (1997). Herzfeld conceptualizes 'cultural intimacy' as insiders' recognition of aspects of cultural identity that are both a source of embarrassment and of common sociality (Herzfeld 1997:3). I also use 'cultural intimacy' to refer to aspects of cultural identity, in my case, insiders' discussions, ideas, imaginations, and stories about their past. These aspects of cultural identity, however, could be a source of embarrassment for both insiders and outsiders, to the extent that outsiders might reject them outright, or contest them. As will become clear below, most of the claims of 'new history' may seem paradoxical to outsiders; for insiders, though, they constitute an additional source of pride, and they nourish their nationalist sentiments.

     https://doi.org/10.11647/OBP.0114.06

in Kyrgyz — booklets or treatises on animal diseases included — were not that numerous. The situation, however, evolved quickly: some fifteen years later, it is no longer possible to buy 'all' that is published in Kyrgyz, for the very simple reason that such publications abound.

In some ways, the growth of publishing in Kyrgyz satisfied my desire to access this 'cultural intimacy': I have discussed elsewhere (Jacquesson 2010) the proliferation of local genealogies and local histories and, though most of the people and places discussed in these publications were completely unknown to me, I still leaf through the books and enjoy a story here and there or learn something new about the country and its people. However, a substantial portion of the local writings on history engaged in intricate reconstructions of a deeper past. These reconstructions were about places and peoples I knew, but these places and peoples were connected to the Kyrgyz and their past in ways quite unfamiliar to me. To give but a taste of such unexpected connections, whereas I had an idea of 'who' Aryans or Indo-Europeans were, I had never heard or thought of the Kyrgyz as Aryans; neither had I read about Atilla or Genghis Khan being Kyrgyz. While I was vaguely aware that, in the very distant past, humans must have crossed the Bering Strait and settled in North America, I had never thought of these humans as being closely related to the Kyrgyz, and as for Germans and Kyrgyz sharing common ancestors, this was a stretch too far for me. Though it is difficult to evaluate the exact volume of such historical writings, they appear frequently in the pages of various news media outlets or on social media forums.

This brand of history — which I will refer to as 'new history'[2] — is produced not only in Kyrgyzstan, but also in Russia and in the other

---

2   Laruelle (2012a) examines similar trends in history making in Russia under the category 'alternate history'. However, alternate history is not only a very dynamic and defined field but also one in which science-fiction tropes (time travel, time splitting, crossing time) predominate. In this regard, the kinds of history making I examine in this chapter differ significantly from alternate history. 'Alternative history' might have been a better denomination for the kind of intellectual endeavour I try to analyze, especially in the way it is conceptualized by Pels (1997:168), i.e., as histories 'that challenge historiographical "hierarchies of credibility" because they derive from street art, spirit possession, oral tradition, rumor, gossip, and other popular or subaltern forms of knowledge production'. But since 'alternate' and 'alternative' history tend to be used interchangeably, I prefer 'new history' as a more neutral denomination.

post-Soviet Central Asian countries. Local academic circles — or at least some of them — refer to it as the 'mythologization of history' and reject it outright (Masanov *et al.* 2007, Galiev 2010, Grozin 2010, Omurbekov 2012.) As an anthropologist I am less inclined to do so, though I do not espouse the claims of new history. In this chapter I experiment with translocality in an attempt to suggest an analytical approach to 'new history' — or at least part of it — that is not limited to its outright rejection.[3] I investigate what new history is about, who its producers are, and how they work. I use 'investigate' on purpose because I do not have any relationships with the authors of new history, and I have not received any revelations from them. Instead, I have been working with the 'evidence' they leave, i.e., their texts, and I reconstruct their 'crimes' based on their methods and claims. I argue that this peculiar brand of history is the outcome of knowledge transfers and interactions that transgress a variety of borders — social, professional, national, and geopolitical — and that its claims as well as its social and political significance can be made analytically meaningful by adopting a translocal research perspective (Freitag and von Oppen 2010). When approached as a 'translocal field', new history provides a telling example of the ways in which new connections between histories, concepts, and actors that were formerly separated in time and space may yield unexpected and controversial results that go against widely assumed ideas about globalization and its effects. As such, new history is an alternative to mainstream global or world history, and demonstrates that the activity at the 'periphery' of globalization may bring about novel agencies and outcomes.

I will start by providing some samples of new history from Kyrgyzstan. I will then analyze its methods, content, and claims, as well as the social background of its authors. In each of the analytical sections I will foreground those aspects of new history that are best captured by adopting a translocal perspective, or the translocal processes and practices that are at the core of new history. In conclusion I will advance some ideas on the epistemological value of new history, and on the insights it provides for a fuller and deeper understanding of globalization and its variations.

---

3   I disagree here with the late Nurbulat Masanov, who maintained that a serious discussion of this kind of history is impossible (2007).

Cases

In an otherwise outrageously critical interview from 2013, Anuar Galiev — a senior researcher at the Kazakh State University of Law, whose Ph.D. explores the mythologization of history in Central Asia — acknowledges that new history owes its success to the writing skills of its authors and that new history is much more enjoyable to read than most of the existing history schoolbooks. I am a little bit more sceptical about the literary qualities of the Kyrgyz new history I have explored: some of the pieces are well-written and read smoothly; others are excessively wordy and convoluted, larded with manifestations of erudition, and so overtly rhetorical that the stories they try to convey are difficult to follow, and even to understand. What I provide here are snapshots that explore some of the claims of new history and how these claims are substantiated.

In 2010, Anarbek Usupbaev — former head of Kyrgyzstan's communist party and current leader of the country's Tengrist movement[4] — published the history of his own clan under the title *The True History of the Kytai Clan from the Left Wing of the Kyrgyz, or the Backbone of Their Genealogy.*[5] This 'backbone', which supports all of Usupbaev's claims, is a statement by a renowned local biologist[6] according to whom the high frequency of two haplotypes among Kyrgyz — called 'Paleo-European' (R1a1) and 'East-Asian' (C3) respectively — can be explained by the fact that the ancient Europoid populations of the Sayan-Altay region, the Dinlin, are among the ancestors of the Kyrgyz of the Left Wing, while the Kyrgyz of the Right Wing have as their ancestors populations of East-Asian origin. In his *True History*, Usupbaev relates this genetic data to local genealogical narratives (*sanjyra*) and concludes that the descendants of the Dinlin are referred to as *Ak uul* or Left Wing

---

4   The Tengrist movement is a pan-Central-Asian religious and political movement promoting an allegedly native religious system — Tengrism. Based on the harmonious co-existence of mankind and nature, these religious beliefs often conflict with the teachings of Islam. Tengrism took shape after the fall of the Soviet Union and is an example of the various identity-building movements that characterise Central Asia in the post-Soviet period.

5   The *True History* was first published as a self-published book (*samizdat*) initially printed in 100 copies. It was then serialized in the pages of *Fabula*, one of the most popular newspapers in Kyrgyzstan.

6   See Aldashev (2009).

by Kyrgyz genealogies while the descendants of the Huns are called *Kuu uul* or Right Wing.[7] In making this argument, he substitutes the well-known Huns for the unnamed East-Asian populations and defends this substitution by claiming that *Hun* is the same as *Kün*, 'East, Orient' in Kyrgyz. As for the backbone of the genealogy of the Kytai clan, it takes the following shape:

> Now, let me provide some more information from historical sources. In his book *Kyzyl Kyrgyz Tarihi* (*The Red History of the Kyrgyz*), volume 1, page 23, the renowned Kyrgyz historian and writer Belek Soltonoev[8] mentions that the Kyrgyz descend from forty women. He refers on this occasion to the works of Radlov[9] and to the annals of the Yuan clan [sic] of the Moghuls [sic]. These annals mention the Kyrgyz, i.e., the *Kyrk Usun*. The Usun are the same as the Kyrgyz Saruu clan, they descend from the Dinlin. Kyrk Usun married forty girls from the Kytai. Here Kytai does not stand for Chinese, but for the Kyrgyz Kytai clan which is the same as the Huns. The union of the Kyrk Usun and the Kytai gave birth to the Kyrgyz. Kyrk Usun is the same as *kyrk ösö* and this is where the name Kyrgyz comes from. Such a conclusion was also reached by Aristov,[10] see page 45 in his work. [...] In one word, isn't it clear that the Kyrgyz have come into being through the association of the Kytai clan, which is of Hun origin, with the Saruu clan, which is of Usun-Dinlin origin, and that this has happened at least 8,000 years ago.

---

7   Left Wing (*Sol Kanat*), Right Wing (*On Kanat*) and Core (*Ichkilik*) are the major genealogical branches among the Kyrgyz, partially overlapping with the geographical and political north-south divide.

8   Soltonoev Belek Soltonkeldi uulu (1878–1938) is the author of the first 'modern' history of the Kyrgyz, called *Kyzyl Kyrgyz Tarykhy* (History of Red [i.e., Bolshevist] Kyrgyz). Soltonoev's *History* is a compilation of oral traditions, European Orientalist writings on the Kyrgyz and the author's own ethnographic notes.

9   Vasilii Radlov (1837–1918), born Friedrich Wilhelm Radloff, is celebrated in Russia and Central Asia as one of the founders of Turkic studies. He was the first to publish the runic inscriptions of Orkhon and a comparative dictionary of Turkic languages in four volumes. In Kyrgyzstan he is best known for his 1868 recording of the Manas epic.

10 Nikolai Aristov (1847–1903) was a high-level official in the Tsarist administration who dedicated much of his life to completing Carl Ritter's volume on Asia in *Comparative Geography* (1816–1832) by collecting data on the history of the western Tian Shan. Aristov was the first to suggest that the Usun are the ancestors of the Kyrgyz in an 1894 article published in *Zhivaia Starina*, the ethnographic journal of the Russian Imperial Geographical Society. Although Aristov's hypothesis on the relationship between Usun and Kyrgyz has been criticized ever since it was formulated, in 2001 his works were republished without any annotations by the Soros Foundation in Kyrgyzstan.

The Kytai then descend from the Huns. Next, Usupbaev brings in further evidence from Belek Soltonoev as well as from the Manas epic itself and claims that the epic's eponymous hero belongs to the Kytai clan.[11] The might and glory of Manas are proved by a long list of places in the world whose names, allegedly, are based on the name of Manas and, thus, demonstrate the worldwide span of Manas' as well as the Kytai clan's fame.[12] Usupbaev explains this worldwide span by arguing that all Kyrgyz clans had to struggle for their existence and that in the course of these struggles they found themselves dispersed between the four corners of the world. Thus, factions of the Kytai clan settled in Mongolia, China, Uzbekistan, Kazakhstan, Tajikistan, Moldavia, and Romania. Serbians and Macedonians, too, descend from the Kytai and, as far as the Russians are concerned, their ancestor Ilya is none other than Yelu Dashi — a Kidan or Khitan khan — and, thus, a Kytai, i.e., Kyrgyz. Usupbaev delights in mentioning that somewhere in North or South Dakota in the United States there is a place inhabited by 56,000 people who claim to be Kytai (Cathay) and not Chinese. Finally, Usupbaev turns to Tacitus. He asserts that in his *Germania* Tacitus indicates that the Germans have come from the East, that they ride horses, drink their milk as well as fermented millet, and that they worship Germanus. After explaining that Germanus is derived from Herr and Manus, and declaring that Herr Manus is a distortion of the Kyrgyz Er Manas, 'Manas the Brave', Usupbaev concludes that the Germans have also been exposed to the civilizing influence of Manas.

---

11   The evidence is encapsulated in just the following sentence: 'According to oral traditions, the ancestors of Manas had some relations with *Kytai,* and the Karakhanid' (Soltonoev 1993:II,143). It is worth emphasizing that it is not clear whether Soltonoev means China, the Chinese, the Khitan or the Kytai clan among the Kyrgyz since one Kyrgyz word — Kytai — refers to all of them. Much of Usupbaev's history is based on the assumption that Kytai stands only for the Kytai clan, and that Kytai refers to the same group as Kidan (also known as Khitan) and Karakhanid (known also as Kara Khitai), an assumption that most historians strongly disagree with.

12   This list seems to have been first drawn up by Dastan Sarygulov, the oldest active member of the Tengrist movement and a prolific history writer. Sarygulov's *Origin of the Kyrgyz* (*Kyrgyz kachan jana kaydan chykkan*) published in 2008 — containing the list of 'Manas' toponyms — was serialized by the Kyrgyz language biweekly *Alibi* and this in part explains the popularity of the list. Since some of the places included in Sarygulov's list are little known to the wider public, the list is both shortened — by the omission of these little-known places — and extended by the efforts of amateur historians who discover better and new correspondences. On amateur historians, see Light (2016).

As proof of this statement, he invites any Kyrgyz who visits Berlin to have a closer look at the quadriga adorning the Brandenburg Gate: this quadriga, Usupbaev emphasizes, is exactly the same as the carts that the ancestors of the Kyrgyz used to ride, and the woman on the quadriga holds not an iron cross but the top (*toono*) of a Kyrgyz yurt (which is also the symbol of Tengri, the master of the universe in the Tengrist tradition).

One year after Usupbaev's *True History*, Amangeldy Bekbalaev — professor of philology and dean of the Faculty of Humanities at the Kyrgyz Russian Slavic University in Bishkek[13]—claimed that the Huns were Kyrgyz as was their leader Atilla, and that Kyrgyz and Germans — or their ancestors, the Huns and the Goths — share a common linguistic and cultural heritage (Bekbalaev 2011). The disappearance of the ethnonym Kyrgyz from Eastern written sources from the 2nd to the 4th centuries BC, according to Bekbalaev, could not be explained except by the Kyrgyz — also called Hunno-Kyrgyz or proto-Kyrgyz — leaving Central Asia to rule in Europe and then, at the death of Atilla, returning to the Tian Shan, i.e., to the territory of present day Kyrgyzstan. Bebalaev's work, as published on the web portal Novaia literatura Kyrgyzstana (New Literature of Kyrgyzstan), spans more than seventy pages. His method, as he himself explains it, consists in 'bringing facts (evidence) from various sciences to support my claim'. These various sciences include history, archaeology, comparative linguistics, folklore, musicology, and genetics. Bekbalaev's work therefore abounds in references to European,[14] Russian,[15] and Kyrgyzstani scholarly works.[16] The compilation of evidence is made reader-friendly by long excerpts

---

13 According to local news media, Bekbalaev is also a member of the Russian Academy of Pedagogic and Social Sciences, a member of the New York Academy of Sciences, and honorary professor of International Relations and World Languages at Kazakhstan's University.

14 Among them: Altheim Franz and Haussig Wilhelm Hans, *Die Hunnen in Osteuropa. Ein Forschungsbericht* (1958); Wolfram Herwig, *Die Goten* (1990); Schreiber Hermann, *Die Hunnen* (1976); Bona Istvan, *Das Hunnenreich* (1991).

15 E.g. historians Vasiliy Bartol'd (1869–1930) and Aleksandr Bernshtam (1910–1956), and linguists Igor Batmanov (1906–1969), Nikolai Baskakov (1905–1955), and Edkhiam Tenishev (1921–2004). Bekbalaev is a fan of Lev Gumilyov (1912–1992) and refers repeatedly to his *Hunny* (1960) and *Geografiya etnosa v istoricheskii period* (1990). He also refers to another well-known Eurasianist, Nikolay Trubetskoy (1890–1938), author of *Nasledie Chingizkhana: vzglyad na russkuyu istoriyu ne s Zapada a s Vostoka* (1925). On Russian Eurasianism, see Laruelle 2012b.

16 Some of these works are quoted below.

from Germanic, Nordic and Kyrgyz legends about Atilla and the
Huns, long quotes from historical novels on the same topics,[17] and the
reproduction of multiple paintings reconstructing Hunnic lifestyle
and warfare as well as some photos from contemporary Kyrgyzstan
demonstrating the similarities in lifestyle between modern Kyrgyz and
ancient Huns.

A substantial portion of Bekbalaev's work is dedicated to the
description of the might and glory of the Huns. The Kyrgyz can lay
claim to this glorious past and its heritage because to this day they share
a range of linguistic and cultural features with the Germans, or with
their ancestors the Goths. By comparing the German and Kyrgyz words
for people, objects, and animals as depicted in a 1976 reconstruction of
a Hunnic camp by Hermann Schreiber, Bekbalaev claims that Germans
and Kyrgyz have the same words for 'camp' (*aul*/*ayil*), 'woman' or
'spouse' (*gattin*/*katyn*), 'father' (*atta*/*ata*), 'man' or 'warrior' (*herr*/*er*),
'camel' (*kamel*/*kaymal*), 'saddlecloth' (*schabrake*/*chüpürök*), 'cattle' (*ockse*/
ögüz), etc., and that they have inherited this shared vocabulary from
their common ancestors. He also emphasizes that beyond this common
vocabulary there exist approximately five hundred corresponding
words between Hun/Kyrgyz and Gothic/German, which can be
found in the trilogy about the Huns by Ammian von Bek.[18] In the final
section of his work, Bekbalaev shames the Kyrgyz for not being proud
of their Hun ancestors and showcases the Kazakhs who — though
incorrectly — 'tell their children wonderful stories about their ancestors
the Huns'. He finds the 'shyness' or 'irresolution' of Kyrgyzstani
historians regrettable. Germans themselves, according to Bekbalaev,
believe that the Huns are the ancestors of the Kyrgyz, as shown by a
photo from present-day Kyrgyzstan that illustrates a catalogue of an
exhibition on Attila and the Huns held in Stuttgart in 2007 and bearing
the caption: 'The nomadic lifestyle of contemporary Kyrgyz dates back
to their ancestors the Huns'.[19]

---

17   Mainly from the Russian translation of John Man's *Atilla the Hun* (2005) and from
      Ammian von Bek's trilogy *Gunny* (2009). Ammian von Bek is in fact the literary
      pseudonym of Bekbalaev himself. The trilogy he refers to is, in his own definition,
      a 'historical novel' (Bekbalaev, aka Ammian von Bek 2009).
18   On Ammian von Bek, see note above.
19   *Attila und die Hunnen: Begleitbuch zur Ausstellung* (Stuttgart, 2007). This and the
      previous two quotations are from Bekbalaev, 2011.

Zamir Osorov is a journalist who until recently was working for *MSN*, one of the most influential Russian language newspaper in Kyrgyzstan. He is also a prolific writer and a poet, and his works — mostly in Russian, with some curious pieces in 'Google-Translate English' are available online.[20] The two pieces that I will discuss here are taken from a collection of 230 works. The first, entitled *Kyrgyzy i Indeitsy* (Kyrgyz and Native Americans, 2012),[21] elaborates on the work of Frederick Louis Otto Roehrig (1819–1908), a German-born philologist fascinated by the study of North American languages. In the late nineteenth century, Roehrig foregrounded the similarities between the Dakota Indian languages and Turkish.[22] Osorov, who discovered Roehrig's work via the Tatar linguist Abrar Karimullin,[23] claims to be well acquainted with the works of several other Western scholars[24] who have engaged in the comparative study of Turkic and North American languages, as well as with all the Soviet scholarship on American Indians[25] and Thomas Maine Reid's and James Fenimore Cooper's novels. An important portion of Osorov's text is dedicated to the description of his sources

---

20　See https://www.stihi.ru/avtor/zamir1 and https://www.proza.ru/avtor/zamir1

21　See https://www.proza.ru/2012/03/28/1437

22　On Roehrig, see Barreiro 2012.

23　Abrar Karimullin (1925–2000) was a philologist and a bibliographer whose interest in Tatar history, literature, and the diaspora was not always welcome during the Soviet period. He was reprimanded for nationalism or Panturkism on several occasions, and was known to have spent five long years in disgrace before being allowed to defend his Ph.D. thesis on the history of early-twentieth-century Tatar printing in the beginning of the twentieth century. In post-Soviet Tatarstan, Karimullin is revered as the founder of Tatar studies. His essay on 'Proto-Turks and American Indians' was first published in Moscow in 1995. The essay, according to the English translation available on the web portal Turkic History (http://s155239215.onlinehome.us/turkic/67Amerind/KarimullinPrototurks1En.htm), was 'the outcome of twenty years of research'. In it, Karimullin claimed that, based on the comparative study of American Indian and Turkic languages, the American Indians and the ancient Turks have a common 'origin'. Karimullin's claim was welcome by Lev Gumilyov who, in turn, argued that the Huns and the Dakota Indians were genetically related. For more on Karimullin, see Khaliullin 2005.

24　E.g., John McIntosh, *The Origin of the North American Indians* (1843); Wikander Oscar Stig, 'Maya and Altaic: Is the Maya Group of Languages Related to the Altaic Family?', *Ethnos* 32 (1967): 141–48; *idem*, 'Maya and Altaic II', *Ethnos* 35 (1970): 80–88; *idem* 'Maya and Altaic III', *Orientalia Suecana* 21 (1972): 186–204; Osorov also refers to Georges Dumézil's articles on the relationship between Quechuan and Turkish (published between 1954 and 1957) but I was unable to identify these.

25　Yurii Knorozov, *Sistema pis'ma drevnikh Maya* (1955) and *Pis'mennost' indeitsev Maya* (1963) as well as all the ethnographic studies of Native Americans published by the (former) Institute of Ethnography at the Russian Academy of Sciences.

and the life of the Indians they refer to, with a strong emphasis on the injustices and suffering inflicted on the latter by white settlers or Spanish conquistadors, and the splendor of the Mayan, Aztec, and Incan empires. Another important portion of his text contains lists of lexical correspondences between various Native American and Turkic languages and descriptions of lexical similarities. In his conclusion, he deals with the importance of this 'genetic relationship' and why it continues to be ignored to this day.

As far as lexical correspondences are concerned, the Turkic language most often referred to is Tatar — which seems to indicate that these correspondences are mostly borrowed from the work of Karimullin — though, in his comments, Osorov repeatedly insists that the Kyrgyz words are closer to Native American than the Tatar ones, because Kyrgyz is the oldest and purest of the Turkic languages. Osorov's own contribution consists in applying Turkic etymologies to as many place names in California and Yucatan as possible as well as in emphasizing that *Ishi*[26] and *Kon-Tiki*[27] have perfect correspondences in Kyrgyz: *ishi* is phonetically and semantically the same as the Kyrgyz *kishi* 'man, person' while Kon-Tiki as 'God of Sun' corresponds to the Kyrgyz Kün-Teke where *kün* means 'sun' and *teke* 'billy-goat' but also 'leader'.

Osorov's ultimate concern is that if the unity of the Indo-European languages is uncontested (though, in his opinion, the evidence is overstretched) the unity of Native-American-Turkic languages remains unrecognized or downplayed. He asserts that the simple existence of five or six lexical correspondences between Native American and Turkic languages should have been 'a thunder from a clear sky' for Western scholars (Osorov 2012a), and slams the latter for disregarding the hundreds of lexical correspondences already established. Osorov insists that these correspondences cannot be haphazard, that they can only be explained by a 'genetic relationship' (*ibid.*) and reinforces this argument by emphasizing that Russians and Tatars have been living side by side

---

26 *Ishi* is the name of the last member of the Yahi Indians made famous by the works of Alfred Kroeber and his wife Theodora.

27 *Kon-Tiki* is the name of the Inca God of Sun, and of the 1947 expedition of Thor Heyerdahl to the Polynesian islands.

for centuries, but that there is not a single similarity between the two languages.

While in *Kyrgyz and Native Americans* Osorov remains inconclusive in his claims and goals, and even in the story he wants to tell, in his second piece entitled *Supersimetriia istiny* (The Super Symmetry of Truth) and published also in 2012, he declares that the Kyrgyz language is the equivalent of the Mandeleev periodic table, and that in the same way as the Mandeleev periodic table derives and predicts the relationships between the properties of chemical elements, the Kyrgyz language can derive and predict relationships between linguistic or cultural elements. After providing a list of the 170 'key' Kyrgyz words that 'encode the world', he offers some demonstrations by supplying Kyrgyz etymologies for Achilles (*akyl* 'mind' and *es* 'master' and thus meaning 'master of minds'), Heracles (derived from *er* 'man' and *akyl* 'mind' and meaning 'wise man') and Zeus/Atheus (the same as the Kyrgyz *atabyz* 'our father'). He also claims that the meaning of the name Jehovah as understood by Jehovah's Witnesses — 'Helping to Become' — is the same as the meaning of the name of the supreme god of the ancient Turks: Tengir, 'Great but Equal'. Osorov concludes that without the knowledge of the Kyrgyz language it is impossible to discover the meaning of human civilization's oldest words and concepts.

Analysis

Methods

Let me start with some observations on the methods of new history. In the first place, etymologization and lexical similarities or correspondences are crucial to new historians. Although etymologization and lexical similarities can be problematic methodologies, they are also scholarly tools that have been widely used for a long time now, for instance in establishing the unity of the Indo-European language family. Their validity is accepted only after systematic and critical consideration of sound-correspondences over time, but this is not without problems: as Osorov himself points out, some of the lexical correspondences within the big Indo-European family are incomprehensible to a non-linguist. However, the language correspondences established by new historians are mostly 'transparent' to lay readers, and new historians do not rely entirely on these lexical correspondences to make their case.

Another observation that strikes the reader — as can be seen by the time I have taken to lay out the sources on which these claims are based — is that new history is not properly described as 'mythology'. Whether we think of 'myth' as opposed to 'logos', following the ancient Greeks, or of 'myth' as 'a charter for the present', or 'an exploration and obliteration of social contradiction', or 'an explanation of origins' in the way anthropologists have done (Herzfeld 2001:85), new history possesses hardly any of the features of myth. Insofar as new historians show a real concern for 'sources' and cite them systematically, new history is not invented, it is, or at least claims to be, based on other 'sources', 'histories', or 'stories'. James Wertsch (2000) conceptualizes such a way of writing history based on textual signifying relations, and distinguishes it from history based on object signifying relations. In the first case, historical narratives are produced in response to other narratives, by reproduction, praise, contestation, mockery, or distortion. In the second case, historical narratives are produced when new evidence or new sources are discovered. Suffice it to mention here that historical narratives based on textual signifying relations are not produced only by amateur historians, and that much nationalist history is written in this style.[28]

As for the sources used by new historians, they are diverse in several ways.[29] First, not all of them are 'historical' in the conventional

---

28   See for instance McNeil (1986:2): 'Yet the limits of scientific history were far more constricting than its devotees believed. Facts that could be established beyond all reasonable doubt remained trivial in the sense that they did not, in and of themselves, give meaning or intelligibility to the record of the past. A catalogue of undoubted and indubitable information, even if arranged chronologically, remains a catalogue. To become a history, facts have to be put together into a pattern that is understandable and credible [...]'. What I refer to as 'emplotment' or 're-emplotment' further in this chapter is the same process as the 'patterning' of historical facts discussed by McNeil.

29   It would be instructive to compare systematically the sources used by Soviet historians, for instance, and the sources used by new historians. However, a quick look at one of the Soviet histories of Kyrgyzstan discouraged me from taking this on since the bulk of the 'sources' comprised the writings of Karl Marx and Lenin, together with different Party resolutions.

sense: not only philology, linguistics, genetics,[30] but also literature and folklore provide the material on which new historians exercise their skills. These texts belong not only to different scholarly traditions — the most recognizable ones being Western and Soviet — but also to very different periods, starting from medieval Chinese annals and ending with recently-defended Ph.D. thesis. These historians also have a noticeable predilection for Western sources as opposed to Soviet or local ones, and for older ones, as opposed to recent ones. Most of the sources they use are also 'legitimate' scholarship because they belong to well-established academic disciplines and can often be associated with well-known scholars.

Content

New history is nourished by ethnic nationalism. Yet, I suggest that there is something qualitatively new in the kind of ethnic nationalism it promotes, at least in the case of Kyrgyzstan. Nationalism in Central Asia shares some common features with classic or European nationalism — the 'blood and soil' variety (Verdery 1993) — in the sense that it seeks to fix historically documented peoples and cultures onto the 'soil' of a present state and is most comfortably endorsed by those who were born on this 'soil'. This 'blood and soil' nationalism has been reinforced and legitimized by the Soviet concept of ethnogenesis, or the unbroken continuity between contemporary ethnic groups and their remote ancestors inhabiting the same territory.[31] The first outburst of new history, and the first divorce with supposedly neatly and solidly established Soviet linguistic, ethnic, and national identities, happened in the last years of the Soviet regime and in the very first years of Kyrgyzstan's independence. At that time, new history was mostly preoccupied with the Aryan myth.[32] Yet this wave of new history was still shaped by classic nationalism because a 'competition for Aryan ancestors' was waged among Central Asian historians who sought to

---

30   The ways in which new historians use genetics to support their arguments is a topic worth covering at length. For other unexpected uses of human genetics, see Simpson 2000, Abu El-Haj 2004.

31   On the Soviet concept of ethnogenesis, see Laruelle 2008.

32   On the Aryan myth in Central Asia, see Laruelle 2007 and Shnirelman 2009.

appropriate, or to incorporate, the earliest Indo-European inhabitants of the region into separate national histories. This kind of nationalism, I would suggest, relies on a 'transtemporal imagination' because it implies the capacity to relate to ancestors distant in time of whom few or no material traces have remained.[33]

The kind of imagination required by new historians more recently is significantly translocal. This translocal imagination operates at two levels: firstly, by referring to places and people outside of Kyrgyzstan; secondly, by inviting readers to embrace the connections to ancient and faraway civilizations and empires, world-renowned cultural monuments, or the past of contemporary powerful states that the historians describe. China, no matter whether admired or feared, represents an ancient empire and an ancient civilization, and even ordinary Kyrgyzstanis know something about China's history. There is glory in both ancient history and ancient civilization, and the idea that part of China's ancient history and civilization were created under the rule of a Kyrgyz clan is, to say the least, exciting. So is the claim that Huns, and, perhaps most importantly, Germans, share common ancestors with the Kyrgyz. While lexical correspondences may be important, what seems decisive is a Kyrgyzized Brandenburg Gate in Berlin because if the correspondences between German and Kyrgyz words may prove too demanding for some readers, the idea that Kyrgyz ancestors are connected to one of the world's best-known monuments[34] is extremely appealing. So is the kind of 'visual comparison' offered by Bekbalaev between contemporary Kyrgyz camps and ancient Hunnic camps in the heart of Europe. Or the idea that the gods of ancient Greece — the cradle

---

33 The Aryan myth and the claims for Aryan origins are still quite popular in new history, as some of Usupbaev's writings demonstrate. However, new historians tend to promote the Aryan myth not by anthropological and linguistic comparisons, nor by comparisons with now extinct lifestyles, i.e., sedentary versus nomadic (cf. Shnirelman 2009), but rather by establishing connections to globally famous monuments or places. Thus, as I have shown elsewhere (Jacquesson 2016), in order to demonstrate that the Kyrgyz are Aryans and not Turks, Usupbaev 'proves' that the pharaohs were among the ancestors of the Kyrgyz, and that the pyramids were built by them. This is not only a striking claim but a flattering one, because it suggests that one of the best-known monuments in the world is in fact Kyrgyz.

34 The monument is familiar to Kyrgyzstanis because of the former division between Eastern and Western Germany, World War Two, and the fact that quite a few local men did their military service in Eastern Germany.

of European democracy and civilization — 'carry Kyrgyz names'. Similarly, there is an obvious appeal to the suggestion that Native Americans and Kyrgyz (or Turks) belong to the same linguistic family and that, though remote, there is a certain Kyrgyz or Turkic essence in the Incan, Mayan, or Aztec civilizations and their heritage. This type of nationalist imagination requires the capacity to connect places and peoples that are separated by national and geopolitical borders. This is why I call new history a 'translocal' discipline. This belief also entails the idea that the sources of national pride can be found elsewhere, outside the territory of Kyrgyzstan proper. Yet, though distant in space, most of the civilizations and monuments to which translocal imagination lays claim are publicized and advertized by the global news media and are therefore perceived as familiar.

Last but not least, this 'translocal imagination' also has a geopolitical dimension: Europe (with Germany as its epitome), the US (as the master of the Americas), and China (which stands only for itself) are major players in the present social, economic and political destiny of Kyrgyzstan in particular, and of Central Asia in general. These players are not always loved, though they are admired or envied for their political and economic might. And if Kyrgyzstan cannot compete with them in the present, new history, at least, suggests that power relations might have been different in the past. The last great power in the region, Russia, is less frequently the object of such 'translocal imagination', perhaps because Russia and Central Asia share some history and this history is too well-known to allow exciting re-emplotments.

Actors and networks

In this section I will focus on the translocal dimensions of the networks produced by new history. To start with, it is worth noticing that the actors who succumb to the temptation to write new history have quite diverse social identities: they can be well-established academics, as the case of Bekbalaev demonstrates; they can be writers, poets or journalists like Osorov; they can also be newcomers to the intellectual field like Usupbaev who has a degree in engineering and who, for most of his life, worked at a construction company. One observation, though, seems to be valid for all new historians known to me: none of them is a professional historian, or a historian holding a position in an official research institution.[35] Even those who are academics — like Bekbalaev — belong to a different discipline, philology in his case. As I have already emphasized while discussing its methods, new history involves the transgression of conventional professional or disciplinary borders and its style and content are, in part at least, shaped by these transgressions.

New history producers and their sources, or the authors whose works they mine for data, form another kind of network. It has both transtemporal and translocal dimensions. As I have already emphasized when discussing their methods, new history writers have a clearly discernible predilection for foreign sources. These foreign sources are appealing, first, because they have long remained inaccessible, or difficult to access.[36] Second, they are appealing because they are believed to be more objective or more truthful than Soviet or local scholarship based on the dictates of Marxist-Leninism. In the last ten or twenty years a lot of these foreign sources have become accessible in various online formats and editions, in Russian translations or in the original. It would not be an exaggeration to state that the movement of knowledge between the 'West' and the 'Rest' has never been as dynamic — or at least as unchecked — as it is now, and new history producers benefit from this 'free flow'. Therefore, new historians interact — even if virtually — with a significant number of scholars whose works and ideas have been shaped in distant and different contexts. Moreover, new history's sources, both foreign and local, are often old: some of them are as ancient as the Chinese or Mongol annals so beloved by Usupbaev; others are simply outdated, such as the dictionaries of American Indian languages used by Osorov to substantiate his claim about the unity of Native American and Turkic languages. Old and foreign sources offer the additional advantage that their authors cannot speak for themselves any longer. Both the transfer of knowledge and the re-emplotments of information that new history undertakes become thus relatively secure,

---

35 Some professional historians also stray from traditional methodologies, but they veer more towards classic nationalism as discussed above.

36 Few Western works were translated into Russian during the Soviet period and their use was limited for fear of accusations of political incorrectness. Translations into the national languages of Central Asia were next to non-existent.

or at least protected from the most legitimate of critiques, those of the scholars who have first collected and analyzed the material.

New historians seem to have strong networks within Kyrgyzstan, but also across Central Asia. The interactions within this network take various shapes. The work of other new historians is openly praised, if not directly cited as Osorov and Usupbaev do when referring to the works of Bekbalaev and Sarygulov respectively. They borrow from each other's 'data' whether they acknowledge it or not. For this reason it is not always easy to establish who was the first one to discover 'new data' or formulate a new claim, as the same 'data' and similar claims are found in the works of different new history authors. A striking example of this kind of cooperation is provided by Osorov and Usupbaev, who joined forces after several years as independent authors to produce a common narrative in English on the glory of Kyrgyz' ancestors. The book, under the title *The Origin of Ancient Kyrgyz Tribes*, was published in July 2015 in Singapore and although it is being sold by a number of online retailers — Amazon included — I have been able to read only excerpts, which are however revealing about the goals and claims of this joint enterprise:[37]

> Technically, all the modern world originated in some way or another from the ancient Kyrgyz tribes, which were in close relation with ancient civilizations such as the Sumerians, ancient Egypt, Israel, Greece, Rome, China, Kushan, the Ottoman Empire, as well as the Aztecs and Incas. Eventually, the Kyrgyz tribes will be able to unite the world again and achieve the long awaited peace between East and West, Israel and Arabs, Russia and Ukraine, China and the U.S., Shiites and Sunnites, Hindi and Urdu, and so on in our currently so divided and unhappy reality.[38]

Finally, new history authors in their turn are used as authorities or sources of inspiration by those who follow them. Osorov's reconstruction of the Native-American-Turkic linguistic community builds upon the work of Abrar Karimullin whose writings enjoyed some recognition in Tatarstan, Russia and beyond since he was an honorary fellow of Harvard University, although his work was not

---

37 This quote is written in English in the original and is therefore reproduced as published.
38 Osorov and Usupbaev 2015.

uncontested. The works and ideas of Lev Gumilyov appear as another source of frequent inspiration among new historians.[39] Last but not least, whether they acknowledge it or not, the works of current new history writers read quite often as more or less successful variations on Olzhas Suleimenov's *AZ i IA*.[40] In the context of the late Soviet period Suleimenov's *AZ i IA* was a provocative cultural manifesto blurring the borders between poetry, historiography and linguistics in an attempt to rethink or rediscover — or as some would have it, 'imagine' or 'reinvent' — the place of the Turks in Soviet Eurasia and beyond. Suleimenov's views are encapsulated by his 1962 statement that 'many obscure aspects of the history of literate peoples cannot be explained without some knowledge of the history of the Turks' and that 'at some point there will appear a genuine, realistic book, "the True History", and that we [i.e., the Turks] too will take part in its birth'.[41] These intellectual networks, or intellectual genealogies, can be extended further back into the past since Gumilyov and Suleimenov were borrowing information and ideas from their predecessors. Therefore, some of the methods, writing styles, facts and even the claims of 'new history' are not as novel as they might appear at a first glance.

Conclusion

At the beginning of this chapter I argued that branding new history as 'historical mythologization' does justice neither to its practices and actors, nor to its significance as a social and political phenomenon. I suggested that a translocal research perspective might provide a better analytical grasp on its actors and practices, and on new history as an intellectual endeavour.

Neither medieval annals, nor Mayan nor Aztec civilizations, nor even the strained or fake language similarities and etymologies are 'myths', according to both the common meaning of the word or from

---

39 Mainly Gumilyov's *Hunny* (1960) and *Geografiya etnosa v istoricheskii period* (1990). On Gumilyov, see Shnirelman and Panarin 2000, Laruelle 2000 and 2001, cf. Titov 2005.

40 On Suleimenov's *AZ i IA*, see Ram 2001, Baker 2016.

41 As quoted in Ram 2001:293.

an anthropological perspective. All national(ist) histories are in some ways 'mythistories' (McNeil 1986). But even so, as McNeil himself emphasizes, the myth is more in the plot than in the facts; in other words, nationalist histories, or mythistories, rely on different emplotments of historical facts rather than on the pure invention of such facts, or on their outright distortion. If we accept that history is to a great extent about the re-emplotment of the past, it is particularly important for an anthropologist to investigate these re-emplotments and not to dismiss them as 'myths', or 'fake history'. In this chapter, I have attempted to do exactly this — to demonstrate that new history does not work with myths but with facts, whether they are borrowed from other historical sources as in the case of Usupbaev, or from other sciences as in the cases of Bekbalaev and Osorov.

I have suggested that new history — at least the way it is practiced in Kyrgyzstan today — greatly resembles Suleimenov's endeavour in *AZ i IA*, though it lacks Suleimenov's erudition and writing skills. I would like to add here that, as distinct from Suleimenov, who wreaked havoc on the Soviet knowledge system, new historians have had a similar effect on European or Western knowledge systems. In a way, while Suleimenov revolted against history as designed by the Soviet state, new historians attempt to claim agency in a world history that is still largely Eurocentric, or that foregrounds some historical perspectives while ignoring or denying others. In this sense, new history is not only an attempt to emplot the past differently, but also an attempt to imagine the present and the future differently, as Usupbaev's and Osorov's proclamation quoted above demonstrates. New history as an intellectual endeavour then sheds light on the different experiences of globalization and on the novel agencies it generates among those who strive to not lag behind.

New history, to put it bluntly, is a non-scholarly body of writings based on scholarly methods and sources. Its practitioners transfer 'facts' from one academic discipline to another, and from Western to Soviet or post-Soviet epistemologies, and in doing so, they emulate conventional scholarly methods. Approaching new history as a translocal and transtemporal field and analyzing the processes and practices that are involved in its production allows a better understanding of its epistemological status and its political stance.

The study of new history leads to a reflexive engagement with sources, methods, and different types of knowledge. New history, therefore, offers a favorable ground for the exercise of sociocultural reflexivity (Herzfeld 2001:45–52). After all, it fulfills the expectations of certain audiences since it is published, serialized, or disseminated on social media forums. It cannot therefore be ignored in the ongoing discussions about hierarchies of knowledge, or the nature of history, and how it should be narrated.

References

Abu El-Haj, Nadia. '"A Tool to Recover Past Histories". Genealogy and Identity after the Genome'. *Occasional Papers of the School of Social Science* 19 (2004): 1–23.

Aldashev, Almaz. 'Etnogenez i genealogiia kyrgyzov. Vzgliad s tochki zreniia molekuliarnoi genetiki'. *Zdravookhranenie i nauka* (11 December 2009), http://www.akipress.org/zdorovie/news:1931/

Baker, Christopher. 'The Power and Significance of the Ethnic Past'. In Svetlana Jacquesson, ed. *History Making in Central and Northern Eurasia: Contemporary Actors and Practices*. Wiesbaden: Reichert Verlag, 2016, pp. 21–40.

Barreiro, Elena. 'Frederick Roehrig: A Forgotten Name in Salish Linguistics', *Northwest Journal of Linguistics* 6.3 (2012): 1–17.

Bekbalaev, Amangeldi. 'Atilla — predok kyrgyzov' (2011), http://www.literatura. kg/articles/?aid=1259

Bekbalaev, Amangeldi, aka Ammian von Bek. *Gunny: trilogiia*. Almaty: Print, 2009, http://www.literatura.kg/persons/?aid=333

Freitag, Ulrike, and Achim von Oppen. 'Translocality: An Approach to Connections and Transfer in Area Studies'. In Ulrike Freitag and Achim von Oppen, eds. *Translocality: The Study of Globalising Processes from a Southern Perspective*. Leiden: Brill, 2010, pp. 1–21, https://doi.org/10.1163/ej.9789004181168.i-452.8

Galiev, Anuar. *Etnopoliticheskie protsessy u tiurko-iazychnykh narodov: istoriia i ee mifologizatsiia*. Doctoral thesis, Kazakhstan's University of International Relations and World Languages, 2010.

Galiev, Anuar. 'Pokazhite mne pasport Chingiza gde napisano chto on Kazakh', *Centrasia*, 27 July 2013, http://www.centrasia.ru/newsA.php?st=1374917100

Grozin, Andrei V. 'Mifologizatorstvo v sovremennoi istoriografii Kazakhstana: politologicheskii aspect problemy', *Vestnik MGU im. M. A. Sholokhova* (2010): 106–20.

Herzfeld, Michael. *Cultural Intimacy: Social Poetics in the Nation State*. New York: Routledge, 1997.

Herzfeld, Michael. *Anthropology: Theoretical Practice in Culture and Society*. Malden: Blackwell, 2001.

Jacquesson, Svetlana. 'From Clan Narratives to Clan Politics', *Central Asian Survey* 31.3 (2010): 277–92, https://doi.org/10.1080/02634937.2012.720868

Jacquesson, Svetlana. 'Genealogies as a Craft: The Search for "Truth" and Authority in Contemporary Kyrgyzstan'. In Svetlana Jacquesson, ed. *History aking in Central and Northern Eurasia: Contemporary Actors and Practices*. Wiesbaden: Reichert Verlag, 2016, pp. 100–21.

Karimullin, Abrar. _Proto-tiurki i indeitsy: po sledam odnoi gipotezy_. Moscow: Insan, 1995. English translation available at http://s155239215.onlinehome.us/turkic/67Amerind/KarimullinPrototurks1En.htm

Khaliullin, Yulduz. 'Abrar Kariullin: vydaiushchiisia syn tatarskogo naroda. K 80-letiiu so dnia rozhdeniia' (2005), http://yulnur.ocean.ru

Laruelle, Marlène. 'Lev Nikolaevič Gumilev (1912–1992): biologisme et eurasisme dans la pensée russe', _Revue des études slaves_ 72.1 (2000): 163–89. https://doi.org/doi:10.3406/slave.2000.6650

Laruelle, Marlène. 'Histoire d'une usurpation intellectuelle: L. N. Gumilev, "le dernier des eurasistes"? Analyze des oppositions entre L. N. Gumilev et P. N. Savickij', _Revue des études slaves_ 73.2 (2001): 449–59, https://doi.org/10.3406/slave.2001.6726

Laruelle, Marlène. 'The Return of the Aryan Myth: Tajikistan in Search for a Secularized National Ideology', _Nationalities Papers_ 35.1 (2007): 51–70, https://doi.org/10.1080/00905990601124462

Laruelle, Marlène. 'The Concept of Ethnogenesis in Central Asia: Political Context and Institutional Mediators (1940–50)', _Kritika: Explorations in Russian and Eurasian History_ 9.1 (2008): 169–88, https://doi.org/10.1353/kri.2008.0005

Laruelle, Marlène. 'Conspiracy and Alternate History in Russia: A Nationalist Equation for Success?', _The Russian Review_ 71 (2012a): 565–80, https://doi.org/10.1111/j.1467-9434.2012.00669.x

Laruelle, Marlène. _Russian Eurasianism. An Ideology of Empire_. Washington, D.C.: Woodrow Wilson Press, 2012b.

Light, Nathan. 'History, Experience and Narration: Novel Accounts and Multiplex Stories'. In Svetlana Jacquesson, ed. _History Making in Central and Northern Eurasia: Contemporary Actors and Practices_. Wiesbaden: Reichert Verlag, 2016, pp. 139–61.

Masanov, Nurbulat, _et al. Nauchnoe znanie i mifotvorchestvo v sovremennoi istoriografii Kazakhstana_. Almaty: Daik-Press, 2007.

Masanov, Nurbulat. '"Kazakhantropov" ne bylo', _CentrAsia_, 8 November 2007, http://www.centrasia.ru/newsA.php?st=1194470340

McNeil, William H. 'Mythistory, or Truth, Myth, History, and Historians'. _The American Historical Review_ 91.1 (1986): 1–10.

Omurbekov, Toktobek. 'V usloviiakh otsutstviia nauchnykh trudov obshchestvu prikhoditsiia verit' rabotam diletantov', _Kabar.kg_, 15 November 2012, http://kabar.kg/science-and-culture/full/43951

Osorov, Zamir. 'Kyrgyzy i Indeitsy' (2012a), https://www.stihi.ru/avtor/zamir1 and https://www.proza.ru/avtor/zamir1

Osorov, Zamir. 'Supersimetriia istiny' (2012b), http://www.proza.ru/2012/03/15/327

Osorov, Zamir, and Usupbaev, Anarbek. *The Origins of Ancient Kyrgyz Tribes* Singapore: Partridge Publishing, 2015.

Pels, Peter. 'The Anthropology of Colonialism: Culture, History, and the Emergence of Western Governmentality'. *Annual Review of Anthropology* 26 (1997): 163–83, https://doi.org/10.1146/annurev.anthro.26.1.163

Ram, Harsha. 'Imagining Eurasia: The Poetics and Ideology of Olzhas Suleimenov's AZ i IA'. *Slavic Review* 60.2 (2001): 289–311, https://doi.org/10.2307/2697272

Shnirelman, Viktor, and Sergei Panarin. 'Lev Gumilev: His Pretensions as Founder of Ethnology and His Eurasian Theories'. *Inner Asia* 3 (2001): 1–18, https://doi.org/10.1163/146481701793647732

Shnirelman, Victor. 'Aryans or Proto-Turks? Contested Ancestors in Contemporary Central Asia'. *Nationalities Papers* 37.5 (2009): 557–87, https://doi.org/10.1080/00905990903122834

Simpson Bob. 'Imagined Genetic Communities: Ethnicity and Essentialism in the Twenty-First Century'. *Anthropology Today* 16.3 (2000): 3–6, https://doi.org/10.1111/1467-8322.00023

Soltonoev, Belek. *Kyzyl Kyrgyz tarykhy*. Bishkek: Uchkun, 1993 [1934].

Suleimenov, Olzhas. *AZ i IA. Kniga blagonamerennogo chitetelia*. Alma-Ata: Engbek, 1975.

Titov, Alexander. *Lev Gumilev, Ethnogenesis and Eurasianism*. Doctoral thesis, University College London, 2005.

Usupbaev, Anarbek. 'Kyrgyzdyn sol kanatynyn Kytay uruusunun nukura tarykhy' (PressKG, 2010).

Verdery, Katherine. 'Whither "Nation" and "Nationalism"?' *Daedalus* 122.3 (1993): 37–46.

Wertsch, James V. 'Narratives as Cultural Tools in Sociocultural Analysis: Official History in Soviet and post-Soviet Russia'. *Ethos* 28.4 (2000): 511–33, https://doi.org/10.1525/eth.2000.28.4.511

7. Informal Trade and Globalization in the Caucasus and Post-Soviet Eurasia

Susanne Fehlings

Introduction

In Central Asia and the Caucasus, one can observe many petty traders, who travel long distances and cross international borders to complete their business. Even though these traders have little financial capital at their disposal, and even though the economic activity of each individual seems rather unimportant, the total effect of such agents, their trade, and their mobility is more than a random phenomenon. They are typical actors of globalization — or, more precisely, of something that has been theoretically framed as 'globalization from below' (Portes 1997, Mathews 2011, Mathews *et al.* 2012), 'grassroots globalization' (Appadurai 2000), or 'translocality' (Freitag and von Oppen 2010, Smith 2011).

During my fieldwork in the Caucasus, conducted between 2008 and 2010, I met many of these traders on the roads between Yerevan (Armenia) and Tbilisi (Georgia) and those between Tbilisi and Baku (Azerbaijan). I remember the day when I crossed the Armenian-Georgian border for the first time. The minibus had just crossed the wild mountains and deep valleys of the Caucasus at breathtaking speed and some passengers had been sick. After I got my passport back from a serious-looking border official, I suddenly felt much like an adventurer — like Tolstoy, who describes the Caucasus as a remote and wild region — and I felt like I was in 'the middle of nowhere'. But

 https://doi.org/10.11647/OBP.0114.07

as I understand now, this perception of the border as a remote place was an illusion of mine. In fact, the borders in the Caucasus (and Central Asia) are very vibrant places and hotspots for all kind of exchanges and economic activity (compare Reeves 2014, Gellner 2013). They are central loci, 'nodes', or 'sites with a lot of transiency' (Hannerz 1998:139) along the travel routes that cross the whole area, traditionally connecting Europe and Asia, and Great Powers like Russia and Persia. In many cases 'border-markets'[1] have developed in their proximity.

On the roads you can find all kinds of people: besides tourists and commuters, you will meet Iranian truck and Georgian minibus drivers, Armenian fruit and vegetable retailers, Turkish businessmen — and, invisible to the eyes of ordinary travellers, smugglers of drugs and weapons. Almost all of these people can be labelled 'petty traders', who obviously form a very heterogeneous group. My aim is to learn more about these people, their economic activity, and their travel routes. In this chapter, I shall first outline the theoretical framework and main research questions of my work, which is conceived as a subproject within the research project 'Informal Markets and Trade in Central Asia and the Caucasus', funded by the Volkswagen Foundation. I shall present some general objectives of the project, and discuss some of its central theoretical concepts such as 'informality' and 'globalization', which I shall then link to 'translocality'. Finally, I shall present some preliminary results from my own recent research trips and my initial fieldwork on local markets in Georgia, which I took as a starting point to investigate the theoretical concepts mentioned above. One of the results was the identification of research units that might help to investigate 'translocal contexts' and 'translocality' in general. Using research units such as location, people, mobility, goods and frequency, which are components of the economic activity I investigated, I describe and pay special attention to my target group: female petty traders, who travel long distances and who exist at the lower end of the scale of informal entrepreneurial activity.

---

1 For literature on 'border-markets' in Central Asia and the Caucasus see, for example, Dabaghyan and Gabrielyan (2008, 2011); Yalcin-Heckmann (2012) and Turaeva-Hoehne (2014).

'Informality', 'globalization', and 'translocality'

One general objective of the project 'Informal Markets and Trade in Central Asia and the Caucasus' is to reach a comprehensive understanding of the 'informal economy' in post-Soviet regions and their bordering countries. These local contexts, which reach as far as from Turkey to the Caucasus and Russia, and from Central Asia to China, have been shaped by the breakdown of the Soviet economic system and its opening up to the world market. The project thus starts from the concept of 'globalization from below' or 'grassroots globalization' that conflates informality and non-elite local actors with global flows, networks, and settings, which have become more and more relevant for local people and economies since the early 1990s (Fehlings and Karrar 2016).

'Globalization from below' is usually distinguished from 'globalization from above' (Portes 1997, Appadurai 2000, MacGaffey and Bazenguissa-Ganga 2000, Mathews 2011, Mathews *et al.* 2012). While the latter is defined as regulated by state institutions and large enterprises, 'globalization from below', according to the literature, encompasses the economic activity of individual entrepreneurs, who usually have little money at hand, rely on their personal networks, and have no formal training. As the everyday exchanges of these people are unregulated by the state or official law, their activity is often associated with 'informality' as defined by Keith Hart (1973). Especially in the aftermath of the Soviet Union, during the process of nation-building in the newly-established and recently-independent republics on former Soviet territory informal practices seem to have substituted for many formal (state) structures that had disappeared or were not yet fully established, implemented, or accepted (Giordano and Hayoz 2013, Morris and Polese 2013, Holzlehner 2014).

'Informality', as used by academics, quite simply describes the absence of 'formality'. But because it is difficult to define clear boundaries between formality and informality, between formal structure, as defined by state bodies, and the individual interpretations of these structures, between formal rules and socio-cultural practice, and between institutionalized and written codes of behavior (legal law) and agency, the definition of informality (and formality) leaves much space for interpretation (Hart 1973, 1986, 1992, Helmke and Levitsky 2006, Chen 2007, Sassen 2001, Giordano and Hayoz 2013, Morris and Polese 2013, Hardenberg and Fehlings 2016). State regulations are usually taken as formal (in the Weberian sense of 'rational government') but there is no doubt, as proven by many examples from Central Asia and the Caucasus, that states, governments and their administrative bodies are not only grounded in rationality and legal law regulations (compare Gupta 1995, 2012). In Uzbekistan, for example, the state and enterprises supported by state institutions extensively use informal practices such as social networking, which is why Kaiser (1997) and Rasanayagam (2011) have described this situation as an 'informalization'[2] manifesting at all levels of society (Hardenberg and Fehlings 2016, Iskandaryan 2014). In contexts like these, 'culture', which, in economics as well as in public media, is often associated with 'backward and primitive behavior' is held responsible for the informal practices that, in a next step, are sometimes equated to corruption. Culture, in this formulation, is perceived as an obstacle to economic growth and welfare, which, according to some (Georgian and Western) economists is a reason for the lack of economic success of Caucasian petty traders and small entrepreneurs, who trust in their kinship networks instead of taking loans from credit institutions, and who spent their money on feasts and family matters rather than on reinvestment.

From an anthropological point of view, culture and 'backwardness', same as culture and informal structures, cannot be equated but need to be treated as separate categories. Just as states are rarely purely formal and based on rational government, so are social practices and organizations, cultural norms and codes of behavior, rarely arbitrary or chaotic — or 'backward' and illegal per se. This is why I use both terms — formality and informality — in a non-dogmatic way. Formality and informality,

---

2   'Informalization' is a concept originally developed by Castells and Portes (1989), describing the growing impact of informality not only in third-world scenarios but also in wealthier economies through, for example, labour migration. For Kaiser and Rasanayagam, on the other hand, the important point is that the formal structures themselves provide the framework within which the informal activities emerge (compare Sassen 2001).

in my opinion, should not be taken as strictly analytical classifications. They are starting points to describe the different facets of structures, of behaviors, of motivations and of practices on all social and spatial levels and in relation to each other. Thus they help to describe these structures, behaviors, motivations and practices as more or less controlled by official bodies, more or less visible, and more or less difficult to grasp through official statistics. From an emic perspective, people involved in economic activities like petty trade or bazaar vending do not at all distinguish between formal and informal practices. For them, their activity is a logical reaction or adaptation to the circumstances shaping the market and the marketplace. These circumstances simply have to be transformed into successful business. State regulations are sometimes perceived as unfair and therefore ignored. Sometimes, traders look for loopholes in the legal framework. But as long as no major crime (such as murder or trafficking) is committed, people (petty traders as well as officials) do not perceive these crossings of regulatory boundaries as significant. Entrepreneurs complete their business and sometimes one has to pay a fee. Thus, the classification of activities into formal and informal categories and the use of such terms are academic rather than practical.

From a theoretical point of view, as already mentioned, 'formality' and 'informality' and 'globalization from above' and 'from below' are related to each other in similar ways. Thus, from an analytical perspective, we need the same tools to understand 'globalization from below' as to understand 'informal practices', which are both important aspects of globalization as a whole. It is the mingling of the two spheres that interests me.

Authors such as Keith Hart (1973, 1986, 1996) have argued that globalization as such to some extent promotes 'informality', because it weakens the role of nation states and their formal regulations. In fact, geographical borders, specifically national borders, are constantly being transgressed and undermined though informal practices: migration, economic activity, tourism, and personal networks (virtual networks, kinship, or other) that escape state control (Portes 1997). Becoming at some point institutionalized, they create new structures beyond or within national horizons. Yet at the same time, there is no doubt that national borders and institutions exist and that people have to deal with them (compare Reeves 2014, Gellner 2013, Harris 2013).

The term 'translocality' is used to engage with similar phenomena and problems. According to Freitag and von Oppen (2010:3), the notion of translocality includes the attempt to focus on actors, connections, flows, places, and processes that range 'below the elite level'. Rather than solely taking into account the perspectives of those with power, researchers using a translocal lens pay attention to marginal mobilities, historical changes, and the dynamics of specific places through flows, relations between local and global connectedness, and local adaptions of translocal experiences. The goal is to write a 'social history from below' and to 'understand the manifold ways in which the world is constituted' (*ibid.*:6).

Here, we face the same problems as mentioned above: on the one hand, we have to consider 'processes of the establishment and institutionalization of cultural, social and political structures'; on the other hand, specifically in an overall situation of mobility, flows, and transition, 'it seems that translocality is often marked by transient, non-permanent and unordered spaces' that are difficult to record (Freitag and von Oppen 2010:7).

The actors, such as petty traders or migrants, are the focus of our interest when examining informality, globalization from below, and translocality, and they have a similar background and use similar networks and practices. But while researchers using the concepts of informality and globalization from below emphasize these actors and their specific practices, movements, backgrounds, behaviors and networks, researchers using a translocal perspective investigate 'the tensions between movement and order' and address 'the attempts to cope with transgression and the need for localizing some kind of order' (Freitag and von Oppen 2010:8). Thus, translocality, as I understand it, deals with new and fluid belongings, new identifications, networks, imaginations, 'livelihoods', and adapted practices. These are linked to the unconventional definitions of space that appear in these contexts, but are still rooted in localities and thus not arbitrary or unbound. As such, translocality, in contrast to transnationalism, takes into account that there are boundaries other than purely political ones. This is, for example, true in the context of trade networks — such as those reaching from Turkey to the Caucasus and from Central Asia to China — that cross the region currently under our investigation (compare Freitag and von Oppen 2010, Schetter 2012, Schröder and Stephan-Emmrich 2014). However, we have to admit that conventional nation-state borders have not ceased to exist. Truck drivers, for example, as I could observe myself, spend hours at border posts. They thus physically experience the existence of borders. There are material blockades, administrative obstacles, language barriers, and, last but not least, socio-cultural boundaries rooted in ethnic backgrounds, social networks like kinship relations, religious and social practices, customs, beliefs, and worldviews that have to be overcome. At the same time, national institutions promote trade and mobility. Local governments build many of the roads on which the traders travel and provide the infrastructure that makes communication, exchange, and economic success possible.[3]

Therefore, the activity we observe takes place in spaces that are neither solely locally bound nor totally 'translocal'; they are neither completely informal nor formal; they are global but usually the actors are embedded in local contexts. Consequently, we have to investigate the points of intersection and the 'linkages of different scales' (Freitag and von Oppen 2010:19), by considering a 'plurality of perspectives', making use of, for example, multidisciplinary attempts and different regional experiences (*ibid*.:18–20).

To summarize, we must keep in mind that the economy is not an 'impersonal (formal) machine' but made and remade by people in their everyday lives (Hart 2010). Therefore, I try to investigate the economy, respectively informal markets and trade, in accordance with anthropological tradition[4] in conjunction with other realms of human existence such as culture, social relations, politics, and religion. Informality, globalization from below, and translocality are simply means to describe some aspects of the interrelation of these fields.

---

3   The importance of infrastructure has been discussed by Cresswell (2006), Dalakoglou and Harvey (2012), Larkin (2013), and Nadjmabadi (2014).
4   See, e.g., Mauss (1990 [1925]), Malinowski (1935), (1972), Bohannon and Dalton (1962), Polanyi (2001 [1944]), Gudeman (2001), (2005), Carsten (1989), Parry and Bloch (1989) and others.

Informal markets and translocal trade
in Tbilisi and beyond

For this chapter, I have used materials from previous long-term research stays in the Caucasus and from two and a half months of fieldwork on local markets in Tbilisi in spring 2014. Based on these experiences and data I started to classify marketplaces, traders, forms of mobility, and the types of the trader's economic activity. My first idea was to get in touch with traders and to travel with them in order to track their trade routes and observe their translocal environment, as well as their behavior and experiences, thus understanding the formal and informal context of their practices, and their socio-cultural background and motivation. But walking through Tbilisi and paying attention to traders, trade, and marketplaces, I was simply overwhelmed by the number of merchants and the amount of goods that flood the city. Globalization from above and below, and the translocal contexts of trading, become most obvious in the local setting of the Georgian capital. Thus, to get an overview, I did not follow individual traders on their travel routes, but tried to understand the variety of economic exchanges and the diversity of social groups involved in trade by investigating the places, which are, besides border markets, the spatial centres and the nodes of economic action in the region.[5]

A specific group of traders attracted my particular attention: female petty traders who travel quite long distances, crossing international borders. These women usually buy a few goods, like furniture or clothes, which, back home, they sell for a small profit. To get a better understanding of the particularity of this group in relation to other groups of traders, I tried to identify parameters that help to describe different aspects of trade, the specific social groups of traders, and their 'embeddedness' in socio-cultural contexts. These parameters can also be interpreted as possible units for investigating formality and

---

5   Compare Bestor's (2001) investigation of the international seafood trade by focussing on Tokyo's Tsukiji seafood market and the local specificity of market and place within a globalized urban setting.

informality, the interrelation of globalization from below and above, and translocality. The parameters consist of: a) the locations where economic activity takes place, b) the people involved, c) their mobility, d) the types of goods that are traded, and f) the exchange volume and frequency of activity. Some additional aspects under consideration include historical and political dynamics.

Location

Tbilisi is full of street vendors, bazaars, markets, small shops, malls, etc., and it is almost impossible to differentiate between them, as they coexist in close proximity without being strictly separated. One can hardly draw a line between territories, the different groups of people working there, and the various types of businesses being represented. Despite these challenges, I tried to understand what distinguishes them.

Let me start with space and sales facilities. The locations of economic exchange in Tbilisi (and in the Caucasus in general), can, as a first step, be classified — even though, as mentioned above, this is a very tentative and problematic classification — as more or less formal or informal. The level of formality, in this case, usually can be defined according to the solidity and durability of the sales facilities and their ability to meet official sanitary standards. Sales facilities and displays range from a cloth that is placed on the soil in front of the vendor, to push carts, booths in roofed and unroofed bazaars of different size and importance, small shops and kiosks, and boutiques, supermarkets, shopping malls, and department stores.

While the less formal traders use public spaces like streets, metro stations, or parks, the more formalized businesses are found in permanent locations explicitly designed and equipped for this purpose. For each of the different spaces of exchange there exists a particular local term, such as, for example, in Georgian, *supermarketi, marketi, maghazia, bazari, bazroba, budiki,* and *budka;* or in Armenian *supermarket, khanuth, shuka, krapak,* etcetera.

Fig. 7.1 Eliava's spare parts market in Tbilisi.
Photo © Susanne Fehlings (2014), CC BY 4.0

The different spaces of exchange have different legal statuses. Some are approved and supported by formal state institutions, such as *Lilo Molli* next to Tbilisi's airport, which is the biggest wholesale and retail market or bazaar in the Caucasus. Here, you can find a market administration, hierarchical organization, and security measures, and the shops within the marketplace are neat, numbered, and listed on a map. The wholesalers and retail traders there will usually rent some space and thus automatically receive an official license to sell their merchandise on their allocated spot. When I asked the manager of a similar market in Tbilisi's centre how the market was organized, the conversation quickly came to an end: 'people pay, they get a booth with a certain number of square meters, and then everything is fine. I do not know how they manage the rest. This is none of my business [it does not concern me.]'.

In other spaces such as public pavements or metro entrances, trade is much more chaotic, only tacitly accepted by officials, or sometimes even prohibited. In Tbilisi there have been several initiatives, which were enforced by the state police, to expel street vendors from public spaces (Khutsishvili 2012, Rekhviashvili 2015). Similar initiatives, which in Tbilisi were eventually dropped by the new government, can be observed all over post-Soviet territories, because informally-operating street vendors and their goods displays are usually perceived as an obstacle to formal urban order and a modern city lifestyle (Stephan-Emmrich and Mirzoev 2016).

All the above-mentioned localities, even the more permanent ones, have in common the appearance of being comparatively transient and disordered. Indeed, the less formally controlled they are, the more they become, at least from the perspective of an outsider, jumbled accumulations of merchandise and people, or chaotic bazaars, which are composed of labyrinths of small corridors and tentative stalls overloaded with commodities. In such places the smells of food mingle with those of rubbish, and music from different stalls competes with the noises and shouts from the street. Many of these locations are in a state of permanent transformation. Shops, goods, merchants, and consumers come and go. Some shops get bankrupt, more successful traders open new shops, changing demand requires new merchandise, and consumers may develop new habits and become attracted by other places and types of shops.

Importance and centrality, of course, are two more key features that should be considered in order to understand the position of marketplaces within local and global geographic, political and economic landscapes, within networks of marketplaces and as part of trade routes both within and beyond the Caucasus (Dannhaeuser 1989).

Interestingly, the women of my target group make use of these webs of marketplaces and profit from price differences that occur within them. But in many cases, they bring the merchandise from a far-away market directly to their clients, which is why they do not necessarily appear in the local markets of the Caucasian capitals. They often do not have a space for selling their goods, but use their villages and private houses as locations for economic negotiation and exchange. Invisible to the eyes of outsiders and to state control, these private places can be interpreted as the complete opposite of formal sales facilities.

Fig. 7.2 Traders next to the railway station and the bus stop in Tbilisi.
Photo © Susanne Fehlings (2014), CC BY 4.0

People

In markets and shops, it is quite common for the salespersons to be hired simply as sellers and to be not at all involved in the process of importation. In other cases, producers and traders are the very same, for example, in the case of farmers (*glechebi* in Georgian), who sell their vegetables and fruits on Tbilisi's streets or on the platforms of Tbilisi's railway station. According to Ketevan Khutsishvili 'their products are known to be extraordinarily fresh and cheap, and this is why consumers buy from them'.

Some traders buy their merchandise at cheap wholesale markets like *Lilo* and re-sell them for a small profit in the city centre, as was the case of an old woman who I saw every day selling costume jewelry on Tbilisi's central Rustaveli Street, where she used the architecture of public buildings as a showcase. Others travel long distances and live translocal lives.

Fig. 7.3 Street vending in Tbilisi: using public buildings as a showcase.
Photo © Susanne Fehlings (2014), CC BY 4.0

The motivations for working as a trader vary widely. Besides entrepreneurs, for whom their business is their 'real profession', there are many people who get involved in trade only out of absolute necessity. The socio-cultural background is essential to understand why people do what they do and how they do it. The socio-cultural context, for me, consists of social relations (such as kinship relations or other social networks) that shape society, social practices and hierarchies, cosmology, beliefs, and shared values. These shape economic practice. In Georgia, many people, especially the elderly, grew up with a Soviet ideology that condemned trade, profit-making, and free-market economics (Mandel and Humphrey 2002). For these people, it was, as far as I could make out from the conversations, a hard and amoral decision to turn to trade. Very typical sentiments were: 'by profession I am an engineer', 'a university teacher', or 'I have [X number of] diplomas'. This is a way to express regret about declining status as a result of external factors (compare Niyozov and Shamatov 2007, Schröder in Chapter Eight). This was the case with many female petty traders, whom I met at local markets or on their travels.

In the 1980s and 1990s, trade and therefore travelling became a strategy of survival for all kinds of people who had lost their livelihoods. Many of them belonged to the so-called *intelligentsia*, whose members were especially vulnerable during this time, and many of them were women (compare Niyozov and Shamatov 2007). These people, who were called *chelnoki*, had very little experience in the field of commerce. Armine, an Armenian university teacher, for example, told me about trade expeditions in the 1990s, which she undertook with small groups of students to Iran. She remembered how they veiled themselves to explore this unknown territory and how they crossed the border for the first time.

The term *'chelnoki'* derives from the term 'shuttle' (*chelnok*), which is a device used in weaving to carry the weft by moving back and forth. This motion recalls the back and forth of the traders' travel (Holzlehner 2014). Mobility, in times of crisis, became the basis of peoples' economic existence. But in contrast to the widespread opinion that translocality, mobility, and flexibility lead to economic success (Stephan-Emmrich and Mirzoev 2016), many of the petty traders under consideration here engaged in trade for their mere survival.

Nowadays, this group of people and their kind of economic activity has decreased. The women I am interested in, their travels, and their special kind of commerce, might be the last remnant of the *chelnoki* phenomenon. It can be classified as highly informal because it is often not even a permanent occupation, since it is based on personal relations, and — at least in large part — operates outside of the state controlled sphere of formally registered business. Almost everyone else from this first generation tried to stop doing this as soon as there were other possibilities. The women of my target group, however, continue this business, but rarely travel very long distances (e.g., to China or India). The women's new and favorite destination is Turkey, which they can reach easily by *marshrutka* (minibus). I wonder if their activity, again, is an outcome of political and economic crisis (in this case, the financial crisis of 2008). I believe this is an interesting hypothesis, which is worth investigating in future work.

However, female traders, especially those who have passed the age of forty, belong to the lowest class of traders (and of society in general). They are perceived (by large parts of society and often by themselves) as the last remnants of the Soviet system and the transition period. Usually, a tragic biography and the absence of support from family members, which is perceived as crucial for a successful and happy life in Georgian society, has forced them to continue this occupation at a time when most other people, thanks to the recovering national economy, have started bigger businesses or other jobs. Thus, for example, I met a woman in the train from Baku to Tbilisi who had just returned from China. Her son and her daughter-in-law had died in a car accident. Having lost her family and all financial support, she had to care for her grandchild, which was the only reason for her to turn to petty trade. Another woman, Marina, who travels to China, lost her husband and has to feed two children, and Hasmik, who trades in vegetables from Turkey, which she buys in Tbilisi and sells in Yerevan, told a similar story.

Younger, so-called *bisnesmeny* have a totally different attitude. For them, trade and economic success is linked to prestige and a 'modern lifestyle'. This lifestyle, as I observed, fits well with the 'new' ideology. It accords with the cultural orientation towards a market economy and a more Western European outlook, and it is also supported by the Georgian Orthodox Church, representatives of which present themselves in the guise of businessmen. In general, elderly people and women work in the more informal and less profitable sectors, whereas men and younger people more often manage to establish themselves in business permanently and profitably. In this context it makes sense to ask, at what point does one become a successful businessmen, trader, or entrepreneur? This is, of course, difficult to answer. Perhaps the level of formalization, which manifests in owning a permanent location like a registered booth or shop among other signals, is an indicator. It is clear, however, that the traders who are forced into trade and an itinerant work schedule do not belong to this category. They are far from being able to accumulate wealth and usually not able to make their business grow.[6]

Mobility

The first discovery during my recent fieldwork was that many traders working in bazaars and markets do not really travel, but sell goods they buy from wholesalers. The more established traders, most of them men, buy their goods by catalogue order. For example, Levan, who sells furniture from China next to Tbilisi's railway station, told me that he had once travelled to China and visited the factory where his merchandise is produced. The Chinese factory had employed a professional Russian translator, and once the business relationship was established, offers and orders for goods were placed via the internet. As soon as one delivery is sold out, Levan orders the next. Payment is made through bank transfer, and transport and payment of custom duties organized through globally operating cargo companies, thus limiting the risk to, and individual mobility of, those involved in this exchange.

The establishment of business relations and the regularity of exchange call for structuring, formalization, specialization, and division of labour, which often leads to the outsourcing of logistics. It follows that personal movement is often linked to a lower degree of formality. Consequently, one could also classify the merchants, their informal or formal character, and their involvement in translocal contexts, with reference to their personal mobility. The farmers mentioned above, for example, usually bring their products from rural to urban areas to sell them on the public streets or in proximity to railway or bus stations. They usually manage their itinerary in less than one day, and hence are

---

6   How modes of entrepreneurship change and which factors influence this change is one subject of the project 'Informal Markets and Trade in Central Asia and the Caucasus' (Fehlings and Karrar 2016).

quite mobile. They are definitely operating on an informal level, but do not feel any tensions between 'being here or there' (Freitag and von Oppen 2010), or movement and order. Thus, their translocal experience is limited to their interactions within the marketplaces.

Yet some farmers, in contrast, stay in Tbilisi for a few weeks or months to try their luck at getting more permanently involved in the process of exchange. The exchange volume of their transactions is very modest. For example, they start with a bag of potatoes that they sell for a few coins. They then use this money for living expenses and to buy some tomatoes, which they sell again to buy other products and so on. With a minimal profit, people can thus afford their daily survival and a dirty room in a shabby hostel next to the railway station, where there is no privacy and where they share the poor conditions with plenty of others.[7] Their day-to-day lives are transient, impermanent, and experienced as uncertain — and the more this is the case, the more such an experience can be classified as translocal and at the same time as belonging to the uncontrolled and unregulated sphere of informality. These people are generally from the lowest levels of society and are not even noticed by state officials, and if they are noticed, they are usually perceived as a blight on the urban landscape.

Other people, especially local women from Tbilisi, buy commodities at *Lilo Molli*, which is not far from the capital. *Lilo* is the commercial centre of the region. Goods from Turkey, China, Iran, Russia or elsewhere are brought here and then redistributed all over the area. Thus many (female) traders use the minibus to bring merchandise from *Lilo* to the city centre, where they sell the goods for a small profit on the streets, or in smaller marketplaces or shops.

As mentioned above, there is a kind of hierarchy of markets linked to importance, centrality, size, and price differentials (see Dannhaeuser 1989). The mobility of traders and the system of markets and bazaars form a (global) web of interrelations, flows, and routes, which is at least as fascinating as the ancient Silk Road. Some traders only transport goods from one end of the city to the other, while others undertake adventurous journeys to neighboring countries or even further (see Karrar 2013). Thus, for example, in the early morning, Georgian

---

7   The Georgian movie director Natia Arabuli-Weg shot an interesting documentary about these traders.

vendors, who have just returned from shopping tours in Turkey, sell their merchandise to *Lilo*'s wholesalers, who resell the goods to traders and middleman, who then bring the goods to Tbilisi or other urban centres in the region. From here, goods travel further, as I could observe myself when travelling in the region as described in the introduction.[8]

Having some more capital at hand, long-distance traders, today, usually fly. For example, a friend of mine travelled to Oman by plane to buy some special scarves for a museum shop in Georgia, while Georgian traders, who do their shopping in wholesale department stores in the centre of Beijing or Guangzhou, all travel by air. But there are still people who travel these distances by bus or train, thereby economizing. Most of the petty traders who travel these distances and then sell their commodities in the Caucasus are Georgian, Armenian or Azerbaijani. Accordingly, Chinese factories and wholesalers in China, and Turkish businessmen in Turkey, have specialized in taking on these traders as clients and have engaged Russian-speaking translators to enable this (as mentioned above).[9]

Many people specialize in certain goods and have institutionalized their business, while others are less committed and only occasionally take the opportunity to make a quick deal. Usually, the latter are much more 'mobile' and 'flexible' than the former, which at the same time correlates with the fact that their business is an informal occupation, which is sometimes even combined with tourism.

Goods

One can also distinguish traders by the kind, quantity, and quality of goods they sell. Usually this also determines the location of exchange (Gell 1982), which in turn determines the clients.[10] High quantities and

---

8   There is a growing literature describing this kind of petty trade in Central Asia, the Caucasus, and the whole post-Soviet region (for example, Werner 2004, Yalcin-Heckmann and Aivazsishvili 2012, Turaeva-Hoehne 2014, Holzlehner 2014).

9   At the same time, foreigners come to the urban or border markets in the Caucasus. There are, for example, a lot of Turkish retailers, who come to Batumi, and also a growing community of Chinese people, who seem to establish permanent shops and trade relations, which they organize through their own exclusive (ethnic) networks.

10 Just as with traders, the group of clients has metamorphosed since independence. As an example, the average citizen who became impoverished during the breakdown

quality of goods usually point to more financial capital, more regulated activities, and hence to more formalized business. Small quantities and low quality often indicate individual initiative, a weak financial background, and thus less recognition by state bodies resulting in informal practices of avoiding regulation and flexibly adapting to changing frameworks. Thus, for example, it is easy (and even legal) to bring small amounts of goods through customs without paying clearance. Petty traders, who deal with small amounts, thus simply ask fellow travellers to carry some of the merchandise through customs control, thus hiding the total number of goods. In 2017, for example, I was asked by Giorgi, who has a small shop in Batumi, to take two furs in my luggage from Beijing to Tbilisi; and almost every time I crossed the Armenian-Georgian border, there was a petty trader who distributed some of his bags among the passengers.

The quality of merchandise is often associated with its country of origin. Although merchandise such as shoes, handbags, and clothes from Turkey had a bad reputation in the 1990s, they recently became much more prestigious than goods from China or India. There are changing trends. A few years ago, for example, most of the furniture and plastic toys were from Asia, while nowadays many items are produced in Iran. Electronic equipment, computers, mobile phones, laptops, perfumes, and the haute couture collections are brought from Dubai, cars from Germany or Japan, and sweets and milk products from Ukraine. The most prestigious products are usually those from Europe.

The merchandise is diverse and at the same time it is always the same. You will find market stalls and shops for food (e.g., fruits and vegetables), for clothes and shoes, for accessories (e.g., handbags, glasses, jewelry), for plastic and soft toys, for electronics, for repair parts, for furniture and building materials, for antiques (e.g., books, porcelain), and for items of daily use (e.g., for cooking). There are whole areas, like the marketplace in the city of *Rustavi*, where one can buy cars, and there are sections in bazaars, where there are about twenty or more stalls advertising and providing the same shoes, the

---

of the political system usually bought at cheap bazaars in the 1990s. As soon as their financial situation recovered, they changed their consumption patterns and turned their attention to supermarkets and boutiques. Buying from street vendors, for many citizens, has turned into an act of charity.

same handbags, and the same winter coats. Everything looks identical and vending is quite competitive. Indeed, many traders I talked to in the bazaar told me that they sell less and less. A friend of mine told me that she was happy about this decline in demand: 'It is a good sign for our economy, that people do not buy on bazaars anymore, but go to shops and buy better brands'.

One more feature that characterizes commodities is, besides their quality, their age. While the prices of antiquities increase with age, second-hand parts and clothes are less expensive than new merchandise. However, there are some items, e.g., some repair parts, that have the reputation of having been produced in a better way in former times, which is why consumers prefer to buy them second hand. In any case, the offered item tells much about the vendor and his social status.

Fig. 7.4 A bazaar in Tbilisi: a huge number of goods, which, at least to the author, all look the same. Photo © Susanne Fehlings (2014), CC BY 4.0

Amount and frequency

How do all these goods come to the Caucasus? As mentioned above, some are simply ordered and then brought to Georgia in huge containers. They are, for example, shipped to the harbour of Poti, and then loaded onto trucks, which bring them to Tbilisi and beyond.

The petty traders who bring the merchandise from abroad themselves usually transport their goods in small quantities by train or *mashrutka* (minibus). Sometimes oral agreements between the traders and the *mashrutka* drivers exist. When I travelled from Tbilisi to Yerevan during my field trip in March 2014, the *mashrutka* started about four hours late because the driver was waiting for a young woman, Hasmik, who was heavily laden with boxes of eggplants. When I asked her about her business, she told me that she travels regularly to Tbilisi to buy vegetables and fruits (which come from Turkey), because they are a little less expensive than in Yerevan. She did not tell me whether she was paying something to the *mashrutka* driver for helping her, but it was obvious that they knew each other pretty well and were 'working hand in hand'. During the trip, Hasmik, who was playing the role of an intermediary, was constantly calling dealers from Yerevan to negotiate prices and to arrange the delivery of her products. Yet she seemed not very happy with her job, especially as she was making this trip twice a week. 'You have to eat and I have two children' was her sober explanation.

Other goods are brought to the Caucasus by individuals who are much less regularly involved in trade than this Armenian woman. Many of my acquaintances told me that they use business trips or holidays to buy reduced-price clothing from designer shops. The dates for seasonal sales in Europe are common knowledge in the Caucasus: according to my experience, almost everybody in the Caucasus is somehow involved in 'doing business', which includes all kinds of economic activities and forms of economic exchange. To classify a group of entrepreneurs or traders it is important to clarify whether trade is a permanent or an occasional occupation.[11] Do traders use established business relations

---

11   Sometimes it is not even a professional activity but a by-product of travelling in the context of business or holiday trips.

and infrastructures? Are they constantly involved in translocal networks? Do they run a shop and do they pay taxes? Does their exchange rely on contracts or oral agreements? What is the economic volume of goods? And do the traders trade for fun or do they live on it?

Many people, such as the elderly women I met between Tbilisi and Baku, only travelled once a year, but brought as much as they could to make their livelihood. Their purchases filled up an entire freight container that had to be shipped to Georgia. Other people just bring a few T-shirts from abroad to sell them to their friends, classmates, or colleagues. It is difficult to classify this kind of 'favour' or exchange as trade, even though the agents make some profit. Many people told me that they used to travel once a year, usually before Christmas, to make some extra money for feasting expenses. The motivation and social background of agents in these interactions usually differ very much from that of the elderly women or the well-established businessmen working in the bazaars.

Most of the cases described above are characterized by the small amount of exchange value — at least in comparison to that of international trade companies. Even the economic activities at the high end of the scale are still managed by individuals, who usually run a business with only the help of their personal networks, including their kin. Dato, for example, who perceives himself as a successful businessman and who owns three shops or booths on *Lilo Bazroba*, still belongs to the category of small entrepreneurs. He and his wife run the business with the help of some relatives, and several times a year, Dato travels to Turkey and his wife to China, to buy the merchandise themselves. In Turkey, Dato cooperates with a Turkish businessman with whom he is friendly. His wife uses a similar social network to complete her business in China. Dato keeps the accounts, pays taxes, and is very religious. In each of his shops, there is a corner with icons. He regularly prays and burns candles in front of them, which might be one reason for his satisfaction in life. To be successful, these traders also need a lot of courage or a wide range of knowledge about global trends and local conditions, which are, as a rule, transmitted and communicated face to face. We can therefore talk of this economic trend as something I would call 'informal globalization' or 'globalization from below', whereby a large amount of goods and the overall frequency of this trading activity indicate more informality than does a small quantity, simply because large-scale and permanent trade is more visible, less flexible, and cannot work without institutional support.

Dynamics, embeddedness, gender

A problem for the investigation of the cases of economic exchange I have described, especially the cases of informal exchange, is the fact that conditions constantly change. The national and international political and economic situation perpetually transforms, which has a direct impact on local markets and exchange patterns. One outcome of this fact is that certain economic activities and places of exchange grow or shrink, that people are forced to leave one kind of business to get involved in another, and that people become rich or impoverished. Thus, for example, in recent years, the bazaars of Tbilisi were modernized and 'formalized', which means that they turned into an accumulation of registered shops and supermarkets (see Jaeger 2016). In a parallel development, many entrepreneurs who were not able to pay taxes were pushed into informality, resulting in a worsening of their situation and a growing amount of 'wild markets' and 'illegal' street vending (Khutsishvili 2012).

It follows that one challenge and risk is that legal frameworks — on the local, national, and international level — change, which is why, for example, travelling to certain countries might suddenly become more complicated and less profitable on the one hand, while restrictions in the one country might make it complicated to sell the goods in the other. Such restrictions can take the form of conflicts and wars (which were an obstacle, for example, for border trade between Georgia and Abkhazia); visa formalities and import duties; rising taxes; or new laws restricting, for example, street vending or the import of certain goods (see, for example, Turaeva-Hoehne 2014). A good example of a law affecting a whole economic branch is the announced introduction of MOT (Ministry of Transport) certificates, which led to a panic among my interlocutors, since it would affect and diminish — or even eliminate — the second-hand car, scrap, and spare-parts trade.

At the same time, tastes and therefore consumption patterns follow fashion trends, which is why certain goods appear and disappear on the market (see Bestor 2001). The economic situation in general, however, and only fashion trends, determines consumption. Thus I was told by a friend of mine that, 'in the 90s all women wore the same black skirts from Turkey, because they were available and cheap. Today, there are more possibilities to create an individual look. There is more choice and people have more money'.

Additionally, the ideological, the economic, the socio-cultural, and the historical contexts are dynamic. Central Asia and the Caucasus, not least because of the Silk Road, have a long tradition of trade (see, for example, Kalandarova 2007). Traders, trade routes, and mercantile expeditions, as well as commercial cities, trading posts and *caravanserais*, are part of the history and identity of the region. Despite this heritage, Soviet ideology has brought all kinds of economic activity into discredit. Traders were classified as speculators (*spekulanty*, *galamchilveli* in Georgian), who had a very bad reputation for being 'immoral' (Mandel and Humphrey 2002). Accordingly, it was not obvious that so many people would turn to commerce after the breakdown of the Soviet Union (Niyozov and Shamatov 2007). Today, by contrast, commerce has almost lost its negative connotations. To be a 'businessman', as it is called now, is an accepted professional occupation. 'Everybody is doing it, currently', I was told as a justification. However, people who are seen as too successful are still suspected of being corrupt or having done something illegal. This might be one reason why economic success in Georgia, as people explained to me, is seldom made public or discussed with others.

Another development over the last few decades has to do with gender and concerns my target group. If it was mainly women who worked as traders in the first years of independence (see Werner 2004), which were years of crisis, it is now mostly men who run established shops and businesses. An Armenian friend of mine, Levon Abrahamian, explained this gender-specific development, which was often mentioned by my interlocutors, as follows: 'in times of crisis people return to primitive modes of economy. In the black years after independence, it was the women who managed to feed the families. What they did, was to go out and to sell some homemade cookies on the streets or to trade'. Indeed, it seems that women were the pioneers of petty trade. This might be founded in the fact that the low end of petty trade is regarded as a low-grade (primitive) occupation and therefore associated with female inferiority (see Werner 2004). Some people argue that women are more talented at negotiating. Women's affinity for gossip and communication is often mentioned as a necessary quality for being a good trader, one which men lack. On the other hand, women working as traders, especially young women, are exposed to all kinds of risks, last but not least of losing their reputation as 'proper girls' (see Stephan-Emmrich and Mirzoev 2016). On the one hand, they gain status through their contribution to family income (see Abrahamian 2007); on the other hand, they have to struggle with socio-cultural norms regarding gender roles, which they violate when engaging in trade. However, in many cases women were the first, after the breakdown of the Soviet Union, to take the risk and discover unknown, unfamiliar territory. Only later, when relations and infrastructure were established, when trade became more formalized, did men take over the business.

Fig. 7.5 Female traders at *Lilo Bazroba* in Tbilisi. Photo © Susanne Fehlings (2014), CC BY 4.0

Taking into account the above-defined research units (location, people, mobility, goods, etc.), most of the female petty traders of my focus group can be described as not being linked to specific marketplaces.

They usually have a social background that positions them on the losing side of historical (economic, political, ideological, and social) change. Having lost most of their previous socio-cultural capital (social networks, professional qualifications, prestige within their community) and their financial capital as a result of the breakdown of the Soviet Union and the following period of upheaval, they usually describe how they were forced into mobility and commerce to make their living. The amount of goods and the frequency of their economic activity are rather limited, and the goods they trade are usually not of extraordinary quality, but rather cheap products from informal markets abroad. All these facts rank the economic activity of these women as highly informal. But because their number is non-negligible, and because they cross half of the globe, we can perceive them as actors of a 'globalization from below', who contribute to the flows of goods, people, and ideas across a vast area.

As far as it concerns the women's translocal experience it is difficult to come to clear conclusions. Female petty traders use networks and their knowledge of translocal communities, and they flexibly adapt their mobility to translocal opportunities and contexts. I am not sure, however, how much they are effectively involved in translocal identities. Their experiences are translocal, but their involvement in translocal belongings and their imagination of translocal space seems rather vague and does not really lead to the accumulation of economic wealth. Just as they perceive their activity as a fall-back plan, even though it might become a permanent occupation, they perceive their engagement in trade and translocal networks as accidental, and therefore not part of their 'real' identity. This is possibly the reason why they are not able to fully exploit the chances linked to translocality as described in the literature.

Conclusion

As one can conclude from my examples, one has to consider many aspects to get a holistic picture of the situation of petty traders and trade in the Caucasus, specifically in Georgia. To understand informal trade activity, or 'globalization from below', it is important to look at the very complicated and changing contexts along the trade chains that cross the region. One has to consider the socio-cultural background of traders and buyers in different locations, and one has to take into account different legal frameworks and historical, geographical, political, and macro-economic circumstances on the different levels of interaction — local and global.

In this contribution, I have tried to suggest some parameters, which, taken together, help to describe and classify economic exchange, marketplaces, and traders at the grassroots level. These parameters, along with their specific character and interrelations, help to cast light on the level of informality, and, in my opinion, give some interesting insights into how globalization from below and translocality become real. As I have shown, the specific locations of economic exchange, the social groups of people appearing there, their forms of mobility, the goods they sell and buy, the volume of exchange, and the frequency of their activity are linked to, refer to, and determine each other. By describing these links and dependencies, we come to a portrayal of specific groups of traders and their forms of economic behavior and embeddedness in socio-cultural contexts, which includes the description of their involvement in translocality and globalization.

In my opinion, although almost all traders described above are somehow involved in 'globalization from below' purely by virtue of the fact that they trade in goods that circulate on the global market, not all of these traders live translocal lives in the sense of being linked to translocal space or belongings. Especially from the perspective of those not participating in mobility, the globalized world is only the backyard of their private homes. This is of course a question of perspective. Even the traders I met on their travel routes, for example the women of my target group, who crossed half of the globe, were very much focused on their own problems and duties at home. Even though they sometimes profited from translocal relations, they did not necessarily feel the tension between the relations of translocal connections. Besides, frequently the poor petty traders are people lacking connections of any kind who have to fight their own individual battles to survive. If they had any 'local' or 'translocal' networks, they would not have to move. Mobility can, as mentioned in the literature, of course result in social mobility.[12] This is probably true for many labour migrants, who are

---

12 Kaufmann *et al.* (2004) have pointed to the linkages between physical and social mobility, thereby introducing the term 'motility'.

comparatively successful and able to accumulate wealth. But in many cases, the mobility of the traders I observed only ensured economic survival or resulted in a small surplus, which was immediately used up for personal or family needs.

Of course, it depends who is travelling and why. While the business trips of successful entrepreneurs or the occasional travels of trade tourists are quite prestigious, the mobility of the lesser group of traders is perceived as a marker of their low social status, which pushes them into informal businesses. This was true for most of the female petty traders of my target group.

Thus, we can conclude that informal practices are usually part of translocality, but do not necessarily lead to translocal identities. Informality includes a huge spectrum of techniques of adaptation, which are particularly useful to those who can easily escape state control. In the case of petty trade, such people generally do not belong in permanent locations, they range at the low level of society, they are forced into mobility, they trade with small amounts of goods of cheap quality, and they perceive themselves as unprofessional, which is why they are active only sporadically and if necessary. Looking at the whole picture, one can observe, at least in the Caucasus, a certain degree of 'formalization' as soon as the overall economic situation improves. Thus, since the 1990s, the low end of informal petty traders has diminished. However, as soon as a new crisis arises (for example in 2008) they reappear.

Simultaneously, we observe that all structures are culturally embedded and that state structures are far from being exclusively formal, which of course calls into question all definitions and dichotomies such as formal vs. informal. State capitalism means something different in Georgia than in Germany. Thus, the market economy, globalization, democracy, nation state, and modernization, etc., have to be considered as local adaptions of pretended neutral notions, which makes classification even more complicated.

References

Abrahamian, Levon. 'Troubles and Hopes — Armenian Family, Home and Nation'. In *Representations on the Margins of Europe: Politics and Identities in the Baltic and South Caucasus States*, ed. by Tsypylma Darieva and Wolfgang Kaschuba (Frankfurt: Campus Verlag, 2007), pp. 267–81.

Antonyan, Yulia, Susanne Fehlings, Roland Hardenberg, *et al.* 'Informal Markets in the Caucasus and Central Asia' (unpublished proposal under review at VW Stiftung, 2014).

Appadurai, Arjun. *Modernity at Large: Cultural Dimensions of Globalization*. Minneapolis: University of Minnesota, 2003[1949].

Appadurai, Arjun. 'Grassroots Globalization and the Research Imagination'. *Public Culture* 12.1 (2000): 1–19, https://doi.org/10.1215/08992363-12-1-1

Appadurai, Arjun. *The Social Life of Things: Commodities in Cultural Perspective.* Cambridge: Cambridge University Press, 1986.

Augé, Marc. *Non-Places: Introduction to an Anthropology of Supermodernity*. London: Verso, 1995.

Bestor, Thodore C. 'Supply-Side Sushi: Commodity Market, and the Global City'. *American Anthropologist* 103.1 (2001): 76–95, https://doi.org/10.1525/aa.2001.103.1.76

Bohannan, Paul and George Dalton, eds. *Markets in Africa*. Evanston: Northwestern University Press, 1962.

Freitag, Ulrike, and Achim von Oppen. 'Introduction: "Translocality": An Approach to Connection and Transfer in Area Studies'. In *Translocality: The Study of Globalising Processes from a Southern Perspective*, ed. by Ulrike Freitag and Achim von Oppen. Leiden: Brill, 2010, pp. 1–24, https://doi.org/10.1163/ej.9789004181168.i-452.8

Carsten, Janet 'Cooking Money: Gender and the Symbolic Transformation of Means of Exchange in a Malay Fishing Community'. In *Money and the Morality of Exchange*, ed. by Jonathan Parry and Maurice Bloch. Cambridge: Cambridge University Press, 1989, pp. 117–41.

Castells, Manuel, and Alejandro Portes, 'World Underneath: The Origins, Dynamics, and Effects of the Informal Economy'. In *The Informal Economy: Studies in Advanced and Less Developed Countries*, ed. by Alejandro Portes, Manuel Castells and Lauren A. Benton. Baltimore: The Johns Hopkins University Press, 1989, pp. 11–37.

Chen, Martha A. 'Rethinking the Informal Economy: Linkages with the Formal Economy and the Formal Regulatory Environment'. DESA Working Paper No. 46 (New York: United Nations Department of Economic and Social Affairs, 2007), pp. 1–12, https://doi.org/10.18356/0634a775-en

Cresswell, Tim. *On the Move: Mobility in the Modern Western World*. New York: Routledge, 2006, https://doi.org/10.4324/9780203446713

Dabaghyan, Artak, and Mkhitar Gabrielyan. 'Rural Transcaucasian Trade before and after National Border', *Acta Ethnographica Hungarica* 56.2 (2011): 333–57, https://doi.org/10.1556/AEthn.56.2011.2.5

Dabaghyan, Artak, and Mkhitar Gabrielyan. *Economy, Trade and Ethnicity in Borderlands: An Ethnographical Survey in Tavush Province of Armenia*. Yerevan, 2008.

Dalakoglou, Dimitris, and Penny Harvey. 'Roads and Anthropology: Ethnographic Perspectives on Space, Time and (Im)Mobility', *Mobilities* 7.4 (2012): 459–65, https://doi.org/10.1080/17450101.2012.718426

Dannhaeuser, Norbert. 'Marketing in Developing Urban Areas'. In *Economic Anthropology*, ed. by Stuart Plattner. Stanford: Stanford University Press, 1989, pp. 222–52.

Fehlings, Susanne, and Hasan Karrar. 'Informal Markets and Trade in the Caucasus and Central Asia', *Working Paper Series on Informal Markets and Trade* 1 (2016), urn:nbn:de:hebis:30:3-415163

Gell, Alfred. 'The Market Wheel: Symbolic Aspects of an Indian Tribal Market', *Man* 17.3 (1982): 470–91, https://doi.org/10.2307/2801710

Gellner, David N., ed. *Borderland Lives in Northern South Asia: Non-State Perspectives*. Durham: Duke University Press, 2013, https://doi.org/10.1215/9780822377306

Geertz, Clifford. 'The Bazaar Economy: Information and Search in Peasant Marketing', *The American Economic Review* 68.2 (1987): 28–32, http://www.asia-europe.uni-heidelberg.de/fileadmin/Documents/Summer_School/Summer_School_2013/Frank_Gruener_text_I.pdf

Giordano, Christian, and Nicolas Hayoz. eds., *Informality in Eastern Europe: Structures, Political Cultures and Social Practices*. Bern: Peter Lang, 2013, https://doi.org/10.3726/978-3-0351-0651-0

Gudeman, Stephen. *The Anthropology of Economy. Community, Market, and Culture*. Malden: Blackwell Publishing, 2001.

Gudeman, Stephen. 'Community and Economy: Economy's Base'. In *A Handbook of Economic Anthropology*, ed. by James G. Carrier. Cheltenham: Edward Elgar Publishing, 2005, pp. 94–106, https://doi.org/10.4337/9781849809290.00013

Gupta, Akhil. 'Blurred Boundaries: The Discourse of Corruption, the Culture of Politics, and the Imagined State'. *American Ethnologist* 22.2 (1995): 375–402, https://doi.org/10.1525/ae.1995.22.2.02a00090

Gupta, Akhil. *Red Tape: Bureaucracy, Structural Violence, and Poverty in India*. Durham: Duke University Press, 2012, https://doi.org/10.1215/9780822394709

Hann, Chris, and Keith Hart, eds. *Market and Society. The Great Transformation Today*. Cambridge: Cambridge University Press, 2009, https://doi.org/10.1017/cbo9780511581380

Hann, Chris, and Keith Hart. *Economic Anthropology. History, Ethnography, Critique*. Cambridge: Polity Press, 2011.

Hann, Chris. 'Moral Economy'. In *The Human Economy: A Citizen's Guide*, ed. by Keith Hart, Jean-Louis Laville and Antonio D. Cattani. Cambridge: Polity Press, 2010, pp. 187–98.

Hannerz, Ulf. 'Transnational Research'. In *Handbook of Methods in Cultural Anthropology*, ed. by H. Russell Bernard. London: Altamira Press, 1998, pp. 235–56.

Hardenberg, Roland, and Susanne Fehlings. 'Informality Reviewed: Everyday Experiences and the Study of Transformal Processes in Central Asia and the Caucasus'. *Working Paper Series on Informal Markets and Trade* 2 (2016), urn:nbn:de:hebis:30:3-415178

Harris, Tina. 'Trading Places: New Economic Geographies of Trade Across Himalayan Borderlands'. *Political Geography* 35 (2013): 60–68, https://doi.org/10.1016/j.polgeo.2012.12.002

Hart, Keith. 'Informal Income Opportunities and Urban Employment in Ghana'. *Journal of Modern African Studies* 11.1 (1973): 61–89, https://doi.org/10.1017/S0022278X00008089

Hart, Keith. 'Market and State after the Cold War: The Informal Economy Reconsidered'. In *Contesting Markets: A General Introduction to Market Ideology, Imagery and Discourse*, ed. by Roy Dilley (Edinburgh: Edinburgh University Press, 1992), pp. 214–27.

Hart, Keith. 'Heads or Tails? Two Sides of the Coin'. *Man* 21 (1986): 637–56, https://doi.org/10.2307/2802901

Helmke, Gretchen, and Steven Levitsky. 'Informal Institutions and Comparative Politics: A Research Agenda'. *Perspectives on Politics* 2.4 (2004): 725–40, https://doi.org/10.1017/S1537592704040472

Holzlehner, Tobias. *Shadow Networks: Border Economies, Informal Markets and Organized Crime in the Russian Far East*. Berlin and Zürich: Lit Verlag, 2014.

Iskandaryan, Alexander. 'Formalization of the Informal: Statebuilding in Armenia'. In *Informality in Eastern Europe: Structures, Political Cultures and Social Practices*, ed. by Christian Giordano and Nicolas Hayoz. Bern: Peter Lang, 2014, pp. 451–84, https://doi.org/10.3726/978-3-0351-0651-0/34

Kaiser, Markus. 'Informal Sector Trade in Uzbekistan'. Working Paper No. 281 (Universität Bielefeld, Fakultät für Soziologie, Forschungsschwerpunkt Entwicklungssoziologie, 1997), pp. 1–50, http://nbn-resolving.de/urn:nbn:de:0168-ssoar-422831

Kalandarova, Mastura S., 'Indian Merchants in Nineteenth-Century Bukhara: Trade Networks and Socio-Cultural Role', *Toronto Studies in Central and Inner Asia* (Traders and Trade Routes of Central and Inner Asia: The 'Silk Road', Then and Now), 8 (2007): 93–198.

Kaminski, Bartlomiej and Saumya Mitra, *Skeins of Silk: Borderless Bazaars and Border Trade in Central Asia*. Washington: The World Bank, 2010.

Kaufmann, Vincent, Manfred M. Bergman and Dominique Joye, 'Motility: Mobility as Capital'. *International Journal of Urban and Regional Research* 28.4 (2004): 745–56, https://doi.org/10.1111/j.0309-1317.2004.00549.x

Karrar, Hasan, 'Markets, Merchants and the State: Informality, Transnationality and Spatial Imaginaries in the Revival of Central Eurasian Trade', *Critical Asian Studies* 45.3 (2013): 459–80, https://doi.org/10.1080/14672715.2013.829 315

Khutsishvili, Ketevan, 'Bazaar Culture in Georgia: Case of Tbilisi'. In *Die postsowjetische Stadt: Urbane Aushandlungsprozesse im Südkaukasus*, ed. by Wolfgang Kaschuba, Melanie Krebs and Madlen Pilz. Berlin: Panama Verlag, 2012, pp. 41–53.

Kopytoff, Igor, 'The Cultural Biography of Things: Commoditization as Process'. In *The Social Life of Things: Commodities in Cultural Perspective*, ed. by Arjun Appadurai. Cambridge: Cambridge University Press, 1986, pp. 64–93.

Larkin, Brian, 'The Politics and Poetics of Infrastructure', *Annual Review of Anthropology* 42 (2013): 327–43, https://doi.org/10.1146/annurev-anthro-092412-155522

MacGaffey, Janet and Rémy Bazenguissa-Ganga, *Congo-Paris: Transnational Traders on the Margins of the Law*. Bloomington: Indiana University Press, 2000.

Malinowski, Bronislaw, *Coral Gardens and their Magic: A Study of the Methods of Tilling the Soil and of Agricultural Rites in the Trobriand Islands*. New York: American Book Company, 1935.

Malinowski, Bronislaw, *Argonauts of the Western Pacific: An Account of Native Enterprise and Adventure in the Archipelagoes of Melanesian New Guinea*. London: Routledge, 1972.

Mandel, Ruth E. and Caroline Humphrey, eds., *Markets and Moralities: Ethnographies of Postsocialism*. London: Bloomsbury Publishing, 2002, https://doi.org/10.5040/9781474215114

Marcus, George E., *Ethnography Through Thick and Thin*. Princeton: Princeton University Press, 1998.

Mathews, Gordon, *Ghetto at the Center of the World: Chungking Mansions, Hong-Kong*. Chicago: University of Chicago Press, 2011, https://doi.org/10.7208/chicago/9780226510217.001.0001

Mathews, Gordon, Gustavo L. Ribeiro and Carlos A. Vega, eds., *Globalization from Below: The World's Other Economy*. London: Routledge, 2012, https://doi.org/10.4324/9780203106006

Mauss, Marcel, *The Gift: Form and Reason of Exchange in Archaic Societies*. London: Routledge, 1990 [1925].

Nadjmabadi, Shahnaz, '"Lost in Transit": Ressourcenförderung und Mobilität in der ostiranischen Provinz Khorassan'. *Internationales Asienforum* 45.1–2 (2014): 193–221.

Niyozov, Sarfaroz and Duishon Shamatov, 'Teaching and Trading: Local Voices and Global Issues from Central Asia', *Toronto Studies in Central and Inner Asia* (Traders and Trade Routes of Central and Inner Asia: The 'Silk Road', Then and Now), 8 (2007): 281–300.

Parry, Jonathan and Maurice Bloch, 'Introduction: Money and the Morality of Exchange'. In *Money and the Morality of Exchange*, ed. by Jonathan Parry and Maurice Bloch. Cambridge: Cambridge University Press, 1989, pp. 1–32.

Polanyi, Karl, *The Great Transformation: The Political and Economic Origins of our Times*. Boston: Beacon, 2001 [1944].

Morris, Jeremy and Abel Polese, eds., *The Informal Post-Socialist Economy: Embedded Practices and Livelihoods*. London: Routledge, 2013, https://doi.org/10.4324/9780203740545

Portes, Alejandro, *Globalization from Below: The Rise of Transnational Communities* Princeton: Princeton University Press, 1997.

Rasanayagam, Johan, 'Informal Economy, Informal State: The Case of Uzbekistan'. *International Journal of Sociology and Social Policy* 31.11–12 (2011): 681–96, https://doi.org/10.1108/01443331111177878

Reeves, Madeleine, *Border Works: Spatial Lives of the State in Rural Central Asia*. Ithaca and London: Cornell University Press, 2014.

Ribeiro, Gustavo L., 'Wirtschaftsglobalisierung von unten'. In *Lexikon der Globalisierung*, ed. by Fernand Kreff, Eva-Maria Knoll and Andre Gingrich (Bielefeld: Transcript Verlag, 2011), pp. 441–42, https://doi.org/10.14361/transcript.9783839418222.441

Sassen, Saskia, *Global Cities: New York, London, Tokyo*. Princeton: Princeton University Press, 2001.

Schetter, Conrad, 'Translocal Lives: Patterns of Migration in Afghanistan', *Crossroads Asia Working Paper Series* 2 (2012): 1–17.

Schröder, Philipp and Manja Stephan-Emmrich. 'The Institutionalization of Mobility. Wellbeing and Social Hierarchies in Central Asian Translocal Livelihoods', *Mobilities* (2014): 1–24, https://doi.org/10.1080/17450101.2014.984939

Smith, Michael P., 'Translocality: A Critical Reflection'. In *Translocal Geographies: Spaces, Places, Connections*, ed. by Katherine Brickell and Ayona Datta (Farnham: Ashgate, 2011), pp. 181–98.

Stephan-Emmrich, Manja and Abdullah Mirzoev, 'The Manufacturing of Islamic Lifestyles in Tajikistan Through the Prism of Dushanbe's Bazaars', *Central Asian Survey* 35.2 (2016): 157–77, https://doi.org/10.1080/02634937.2 016.1152008

Thompson, Edward P., *Customs in Common: Studies in Traditional Popular Culture*. New York: New Press, 1991.

Turaeva-Hoehne, Rano, 'Mobile Entrepreneurs in post-Soviet Central Asia: Micro-orders of Tirikchilik', *Communist and Post-communist Studies* 47.1 (2014): 105–14, https://doi.org/10.1016/j.postcomstud.2014.02.001

Werner, Cynthia, 'Feminizing the New Silk Road: Women Traders in Rural Kazakhstan'. In *Post-Soviet Women Encountering Transition: Nation-Building, Economic Survival, and Civic Activism*, ed. by Kathleen Kuehnast and Carol Nechemias. Baltimore: The Johns Hopkins University Press, 2004, pp. 105–26.

Yalcin-Heckmann, Lale and Nino Aivazsihvili, 'Scales of Trade, Informal Economy and Citizenship at Georgian-Azerbaijani Borderlands'. In *Subverting Borders: Doing Research on Smuggling and Small-scale Trade*, ed. by Bettina Bruns and Judith Miggelbrink. Wiesbaden: VS Verlag für Sozialwissenschaften, 2012, pp. 187–205, https://doi.org/10.1007/978-3-531-93273-6_10

8. The Economics of Translocality – Epistemographic Observations from Fieldwork In(-Between) Russia, China, and Kyrgyzstan

Philipp Schröder

Introduction: my translocal field and epistemography

My current research project attempts to capture the 'translocal livelihoods' of Kyrgyz business(wo)men who are involved in the trade of consumer goods 'made in China'. Twenty-five years after the dissolution of the Soviet empire and in times of an emerging 'New Silk Road' through Eurasia, I engage with a broad range of economic agents: Kyrgyz traders in Novosibirsk, who sell Chinese merchandise in one of Russia's largest bazaars; Kyrgyz middlemen in Guangzhou, who guide their clients through the thick of Chinese manufacturing landscapes hunting for profitable wholesale deals; and, finally, Kyrgyz entrepreneurs in their nation's capital, Bishkek, some of whom are, in addition to importing 'raw materials' (e.g., fabric) from China, processing these materials into consumer goods (e.g., dresses). Along these various commodity chains originating in China, my aim is to trace how ethnic Kyrgyz earn their everyday living at home and abroad within their niche of post-Socialist capitalism as well as how their senses of wellbeing and identity are shaped by the myriad flows of things, people, and ideas across the borders of nation states and the boundaries

 https://doi.org/10.11647/OBP.0114.08

of diverse linguistic, cultural, and other environments (see Schröder and Stephan-Emmrich 2014).

In the following paragraphs, I want to expand the analytical gaze of economics — which is said to be about the production, distribution, and consumption of something more or less valuable — into the domain of epistemology. To arrive at an understanding of what my research 'can know' about current trading and other business practices in Eurasia, I will present different ethnographic vignettes that illustrate both methodological possibilities and limitations. In this way, I return to the original etymology of the term economics, which in Greek referred to the 'rules of the house' (*oikos* = house and *nomos* = rule/law). Examples of such vernacular house rules that came to guide my fieldwork include the management of my ambitions for participant observation among traders, the accessing of online 'homing desires' among younger Kyrgyz abroad, and the adjustment to differently 'sized' and 'rooted' Kyrgyz diaspora groups in China and Russia.

My contribution thus conflates two genres that conventionally are kept apart in social and cultural anthropology: so-called 'professional ethnography', i.e., a researcher's (re-)presentation of the lifeworlds of his or her interlocutors as they express them, and a more self-reflective commentary on how this same researcher assesses such self-induced processes of knowledge generation. To capture this, I will employ the term 'epistemography', which Peter Dear (2010:131) has identified as 'an enterprise centrally concerned with developing an empirical understanding of scientific knowledge, in contrast to epistemology, which is a prescriptive study of how knowledge can or should be made'. Returning to economics, the epistemographic notes on the following pages will provide some descriptive insights into my ways of working towards a translocal ethnography; i.e., how I accessed, selected, negotiated, and tailored information for (scientific) consumption in the different sites of my field. This will show that when mapping translocal assemblages, it is essential not only to identify (the transgressions of) factual boundaries of state regimes, social belongings, and so on, but also to reflect on how the particular house rules of a fieldworking reality, as established between interlocutors and researchers, shape the very contours of knowledge production.

Vignette 1:
'He shouldn't see us trade, it would be shameful' — lost (authenticity) in participation

Since the early twentieth century, 'participant observation' has been the key data-gathering tool of cultural and social anthropology. Located right at the heart of this discipline and its fieldwork practice, the professional identity of most ethnographers still crucially rests on engaging in long-term, face-to-face, and close relations with their interlocutors. Most significantly, this cultural proximity — in terms of knowing local traditions and languages — is commonly believed to allow deeper insights into the lifeworlds of others, but also claims to allow for more 'authentic' representations of emic views.

Clifford Geertz (1968:54) once argued that successful fieldwork is about a common fiction, which the researcher and the researched agree upon regardless of the social distances between them and their awareness of these distances. Aside from calling attention to this irony, Geertz identified such anthropological research as a 'form of conduct' (see also Schröder 2014). This again reminds us that, just like any shared narration aiming for validity, the practice of fieldwork draws on certain conventions and strategies. As the following example from Russia shows, one such rule of thumb may be that an enforced 'witnesshood', i.e., an exaggerated connection to a witness identity (analogous to victimhood), which rests on the mantra 'more participation = more authenticity', may in fact endanger the stability of field relations.

In Novosibirsk, the primary topic of my interest is trading. Mostly, this occurs in the city's main bazaar, which, as in other places in the post-Soviet sphere, is commonly referred to as the *baraholka* ('flea market' or 'rag fair'). At the time of my research, Novosibirsk's *baraholka* featured about 10,000 sellers, and with its enormous wholesale capacity it was said to supply 'the whole of Siberia' with goods. At night, when the larger-scale trading set in at 2am, busses with re-sellers from cities such as Tomsk, Krasnoyarsk, and even from Yakutsk — 5,000 kilometers away — could be spotted.

The majority of traders working the bazaar are 'non-Russians' and belong to different ethnic groups from Central Asia. Among them, the

Kyrgyz have the largest presence in Novosibirsk's *baraholka*, and their long-time establishment here is exemplified by the fact that the bazaar's prime restaurant is called 'Bishkek' (after Kyrgyzstan's capital). The earliest Kyrgyz traders — the self-acclaimed 'pioneers' — had already settled in Novosibirsk in the 1990s. Most of them originate from the southern regions of the Kyrgyz Republic, which, due to structural neglect and demographic pressure since the Soviet era, has been hit harder by the later transformation period than the country's northern part. Within the two decades that have passed since this first generation of migrants arrived and settled down, the Kyrgyz ethnic communities in different parts of Russia have grown. Currently, an unofficial 1 million Kyrgyz (of Kyrgyzstan's approximately 6 million total population) reside in Russia, about 30,000 of them in Novosibirsk.

Timur *aka* is one of these traders. I was introduced to him during a fieldwork trip to Novosibirsk in 2013 by a mutual Kyrgyz acquaintance of ours, who I had been in touch with since my first research in Kyrgyzstan six years before. This 'friend-of-a-friend' scenario proved to be a very fortunate door-opener for me, as I was credibly vouched for as a trustworthy interlocutor: one who meant no harm, who was not a 'Western spy', and, most importantly, who already knew about the Kyrgyz and had even 'written a book about our capital city' (see Schröder 2012).

On that ticket, I was first granted access in Novosibirsk and quickly learned more about the business that Timur *aka* and his wife Gulmira *eje* were running together. Specializing in men's underwear, it was part of their (gendered) labour-sharing agreement that Gulmira *eje* was the one to travel back and forth between Novosibirsk and Kyrgyzstan's big *Dordoi* bazaar, where she purchased their goods and sent them north to Russia via cargo. While she was considered better qualified for this task due to 'a woman's better taste in fashion', Timur *aka* was the one who opened up their selling container at 2am and who received and unloaded the cargo.

Similar to many fellow Kyrgyz traders of their generation, Timur *aka* and Gulmira *eje* stressed that 'trading is not our actual profession' and that 'life forced us to get into this'. With Timur *aka*'s background in engineering and Gulmira *eje*'s training to be a nurse, the two indeed belong to a category that has been described as 'accidental traders' (Sahadeo 2011). This categorization alludes to the fact that, ever since

Fig. 8.1 Novosibirsk's *baraholka*. Photo © Philipp Schröder (2017), CC BY 4.0

the later years of the Soviet Union, the shrinking economic opportunities in the empire's peripheral areas have led sizeable numbers of the local population to abandon their original professional education and instead go into trading (e.g., Yurkova 2004, Kaiser 2003, 2005). In this way, many who had envisioned working in Soviet schools or factories became 'speculators' and merchants due to the accident of the regime's 1991 collapse.

For Timur *aka* and Gulmira *eje*, Russia became a lucrative option because, in their native Kyrgyzstan, goods made in China were available at low prices, the borders in between the countries of the region were manageably porous, and because they already had a reliable set of relatives and friends in place among Novosibirsk's Kyrgyz diaspora. Aside from such advantageous conditions of economic development (especially Kyrgyzstan's WTO membership), corruption (cheaper to pay a bribe than the actual customs tariffs), and social networks (who provided initial loans and shared local knowledge), there are matters of identification to keep in mind when doing — and when researching — business. In the self-presentations of Timur *aka* and other Kyrgyz interlocutors, any mention of their hard-earned material success, apparent, for example, in their ownership of several apartments in Bishkek and Novosibirsk, was subordinate to their subjective perceptions of belonging to a collective with distinct features and what they called their 'unique cultural mentality'.

Much has been written about the feeling of shame that such newcomers to trade and the market economy in formerly socialist countries experienced during the transformation years (e.g., Heyat 2002, Hohnen 2003). For the most part, this refers back to Socialist ideology, according to which private trade was condemned as 'capitalist exploitation' and 'criminal speculation' for about six decades. While all traders, who soon operated between the very western and the very eastern end of the former Socialist orbit, shared this background, for the likes of Timur *aka* and Gulmira *eje* there were additional stigmatizations to face. In Russia, just like the members of other ethnic minorities from the Caucasus and Central Asia, they were often derogatorily referred to as 'blacks' (Sahadeo 2012); and for a long time, such everyday racial discrimination made them feel 'as if we are a second class of people'.

During my fieldwork in Novosibirsk, however, none of these aspects caused me to reflect on when and where to approach the topic of trading with my Kyrgyz interlocutors. Ahead of my first visit to the *baraholka*, thanks to the stories I had heard from Timur *aka* and others about their challenging beginnings, about the big risks and even larger profits that seemed to be part and parcel of this place, I was excited about the moment when I would actually see them 'in action'.

In light of this, the first hours I spent in between the rows of containers that make the *baraholka* its bustling and noisy self were a disappointment. When I arrived at the bazaar, after an enthusiastic welcome and a hurried tour of his trading spot, Timur *aka* slowed things down pretty quickly. I could see no obvious reason for that, because Timur *aka*'s business was legal and registered, and he had a license with his name and picture hanging inside his container. Also, there were few customers around at the time, as I had deliberately come towards the end of the trading day. Still, Timur *aka* remained hesitant.

This surprised me, because before, whenever we had met in his home over tea and snacks, he had not been shy about revealing his trade secrets to me (on handling customs, profit margins, etc.). Yet now Timur *aka* was far from his usual proactive self, and despite the fact that my questions did not touch on any themes that I imagined could be too delicate to discuss in this half-public setting, he responded very briefly and with a lowered voice. A final and more obvious hint was necessary for me to finally grasp the origin of Timur *aka*'s distancing in the bazaar. Some days later, Timur *aka* and I had agreed that he would pick me up that night in order for me to join him for a whole working day. But about three hours before our meeting, I received a call from Timur *aka*'s wife Gulmira *eje*. Obviously embarrassed about the situation, she let me know that her husband could not take me with him, because, and then she began to whisper, 'he said that you should not see them trade, especially not at night [...] this will be *uiat*'.

Uiat in Kyrgyz is governed by strong moral guidelines referring to shameful behavior and to the anxiety that someone might lose social face. At that early stage of my fieldwork, it was the first time that *uiat* was mentioned to me in regard to trading. Judging from Gulmira *eje*'s words, the main issue here was not only that Timur *aka* himself would trade in front of me, but also that he would bring a foreigner to the *baraholka*, thereby exposing all his fellow traders to that shameful situation. Whereas during the day, this could be represented as a social visit among acquaintances, at night the obvious purpose of my presence would be to witness people trade.

For my further research, this incident provided me with a valuable clue about an essentialized ethnic identity, which was maintained by Timur *aka* and others from a pre-Soviet and Soviet ethnogenetic template (Jacquesson, Chapter Six). As part of this primordialist perspective, trading was depicted as unusual for those with a nomadic heritage, like the Kyrgyz, but rather was associated with sedentary groups, such as their Uzbek neighbors.[1] Abramzon (1971:109) remarks accordingly in Soviet ductus:[2] 'Despite some developments of trade and exchange with neighboring settled people [ethnic groups, P.S.], the commodity-production of the nineteenth century Kyrgyz society was in a rudimentary [*zachatochnyi*] state'.

During the following decades of Soviet social engineering, such 'perceptions of nationally constructed imagined communities' (Gullette 2010:132)[3] were continuously reinforced, and among many Kyrgyz traders of Timur *aka*'s generation they have shaped attitudes to the bazaar as a (morally) 'dirty place' and given rise to statements such as 'trade is not in our blood'. In the reasoning of my Kyrgyz interlocutors in Novosibirsk, that ethno-cultural element, framed as 'our Kyrgyz mentality', was felt more strongly than the repercussions of the more general Marxist-Leninist ideology, which had condemned private trading as 'illegal, illegitimate, and immoral' (Hohnen 2003:32). (Quite fittingly, I encountered a more welcoming environment with Kyrgyz businessmen in Novosibirsk who were active in the service sector — e.g., selling SIM cards — and who revealed considerable pride in their work when receiving me in their offices.)

In fact, this experience of the trade-shame nexus that I shared with my interlocutors marked an instance of 'cultural intimacy', which has been described by Herzfeld in reference to discourses on nationalism (1997:3) as: 'the recognition of those aspects of a cultural identity that are considered a source of external embarrassment but that nevertheless provide insiders with their assurance of common sociality [...]'.

---

1   Drawing on earlier work, Finke (2014:45) shows that distinctions between nomads and settled groups, the latter, for example, (derogatively) labelled '*Sart*', had existed prior to the Soviet period.

2   Ductus refers to a characteristic way of expressing oneself, either orally or in writing: https://en.wikipedia.org/wiki/Ductus_(linguistics)

3   Gullette (2010:132) identifies ethnogenesis as an important tool in Soviet attempts to socially engineer group boundaries: 'The establishment of ethnic groups, the ideological construction of those ethnicities into nationalities and the development of the nationalities policy by Lenin (which was continued by subsequent leaders of the Communist Party) eventually led to a situation where perceptions of nationally constructed imagined communities became markers of identity. Ethno-national leaders began to use Gumilev's theory [of ethnogenesis, P.S.] to emphasize ethnic distinctiveness and their place in history'.

Translated into a methodological insight, such encounters prompted me to be sensitive about the frequency and duration of the visits that I paid to the *baraholka*. I learned as a first 'house rule' for the Novosibirsk site of my translocal research field that I should assess carefully which of my Kyrgyz interlocutors did not feel ashamed while trading, and which of them did. The latter, just as Timur *aka*'s example showed, may be better suited for an after-work conversation outside of the bazaar. In any case, I took Gulmira *eje*'s call — to which similar such indications were added over time from other sources — as a well-meant warning that otherwise solid relations might collapse as a consequence of trespassing too far into '*uiat* territory'.

Taking this concern seriously, in my estimation, meant that 'travelling with' my interlocutors and their goods, or aiming for an 'apprenticeship' in their trading containers, was far from feasible. Thus, in order to reach 'satisficing' ethnographic data, according to Herbert Simon's (1956) original sense of retreating to a non-optimal but attainable solution that both 'satisfies' and 'suffices', I refrained from an overambitious 'witnesshood': i.e., what I understood as the eagerness to get a glimpse of something that my interlocutors thought should not be seen. I accepted this inability either to 'follow the people' or 'follow the thing', which Marcus (1995) discusses as two of the basic 'practices of construction' for multi-sited ethnographies, as a particularity of researching Kyrgyz trading. I expected, on the other hand, that fieldwork might have progressed differently had I researched an ethnic group with a longer historical involvement in trade, for example the Igbo traders of Nigeria, who have established institutions to bring people into trade, and who thus might have expressed more pride and appreciation for this line of work (see Abimbola 2011).

Vignette 2:
'My Divine Land — Kyrgyzstan'

The previous vignette illustrates that regardless of the material success they have achieved in Russia, many Kyrgyz accidental traders still present their current status as a part of post-Soviet decline. A friend of Gulmira *eje* once commented: 'We [the ethnic Kyrgyz] had been an elite in the Kyrgyz SSR![4] The Soviet Union educated us well and we were on our way to a good future... but now we have to do this!'

Eliza Isabaeva (2011) has made a fitting observation here, arguing that those Kyrgyz abroad who do not work in their actual profession — e.g., a doctor who turned into a merchant (*kommersant*) — are categorized as just 'being in the field' (*talaada*). Furthermore, this is understood as a term with a distinctly negative connotation: 'Being 'in the field' — that is, being somewhere uncertain, unmoored from home, is often used to refer to being lost. The field is not a place of safety but is rather unbounded and dangerous, exposed to social and climactic extremes; owned — and therefore protected — by no one' (*ibid.*:544).

I heard such reflections on the uncertainties and dangers of life abroad mainly from those who had remained behind in Kyrgyzstan and for this reason were worried about a relative or friend in Russia, or from those who were recent or illegal migrants there and thus were jeopardized by racial or administrative discrimination or even the threat of deportation. In contrast, I could not sense any such anxieties among the long-term Kyrgyz residents in Russian cities, who, just like Timur *aka* and Gulmira *eje*, had lived there for almost two decades and might even have obtained Russian citizenship. On the day when I first arrived in Novosibirsk, the friend of Gulmira *eje* who met me at the airport welcomed me with the words: 'Well Philipp, this is our home now, this is where we live'. And, indeed, it felt like that right away, once we drove in her husband's car into the city, continued to a modern 'Sushi-and-Grill' restaurant for a snack, and then had tea sitting on Kyrgyz *töshöktör* (mats) in the family's apartment, which they had already owned for several years.

Although nowadays the likes of Timur *aka* certainly are established in Novosibirsk, all of them still remember quite well the initial stages of adapting to Siberian urban life. To a limited extent, this was a matter of language, as most of them had learned Russian during their school and university days back in Soviet Kyrgyzstan (where the knowledge of Russian was more widely spread than, for instance, in Tajikistan or Uzbekistan). Still, to be limited for the most part to speaking Kyrgyz at

---

4   The statement refers to Soviet policies that aimed to develop local cadres through 'indigenization' (*korenizatsiia*), which Northrop (2004:48) clarifies was an 'elaborate affirmative action program' to 'create educated indigenous elites'.

home, while switching to Russian in any public situation, was commonly depicted as a challenging experience. Among this elder generation, the Kyrgyz language is thus regarded as providing a crucial link back towards the ancestral homeland (*ata-meken*). Furthermore, some respondents, most often men in their fifties, revealed to me romantic fantasies about their imminent return to their native Kyrgyz village, where, as one interlocutor put it: 'I would take the money I earned here to buy a tractor, then rent it out to my fellow farmers and have a quiet life'.

Novosibirsk's younger Kyrgyz provide a clear contrast to this. As regards the sons and daughters of Timur *aka*'s generation, it is essential for their lifeworlds that they moved there as little children, or even grew up in Russia entirely. One notable aspect about these 'second generation' Kyrgyz is the relevance of education, which is projected onto them by their parents, many of whom — as Gulmira *eje*'s friend phrased it — had been 'good specialists' during the Soviet era. For their offspring, instead of dragging them into the 'dirty *baraholka*', this parental generation is prepared to spend significant amounts of money — sometimes up to 500 USD per month and per child — for private schools, tutoring lessons and 'cultural' hobbies (such as playing the piano).

Aizhana is one of these bright, next-generation Kyrgyz. When I first met her in 2013, she was studying to become a lawyer. Equipped with a stipend from one of the more prestigious universities in the city, Aizhana was among the best in her class, admittedly in part because, as a 'non-Russian', she was determined to prove her worth and felt 'obliged' to succeed. Aizhana was certain to be well-integrated in Russia. She held Russian citizenship, and envisioned a future working for 'our government', meaning the Russian one. As is known from other diaspora contexts, the flip side of a child's successful integration might be parental anxieties about a loss of culture (e.g., language) and tradition (e.g., what is 'shameful behavior', or who should marry whom).

Although such inter-generational dilemmas have been part of my fieldwork experience, what interests me here is the setup and expression of a 'homing desire' (Brah 1996) among young Kyrgyz in Russia, i.e., their search for a place of belonging beyond simple geographic location in or outside of the Kyrgyz Republic. In this regard, for Aizhana and her peers, it is not so much language, as among themselves they predominantly converse in Russian, and it is definitely not 'working the land', that drives their attachment to Kyrgyzstan. Furthermore, unlike Darieva (2011) has noted for 'US Armenian Americans', who consider environmental work in their ancestral home to be part of a global framework for improving the future of Mother Earth, among second-generation Kyrgyz there were no similar grand 'cosmopolitan' aspirations. And finally, although my Kyrgyz interlocutors would commonly self-identify as Muslims, only few articulated their homing desire in terms of religious ideals that were directed towards the traditional centres of Islam in Saudi Arabia (Stephan-Emmrich, Chapter Nine).

Rather than being linguistic, cosmopolitan, or religious, the charitable projections of young Kyrgyz in Russia were straightforwardly ethnic and aimed at lending a hand to the 'Kyrgyz nation' (kyrgyz el). Aizhana and her compatriots in Novosibirsk were vocal about the patriotic commitment they felt towards their fellow Kyrgyz, which is in line with the social phenomenon of a 'globalizing ethno-nationalism' that currently can be observed in Kyrgyzstan (Jacquesson, Chapter Six). From my early conversations with them, I learned, for example, about the work of the organization 'Manas'. Named after the main hero of the Kyrgyz traditional epic poem, this group of young compatriots offers free-of-charge legal and other support to recent migrants to Novosibirsk.[5] I also participated in some of Manas' activities myself, such as when, in summer 2013, they collected gifts to be handed to 'respected elders' of the Kyrgyz Novosibirsk community during the celebrations for Kyrgyzstan's Independence Day on 31 August.

As regards fieldwork methodology, my involvement quite closely resembled the classic approach of face-to-face interviewing and following up via participant observation. Still, it was for quite a while that I missed a key dimension through which the Kyrgyz youth of Novosibirsk both organized social support and framed their homing desire: the internet. It was by ways of this virtual vehicle that significant diaspora resources were mobilized and the emotional attachment to an ethnic homeland found expression. For instance, this occurred in the group 'Keremet Jerim — Kyrgyzstan', which translates as 'My Divine Land — Kyrgyzstan', and is hosted on the Russian social networking website 'vkontakte.com' ('In Touch')[6]. Its members, mostly Kyrgyz who

---

5   http://rus.azattyk.org/content/article/25395675.html
6   http://vk.com/edinyi_kyrgyzstan

reside in Russia, share news from Kyrgyzstan, post pictures and video files of Kyrgyzstan's landscape and of traditional food and cultural dresses, and discuss aspects of migrant life in Russia.

Fig. 8.2a 'My Divine Land — Kyrgyzstan'. © VK (2018), all rights reserved

Fig. 8.2b 'Kyrgyzstan's tallest man'. © Novosti Kyrgyzstana Kloop.kg (2014), all rights reserved

In 2014, one of the prevalent stories, both online and in personal conversations, concerned the group's partaking in the support effort for 'Kyrgyzstan's tallest man'[7]. Standing at more than 230 centimeters, Jenishbek Raiymbaev can move only with crutches and in addition suffers from diabetes and other illnesses. After a local news outlet first covered his tragic story, and captured on video how, for 100 Som (€1.50), people could take a picture with 'the giant' in a Bishkek bazaar, it was primarily through the *vkontakte* website that donations for Jenishbek's treatment were raised. In total, a sum of 20,000 Som (€300) was collected, most of it from young Kyrgyz in Russia. In a small ceremony held in a holiday resort at Kyrgyzstan's lake Issyk-Kul, Jenishbek Raiymbaev was handed this donation by a representative of the Kyrgyz diaspora.

The commentaries on this event celebrated it as proof that the Kyrgyz abroad could not only affectively but effectively reach back home. This again must be seen in light of the fact that some of these second-generation Kyrgyz might themselves only rarely travel to Kyrgyzstan. Furthermore, and in contrast to their parents, many

---

7 https://youtu.be/nOgIBtlbo8o

young Kyrgyz like Aizhana do not imagine that they will permanently return to their fatherland. Instead, they have attuned themselves, both pragmatically and emotionally, to lead a 'better life in Russia', where higher living standards join individualized freedoms and meritocratic aspirations to shape their distinctly non-Kyrgyz social imagination. This then underlines Brah's (1996) insight that a (emotion-driven and performative) *desire for home* may be something entirely separate from a (strategically considered) *desire to return home* (see also Budarick 2011:6).

Regardless whether this concerns the present analysis of a virtual homing desire among second-generation Kyrgyz, as expressed within the online group 'Keremet Jerim — Kyrgyzstan', or perhaps the future internet-based negotiations of ethnic moralities among (extended) families that are split between two nation states, when producing my own tri-local ethnography it will be imperative to engage further with the field of 'digital anthropology' (see Horst and Miller 2012). As Kuntsman (2004) notes, aside from the opportunity to create a deterritorialized, yet still 'homey' place, 'cyberspace does not simply reflect existing off-line identities and power relations, but can silence, sublimate or exaggerate them'.[8]

When negotiating 'Kyrgyzness' abroad online, one such sensitive theme involves gender hierarchies and a widespread patriarchal quest to control female behavior and bodies. Gathered in groups such as 'Stop debauching KG [Kyrgyzstan]',[9] cyber-vigilantes make it a matter of 'national shame' and 'Muslimness' if Kyrgyz girls upload provocative nude pictures in social networks. More violently, Kyrgyz men belonging to self-acclaimed 'patriot' groups have spread video files — to be seen by compatriots back home — of their raids through the streets of Moscow and other Russian cities, where they interrogate and chastise Kyrgyz women who they accuse of dating men of other ethnic groups.[10]

---

8   http://www.anthropologymatters.com/index.php/anth_matters/article/view/97
9   http://vk.com/stoprazvrat_kg
10 https://youtu.be/Y_t3gTt4vAQ

Vignette 3:
Dungan kitchen and the Italian pub —
a shallow diaspora

While the previous vignette has shown how young, second-generation Kyrgyz in Novosibirsk advance their 'homing desires' through social media, for those Kyrgyz who operate as middlemen in Guangzhou, the internet serves an economic function. It is not surprising that a person like Azamat, who has resided in this southern-Chinese metropolis for some years now, is involved in multiple Kyrgyzstan-oriented online communities and keeps in touch with his relatives 'back home' through online technologies such as Skype. Despite this, Azamat's digital profile strongly contrasts with that of Aizhana.

To begin with, this is because Azamat is not a student like Aizhana. Fifteen years older, he perceives himself as the family breadwinner and an established business professional, which is also the capacity in which I first met him through a mutual acquaintance in Bishkek. Therefore, Azamat sees the internet primarily as a business tool, through which he can connect to clients, prepare their buying trips, and find essential information about local manufacturing sites. 'In between my trips with these businessmen who I show around in China', Azamat says, 'I basically live on the internet'. To capture this in my research, I was lucky that Azamat allowed me to partially observe his online behavior — not from log files or other secondary documentation, but in person, by letting me join him in his Guangzhou apartment. There, I could quite literally look over his shoulder while he chatted with multiple clients and Chinese factory managers simultaneously, switching languages from Russian to Mandarin and back, just as he switched between the different screen windows of his laptop.

Aside from the invaluable insights I obtained about how Azamat ran his small enterprise, my sessions with him gave me a clear view of the spatial organization of the world-wide web as he uses it. Azamat lives somewhere other than Aizhana, not only geographically but also because he frequents another corner in cyberspace. While in China, Azamat forages for reliable producers and the best commodity deals on regional e-commerce platforms, such as taobao.com (consumer-to-consumer, C2C) or alibaba.com (business-to-business, B2B). He communicates with his clients and factory representatives via specific software applications such as 'WeChat', which is an instant messenger that has most of its 400 million users in China. Knowledge of Mandarin and local search engines like 'Baidu' therefore remain key to navigating within China's state-censored virtual landscape, which is shielded from other international social communication platforms by the 'Great Firewall of China'.

Offline, parallels also emerge to an essentially different private life that the Kyrgyz in Guangzhou experience as compared to the diaspora community in Novosibirsk. By definition, in his profession as a middleman who facilitates business deals between Chinese manufacturers and his various Russian-speaking clients from Central Asia, the Caucasus, and Russia, Azamat's primary task and skill is translating (see Introduction and Stephan-Emmrich, Chapter Nine). This translation work, if successful, bridges multiple translocal gaps among borders, languages, and forms of knowledge. Azamat thereby addresses a divide, which at first glance might be surprisingly large, given that both Russia and Kyrgyzstan share a border with China, and that all of these countries look back at a Socialist past. Yet, on the other hand, China's isolationism is historically well-documented, and from the 1960s until well into the 1980s this was related to the country's deteriorating politico-ideological relations with the Soviet Union (Karrar 2016).

Despite the so-called 'Sino-Soviet split', once Kyrgyzstan became an independent Republic in 1991 it could revive its relations with China (Tang 2000). Still, during the harsh early years of transformation, those Kyrgyz who plunged into an emerging post-Soviet capitalism did not turn first to China. One reason was that none of these pioneering Kyrgyz business people could draw on a similarly strong historic connection to China as was the case for the Dungans of Shortobe in Kazakhstan, for example (Alff, Chapter Five). As a group of Chinese-speaking Muslims, who had fled the Qing Empire in the late nineteenth century to travel to Russian Tsarist territories, Shortobe Dungans managed to reestablish links with Hui and Han Chinese business circles in the late Soviet days. Aside from a head start, the more favorable positioning of these Dungans in the middleman-game, as compared to the Kyrgyz, goes beyond Mandarin language abilities. It entails a more intimate acquaintance with local customs in mainland China and the official status of Dungans as an 'overseas Chinese ethnic minority'.

For the Kyrgyz, on the other hand, the familiarity of shared Soviet history, Socialist values, and Russian language — plus, for some, the existence of personal networks between Central Asia and the empire's northern region due to both Soviet workforce and student mobility — made them see Russia and its burgeoning consumer market as a way out of their own collapsing national economies. As the previous vignettes have indicated, within the last two decades Kyrgyz diaspora life in Russia has become visible, vibrant, and vigorous. In Novosibirsk, for example, there exists a 'Kyrgyz Cultural Center', different Kyrgyz cargo companies and travel agencies, Central Asian restaurants, and a neighborhood nicknamed MZHK (*Mesto zhitelstvo Kyrgyzsov* or 'Place of residence of the Kyrgyz').

Nothing like this has yet appeared in China. In fact, Azamat and the other Kyrgyz I spent time with in Guangzhou do not identify themselves as belonging to a 'diaspora'. Mostly, they relate this to their small size, estimated at less than 1,000 Kyrgyz in the metropolis of 14 million people, as well as to their rather recent arrival, with reports that date the first Kyrgyz relocating there to 2006. Furthermore, with knowledge of Mandarin being so integral to success in the Chinese economy, all the Kyrgyz middlemen I encountered had studied the language, first at a university in Kyrgyzstan and then again in mainland China (often in Urumqi). This again sheds light on why my interlocutors in Guangzhou were rather young, ranging from students in their twenties to the likes of Azamat, who in their mid-30s already call themselves the 'old guys'.

Unlike in Novosibirsk, where bold weddings attended by a mix of local 'honorary' guests and relatives from back in Kyrgyzstan are examples of an extensive diaspora, in Guangzhou I found rather patchy small networks of young families. With only such weak ties to an imagined community of co-ethnics in their immediate living environment, some of the Kyrgyz there expressed enjoying this as a 'life with more freedom' and fewer worries about mechanisms of social control in regard to what a 'Kyrgyz society' would consider appropriate or shameful behavior (*uiat*). 'Here', a common joke had it among Azamat and his friends, 'you just have to avoid being considered an Uighur [and thus a potential Turkic separatist], then you are fine in China'.

This situation opened up new avenues for the Kyrgyz of Guangzhou to integrate beyond their own ethnic group. Some therefore engaged in loose friendships with 'other Muslims', e.g. from Lebanon. 'For food', I was told, 'the closest we can find around here to our national cuisine are Dungan restaurants, so we go there'. And in early 2014, for the occasional evening out among men, the choice of Azamat and his friends was the Italian pub that had recently opened around the corner in their neighborhood.

Fig. 8.3 Zhongshanba neighbourhood in Guangzhou.
Photo © Philipp Schröder (2017), CC BY 4.0

All in all, the Kyrgyz in Guangzhou — and consequently my research — had to adapt to something that in comparison with the situation in Novosibirsk may be called a 'shallow' ethnic diaspora. Among China's Kyrgyz middlemen, belonging was performed less as a distant, virtual 'homing desire' similar to that of Aizhana and other second-generation Kyrgyz in Russia. Rather, Azamat and his peers — partly because they had the financial means to do so — regularly travelled between China and Kyrgyzstan. Usually, they spend their summer holidays and a whole month around the Chinese New Year back home; they also return for important cultural events, such as weddings and funerals. As regards their futures, most young families like that of Azamat clearly expect to spend them in Kyrgyzstan. With fewer opportunities to actually settle down in China, where for instance they are not eligible for citizenship and consequently not able to acquire property, there are greater incentives for Azamat and his peers to try and earn their fortunes in Guangzhou now, then to invest these into Bishkek's real-estate market or another post-China business endeavour across the border.

As for the final 'house rule' of my fieldwork, the previous vignette followed a switch I had to make after relocating from Novosibirsk to China: to look for less 'Kyrgyzness' or a coherent diaspora community in Guangzhou, and instead to follow up on the individual 'translocal livelihoods' of Azamat and other such middlemen during one of their frequent trips 'back home' to Kyrgyzstan. As regards my own positioning, both towards my interlocutors and the themes I could tackle, this substantiates George Marcus's (1995:112) early insight that: 'In practice, multi-sited fieldwork is thus always conducted with a keen awareness of being within the landscape, and as the landscape changes across sites, the identity of the ethnographer requires renegotiation'.

Conclusion: the economics of translocality and satisficing ethnographic data

In this contribution, I made an attempt at epistemography. Lynch (2006:779) eloquently summarizes this as: 'an empirical study of particular historical and institutional settings in which participants organize and deploy what counts, for them, as observation, experimental evidence, truth, and knowledge'. The above pages entwined my own (researcher's) positionality with the situatedness of my interlocutors in different localities of Eurasia. From this I have identified three key house rules that shaped my fieldwork and thus the production of such a translocal ethnography.

The first of these, which debated the essentializing ethno-cultural (self-)stigmatization of trading activities among the older generation of Kyrgyz abroad, cautioned against an overambitious 'witnesshood' that might push the limits of what interlocutors consider appropriate participant observation. The second house rule may be summarized as 'go online!', and it drew attention to the role of cyberspace in regard to a 'homing desire' among second-generation Kyrgyz who have grown up in Russia. Shifting my focus to China, I entered a less intense diaspora context than I had experienced in Novosibirsk where many 'pioneers' had settled already in the 1990s. Given the Kyrgyz' shorter migration history in Guangzhou, which began only around the mid-2000s, and because of the smaller and rather dispersed nature of their social networks there, the third house rule led me to expand from the local gaze, most importantly by following up these middlemen's 'homeland connection' during their frequent return trips to Kyrgyzstan. Some of these house rules, then, relate to accepting the boundaries of knowledge production, for example as regards the observation of trading or the adaptation to a 'shallow' ethnic diaspora. Other house rules are about exploring alternative avenues by which boundaries could be expanded, for example by covering social media platforms or by meeting face-to-face when a Kyrgyz middleman residing in China spends some time in Bishkek.

What these house rules reflect as well are the dialogical experiences which I shared with my interlocutors. These involved diverse negotiations in which the eventual flow of information depended on aspects such as credible access, relative age, the location of the encounter, and, finally, on power constellations. In comparison to my previous research among young Kyrgyz males in urban Bishkek, when mutual and straightforward proofs of solidarity dominated our relatedness (Schröder 2014), the translocal assemblages of my current research comprises diverse sites and types of actors, and turns out to be more multidimensional and complex.

Regardless of whether the setting was Russia, China, or Kyrgyzstan, within the circles of business and entrepreneurship that I attempted to associate with, access depended primarily on credible long-term relationships with mutual acquaintances who vouched for me, and on the professional credentials of possessing a doctorate and being known to do scientific work on 'the Kyrgyz'. Being introduced as 'our already half-Kyrgyz professor' enabled entry into the field, which gained even further traction whenever outside of Kyrgyzstan it was remarked that 'he specifically came here [to Russia or China] to write about us'.

From there, however, my affiliation with certain groups of interlocutors evolved differently. With Timur *aka* and other first-generation Kyrgyz traders in Russia, who were ten to fifteen years my senior, I started off on a quite formal basis that was as much about the etiquette of proper hospitality within the Kyrgyz diaspora as about providing me with accurate, objective information on everyday business life. Only over time, and due to my repeated visits to Novosibirsk, did the likes of Timur *aka* begin perceiving our conversations as an opportunity for subjective self-presentation and intimate reflections on their own biographies. With the younger generation of Kyrgyz in Russia, our relative ages were reversed. As I was their senior by at least fifteen years, it was only upon my initiative that regular barriers of socializing and communication existing between members of different age-groups were lowered in order to encourage Aizhana and her peers to be vocal and expressive about their everyday life abroad. China, in that regard, proved to be an easy-going site. With interlocutors such as Azamat I shared the same position in an idealized Kyrgyz social lifecycle, that of a married family man in his thirties, which enabled us to interact on an equal level. Furthermore, because in Guangzhou there was no one 'elder' to Azamat and his peers, the degree of (re-)presenting 'Kyrgyzness' to me did not compare to that of the larger diaspora community in Novosibirsk, but was confined to dinner invitations at home with some traditional Kyrgyz dishes.

Despite the geographic distance and age differences between them, most of Timur *aka*'s peers in Novosibirsk and those of Azamat in Guangzhou shared membership of what they referred to as an 'upper middle class'. The corresponding discourse of their social mobility from humble beginnings was expressed modestly, yet still it reflected a strong confidence in their achievements. In my fieldwork practice this meant, for example, that I was not to define where, when, and for how long to meet, but that I should conform to their schedule, or that for a meaningful conversation to evolve, I needed first to demonstrate to know the basic methods and terminologies of doing business within post-Soviet capitalism. In these moments, I sensed I was not dealing with interlocutors who would be disempowered by my ability to objectify them in an ethnographic text, but more immediately I understood them to be firmly in the driver's seat during the process of data-gathering.

By considering the origins and consequences of my fieldwork's house rules, this chapter aims for more than a standard representation of my interlocutors' 'translocal livelihoods' in between three countries. Blending personal constellations with historical, cultural and other aspects of these contrasting (fieldwork) locales, in my view, allows for some rewarding insights into the very process of producing knowledge. To document how these always only imperfect and 'satisficing' results are achieved under such particular circumstances may enhance the validity of the written accounts that we offer of our ethnographic experiences. Such insights, of course, are not at all new to the anthropological discipline. They go back to early efforts at self-reflection such as those of William F. Whyte (1943), who elaborated on his ways into and around the 'Street Corner Society' of a 1930s Boston neighborhood in an impressive eighty-page appendix to his seminal study.

However, as the vignettes assembled here have shown, the ethnographic field has shifted significantly, not only with time and the dawn of new technological advancements, but also because nowadays often there is more than one fieldwork location in play. As Barak Kalir (2012) has argued recently, one of our tasks ahead will be to move beyond conceiving of migration primarily in terms of international border-crossings and state regimes that facilitate or impede these movements. Instead, to overcome such 'stagnant' fixation on the paradigm of 'methodological nationalism', we need to expand the ethnographic gaze and embed mobile trajectories within the wider context of their various translocal institutionalizations (Schröder and Stephan-Emmrich 2014).

This chapter offered some illustrations of how this occurs within personal biographies, informal networks, and social hierarchies (e.g., of gender and generation), within imaginations of the future, and, finally, with regards to how belonging is performed and how emotional wellbeing (or discomfort) is negotiated both on the ground and in cyberspace. The house rules of fieldwork that emerge from the various instances of translation and mediation that occur among the interlocutors themselves, as much as between these and the researcher (see Introduction) are part of such institutionalizations. My contribution here emphasizes the translocal aspects of epistemography, i.e., of what can be perceived as observation, evidence, or knowledge in cases when everyone involved in a research project (the researcher included) has been engaging in multiple re-locations and re-adaptations to different national and regional contexts.

References

Abimbola, Olumide. *Okrika — Igbo Trade Networks and Secondhand Clothing.* Doctoral thesis, Martin-Luther-Universität, Halle-Wittenberg, 2011.

Abramzon, Saul Matvei. *Kirgizy i Ikh Etnogeneticheskie i Istoriko-kul'turnye Svyazi.* Leningrad: Nauka, 1971.

Brah, Avtar. *Cartographies of Diaspora: Contesting Identities.* London: Routledge, 1996.

Budarick, John. *Media, Home and Diaspora.* MEDIA@LSE Electronic Working Papers No. 21. London: London School of Economics and Political Science, 2011, http://www.lse.ac.uk/media@lse/research/mediaWorkingPapers/pdf/EWP21.pdf

Darieva, Tsypylma. 'Rethinking Homecoming: Diasporic Cosmopolitanism in Post-Soviet Armenia'. *Ethnic and Racial Studies* 34.3 (2011): 490–508, https://doi.org/10.1080/01419870.2011.535546

Dear, Peter. 'Science Studies as Epistemography'. In Jay A. Labinger and Harry Collins, eds. *The One Culture? A Conversation about Science.* Chicago: The University of Chicago Press, 2010, pp. 128–41, https://doi.org/10.7208/chicago/9780226467245.003.0010

Finke, Peter. *Variations on Uzbek Identity. Strategic Choices, Cognitive Schemas and Political Constraints in Identification Processes.* Oxford and New York: Berghahn Books, 2014.

Geertz, Clifford. 'Thinking as a Moral Act: Ethical Dimensions of Anthropological Fieldwork in the New States'. *The Antioch Review* 28.2 (1968): 34–59, https://doi.org/10.2307/4610913

Gullette, David. *The Genealogical Construction of the Kyrgyz Republic: Kinship, State and Tribalism.* Leiden: Brill, 2010, https://doi.org/10.1163/ej.9781906876104.i-220

Herzfeld, Michael. *Cultural Intimacy. Social Poetics in the Nation-State.* New York and London: Routledge, 1997.

Heyat, Farideh. 'Women and the Culture of Entrepreneurship in Soviet and Post-Soviet Azerbaijan'. In Ruth Ellen Mandel and Caroline Humphrey, eds. *Markets and Moralities: Ethnographies of Postsocialism.* Oxford: Berg Publishers, 2002, pp. 19–32, https://doi.org/10.5040/9781474215114.ch-002

Hohnen, Pernille. *A Market Out of Place? Remaking Economic, Social, and Symbolic Boundaries in Post-Communist Lithuania.* Oxford: Oxford University Press, 2003.

Isabaeva, Eliza. 'Leaving to Enable Others to Remain: Remittances and New Moral Economies of Migration in Southern Kyrgyzstan'. *Central Asian Survey* 30.3–4 (2011): 541–54, https://doi.org/10.1080/02634937.2011.607917

Kaiser, Markus. 'Forms of Transsociation as Counter-Processes to Nation Building in Central Asia'. *Central Asian Survey* 22.2–3 (2003): 315–31, https://doi.org/10.1080/0263493032000157799

Kaiser, Markus. 'Cross-Border Traders as Transformers'. In Raj Kollmorgen, ed. *Transformation als Typ sozialen Wandel. Postsozialistische Lektionen, historische und interkulturelle Vergleiche.* Münster: LIT Verlag, 2005, pp. 191–214.

Kalir, Barak. 'Moving Subjects, Stagnant Paradigms: Can the "Mobilities Paradigm" Transcend Methodological Nationalism?' *Journal of Ethnic and Migration Studies* 39.2 (2012): 311–27, https://doi.org/10.1080/136918 3X.2013.723260

Karrar, Hasan. 'The Resumption of Sino-Central Asian Trade, c.1983–94: Confidence Building and Reform Along a Cold War Fault Line'. *Central Asian Survey* 35.3 (2016): 334–50, https://doi.org/10.1080/02634937.2016.115 5384

Kuntsman, Adi. 'Cyberethnography as Home-Work'. *Anthropology Matters* 6.2 (2004): 1–10.

Lynch, Michael. 'Social Constructionism'. In Sahotra Sarkar, and Jessica Pfeifer, eds. *The Philosophy of Science. An Encyclopedia.* New York: Routledge, 2006, pp. 774–79.

Marcus, George E. 'Ethnography in/of the World System: The Emergence of Multi-Sited Ethnography'. *Annual Review of Anthropology* 24.1 (1995): 95–117, https://doi.org/10.1146/annurev.an.24.100195.000523

Northrop, Douglas. *Veiled Empire. Gender and Power in Stalinist Central Asia.* Ithaca: Cornell University Press, 2004.

Sahadeo, Jeff. 'The Accidental Traders: Marginalization and Opportunity from the Southern Republics to Late Soviet Moscow'. *Central Asian Survey* 30.3–4 (2011): 521–40, https://doi.org/10.1080/02634937.2011.602563

Sahadeo, Jeff. 'Soviet "Blacks" and Place Making in Leningrad and Moscow'. *Slavic Review* 71.2 (2012): 331–58, https://doi.org/10.5612/slavicreview.71.2.0331

Schröder, Philipp. '"Der deutsche Bruder in unserem Hof": Respekt, Solidarität und andere Aspekte meiner Verortung in einer Nachbarschaftsgemeinschaft kirgisischer Männer'. *Sociologus* 64 (2014): 155–78, https://doi.org/10.3790/soc.64.2.155

Schröder, Philipp. 'From Shanghai to Iug-2: Integration and Identification Among and Beyond the Male Youth of a Bishkek Neighborhood'. Doctoral thesis, Martin-Luther-Universität Halle-Wittenberg, 2012.

Schröder, Philipp, and Manja Stephan-Emmrich. 'The Institutionalization of Mobility: Wellbeing and Social Hierarchies in Central Asian Translocal Livelihoods'. *Mobilities* 11.3 (2014), https://doi.org/10.1080/17450101.2014.9 84939

Simon, H. A. 'Rational Choice and the Structure of the Environment'. *Psychological Review* 63.2 (1956): 129–38, https://doi.org/10.1037/h0042769

Tang, Shiping. 'Economic Integration in Central Asia: The Russian and Chinese Relationship'. *Asian Survey* 40.2 (2000): 360–76, https://doi.org/10.2307/3021137

Whyte, William Foote. *Street Corner Society: The Social Structure of an Italian Slum.* Chicago: The University of Chicago Press, 1998 [1943].

Yurkova, Irina. *Der Alltag der Transformation. Kleinunternehmerinnen in Usbekistan.* Bielefeld: transcript, 2004, https://doi.org/10.14361/9783839402191

PART 4

PIOUS ENDEAVOURS:
NEAR AND FAR

9. iPhones, Emotions, Mediations: Tracing Translocality in the Pious Endeavours of Tajik Migrants in the United Arab Emirates

Manja Stephan-Emmrich

Digital practices

Mona, a thirty-year-old Tajik woman whom I met during my field trip to the United Arab Emirates in November and December 2013, lives with her family in a comfortable apartment complex in the emirate of Sharjah. Ma'ruf, her husband, is a graduate of Sana'a University in Yemen, where he studied Koran exegesis (*tafsir*) and Islamic law (*fiq*) from 1999 until 2006. In 2001, he married Mona and encouraged her to join him in his religious studies. Five years later and after the birth of their first son, they returned to Tajikistan and Ma'ruf started a journalism course at the National University in Tajikistan's capital city Dushanbe. After an unexpected three-week spell of medical treatment in an Iranian hospital, the university board suspected him of joining radical Islamic networks abroad and deregistered him from the National University. After 2009 the Tajik government's control over the religious activity of Tajikistan's Muslims further increased, and the Soviet legacy of fearing Islam as 'dangerous' to the secular state resulted in a wide range of media campaigns and amendments of the law on religion. As a result, the family decided to emigrate to the United Arab Emirates. With the help of two former Tajik classmates from Sana'a University, who after graduation moved to Dubai to work and live, Ma'ruf established a

  https://doi.org/10.11647/OBP.0114.09

business trading spare car parts in Dubai. Later, he became a successful entrepreneur selling fur coats to Russian tourists (see Mirzoev and Stephan-Emmrich, Chapter Three). Consequently, he brought his family to the Emirates in order to continue his business and live a pious life according to Islamic principles in a 'Muslim-friendly' environment, far away from a secular state regime that classifies Muslim practices as 'good' or 'bad'. During the two weeks that I stayed with Mona and Ma'ruf in their Sharjah apartment, we had many conversations about the family's mobile life, which in 2013 was centred upon Dubai and Sharjah as their main places of residence and work.

Strikingly, while I shared time with the couple and their (non-) Tajik neighbors and friends, as well as Ma'ruf's Tajik coworkers, our conversations were often facilitated by the use of smartphones (mostly the latest iPhones that the students buy in Dubai). Mona and Ma'ruf's smartphones served as an entry point into stories about their lives and so introduced me to the mobile lifeworlds and multiple situatedness of the couple and their Dubai friends. Furthermore, their smartphones triggered memories and created an atmosphere of shared experience or, as I will argue in this chapter, created a sense of immediacy of spatial experience that was linked to places my interlocutors had inhabited in the past. Thus, in the digital representation of their mobile lives, these far-off places turned into virtual landmarks that formed my interlocutors' emotional geographies and acted as reference points to help them to narrate their religious biographies.

When meeting Ma'ruf in his shop in Dubai's Deira district, or having a business lunch with him and his coworkers in one of the city's numerous Afghan, Iranian, or Central Asian restaurants, or when chatting with Mona and her close friend Gulnora in the couple's apartment kitchen, I was introduced to their Facebook or classmate (*odnoklassnik*) contacts and their favorite mobile prayer or Koran apps. Furthermore, they showed me the online forums and the blogs of former Koran or Arabic teachers in Yemen that they use when discussing religious issues or searching for advice. Moreover, I learned about the latest smartphone cases with Islamic symbols and ringtones imitating the *a'zan*.[1] I listened to the women's favorite Koran recitations and Islamic songs (*nasjid*),

---

1   The call for the daily prayer (Arabic *salat*, or Tajik *namoz*).

and the women shared their digital cake recipes with me, recipes which had been shared by their friends in Sana'a, Dubai, or elsewhere abroad.

By drawing on such digital practices from my multi-sited fieldwork in Tajikistan and the United Arab Emirates between 2010 and 2014,[2] in this chapter I trace the entangled study and work trajectories of my mobile interlocutors. Furthermore, I am interested in how these trajectories intersect with my interlocutors' religious biographies, which evolved over the course of their mobile lives, and which result from their multiple situatedness in different geographic places. While studying in Sana'a's Al-Imam or Cairo's Al-Azhar University, or in one of the Islamic universities in the Hejaz, or while working as shopkeeper, street broker, or tourist guide in Dubai Deira, many Tajiks are exposed to a globally circulating Muslim reformism (*isloh*) while abroad. Consequently, like Mona and Ma'ruf, they become engaged in religious self-making projects that involve moral self-perfection and spiritual progress. As they gain religious knowledge and shape their work ethic and daily practices according to the teachings of Islam, many former mobile Tajik students combine spiritual self-improvement with economic strategies, educational goals, and social aspirations (Stephan-Emmrich and Mirzoev 2016).

The role of new media technology in the migration process is now well-documented. Email, Skype, and social media facilitate virtual travel, i.e., a 'virtual mobility' (Hannam *et al.* 2006:4), and thus connect distant people and places and create a proximity that helps to maintain transnational family ties and navigate the often ambivalent experiences of multiple belongings (Madianou and Miller 2012). However, shifting from the movement of people to their social lives and the use of mobile devices such as smartphones, I show how digital representations of mobile lives enable an exploration of the intersections between mobility, religion, and emotion, or what I call translocal piety. Translocality, as I will argue, can be best understood as capturing processes and practices of material mediation, i.e., of mediating immediacy. I borrow this term

---

2   Multi-sited fieldwork for this project was done between 2010 and 2014 in Tajikistan's capital city Dushanbe and in several regional centres in the Central and Southern parts of Tajikistan (Hisor, Kolkhozobod, Kofarnihon), as well as in the United Arab Emirates, mainly in Dubai and Sharjah. The ethnographic case studies presented in this chapter were chosen from about forty (former) students of Islamic subjects I met in either Tajikistan or the Emirates, or with whom I stayed in both places.

from media and religious studies in order to illuminate the ways my interlocutors articulate affiliation, or at least a longed-for affiliation, with particular places. They therefore make these places, as well as the past religious experiences linked to them, 'real' or 'immediate', for themselves, their social environment, and for the ethnographer (O'Sullivan *et al.* 2004, Lundby 2013a/b, Meyer 2013).

In the second part of this chapter, I take the locales of Mona and Ma'ruf's mobile livelihoods as geographic reference points and highlight how they produce, perform, and strive for piety through narrative references to these locales. Thus, as I will show, they use new communication technologies to underpin their emotional connection to these places. Arguably, these digital mediations produce a piety that is *translocal* because it integrates the locales and the movements between them that form part of Ma'ruf and Mona's mobile biographies and their religious experiences. Moreover, in their pious endeavours, Ma'ruf and Mona relate these locales to each other in order to create or sustain coherence and continuity in their ruptured and fragmented lives (see Giddens 1991:53–54).

As I will argue further, through nostalgic narrations about religious experiences linked to previous places of study, work, and pilgrimage, Mona, Ma'ruf, and the other student travellers I met 'produce' (trans-) locality and thus generate a space to articulate religious ideals, belonging, and an elusive 'homing desire' that is tied to ideal Muslim places somewhere else (see also the virtual 'homing desire' of Kyrgyz traders in Novosibirsk explored by Philipp Schröder in Chapter Eight). This turns their pious endeavours into a highly emotional enterprise. Moreover, later in the chapter I clarify that physical movement between different geographic, social, cultural and other contexts facilitates a mobility *within* religion that creates new forms of belonging, and that expands beyond local or national templates and thus produces hybrid and flexible Muslim identities. At the same time, Mona and Ma'ruf's translocal lives promote a heightened mobility *through* religion, i.e., they are mobilized by their desire to live, work, and study in Muslim-friendly and 'pure' Islamic environments that are in accordance with their religious ideals.[3] The chapter concludes with some epistemological

---

3   While some of the students decided to leave their home country in search of
     a Muslim environment that facilitates the pursuit of their religious ideals, i.e.,
     performing *hijra* (the Prophet Muhammad's exodus from Mecca to Medina in 622

thoughts on how to study the making of religious selves in translocal settings.

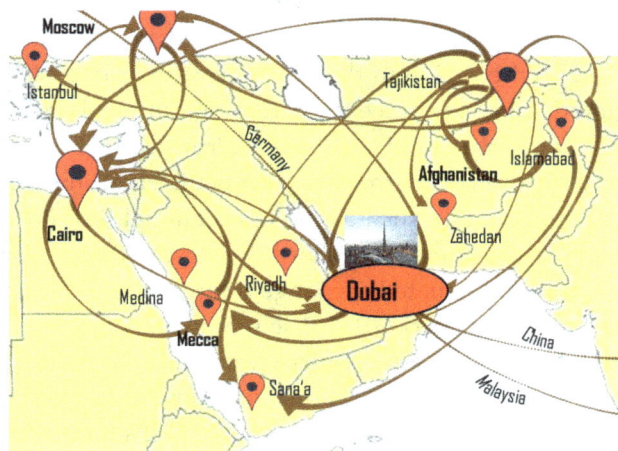

Fig. 9.1 Mobile life trajectories of former Tajik students from Islamic universities in the Middle East. Map © Karin Teuber and Manja Stephan-Emmrich (2013), CC BY 4.0

Entangled pathways to Dubai

In the short period of post-Soviet religious liberalization between 1991 and 2006, many young Tajiks like Mona and Ma'ruf travelled abroad to study Islam in foreign Muslim countries such as Egypt, Yemen, Saudi Arabia, the United Arab Emirates, Pakistan, Iran, and Turkey.[4] Their religiously motivated travel both enables and is enabled by a variety of cross-border mobilities that have reconnected Central Asian

AD) others turned their religious labour, i.e., their piety, into a religious activism that entails missionary activities or religious teaching.

4   The majority of students I met graduated from, or at least studied in undergraduate programs in Cairo's Al-Azhar University. Only a minority of all student migrants managed to earn a degree. Most of them dropped out or interrupted their studies due to financial problems or lack of motivation. In addition, those student travellers in Pakistan, Egypt, and Saudi Arabia who took up their studies in the early 2000s had to cancel their education abroad and return home without an official degree after President Rahmon launched his campaign on Tajik TV in 2010 in order to prevent any form of 'radicalization' of Tajikistan's Muslim youth abroad. Besides Arabic, most Tajik students abroad have studied classic subjects of Islamic education, namely Koran reading (*hifz* or *tajvid*) and Koranic interpretation (*tafsir*), Islamic law (*fiq*), philosophy (*falsafa*) and other subjects.

Muslims with their fellow believers in South Asia, the Arab Middle East, and Eurasia since the collapse of the Soviet Union. In the course of the Tajik Civil War (1992–1997), over 75,000 to 100,000 Tajiks fled to neighboring Afghanistan. There, they reunited with distant relatives who migrated to the region in the late nineteenth and early twentieth centuries (Abdulaev 2009, see also Kamoludin Abdulaev, Chapter One). From their Afghanistan base, like Ma'ruf's distant relative, many became attracted by the international academic environment of South Asian Islamic universities such as the International Islamic University of Islamabad. There, they met fellow countrymen and women who participated in state-regulated exchange programmes with universities in Pakistan and India (Reetz 2014). The religiously-motivated journeys of students to Middle Eastern countries were also triggered by Muslim encounters that occurred in the course of labour migration to Russia. While working seasonally there, many young Tajiks found their way to Cairo's Al-Azhar University through cross-border Tajik or Tatar Muslim networks established in urban hubs such as Moscow (see Roche 2014). Others, however, undertook Islamic study at a university in Medina or Riyad after performing the *hajj* to Mecca.

The new 'objectification of Muslim consciousness' (Eickelman and Piscatori 2004:37ff) in the post-Soviet era has led to a heightened identification with the Muslim community (*umma*) and thus helped to overcome the perceived Soviet isolation of Tajikistan's Muslims from the rest of the Muslim world. The new cross-border mobility refreshed historical socio-spatial relations and facilitated new forms of Muslim belonging that cut across the boundaries of local, regional, and national identities forged by the former Soviet elite and later maintained by the post-Soviet government (Heathershaw and Herzig 2012). Consequently, for many, Islamic study abroad served as a welcome escape from a state secularism that increasingly regulates, limits, and criminalizes any Muslim religious expression not in accordance with the official interpretation of Islam promoted by the government. As I have argued elsewhere, Tajikistan's youth has been influenced by aspirations associated with the internationalization of higher education. While both young men and women sought alternative routes to gain the skills needed for international education (i.e., foreign language skills) (Stephan-Emmrich 2017), Tajik male youth simultaneously accepted international labour migration (to Russia or the Arab Emirates) as a regular stage during the transition to maturity. However, these work- and study-related Muslim mobilities not only opened up new possibilities to pursue individual careers; they also produced a wide range of constraints and limitations. These include the existence of a rigid secular state regime that hampers the professional or educational evolution of Tajik citizens and stigmatizes them due to their religion as carriers of a 'foreign' or 'alien' Islam and thus dangerous to national culture.[5]

While they began as individual religious enterprises that revitalized the Muslim tradition of travelling to 'seek Islamic knowledge unto China',[6] for many Tajiks their study-abroad trips therefore became wide-ranging mobile livelihood projects that link religious pursuits with educational aims, economic needs, and social aspirations. Moving between different studying, living, and working places and thereby manoeuvring within the complex interplay of local, national, and international regulation regimes thus became 'a way of life' that shapes the mobile biographies of Tajik student travellers such as Mona and Ma'ruf. Dubai thereby became an 'ideal place' to realize and combine their study, work, and religious intentions.

When Dubai's oil, property and tourism boom reached Tajikistan in the very late 1990s, a transnational trading sector evolved and integrated Tajikistan's local markets into the global circulation of lifestyle goods. These consumer goods promote Dubai's hyper-image of Gulfian

---

5   In 2001, as a response to the rise of the Taliban regime in neighboring Afghanistan, President Rahmon ordered hundreds of Tajiks to return from their studies at Islamic institutions in Pakistan. The government's fear of Islamic fundamentalism in and outside the country, and of radicalization among its Muslim population, increased further around 2005, when Salafi ideologies became more powerful in Tajikistan's religious environment. As a result, travel regulations became stricter and increasingly aggressive rhetoric against the practice of religious instruction abroad was launched in the public sphere. Popular places of study such as Zahedon in South-Eastern Iran, Pakistan, and Arab countries, where religious instructions is offered to large degree in unregistered institutions outside state-run universities, were placed on so-called 'blacklists' that were spread through state TV and print media, and declared 'not law-compliant' (*ghayriqonunī*). Educational travel to these places without state permission was officially banned.

6   The term refers to a well-known hadith, in which the Prophet Muhammad appeals to Muslims 'to seek knowledge even unto China' ('*Utlub il 'ilma wa law fis-sin*').

Muslim modernity and thus stimulate local Muslim aspirations and desires for social mobility (Stephan-Emmrich and Mirzoev 2016). For many Tajiks such as Ma'ruf and his Dubai coworkers, Dubai has become a lucrative economic hub that transforms their language skills (Arabic, Russian, English, Persian) and their study experiences in a Muslim country into economic capital. Hence, many started to work seasonally in smartphone and souvenir shops or as street brokers hunting for lucrative commissions in order to pay for their tuition. Others cancelled or interrupted their studies and became involved in the transnational trade of modern communication technologies, luxury cars, and automotive spare parts. Still others started a career as middlemen in Dubai's booming tourist sector (see Abdullah Mirzoev and Manja Stephan-Emmrich, Chapter Two). In that way, Dubai became an important spatial node connecting educational networks with business worlds, and Tajiks with Muslim people and places in Central Asia, Russia, Iran, Afghanistan and elsewhere in the Middle East. Working and residing in the United Arab Emirates enabled the pursuit of a career as religious entrepreneur (Stephan-Emmrich and Mirzoev 2016:167ff), or like Mona and Ma'ruf, the undertaking of the *hajj* to Mecca.

Fig. 9.2 Al Nasr Square in Dubai Deira: tourist destination, migrants' living area and Tajiks' workplace. Photo © Manja Stephan-Emmrich (2013), CC BY 4.0

Tracing translocality…

In his provocative reflections on 'multi-sited ethnography', Ghassan Hage concludes that for the study of social realities shaped by globalization, migration, and mobility the anthropologist needs an 'analytical double gaze'. This gaze should be capable of descriptively capturing lived cultures and analytically capturing the global-local relations that structure them, and at the same time apprehending both mobile people's experiences and the micro-social environments and macro-global structures in which these experiences are grounded (Hage 2005:474). In order to track the multiple entanglements of the local and global in this multi-sited human experience, Hage draws on earlier demands for an epistemological shift as voiced by proponents of an anthropology of globalization. In line with this, he also advocates a fundamental rethinking of the spatiality of culture and identity and thus argues for a redefinition of the anthropological field as a 'global site' (Marcus 1995, Gupta and Ferguson 1992, Appadurai 1996, Burrawoy 2000).

However, the term 'multi-*sited* ethnography' reminds us that even in times of advanced global connectedness and in the 'post-national' and 'de-territorialized' state of modernity (Appadurai 1996), the ethnographer still deals with lifeworlds, social experiences, and identity politics that are grounded in very particular localities. Places thus continue to be important as sources of meaning and identity for mobile actors. Translocality, therefore, is both an ethnographic angle and an object of study that responds to the multiple situatedness of mobile actors. The researcher must make sense of ethnographic facts by relating them to the lifeworlds of her interlocutors through an array of multi-sited social, discursive, and semiotic relations (Schröder and Stephan-Emmrich 2014:3). This chapter follows Appadurai's (1996:186) now-classic observation that all 'locality-producing activities' are 'context generative'. That is, they are shaped by the social, cultural, and other politics of a community. At the same time, they are 'context driven'; that is, any such community responds or adapts to wider 'material contexts' (Peleikis 2010) shaped by the nation state, international politics, and global phenomena. Emphasizing the multiple connections rather than multiple sites that shape the Tajik students' mobile livelihoods, I argue for a 'translocal' rather than 'multi-sited' research perspective, because it is the conjunctions, interconnections, juxtapositions, and associations among sites and places that matter most, and which in fact define the argument of a 'translocal ethnography' (Marcus 1995:105, Hannerz 2013). While the term 'multi-sitedness' originated in a methodological discussion, 'translocality' can serve as the analytical 'double gaze' sought by Hage in order to trace the dialectic process of movement and placemaking, but also to illuminate the significant conjunction of place, space, mobility, and the social (or, as in the present case, the religious). Even more, translocality as an analytical gaze detects the multiple ways in which micro-social or local environments and global dynamics permeate mobile lifeworlds.

...through things

Taking these methodological reflections as an ethnographic angle that helps to transform abstract objects of study into observable practices (Ferguson 2011:200), the next pages will focus on specific mobile things, or things 'on the move', and how, through their usage, these things support the production and performance of translocal piety. Tracing how my interlocutors use smartphones (mostly the latest model of iPhones) as a prestigious lifestyle commodity to narrate their life stories and travel experiences, I take seriously what Marcus identified as the core mode for constructing translocal ethnography; namely 'following people, things and biographies' to track the chains, paths, conjunctions, or juxtapositions of locations that shape mobile people's lifeworlds (Marcus 1995:105).

'Following things' also means focusing on a strategically situated (single-site) research object, which unfolds into an emerging multi-sited, or even digital, world (Robben 2013:368), thereby materializing the junction of place, life history, human experience, and subjectivity. Furthermore, tracing aspects of my interlocutors' material culture, and more precisely the way they integrate new communication technology in discursive practices that produce and connect localities, may help us to discern the emotional dimension of their translocal lives (Hannerz 2013). Even more, this chapter illustrates how smartphones support biographical narrations and trigger certain memories and nostalgic moments related to particular Muslim places that my interlocutors know either from their studies, as a place to travel for work, or, in the case of Mecca, as a pilgrimage site. These places provide significant landmarks in their long-term attempts to remake their Muslim selves.

Migration studies have sufficiently described human mobility as an intense emotional and transformative experience. The complex range of feelings that emerge as a consequence of both dwelling within and movement through places produces 'emotional geographies' that play a major role in the ongoing constitution of mobile subjectivities (Conradson and McKay 2007:168), and that provide new forms of religious experience and identity (Silvey 2007). Within these emotional geographies, the material objects that travel with migrants are significant, because they operate both as 'patients', i.e., social agency can be exercised in relation to things, and as 'agents', i.e., social agency can be exercised by things (Svašek 2012:14). For example, mobile material objects may increase feelings of wellbeing and belonging, but they also may evoke feelings of homesickness, triggering memories and a strong sense of home that is then generated in new places (Cierraad 1999). Beyond that, the transportation of objects may contribute to a sense of continuity and 'carry along' memories and feelings from past times and places because they are 'conditioned by emotional discourses and practices already learned' (Svašek 2012:13, 17). Thus, following the 'social life' (Appadurai 1986) and the 'mobile career' (Zolberg 1990) of smartphones helps us to explore the connection between emotional dynamics, personal memories, and religious experiences that strongly shape the multi-sited lifeworlds and modes of mobility among Tajik student travellers (Svašek 2012:13).

Mediating immediacy

The specific articulation of emotional geographies through digital practices guides us to what media theories have framed as 'mediated immediacy'. The term refers to communicative behaviors or cues supported by mediated channels that reduce physical or psychological distance between individuals (and places), convey affiliation, and develop perceptions of closeness (O'Sullivan *et al.* 2004:471, Mehrabain 1971). Accordingly, through mobile devices such as smartphones, student travellers may translate their intimate experiences of belonging to a social environment and thus articulate new forms of connectivity, proximity, and affiliation.

The mediating role of smartphones invites a further conceptual note that addresses the link between religion and media. The availability of new media technology at a given historical moment, as Meyer (2013:10) states, can be taken as a gateway to explore religious changes such as new forms of belonging or the remaking of religious experiences that result from mobile livelihoods. Even more significantly, media that is intrinsic to religion plays a role in practices of religious mediation that link human beings with each other and with the divine (Meyer 2011:23, 27). From such a religious-studies perspective, smartphones and other digital devices are instances of the everyday, and their usage, valorization, and appeal are not 'something added to religion but inextricable from it' (Meyer and Houtman 2012:6–7). Studying the use of digital media devices and how they trigger nostalgic narrations therefore helps to materialize the students' interior spiritual experiences, moral assessments, and the emotional states that strongly inform their translocal piety. Moreover, by narrating with or through smartphones, my interlocutors enabled my study of their religious practices and how religion permeates the everyday of their mobile lifeworlds.

Smartphones and the remaking of religious experience

A growing body of literature explores piety and consumption through the religious appropriation of new media technologies, examining how media engagement, and processes of commodification and commercialization, inform the making of pious subjects, the reproduction of religious experiences, and the formation of religious communities (Piacenza 2009, Meyer and Moors 2006, Armbrust 2006, Schulz 2006).

Schulz, in her study on broadcast media and Islam in Mali (2006:211, 218) for example illustrates how new religious leaders gain prominence and claim authority through their success as a new type of religious entrepreneur. Through various media performances, they 'publicize' Islam, facilitate the adoption of various Muslim identities, and promote religious identity through consumption practices. In her work on 'online Buddhism', Piacenza (2009) shows how digital religion in the form of meditation apps facilitates a shift from an institutionalized and organized religious tradition to individualized, self-tailored, and hybrid religious practices embedded in everyday routines that may induce psychological wellbeing. Moreover, mobile or digital religion allows for greater flexibility in constructing religious identity than traditional forms of religiosity and emphasizes a personal authority to align oneself with self-defined ideals and aims (*ibid.*:11–12).

Tajik student travellers consume the media performance of a great variety of locally and globally active Muslim leaders. These global leaders, either known personally or from Muslim blogs and online forums, serve Tajik student travellers as an important point of reference in their biographical accounts. As the following case study illustrates, photographs or images stored in smartphones become 'chronotopes' that structure time and space, and that map the students' emotional geographies on a semantic landscape. Thus, digital photographs link my interlocutors' religious evolution with places they imagine as future destinations, or that they inhabited during their study or work time abroad.

During the two weeks that I stayed with Mona, Ma'ruf, and their three sons in their Sharjah apartment, we had many conversations about the family's mobile life: their study in Yemen, their family life and work in the United Arab Emirates, the Tajik home they had left behind in 2006, and their *hajj* to Mecca in 2012. Personal photographs played a key role in these discussions. Mona showed me extensive collections of images on her iPhone from close kin that stayed behind in Tajikistan, family photos from Mecca, and selfies showing the couple as students in Sana'a dressed up in typical Arab clothing: for men the traditional garment (*thawb*), long beard, and headgear, and for women the black garment (*abaya*) and face veil (*niqob*). The smartphone thereby operates both as 'agent' and 'patient': when storing personal photographs, the smartphone enables the transformation of memories, experiences, and imaginations into a resource Mona can fall back on to 'make sense' of their travel trajectories. Thus, Mona assembles the fragments of her religious experiences at home and abroad into a coherent story of religious awakening and refashions herself and her husband as pious Muslims.

Once, while sitting together with a Tajik neighbor and close friend Gulnora, Mona showed me a self-made digital compilation of photographs of her favorite Islamic preachers (*olimhoi muqaddastarin*). Merging the great variety of Islamic doctrines that shape Mona's educational biography and spiritual progress, some of the personalities assembled on her iPhone also connect the core locations of the couple's mobile pathways.

Among others, the photo compilation showed Hoji Akbar Turajonzoda, one of the most influential Muslim leaders in Tajikistan today. Turajonzoda is from Mona's natal village in the Kofarnihon region, and his image triggers childhood memories connected with her strict religious upbringing in a respected, religiously educated family (*makhsum*) (see Malikov in Chapter Three) that cultivated close contacts with Turajonzoda, his family, and other currently influential Islamic figures in Tajikistan. Storing his photo in her mobile phone expresses Mona's religious attachment to the local Islamic tradition of a religious nobility and maintains her emotional connectedness to her natal family and village community. At the same time, when viewing Turajonzoda's image, Mona produces a sense of the immediacy of her lived experiences and the childhood memories attached to her birth place. But this is above all a place she had to leave due to a political environment that obviously disadvantages Muslims whose religious biographies do not match the official interpretation of a 'homegrown' Tajik Islam. At the same time, Mona is from a region suspected to be the base for political opposition during and after the civil war. This fact hampers the couple's ability to pursue an educational or professional career in Tajikistan's public sector. Obviously, and as the following short conversation between Mona, her friend Gulnora, and me shows, translocality can be a highly ambivalent experience, requiring substantial emotional work to balance both the joys and constraints of multiple belonging.

> Mona: 'Sometimes, I miss my mother and my sisters so much that I start crying. We only see each other once a year, if at all. We travel to Tajikistan to visit 'our folk' (*avdlodamon*) (only) during Ramadan. [...] I gave birth to two of my sons in Tajikistan. I convinced (Ma'ruf) to travel home to give birth there. That's where my mother is, my sisters are, that's the place where I was born'.

Thereafter, Gulnora explains jokingly: 'That's why she wants so many children. That's a good reason to travel home and stay with her folks for a long period of time'. (*Both women laugh.*)[7]

Another photo in Mona's iPhone shows the so-called 'global mufti' Yusuf al-Qaradawi, an Arab Islamic scholar and TV preacher (see Skovgaard and Gräf 2009), and the Saudi Arabian preacher Muhammad al-Arifi. Both are popular authorities among Tajiks working and living in the Arab Emirates. Al-Arifi's visits to Dubai's city centre mosques, or Al-Qaradawi's sermons broadcast on TV and internet channels such as YouTube, awaken feelings of belonging in the followers of rising Muslim media stars who claim 'global authority' and facilitate the adoption of supranational and cosmopolitan orientations. The latter find expression in Mona's enthusiastic descriptions of a sermon that Al-Arifi delivered in Dubai in 2012. The sermon was extensively discussed by Mona, Gulnora, and other Muslim women from Tajikistan, Afghanistan, Lebanon, Egypt, and Pakistan who regularly attend a Koranic reading group in the neighborhood mosque close to Mona's apartment block in Sharjah. Such religious events confirm the women's belonging to and 'feeling at home' in the culturally mixed urban environment amid the conviviality of Muslim friends, neighbors, and students who share similar mobile biographies, and who, by sharing memories, enhance their religious experiences abroad.

The photo of Abd al-Madjid al-Zindani, founder of the Yemeni Muslim Brotherhood and al-Imam University in Sana'a, reminds Mona of her years of studying in Yemen. After getting married in 2000, she joined her husband and studied Arabic, Koranic recitation (*tajvid*), and Islamic principles (*aqidai Islom*) at an Islamic learning centre in Sana'a. Having been taught by Al-Zindani himself, Mona cultivates a piety that centres around the daily reading and reciting of the Koran as a practice of self-discipline, self-perfection that helps her to become a pure Muslim (*musulmoni pok*). Placing Mona's religious experience within the context

---

7   In Tajikistan, many of the student travelers who return from their Islamic studies in Arab countries are suspected of having joined foreign radical Islamic movements and are therefore placed under state surveillance. Under these political constraints and in order to build trust I did not record my conversations. As a result, the conversations or statements are given as paraphrases but not as direct speech.

of a purist, script-based, and formal religious instruction, the photo also 'carries along' positive memories of, and nostalgic feelings for, her past studies. These include her assessment of her personal freedom, her view of her encounters with other Muslims as an exciting adventure, and the hard intellectual labour and focused learning that made her a new, more conscious, and pious Muslim woman (*mu'min*). Moreover, through her nostalgic memories, Mona imagines her study place as an ideal Muslim place. Thus these memories support her articulation of religious ideals and longing for a joyful past and her nostalgia provides the parameters with which to evaluate her current imperfect pious life in Sharjah. She thereby articulates the 'idea' of an ideal Muslim place somewhere else that facilitates the best conditions for learning and for becoming a devoted believer (*mu'min, musulmoni haqiqiy*):

> 'Our life in Sana'a was perfect, full of happiness. I had the whole day to devote to my studies. Nothing and nobody distracted me. At the time when we left for home (to Tajikistan), I had mastered both reading and writing Arabic and reciting the whole Koran. But here (in Sharjah), being occupied with child-care and housework, I have difficulties reciting the Koran consistently. I cannot gather myself and I don't improve my reading. I am weak (*zayf*)'.

Another ideal Muslim place can be found in the nostalgic reminiscences evoked by the image of the current Imam of the Al-Haram mosque in Mecca, Abdel Rahman al-Sudais. The image, taken from a webpage, reminds Mona of her and her husband's pilgrimage to Mecca in 2012. Describing the *hajj* as the peak of her pious endeavours, Mona completes her religious biography with an intense spiritual experience, and a religious awakening that symbolizes the 'immaterial' success of her study enterprise. The pilgrimage, however, led to a moral reassessment of the couple's former pious pursuits, which were focused on Dubai as a Muslim-friendly place and stimulated Mona's longing to relocate to Mecca, for her the purest and most sacred site in the Muslim world:

> 'When we left our home (in Tajikistan), I imagined Dubai as a paradise (*bihisht*). Many mosques within walking distance, no alcohol, women's space in public transport, no Islamic dress regulations (as governing the expression of Muslim piety in the public space in her home country Tajikistan). [...] But the *hajj* opened my eyes. Back at Dubai airport I realized, Dubai is not a paradise; it is a hell (*duzakh*). The many unbelievers (*kofirho*), the many drunken and uncovered Russian tourists,

the streets full of prostitutes. Also, our neighborhood changed. When we settled here, we were only Muslims, from Pakistan, Afghanistan, Egypt, Syria, Tajikistan. But now, more and more *kofir* are occupying our area. I don't feel comfortable here any longer. That's why we are going to leave in the near future. My husband already started looking for work in Saudi Arabia (*Arabiston*). We wish to live in Mecca. For us, it is the best place (*joyi muqaddastarin*), the purest place (*joyi poktarin*) in the world'.

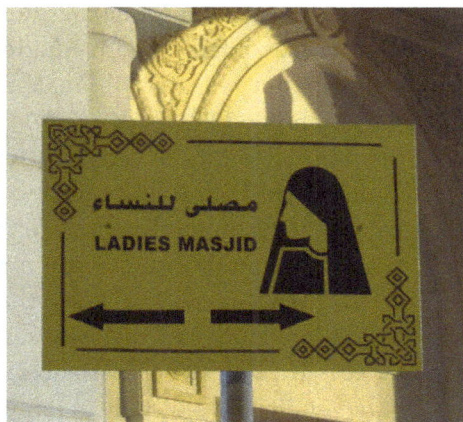

Figs. 9.3 and 9.4 The United Arab Emirates as the 'ideal Muslim place': a neighbourhood mosque in the emirate Sharjah, a signpost near a women's mosque in Dubai. Photos © Manja Stephan-Emmrich (2013), CC BY 4.0

Religious reform, emotion, and a 'mobility within religion'

The nostalgic stories elicited by the images of Islamic personalities exemplify the important role that digital media play in the Tajik students' mobile everyday lives, and also in the formation of their religious selves. Narrating life stories through prestigious lifestyle commodities such as the latest iPhone is also a common discursive practice in Mona's social environment in Dubai, through which her multiple belongings and her virtual, spatial, and imagined movements between different locales and times are substantiated.

New forms of media introduce novel ways in which the 'religious' is circulated, or mediated (Lundby 2013b:190–91). It follows, then, that the contemporary mediation of religion needs to be seen in terms of its 'aesthetic capacities' or 'sensational forms' that materialize the divine (see Lundby: *ibid.*, Orsi 2012:147, see Meyer 2013:7). Tracing the aesthetic and sensational capacity of Mona's digital photo compilation to trigger biographical narratives thus helps to explore how the religious reform projects that Mona, her husband, and other former students of Islam pursue intersect with emotional engagement. Muslim reformism is above all a reflexive self-making project based on education (Frisk 2009, Mahmood 2011, Janson 2014). 'Knowing Islam' thus results from the intensive study of religious texts combined with learning Arabic, frequently reciting the Koran, and strictly following Islamic principles. According to Mona, Ma'ruf, and their Muslim friends in Dubai and Sharjah, individual religious improvement leads to increasing 'inner belief' (*iymon*) and facilitates the experience of a deep feeling of closeness to God (*ba khudo nazdik, taqvo*). Mona's efforts to increase and perfect such religious experiences, as well as her critical self-evaluation of the religious work done in daily life, turn her pious endeavours into a highly emotional enterprise. This accords with Meyer (2013:9) who states that global religious reform movements are strongly related to the body and mobilize it as a sensorial and material ground of religious experience and sensation. Moreover, it shows that emotions can be part of a strategy for involvement in Islamic revitalization. Thus, the self-conscious cultivation of feeling is part of a long-term religious program (see Gade 2008:44, 47).

At the same time, Mona's emotional attachment to certain Muslim locales produces a hybrid religious belonging and positioning within different and often contradictory discursive fields of Islamic tradition. Moving in, through, and between these discursive fields, i.e., being 'mobile within religion', the former student navigates her pious ideals through the various mobility regimes that affect her and her family's mobile livelihood. In this way, Mona and her husband are taking an active part in the 'constant struggles to understand, query, embody, celebrate, and transform categories of […] difference, belonging, or otherness' pushed by the government and the hegemony of these very regimes (Salazar and Glick Schiller 2013:189, Ong 1999:16).

Translocality thus becomes a process of mediating, translating, and transforming religious experience and imagination. Following Lundby (2013b:193) and Latour (2005:39), Tajik student travellers such as Mona and Ma'ruf appear as 'mediators' who carry the meaning of the cultural and social activities in which they are involved during their travel. More than that, in the dialectic process of movement and placemaking, the students transform, translate, modify, and distort these very meanings and thereby contribute to or initiate religious change. Returning then to the entangled relationship between digital technology and religion, Lundby (2013b:192) rightly points to the transformative effect of digital media. With its multimodality, interactivity, and flexibility, digital media shapes the religious subject, creates new spaces to mediate religious experience and imagination, and thus serves the expression of religiosity (see also Campbell 2012 and Hover 2012), or more specifically, translocal piety.

However, by using not just any smartphone but specifically the latest iPhones,[8] Mona, Ma'ruf, and the other student travellers I met in Tajikistan and the United Arab Emirates narrated their religious biographies through a 'sign-commodity', i.e., a prestigious object that gained its economic value in the course of the 'Dubai boom'. Smartphones (and in particular iPhones) have therefore become associated by compatriots at home with the economic success, the modern lifestyles, and the spiritual progress of the many Tajiks who like Ma'ruf have become involved successfully in Dubai's various business sectors (Stephan-Emmrich and Mirzoev 2016). As Meyer *et al.* (2010:209) state, the meaning of a material object draws from 'its circulation, its local adaptation, from what people do with it, and from the affective and conceptual schemes whereby users apprehend an object'. Combining the study of mobile actors and their existential experiences in migration with that of mobile things, and examining how such mobile things as smartphones are used to refashion Muslim selves, may therefore also help us to understand the social contexts in which these politics of representation take place. These contexts also frame how my interlocutors link their spiritual achievements with

---

8   Most of the iPhones in use, however, were inexpensive fakes 'made in China' and
     are sold either in Dubai's streets or by traders in Tajikistan's bazaars and city malls.

aspirations for social mobility and economic success in sensational ways, and how they thereby also materialize their sense of wellbeing.

Some epistemological notes on 'translocal ethnography'

Having explored the translocal piety of Tajik student travellers from the angle of digital practices, I will turn now to ongoing epistemic reflections on the production of anthropological facts about mobile people's religious experiences in globalized lifeworlds. To sum up the ongoing methodological debates caused by the notion of 'multi-sited ethnography', one core issues stands out: if we acknowledge the difficulties of mobile ethnography as guided by classic, Malinowskian ideals and norms, according to which one conducts anthropological fieldwork at a single geographical and territorial field site, we must also acknowledge the urgent need to redefine the idea of the anthropological field site and its privileged status in the construction of anthropological knowledge.

Hage (2005) has illustrated the ethnographer's limited time, material, and mental capacities to follow his or her mobile interlocutors to their numerous geographical locations in order to produce 'thick descriptions' of their complex, multiply-situated lived realities. Taking up Hannerz' (2013) plea for a 'translocal' rather than 'multi-sited' research perspective that traces the multiple connections, conjunctions, and associations of the places inhabited by mobile people, I instead argue that following people and things does not necessarily condition the ethnographer's spatial movement and physical presence at *all* locales. In fact, as Philipp Schröder shows in Chapter Eight, if the ethnographer is too much of witness, i.e., too present, this may even endanger fieldwork relations.

In order to produce ethnographic facts about multi-sited lives, we must question the holistic ambitions of classic anthropology and admit that 'ethnography is an art of the possible' (Hannerz 2013:407). Hannerz' epistemic contribution is in line with Ferguson's (1999:208) argument that because, in some field contexts, more people are strangers, or outsiders, just like the anthropologist herself, anthropological understanding takes on a different character when trying to understand things in the way my interlocutors do. That is, like her interlocutors the anthropologist misses most of what is going on in her field site. This, as Hannerz states, can be as true in both single-site and multi-site ethnographies because this insight problematizes the general relationship between the knowledge of the interlocutor and the ethnographer (Hannerz 2013:405). Such considerations should by no means obscure the fact that the ethnographer's presence in the field determines how, why, and by whom things are said (or not). But they may open up new epistemological avenues to track how anthropological knowledge about individual translocal religious experience is produced in digitalized fields.

Following van de Port (2011:316) and Meyer (2013:5–6), cultural mediation is the practice of world-making that engenders shared worlds of lived experience. Thus, mediation is a communicative process through which social (or, as here, religious) worlds are made. Mediation produces a shared world to be inhabited, taken for 'real' and experienced as 'immediate'. Accordingly, the discursive practices of Tajik student travellers whom I met in the United Arab Emirates not only enabled me to explore how translocal religious subjects are produced or 'made' through digital practices. The invitation of Ma'ruf, Mona and other interlocutors to share their digital worlds of nostalgia, memory, and spiritual longing, even after my return home to Germany, turns the processes of mediating immediacy into an intersubjective and continuous process of communicating individual religious transformation. I stay connected virtually with Mona, her family, and friends. Tracing them online through my own smartphone induces the methodological transition from the ethnographer's physical to a virtual co-presence that transcends the geographic and conceptual boundaries between the 'fieldwork site' and the ethnographer's 'home place'.

To sum up, the significant role played by the researcher's involvement in the digital practices of her interlocutors in mapping emotional geographies illustrates that the idea of 'translocality' is not restricted to the dialectic process of movement and placemaking. Instead, by tackling the spatiality of mobile people's experiences and biographies, translocal ethnography invites the inclusion of other, i.e., virtual, imagined, or affective 'fieldsites' to capture people's movement and connectedness *through space and time.* Such 'alternative spatialisations', as shown in this chapter, help to understand religious being, becoming, and having-been in the complex reality of peoples' lives on the move. Consequently, translocality, both as a research object and a perspective, also covers interlacing temporalities, or transtemporality, as described in the introduction to this edited volume. Nostalgia, as an attachment to the past, helps make sense of people's present lives and futures, but at the same time plays a major role in the conservation of a 'sense' of locality. Demonstrating how the discursive production of locality is bound to inhabited pasts, and, conversely, how the past is materialized through the production of locales, Mona's photo compilation exemplifies what Smith (2011:190) describes as an 'iconic rendering of past experience' that also constitutes markers of translocal connectivity. In other words, by 'freezing the past', the iconography of Mona's mobile photo library also represents a 'nostalgic longing to belong to somewhere else' (*ibid.*). Following this continuous reprocessing of 'home' across different sites of mobility (Taylor 2013), translocal ethnography produces 'field sites' that are not only 'geographically non-contiguous' (Hage 2005:467), but also encompass multiple temporalities. These temporalities, however, become increasingly facilitated by the flexibility, multimodality, and 'deterritoriality' of digital media. Sharing my interlocutors' mobile lifeworlds virtually while physically absent from the field site, I am thus able to trace not only the narrated past and present of their religious reform projects but to follow how their translocal piety merges into articulated moral, social, and economic futures.

Tracing the significance of time and place to the pious enterprises that Tajik migrants create when they move within their virtual emotional geographies, pious enterprises that are managed by their mobile phones, translocal ethnography turns the field into a single 'global site', or more concretely, *the* global site occupied by my mobile interlocutors (Hage 2005:466). Following the notion of a single global field site, the usage of new media and communication technology encourages an 'exploratory freedom' away from the Malinowskian paradigm and complements the ethnographer's physical presence in a (here: religious) field that has become highly virtual and mobile (Marcus 2009).

References

Abdulaev, Kamol. *Ot Sintsiana do Khorasana. Iz Istorii Sredneaziatskoi Emigratsii 20 veka*. Dushanbe: Irfon, 2009.

Appadurai, Arjun. *Modernity at Large: Cultural Dimensions of Globalization*. Minneapolis: University of Minnesota Press, 1996.

Appadurai, Arjun, ed. *The Social Life of Things. Commodities in Cultural Perspective*. Cambridge: Cambridge University Press, 1986.

Armbrust, Walter. 'Synchroning Watches: The State, the Consumer, and Sacred Times in Ramada Television'. In Birgit Meyer and Annelie Moors, eds. *Religion, Media, and the Public Sphere*. Bloomington: Indiana University Press, 2006, pp. 207–26.

Burrawoy, Michael, ed. *Global Ethnography. Forces, Connections, and Imaginations in a Postmodern World*. Berkeley: University of California Press, 2000.

Cierraad, Irene. 'Durch Windows: Female Virtue and Female Vice'. In Irene Cierraad, ed. *At Home. An Anthropology of Domestic Space*. Syracuse: Syracuse University Press, 1999, pp. 31–52.

Conradson, David, and Deirdre McKay. 'Translocal Subjectivities: Mobility, Connection, Emotion'. *Mobilities* 2.2 (2007): 167–74, https://doi.org/10.1080/17450100701381524

Eickelman, Dave F., and James P. Piscatori. *Muslim Politics*. Princeton: Princeton University Press, 1996.

Ferguson, James. 'Novelty and Method. Reflections on Global Fieldwork'. In Simon Coleman and Pauline von Hellermann, eds. *Multi-sited Ethnography. Problems and Possibilities in the Translocation of Research Methods*. New York: Routledge, 2011, pp. 197–207.

Ferguson, James. *Expectations of Modernity. Myths and Meanings of Urban Life on the Zambian Copperbelt*. Berkeley: University of California Press, 1999.

Findlay, Allan M. 'Skilled Transients. The Invisible Phenomenon'. In Robin Cohen, ed. *The Cambridge Survey of Work Migration*. Cambridge: Cambridge University Press, 1995, pp. 510–15.

Freitag, Ulrike, and Achim von Oppen, eds. *Translocality. The Study of Globalising Processes from a Southern Perspective*. Leiden: Brill, 2010.

Frisk, Sylva. *Submitting to God. Women and Islam in Urban Malaysia*. Copenhagen: NIAS Press, 2009.

Gade, Anna M. 'Islam'. In John Corrigan, ed. *The Oxford Handbook of Religion and Emotion*. Oxford: Oxford University Press, 2008, pp. 35–50, https://doi.org/10.1093/oxfordhb/9780195170214.003.0003

Giddens, Anthony. *Modernity and Self-Identity: Self and Society in the Late Modern Age*. Stanford: Stanford University Press, 1991.

Gupta, Akhil, and James Ferguson. 'Beyond "Culture": Space, Identity, and the Politics of Difference'. *Cultural Anthropology* 7.1 (1992): 6–23, https://doi.org/10.1525/can.1992.7.1.02a00020

Hage, Ghassan. 'A Not So Multi-Sited Ethnography of a Not So Imagined Community', *Anthropological Theory* 5.4 (2005): 463–75, https://doi.org/10.1177/1463499605059232

Hannam, Kevin, Mimi Sheller, and John Urry. 'Editorial: Mobilities, Immobilities, and Moorings'. *Mobilities* 1.1 (2006): 1–22, https://doi.org/10.1080/17450100500489189

Hannerz, Ulf. 'Being There... and There... and There! Reflections on Multi-Site Ethnography'. In Antonius C. G. M. Robben and Jeffery A. Sluka, eds. *Ethnographic Fieldwork. An Anthropological Reader*. West Sussex: Wiley-Blackwell, 2013, pp. 399–408, https://doi.org/10.1177/14661381030042003

Heathershaw, John, and Edmund Herzig, eds. *The Transformation of Tajikistan. The Sources of Statehood*. London: Routledge, 2013, https://doi.org/10.4324/9780203718247

Janson, Marloes. *Islam, Youth and Modernity in the Gambia: The Tablighi Jama'at*. New York: Cambridge University Press, 2014, https://doi.org/10.1017/cbo9781139629133

Latour, Bruno. *Reassembling the Social: An Introduction to Actor-Network-Theory*. Oxford: Oxford University Press, 2005.

Lundby, Knut. 'Introduction: Religion Across Media'. In Knut Lundby, ed. *Religion Across Media: From Early Antiquity to Late Modernity*. New York: Peter Lang, 2013a, pp. xi–xxiii.

Lundby, Knut. 'Media and Transformations of Religion'. In Knut Lundby, ed. *Religion Across Media: From Early Antiquity to Late Modernity*. New York: Peter Lang, 2013b, pp. 185–202.

Mahmood, Saba. *Politics of Piety: The Islamic Revival and the Feminist Subject*. Princeton: Princeton University Press, 2011.

Madianou, Mirca, and Daniel Miller. *Migration and Media. Transnational Families and Polymedia*. New York: Routledge, 2012.

Marcus, George E. 'Multi-Sited Ethnography: Notes and Queries'. In Mark-Anthony Falzon, ed. *Multi-Sited Ethnography: Theory, Praxis, and Locality in Contemporary Ethnography*. Farnham: Ashgate, 2009, pp. 181–96.

Marcus, George E. 'Ethnography in/of the World System: The Emergence of Multi-Sited Ethnography'. *Annual Review of Anthropology* 24.1 (1995): 95–117, https://doi.org/10.1146/annurev.an.24.100195.000523

Mehrabian, Albert. *Silent Messages*. Belmont: Wadsworth Publishing Company, 1971.

Meyer, Birgit. 'Material Mediations and Religious Practices of World-Making'. In Knut Lundby, ed. *Religion Across Media: From Early Antiquity to Late Modernity*. New York: Peter Lang, 2013b, pp. 1–19.

Meyer, Birgit. *Mediation and the Genesis of Presence: Towards a Material Approach to Religion*. Utrecht: Universiteit Utrecht, Faculteit Geesteswetenschappen, 2012.

Meyer, Birgit, and Dirk Houtman. 'Material Religion — How Things Matter'. In Birgit Meyer and Dirk Houtman, eds. *Things. Religion and the Question of Materiality*. New York: Forham University Press, 2012, pp. 1–26, https://doi.org/10.5422/fordham/9780823239450.003.0001

Meyer, Birgit, David Morgan, Crispin Paine, and Brent S. Plate. 'The Origin and Mission of Material Religion'. *Religion* 40.3 (2010): 207–11, https://doi.org/10.1016/j.religion.2010.01.010

Meyer, Birgit, and Annelies Moors, eds. *Religion, Media and the Public Sphere*. Bloomington: Indiana University Press, 2006.

Nazpary, Joma. *Post-Soviet Chaos: Violence and Dispossession in Kazakhstan*. London: Pluto Press, 2002, https://doi.org/10.2307/j.ctt18fs75z

Ong, Aihwa. *Flexible Citizenship: The Cultural Logics of Transnationality*. Durham: Duke University Press, 1999.

Orsi, Robert. 'Material Children. Making God's Presence Real through Catholic Boys and Girls'. In Gordon Lynch, Jolyon Mitchell and Anna Strhan, eds. *Religion, Media and Culture: A Reader*. London: Routledge, 2012, pp. 147–58.

O'Sullivan, Patrick B., Stephan K. Hunt, and Lance R. Lippert. 'Mediated Immediacy: A Language of Affiliation in a Technological Age'. *Journal of Language and Social Psychology* 23.4 (2004): 464–90, https://doi.org/10.1177/0261927X04269588

Peleikis, Anja. 'Heritage and the Making of (Trans-)Local Identities: A Case Study from the Curonian Spit (Lithuania)'. In Ulrike Freitag and Achim von Oppen, eds. *Translocality. The Study of Globalising Processes from a Southern Perspective*. Leiden: Brill, 2010, pp. 229–48, https://doi.org/10.1163/ej.9789004181168.i-452.61

Piacenza, Joanna. 'Mobile Mindfulness: Practicing Digital Religion on Smartphones with Buddhist Meditation'. Master's dissertation, University of Colorado, Faculty of Graduate School, 2013.

Pries, Ludger, ed. *New Transnational Social Spaces. International Migration and Transnational Companies in the Early Twenty-First Century*. London: Routledge, 2001, https://doi.org/10.4324/9780203469392

Reetz, Dietrich. 'Mediating Mobile Traditions: The Tablighi Jama'at and the International Islamic University Between Pakistan and Central Asia (Kyrgyzstan, Tajikistan)'. Paper presented at Crossroads Asia Workshop, Berlin: Zentrum Moderner Orient, 2014.

Robben, Antonius C. G. M. 'Introduction: Multi-Sited Fieldwork'. In Antonius C. G. M. Robben and Jeffery A. Sluka, eds. *Ethnographic Fieldwork. An Anthropological Reader*. West Sussex: Wiley-Blackwell, 2013, pp. 367–73.

Roche, Sophie. 'The Role of Islam in the Lives of Central Asian Migrants in Moscow'. *CERIA Brief* 2 (2014): 1–5, http://centralasiaprogram.org/wp-content/uploads/2015/04/CERIA-brief-2-October-2014.pdf

Salazar, Noel B., and Nina Glick Schiller. 'Introduction. Regimes of Mobility Across the Globe'. In Noel B. Salazar and Nina Glick Schiller, eds. *Regimes of Mobility. Imaginaries and Relationalities of Power*. Routledge: London, 2013, pp. 1–18.

Schröder, Philipp, and Manja Stephan-Emmrich. 'The Institutionalization of Mobility: Well-Being and Social Hierarchies in Central Asian Translocal Livelihoods'. *Mobilities* 11.3 (2014), https://doi.org/10.1080/17450101.2014.9 84939

Schulz, Dorothea E. 'Promises of (Im)mediate Salvation: Islam, Broadcast Media, and the Remaking of Religious Experience in Mali'. *American Anthropologist* 33.2 (2006): 210–29, https://doi.org/10.1525/ae.2006.33.2.210

Silvey, Rachel. 'Mobilizing Piety: Gendered Morality and Indonesian-Saudi Transnational Migration'. *Mobilities* 2.2 (2007): 219–29, https://doi.org/10.1080/17450100701381565

Skovgaard-Petersen, Jakob and Bettina Gräf, eds. *The Global Mufti. The Phenomenon of Yusuf al-Qaradawi*. London: Hurst/Columbia University Press, 2009.

Smith, Michael Peter. 'Translocality: A Critical Reflection'. In Katherine Brickell and Ayona Datta, eds. *Translocal Geographies: Spaces, Places and Connections*. Burlington, VT: Ashgate, 2011, pp. 181–98.

Stephan-Emmrich, Manja. 'Studying Islam Abroad: Pious Enterprises and Educational Aspirations of Young Tajik Muslims'. In Pauline Jones Luong, ed. *Islam, Society, and Politics in Central Asia*. Pittsburgh: University of Pittsburgh Press, 2017, https://doi.org/10.2307/j.ctt1r6b097.15

Stephan-Emmrich, Manja, and Abdullah Mirzoev. 'The Manufacturing of Islamic Lifestyles in Tajikistan through the Prism of Dushanbe's Bazaars'. *Central Asian Survey* 35.2 (2016): 157–77, https://doi.org/10.1080/02634937.2 016.1152008

Svašek, Maruška. 'Introduction. Affective Moves: Transit, Transition and Transformations'. In Maruška Svašek, ed. *Moving Subjects, Moving Objects. Transnationalism, Cultural Production and Emotions*. New York: Berghahn, 2012, pp. 1–40.

Taylor, Steve. '"Home is Never Fully Achieved… Even When We Are In It": Migration, Belonging and Social Exclusion Within Punjabi Transnational Mobility'. *Mobilities* 10.2 (2013): 193–210, https://doi.org/10.1080/17450101.2 013.848606

van de Port, Mattijs. *Ecstatic Encounters: Bahian Candomblé and the Quest for the Really Real*. Amsterdam: Amsterdam University Press, 2011, https://doi. org/10.5117/9789089642981

Zolberg, Vera L. *Construction a Sociology of the Arts*. Cambridge: Cambridge University Press, 1990.

10. Translocality and the Folding of Post-Soviet Urban Space in Bishkek: *Hijrah* from 'Botanika' to 'Botanicheskii Jamaat'

Emil Nasritdinov

Somewhere beyond right and wrong there is a garden. I will meet you there.

Rumi

Botanika: 70–80s, 90s and 2000s

I live in the ninth micro-district in Bishkek, the capital of Kyrgyzstan. Every Friday, I come home from my work around 1pm, take a shower and go to the mosque, which is located just across the small Ala-Archa River in Ata-Tyurk Park, formerly known as Park Druzby (Friendship Park). The official name of this mosque is Toiiba, but it is better known as the KASI Mechet.[1] It is a large mosque, and on my way to it I can see how the parked cars of people who come to pray fill up both banks of the river and one adjacent street. There are so many cars that there is often a traffic jam, and the traffic police have to come in advance to control the flow of vehicles and keep the street open for movement. Among

---

1   KASI is the former name of Kyrgyz State University of Construction, Transport and Architecture, which is located on the same side of the river as the ninth micro-district.

          https://doi.org/10.11647/OBP.0114.10

the worshippers, there are many students from the nearby university. Together with the residents of the local micro-districts, they form a very large crowd that fills the two buildings of the mosque, with its large yard covered by a plastic roof, and then spills into the space outside.

Because of my work, I usually come just before the prayer starts and I have to pray in the courtyard. Once the prayer is finished and this huge crowd moves from the mosque, I make my way against the flow of people to a place inside, where my friends meet every week to greet and catch up with each other. By the time I get there, they are usually already standing in a circle joking and teasing one another. '*Assalam aleikum, Botanika*! (peace be upon you, Botanika!)' — I exclaim, and then greet each person in a circle with handshake and triple hug. '*Walekum salam* (and upon you, peace)', — they respond: the warmth of their hugs and their smiles make me happy. We stand there for twenty to thirty minutes, exchange news, make jokes, and then either go our own ways or, as often happens, continue to one of our houses for a meal and more socializing. Some men stay in the mosque to join the three-day *davaat* trip,[2] which is organized every Friday.[3]

This chapter is about Botanika, a term that in the context of this research represents two phenomena: this particular group of men who are now in their early fifties, and the specific territory near the mosque (across the park), where these men were born, spent their childhood and youth, and where many of them still live. Jointly, these two phenomena represent a unique form of urban identity, while their story offers us a new perspective on a very special form of urban translocality that, in interesting ways, connects people and their narratives to a specific urban

---

2   Three-day trips are an important part of *davaatchi* (Tablighi Jamaat). If *davaat* is the trip, then we still need to define *davaatchi* and Tablighi Jamaat practices. A group of between eight and twelve men travel from their own mosque to a different one, usually located in the same city or in the nearby settlements. During the trip, the group (*jamaat*) stays in that mosque and engages in worship, learning, and meeting locals. All members travel using their own money for transportation and food. During these trips, it is strictly forbidden to talk about politics. The main purpose of a trip is not preaching, but personal improvement and development.

3   I am not an insider to this group. I am approximately ten years younger than the others and I grew up in a different city in Kyrgyzstan. However, I have developed relationships of friendship and trust with the members of this group over the last nine years, since I moved here.

place in transformation. By exploring this, I hope to make a contribution to the main debates developed in this volume about translocality and to offer an alternative perspective on post-Soviet transition and urban transformation. To do so, I first present the main ethnographic account of Botanika in chronological order: tracing its history from the 1970s to the present day. I then engage with the French philosopher Gilles Deleuze's book *The Fold* to develop a more complex theoretical explanation for this phenomenon of post-Soviet urban transformation. The fold, described by Deleuze as the intricate internalization of external change and vice versa, is a concept that represents the complexities of transition very well. It shows how the path of individual transformation towards becoming 'a better person' is embedded in the complex territoriality of flows, folds, and obstacles in space, time, and society. To start, I need to take the reader back almost forty years, into the 1970s and 1980s, when Kyrgyzstan was still a part of the Soviet Union, Bishkek was called Frunze, and these men were ten- or twelve-year-old boys.

Fig. 10.1 People returning from the Friday prayer.
Photo © Emil Nasritdinov (2016), CC BY 4.0

Soviet youth street culture:
Botanika in the 1970s and 1980s

Frunze's youth culture was very territorial during the Soviet period. In my previous research with Philipp Schroeder (Nasritdinov & Schroeder, 2016), we were able to locate and map nearly fifty unique youth *rayons* (districts) with clear spatial boundaries and interesting histories. These *rayons* played a very important role in the lives of almost all young people in Frunze in the 1970s and 1980s: they were a part of their urban identity and everyday socialization. The phenomenon of territorial youth culture in Frunze followed the trends common to other Soviet cities and towns, yet Frunze *rayons* had many unique features of their own.[4]

Botanika was one such unique *rayon*. The informal name derives from the Botanicheskaya (Botanical) Street that ran through the middle of the *rayon,* connecting its upper and lower parts. The street was later renamed Dushanbinskaya, but the *rayon* kept the name Botanika. Botanika was one of the largest youth *rayons* in the city and it consisted of three smaller territories: Verhnyaya (upper) Botanika, Nizhnyaya (lower) Botanika, and Treugolnik (triangle) Botanika. The core of Botanika was the yard of one particular house in Verhnyaya Botanika called Shmal Dvor, where the toughest and most active boys used to live. The following maps show the territorial composition of Botanika and its neighboring *rayons*; the aerial photo shows its boundaries, urban fabric, and the park.

Botanika was not known only for its size, but also for the physical abilities of its boys. The territory had several sport facilities: the Dynamo Stadium, sports school #48, and a number of sports clubs, the most popular of which were dedicated to boxing and wrestling. Many local boys were involved in sports clubs from a very young age; many of them had become very good fighters by the age of around ten or twelve and joined 'the army' of Botanika when they fought other *rayons*. Their biggest rival was the neighboring *rayon* to the west of Botanika called Porta, but the boys of Botanika also fought the members of *rayons* from other parts of the city from time to time. Almost all of my interlocutors mentioned one important feature that made Botanika unique — a strong sense of

---

4   For a more in-depth discussion of the Soviet territorial youth culture see Nasritdinov and Schroeder (2016).

Figs. 10.2 and 10.3 Territorial composition of Botanika and its
neighbouring youth *rayons* and an aerial photo. Map and photo © Emil
Nasritdinov (2016), CC BY 4.0

Fig. 10.4 Boys of Botanika in the early 1980s (shared by interlocutors).
Photo © Emil Nasritdinov, CC BY 4.0

friendship and internal solidarity, which, according to them, did not exist in other *rayons*. Together, the large size of the *rayon*, and its members' strong fighting skills and solidarity, contributed to Botanika's reputation as the *rayon* to be respected.

My main group of interlocutors from Botanika includes seven men, all within one or two years of age of one another, who were very close friends from very early childhood. In fact, some of them were *druziya s gorshka* (potty friends); they went to the same kindergarten and later to the same class in school. Today, between forty to fifty years later, they remember how they spent their days as kids *'na rayone'* (in the neighborhood). Nobody sat at home and most of their free time after school, at the weekends, and during school breaks was spent playing outside. The *rayon* had a lot of greenery, including a large park (Park Druzhby), a botanical garden with lots of fruit trees, and a big lake, where they went swimming in summer time. These green spaces belonged to these kids. They played there, ate fruit in the gardens, and collected wood to cook stolen geese and bake potatoes at night. They could also hide in these green spaces when running from the police.

> 'There was an old airport near Botanika and we used to steal magnum there to make mini bombs. Once we noticed that two of our friends had a lot of magnum, but they were hiding it somewhere and not sharing it with us. We decided to track them secretly and saw one of them climbing a large tree in the park. "This is it", we thought, "this is where they hide their magnum — in the crow's nest all the way at the top". The same evening one of us climbed this tree and guess what he found in the nest? A piece of paper, which said: "Screw you! No magnum here!"' (Botanika member, male, Spring 2015)

The boys diligently guarded the park against trespassers from other *rayons*. They never touched an outsider if he was with a girl; this was an unwritten rule of the informal street code, but all other boys would be chased and beaten. As boys got older and became teenagers, the park became a place where they would bring girls, drink alcohol, or smoke weed.

> 'We started drinking in the eighth grade — the first time it was some kind of punch. After we graduated with an eighth grade diploma, we bought vodka and wine and drank so much that we felt very bad and had to vomit — right there in the park, in the apple orchard by the white-brick fence, where our boys had once killed a cat' (Botanika member, male, Spring 2015).

Fig. 10.5 Boys of Botanika in the early 1980s (shared by interlocutors).
Photo © Emil Nasritdinov, CC BY 4.0

Fig. 10.6 Russian[5] boys and girls of Botanika having a picnic in the park
(shared by interlocutors). Photo © Emil Nasritdinov, CC BY 4.0

5   Botanika was ethnically mixed. The majority of members were Kyrgyz and Russian.
     However, my main interlocutors are predominantly Kyrgyz with only one man of
     Tatar ethnicity.

The empty space to the east of the park (where the mosque is currently located) was a common location for fights between the residents of the student dormitory belonging to the university and boys from other *rayons* across the river. During these fights and other adventures, Botanika boys solidified their friendship and social ties.

> 'We once went to the night club (*diskoteka*) in school #62 [across the river from the park]. We were ten boys and at some point, somebody from the school pushed our circle and a fight started. There were too many of them — a whole school — and too few of us, so our boys eventually had to escape, but my friend and I got stuck. We fought back to back for as long as we could, until I realized that we would not survive, so I pulled my friend out and we ran too. He had a new suit, which was completely torn and we both had big bruises on our faces. At home I told my parents that I played soccer and got hit. Next day, we put together a huge crowd from the whole of Botanika and several other friendly *rayons*, went to that school and started beating everyone, including their sports teacher. However, the police came very soon and we all had to run. This was useless — there were a few hundred boys, but we were able to beat only ten or so because the rest of them managed to hide inside the school and the police came too soon' (Botanika member, male, Spring 2015).

With these kinds of adventure, Botanika boys slowly matured into young men, finished school, and most of them entered university. As students, they were less active in street life, but they still retained close links with each other and shared a few exploits as students, including a big fight in a student dormitory, in which Botanika members once again fought to protect their fellows. By the time the Soviet Union broke up in 1991, many of them had completed their university degrees and started working.

'Lihie 90-e' ('The wild 90s')

When the Soviet Union collapsed, the whole country entered a deep crisis. Whole industries collapsed and many people became unemployed, while those who still had jobs saw their salaries shrink. In order to survive, people traded with China, Turkey, Russia, and Kazakhstan. Many migrated to Russia and Kazakhstan for work. The term 'lihie 90-e' ('wild 90s') was common across all post-Soviet republics. The phrase encapsulated the crisis and chaos in many people's lives. Frunze was renamed Bishkek, and Botanicheskaya Street was renamed once again — this time it became Toktonalieva Street. The street culture also changed significantly. High rates of unemployment and growing ethno-nationalistic sentiments caused a large number of Russian families to sell their properties and migrate to Russia. This ruptured the social fabric in all parts of the city: old residents left and their apartments and houses were bought by the Kyrgyz migrants coming to Bishkek from other regions (Schroeder, 2010). As a result, neighbors no longer knew each other and, in a very short period, the identity of the *rayons* as cohesive neighborhoods with strong degree of internal socialization was destroyed. The system of values changed as well: friendship and solidarity were no longer the norm, and cheating and impudence became characteristic of the behavior of young people:

> 'My conscience never bothered me in the 90s. In the eyes of my friends it was cool to cheat someone. The highest degree of cheating and impudence was considered the most prestigious quality a person could attain. In some circles, those who could drink a lot were the coolest; in my circle, those who could cheat others best were the coolest. These were the kinds of values we had then' (Botanika member, male, Spring 2015).

This captures the dilemma of the collective attitudes prevalent in the Soviet Union versus the individualization of the 1990s.

Soviet youth culture also created many delinquents and possessed many links to the criminal world. However, post-Soviet street culture was more aggressive, violent, and criminal. New criminal gangs emerged and participated in the growing drug trade and in the racketeering practiced by newly emerging businesses and small enterprises. Young people were among the most affected; during the early 90s, a large number of teenagers and men in their twenties died from alcohol poisoning and drug overdoses on the streets and in the basements of Soviet residential buildings. Many were killed or injured in skirmishes between gangs.

The story of Botanika is not very different. The boys of Botanika did not become a criminal gang, but because they were very good fighters they were recruited by others,[6] and some did take part in criminal

---

6   These other gangs were not territorial and included boys from all parts of the city. Some gangs involved the new migrants. One of the most notorious was the *Ryspek*

activities. At the same time, many became heavy drinkers and drug addicts. Today, when they remember the past, they say 'those who survived the 90s', or 'those who are still alive'. The following photo of Botanika was taken in 1999 at the funeral of one of its relatively young members.

Fig. 10.7 Members of Botanika at the funeral of one of their friends (shared by interlocutors). Photo © Emil Nasritdinov, CC BY 4.0

This is how one Botanika member describes the atmosphere of the 90s:

'There was one elderly man who went jogging every morning. He would jog with a knife or nunchaku in his hands. I used to look around and think that the air was different — it was very tense. The money had just changed [from the ruble to the som]; heavy drinking, theft, and robbery were very common' (Botanika member, male, Spring 2015).

Many of my interlocutors are not proud of this part of their lives and share it with some hesitation.

---

gang, founded by a criminal from Issyk-Kul, who recruited members from among the students of *Inkub* (a residential sport school in Bishkek), the majority of whom were from outside of Bishkek.

'When I divorced my wife, I came back to Botanika to live with my parents. The whole *rayon* was drinking and everyone was saying to me: 'Hey, take a glass and let's go!' My mother used to lock the door, but what was the use? We lived on the first floor, so I would jump out through the window. My sister also divorced and lived with us. I remember one day, I came home drunk. My younger brother came after me — drunk. Then my dad — drunk! Finally, my sister — drunk as well! My Mom was pulling her hair: "What a drunkards' family!" Later, I got a Russian girlfriend from Botanika and we rented a corner in the dormitory in the completely opposite part of the city, but Botanika boys would still come all the way, because for some reason, shopkeepers used to trust me and give alcohol on credit [...]. By the early 2000s, I did nothing but drink. I used to drink several bottles a day. I had to drink continuously to be able to walk and not to shake. I couldn't even sleep. It was a complete intoxication' (Botanika member, male, Spring 2015).

Other members of Botanika were involved in criminal activities: some in racketeering and some in petty theft and drug trading. One of my interlocutors was imprisoned four times:

'I was always jailed because of vodka. There was this guy in our *rayon*, one day he gave me a drink and asked me to pass a bag to someone. I was drunk and did not know there was heroin inside. I went there and the police were already waiting for me. It turned out he was from the police and I was not the first one to be framed like that. This was my first conviction. For my last conviction I was framed for stealing fifteen cell phones. I once got into the police[7] and they asked me take them on myself.[8] I thought: they will beat me first and then frame me anyway. So, I agreed and for several days during the investigation, they fed me, gave me lots of vodka and took me to court from time to time. The judge knew I was framed. Everyone was looking at me and laughing: "What kind of thief is this? He is just an old drunk!" Ehhh, everything was because of vodka'[9] (Botanika member, male, Spring 2015).

Another member of Botanika shared the story of his life from the early 90s to 2008: it was all about vodka and weed. He used to work in several businesses and state enterprises and earn very large sums of money

---

7   I.e., he was taken to the police precinct for a minor violation, such as being drunk.
8   The police asked him to admit that he had stolen the phones.
9   The police often framed people because they had to show their superiors that they had dealt with the reports of crime in their locality.

through various corrupt schemes, but he drank all of this money with his friends:

'In the 90s, three of my friends and I started doing business together. Once, in the fall, we bought the whole KAMAZ [large Soviet truck] of cognac to sell. We did not sell a single bottle — we drank it all over the winter, not just by ourselves of course. We also used to smoke weed. Once we sat and counted how much weed we would need for a winter and according to our calculations we needed thirty small boxes of hashish. We went to Issyk-Kul, where I had some friends and bought the boxes. Well, they did not last for a winter. We finished all thirty boxes in one week [...] Later [in a different job] my regular day would start with a bottle of vodka on my table, which I drank with my subordinate. He then would go to work, while I would go to sleep. If I finished my cigarettes, I would just call him through the window and he would send someone to get me a pack. At lunchtime we would finish our second bottle. After work we would drink as much as we could. I remember once we had very good food for a snack and we finished a whole box of vodka [twenty bottles] overnight [...] I lived like that for almost twenty years' (Botanika member, male, Spring 2015).

The same interlocutor explained that during one of those drunken nights, he quarrelled with his very good friends from Botanika; their relationship was spoiled for a long time after that. Many of my interlocutors share similar experiences; during the 90s, many of them lost friendships and rarely saw each other.

'In the 90s we did not communicate. Those were wild times, and everybody was a lone wolf.[10] Why would you share your own piece with someone else? Every wolf had his own territory' (Botanika member, male, Spring 2015).

By the end of the 90s the members of Botanika were drunk, doped, imprisoned, exiled, dangerous, criminal, isolated, or dead. There was little hope of recovery. However, in the early 2000s, suddenly things started to change.

---

10   As a result of the retreat of the state during this period, everyone had to take responsibility for themselves.

Davaat and the spiritual enlightenment of the 2000s

In the mid-90s, the first representatives of the Tablighi Jamaat[11] movement arrived in Kyrgyzstan (Balci, 2012). This was a difficult period for them because the majority of the population did not know anything about Islam and the first Kyrgyz *davaatchiler* (followers of Tablighi Jamaat) experienced a lot of hostility. However, in a relatively short period of time, *davaat* became very popular; by the early 2000s, the number of followers who enjoyed regular three-day, forty-day, and four-month spiritual journeys had reached its peak (Ismailbekova and Nasritdinov, 2012). The *jamaats* (travelling groups) were often organized on the basis of language: Kyrgyz-speaking and Russian-speaking. The city boys usually joined the Russian-speaking groups and on these trips they learned the basic premises of Islamic teachings and practices.

Botanika was one such Russian-speaking urban community and, one by one, they became involved in *davaat* practices and started changing their lives on the basis of Islamic teachings. The very first person who became interested in religion did so because of the influence of his uncle. All the others joined gradually, one after another, like a snowball, over a period of approximately eight years. The individual stories of how Botanika members became religious are very unique and extremely interesting. The first is from an interlocutor I discussed earlier, who in the late 90s did nothing but drink:

> 'I was permanently drunk and extremely intoxicated in those times. Two of our Botanika friends came to me. One of them was already going to Friday prayers, but they were both still into racketeering — they used to 'bomb' [racketeer] everyone. So, they came to me and said 'You have to

---

11 Tablighi Jamaat is an apolitical movement that works towards the revival of Islam. It originated in India in the 1920s and has since become widespread all across the globe. Its main principles, summarized by its founder Maulana Ilyas Kandahlavi, are based on the idea that Muslims can only improve their own condition and that of the society they live in through worship (not by engaging in politics or fighting *jihad*). That is why the main purpose of Tablighi Jamaat practice is to improve oneself and remind other Muslims about their duties to Allah. It is not a proselytizing group — they do not preach to non-Muslims. One of the most important Tablighi Jamaat practices is three-day, forty-day, and four-month trips, when a group of Tablighi moves from one mosque to another and engages in worshipping, learning, and inviting local people to the mosque.

go for *davaat'*. I asked them 'What is it?' 'You will sleep for three days in the mosque'. 'Is that it? I can sleep anywhere. What will we do there?' They themselves did not know. Muhammad Sharif gave them *targib* [encouragement] to be concerned for others, so they came to me. They told me to take something to cover myself. I took a tiny kids' blanket and I almost died in that mosque: it was snowing, it was very cold inside, and someone stole my boots. All three days I was shaking — from my alcohol withdrawal and from cold because of this little blanket. "Bastards!" — I was very angry with my friends. However, I slowly started recovering and on the third day I even ate soup. During these three days I didn't understand anything. The boys in the group told me: 'Say *subhanallah'*. I couldn't even pronounce that and asked them to write it down. Then at night, one other friend from Botanika who was with us woke me up and said 'Go pray *tahajud'*.[12] I did not understand where to go and how to pray, and water for ablution was so damn cold. Anyway, I did my ablutions, came inside the mosque — everyone was asleep. I woke him and asked why nobody else was praying. He said: "This is voluntary". I said: "You dummy, I'll break your neck! Then you come and pray with me". He said: "Let's go and eat instead". Stupid guy, I couldn't eat even in the day time. That is how I suffered for three days. When I came back, I did not start praying five times a day right away, but I started going to Friday prayers, and most importantly, after these three days I quit drinking and I have never ever had a drop since then' (Botanika member, male, Spring 2015).

Some stories are told with humour, such as this example from a man who used to be involved in various commercial frauds:

'One day I met some friends in Botanika. They were going to the funeral ceremony for a Botanika boy's father and they invited me to come with them. This was in the 2000s. I thought, well, it is a good occasion to have a drink. We drink a lot anyway, but here is a good reason. I went with them and saw a lot of men with beards in the room. I thought that this might be some kind of fashion or maybe they just didn't have razors. Anyway, I sat and waited for my drink. Instead, they all came to me one by one and talked: one talked about Allah, another about angels, the third about hell, and the fourth about *sahabas*.[13] I was thinking: "It is ok; 100 grams of vodka is worth all this listening". I waited and waited, but didn't get anything. What kind of funeral was this without any alcohol? A couple of weeks later, my other friend from Botanika told me I needed to go for *davaat*. I thought, I have been in many extreme situations in

12   *Tahajud* — voluntary night prayer.
13   *Sahaba* — companion of the Prophet Muhammad (SAW).

life, I can handle that too. So, I went. All the boys in the group were young. I didn't understand anything. I was just mechanically repeating all their moves. However, on our way back to the KASI mosque, I felt as if I was flying above the ground, and I felt as if everyone was like a brother to each other. I wanted to hug and kiss everyone. So, after this first *davaat* 'the ice moved'. That is how they got me in. However, you can understand the essence of religion only in the forty-day trip, and *dua* [supplication] during forty days is also stronger. My daughter was studying in England and in my forty-day journey, I asked Allah to give her a Muslim husband. When I came home, she called and told me that she'd got a boyfriend and that he was a Muslim from Albania. That is how the wisdom of religion comes, and its understanding. This is all from Allah, of course' (Botanika member, male, Spring 2015).

Another member of Botanika was involved in racketeering and at some point, he crossed paths with a notorious criminal, Ryspek, who gave an order to kill him. He says:

'I knew I was a dead man. I moved my family to a different place, got several guns and waited at home. This is when a friend told me that *duas* [supplications] are accepted in the path of Allah and if I go for a three-day *davaat* and make *dua*, I can solve all of my problems. I had nothing to lose and decided to give it a try. I went and for three days I was asking Allah for help. When I came back, the issue was miraculously resolved, and a few weeks later, Ryspek himself was killed. Everyone was like: "Hey, what kind of *dua* were you making there?"' (Botanika member, male, Spring 2015)

One other member of Botanika had serious problems with his health and with his family: he was jobless and his wife wanted to divorce him. Some time after he went for his first three-day trip, his health improved and his wife returned.

In 2008, the Botanika interlocutor who used to drink and had smoked weed for twenty years was living in a Western country as a refugee. His salary was about 2,000 USD a month but he was living there alone and his normal working day would usually finish with a litre of gin and a joint. He started seeing his Botanika friends in his dreams a lot, so he decided to give one of them a call. This is how he described their conversation:

'We just talked about nothing. He asked: "What are you doing there?" I said "I work, what about you guys?" "We do nothing, get together every day, drink tea, and enjoy ourselves. Why don't you come back?"

"And what will I do there?" "There is plenty of work here and you will also spend time with us, drink tea, and have *plov, kuurdak*".[14] This conversation strongly affected me. I really wanted to go back. I thought about it every night and one day I just packed my things and flew back to Bishkek' (Botanika member, male, Spring 2015).

He came back in January 2009 and for five days he met his friends and visited relatives. On the fifth day (Thursday) he had his last drink and on Friday, Botanika sent him for his first three-day *davaat* trip. After he returned, this man, who had drank almost every day for twenty years, quit drinking. Not long after he went for a forty-day trip and during this journey he asked Allah for a good Muslim wife. He explains that a week after his return he married a very pious Muslim woman. Nowadays he drives a taxi; they live happily and have two children.

The Botanika brother who was jailed four times learned about Islam in jail. He said that during his last imprisonment, out of one thousand prisoners, one hundred identified themselves as practicing Muslims. They represented diverse Muslim groups. He quit drinking and smoking on January 10, 2012 and in 2014 when he was released, boys from Botanika helped him to go on a trip, first for three days and then for forty days.

The lives of all seven men have slowly improved since then. Nobody drinks or takes drugs anymore. Two of them smoke, but they are trying to give it up as the others have. None of them are involved in criminal activities; they all have jobs or businesses: one runs an Islamic kindergarten, one drives a taxi, three are engaged in commerce, and two work as security guards. Four of the seven have families and their wives are also practicing Muslims. Some of them travel for three-day *davaat* trips every month and travel for forty days every couple of years. Others travel only from time to time. However, all of them pray five times a day, fast during Ramadhan and attend Friday prayers.

Most importantly, they all maintain very close connections with one another. They call each other on an almost daily basis and they meet every few days for tea or full meals. Sometimes, they invite some religious scholars or experienced Tablighi practitioners to these meals and listen to their talks. In addition, they spend a lot of time

---

14   Traditional Kyrgyz meals.

talking to other former residents of Botanika whom they have known since childhood and encourage them to join in with their religious practices. Their friendships have evolved from the loyal relationships of childhood, through their comparative estrangement in the 1990s, to a new closeness that has been established on a very different foundation. This time their friendship has a spiritual basis and according to their explanations, this relationship is much deeper; they say that Allah puts *mahabbat* (brotherly love) in their hearts and this connection is a great source of support. Botanika — as a group — has reemerged, stronger than it ever was. Now it is known among the local residents and in the wider community of *davaatchis* in Bishkek as *Botanicheskii Jamaat* (Botanical religious group).

Similarly, Botanika as a place has changed significantly. During Soviet times, it was a place of internal solidarity and cohesion. However, it was also a place where outsiders were beaten, while its boundaries were the scene of conflicts with boys from other *rayons*. During the 90s, the place was completely run down: it was not safe; it was full of drunks, drug addicts, and hooligans, and there was a lot of litter in the streets and parks. Nowadays, it looks very different. The mosque, which was built on the empty field between the park and Ala-Archa River is now one of the four *marqases* (regional centres) of Bishkek: it regulates the activities of all mosques located within its wider sphere of influence. Every day, *davaatchiler* from this mosque make *gasht* — knocking on the doors of nearby apartment buildings and inviting men to the mosque. In the streets, there are lots of small shops, cafes, and businesses. The park was renovated by Turks[15] (and for this reason renamed Ata-Turk Park), and today it attracts lots of visitors from the nearby residential districts and even from other parts of the city. Botanika has become very safe: one can easily walk through the area even in the middle of the night. People are reclaiming the public spaces inside the yards of Soviet apartment blocks and, just as in Soviet times, children are among the first to make use of them. Most of my Botanika interlocutors still live in

---

15   Turkish investors gained influence in post-Soviet Bishkek, particularly in the spheres of construction, trade, and education. They own several large construction companies and shopping malls and there are now many Turkish cafes in the city. In addition, Turkish *lyseums* (secondary and high-school) and Turkish universities are quite popular.

the neighborhood. They participate in the activities of the mosque and try to recruit more people, particularly their former friends of the same age.

This is the happy conclusion to the Botanika story and its ethnographic aspect. The end might look somewhat 'too happy'. As I mentioned earlier, many boys from Botanika did not survive the 90s and early 2000s and died from alcohol poisoning, drug addiction, and criminal activities. Many still continue the same lifestyle. There were many others who did not become drunkards or criminals, but also did not become religious, while there are others who join in with religious activities but are still struggling, trying to improve their lives. In short, their individual paths are very diverse. However, the lives of the particular group I have focused on in this chapter share striking similarities, and they represent a unique and extraordinary transformation, both of a community and of a space. My next task is to try to make sense of this transformation from a theoretical perspective. In order to do so I shall engage with the philosophy of Gilles Deleuze, to develop a complex and nuanced understanding of the broader post-Soviet urban transformation and the more specific theme of urban translocality.

Deleuze's fold and the transformation of Botanika

Many academic and policy-based explanations for the changes brought about by the post-Soviet transition can be criticized for being simplistic and ideological: from socialism to capitalism, from a planned to a market economy, from atheism to religiosity. These explanations fail to recognize the complexity and unpredictability of developments in specific post-Soviet contexts. In Central Asia today, twenty-five years after the break-up of the Soviet Union, we can trace a multitude of diverging and converging paths, which together form a very uneven, complex, and interesting pattern of development.

To grasp this complexity, we need a new theoretical perspective that extends beyond the traditional positivistic approach to the social sciences. Postmodern French philosophy can offer a lot in this regard, particularly the ideas of French philosopher Gilles Deleuze, which he developed in his book *The Fold*. The writings of Deleuze and his co-author Félix Guattari are extremely rich in regard to the interpretation of contemporary transformations of space, such as the changes I have described taking place in Botanika. Furthermore, Deleuze's concept of the fold offers a way to challenge linear, one-dimensional treatments of post-Soviet transition in Bishkek and elsewhere. Deleuze engages in a very complex discussion about how different worlds fold and unfold into each other and how the boundary between them has a life of its own. Deleuze conceptualizes the fold as an intermediate zone between physical and metaphysical, animal and spiritual, inside and outside, and this model can be used to understand the spiritual transformation of Botanika and the stories of my interlocutors.

Deleuze treats transition as a process with infinite variation. He rejects universality and writes that all organisms have the quality of irreducible plurality. He is in favour of epigenesis (the view that perceives form as shaped by process) as opposed to preformation (the view that form develops simply by growth in size). This is also useful to consider in relation to transition: it is a process that is impossible to predict or describe in a one-dimensional fashion (e.g., the transition from a planned economy to a market economy) but instead must be conceptualized as something that can develop in any possible and unpredictable direction. I shall apply these and other Deleuzian concepts to Botanika's transformation from the 1990s to the present.[16]

Caterpillar, cocoon, and butterfly

Deleuze describes transformation as a constant shift from the material to the spiritual and back. During the Soviet period, communist ideology shaped the materiality of existence. Boys from Botanika were predominantly working class. They did not have many opportunities to realize material aspirations even if they had them. Although they were not strong believers in communist ideology and, in fact, youth street culture can be seen as an ideological alternative to it, these boys were still driven by the romanticism of street life and by such spiritual values as friendship, solidarity, courage, and heroism, rather than by material incentives.

---

16   All citations in the remainder of this chapter are from *The Fold: Leibniz and the Baroque* (London: Athlone Press Ltd, 1993), unless specified differently.

'Values were different in the Soviet times. We did not divide into rich
and poor. To strive for wealth was considered abnormal; nobody was
after money. One the contrary, if a person was rich, people would say:
"He is *hapuga* [a greedy person], a thief". We had *uravnilovka* [levelling];
wages were similar and sufficient for everyone. The future was secure
and we did not have material aspirations; nobody taught us to pursue
financial success. We were more motivated by prestige. For example,
it was prestigious to study economics in university and the whole
city was trying to get in. The history department was also popular
because you could then progress along the communist party line. The
law faculty — not so much; who wants to be a *ment* [police officer]?'
(Botanika member, male, Spring 2015)

If the Soviet Union did not collapse, perhaps, these boys would have
slowly turned into regular Soviet citizens with a more traditional Soviet
outlook. However, as the formal Soviet ideology collapsed in the 1990s,
the informal ideology of street life also began to erode. No more the
street 'code of honour', but 'survival of the fittest': material 'derivative,
mechanistic, machinic forces' (p. 12) and animal instincts became more
dominant. People survived the ideological, economic, political and
socio-cultural crisis but they abandoned spiritual and moral values.
Moral chaos, deception, betrayal, and cheating became very common. It
was a period when 'every man was for himself' (*kazhdyi byl sam za sebya*).
According to Deleuze, such changes are accidental and they happen as a
result of the influence of external factors, which, in the case of Botanika,
would be the actions of the state and various international actors.

Deleuze compares *life* and *death*, portraying life as something that
unfolds and death as something folding in on itself. In Botanika in the
1990s, young people in the urban areas of Kyrgyzstan were dying in
great numbers due to alcohol poisoning, drug overdoses, and criminal
activities. This was the period accurately described by Joma Nazypary
(2002) as post-Soviet *bardak* — chaos — and as a result many Botanika
members died young, became addicted to drugs and alcohol, and
joined urban gangs. During this time, the group dynamics broke down:
everybody lived his own life and there was very little communication
between them. In this desperate situation, the salvation ideology
promoted by Tablighi Jamaat offered an escape for my interlocutors.

Farideh Heyat (2004) and Mathijs Pelkmans (2007) show that the
chaos in Kyrgyzstan during this period was one of the main reasons

people turned to religion in search of spiritual, moral, psychological, and socio-economic support. The stories I explored in the first part of this chapter reveal how, one by one, 'demoralized' members of Botanika started practising religion and improving their lifestyles, quitting drinking, drugs, and criminal activities. They also became more united again, regularly meeting each other, organizing religious activities together, and reestablishing a sense of community and communal identity as Botanika. Deleuze introduces the concept *socius* — process, in which the world as 'a theatrical basis, a dream, an illusion' (p. 125) unfolds into 'collective spiritual unity' (p. 125). Horizontal unity based on friendship, shared memories and experiences, translates itself into a vertical[17] spiritual unity that connects many of the members of Botanika in a shared spiritual quest.

In the first years of the new millennium, the whole country, including Botanika, began to recover. Life began to unfold in many spheres: people became more economically secure; two revolutions (in 2005 and 2010) brought more democratic governance; and it became safer to walk the streets. The regular monitoring of public opinion conducted by the Center for Baltic Research[18] reveals that the population of Kyrgyzstan has the most positive perception of life in their country in comparison to all the other former Soviet countries, and this perception has remained fairly constant over the last several years.

Deleuze explains how the seventeenth- and eighteenth-century Baroque artistic style evolved in response to the theological collapse that occurred under the influence of capitalism, in order to save theological ideals from the new forces of materialism through the multiplication of existing perspectives and the invention of new ones. We could argue that Botanika's spiritual reemergence is a response to the collapse of Soviet ideology in the context of post-Soviet chaos and *dikii kapitalism* (wild capitalism). Post-Soviet society survived by multiplying existing perspectives and creating new concepts, therefore in Kyrgyzstan today we see a great diversity of religious practices and communities (Pelkmans, 2006).

---

17   According to Deleuze, 'vertical' refers to the connection between the physical and metaphysical or spiritual worlds.

18   Dr Rasa Alishauskene, Center for Baltic Research, presentation organized by the Tyan-Shan Policy Center, American University of Central Asia, 14 March 2016.

Deleuze calls this process 'schizophrenic reconstruction' by 'characters, who reconstitute the world through their inner, so-called auto-plastic modifications' (p. 68). This is exactly how the members of Botanika reconstitute society and space — by engaging with their inner landscapes, by rediscovering a metaphysical basis for their existence and nourishing their spirituality — and it is in this flux the permanence is born (p. 79). This calls to mind theories of chaos and complexity, which argue that when systems collapse, in the context of overall chaos, new centres emerge, so-called 'strange attractors', which become the main nodes of a new system emerging out of this chaos. According to Deleuze, these strange attractors are not of material origin. They are ideas, which actualize themselves in physical matter: 'it is not the body that realizes, but it is in the body that something is realized' (p. 105). So, Botanika is the body, both communal and spatial, in which Botanika as a spiritual concept is actualized.

To illustrate the relationship between life and death as a process of folding and unfolding, Deleuze uses the analogy of a caterpillar metamorphosing into a cocoon and then to a butterfly. This analogy is very apt to describe Botanika: in the 1970 and 1980s it was like a caterpillar, which in the 1990s folded itself into a cocoon, and in 2000s emerged from this cocoon as a butterfly.

Infinite variation in transition

Deleuze distinguishes three main forms of transformation. The first — *vectorial* — is similar to a straight line from point A to point B; it is akin to a simplistic understanding of the transition from socialism to capitalism. It is very limited, like many such transitological perspectives. The second — *projective* — is based on the projection of internal space onto external space, such as an individual explanation or account of change. This is similar to one of the Botanika member's accounts of transition. But the third perspective, described by Deleuze as the *infinite variation* that portrays transition as a bundle of curves, each constructed through an infinite number of angular points, gives the most complex, rich, and diverse interpretation of reconstructed change.

Transition as infinite variation conceptualizes wholes and parts of the world using the principles of similitude and extension of time, number and matter, which is the 'original formula of derived infinity'

(p. 46). Transition is the result of the folding and unfolding of space, time, and narrative, creating great diversity in a specific place. Due to this infinite diversity or fractal complexity, society becomes more and more complex and interesting. It is not a transition from one condition into another, but from outside to inside, from material to spiritual, from simple to more complex. It is an implosion, not explosion, and the story of Botanika is one of such multiple diverse trajectories.

Such implosion happens in two directions identified by Deleuze. The first is a converging series, in which individuals come together to form one world and create communities with similar visions, practices, and lifestyles. Botanika is one such community, which Deleuze would call 'compossibles' (p. 60). The second direction is a diverging series, in which individuals create different worlds, which leads to differentiation between communities whose primary principles, concepts, and metaphysical bases are different. This model illustrates the great religious diversity in Kyrgyzstan today.

Interestingly, this diversity does not generate conflict because the world is reconstituted by first being decomposed into the multiple diverging paths of individuals and then by the discovery of the 'florescence of extraordinary accords' (p. 82) in which multiple diverging actors play in accord with each other and create a 'polyphony of polyphonies' (p. 82) or concertation of life. It is a new world in which diverse communities with their unique features and distinctions coexist without conflict because their main driving force is not external, but internal or spiritual. This is where the situation in Kyrgyzstan becomes so different from the situation in other Central Asian republics,[19] which are still ruled by authoritarian regimes, and where the external powers of the state still dominate internal sources of change. This kills diversity and results in artificial *unison* instead of *polyphony*. These countries could be said to lack freedom because freedom, according to Deleuze, is first of all the moment of a soul.

---

19 There is not enough space here to describe how diversity and freedom in Kyrgyzstan are more established compared to other Central Asian states. Kyrgyzstan is often referred to as 'the island of democracy in the sea of authoritarian states'. Although this statement has been rightly criticized, I believe in that if one takes a more comparative view it still makes a lot of sense. For example, today in Kyrgyzstan there are more madrasas (Islamic religious schools) than in all other Central Asian states together.

The metaphysical dimension of transition
and the power of agency

As he develops this understanding of transformation, Deleuze examines three forms of singularity within it. The first singularity is a *physical point*, an elastic or plastic point-fold. These are real singular events from the life stories of the participant, often connected to specific points in space. The second singularity is a *mathematical point*, a position, a site, or a point of view. We can understand it as the material explanation of change, an explanation based on common-sense logic and physical, non-spiritual reasoning, which characterizes many existing ethnographic accounts of transition. The third singularity is of particular interest; it is a *metaphysical point* and it focuses on 'the soul or the subject'; it is 'a higher point of another nature', a 'point of inclusion' (p. 23).

From this perspective, one perceives change not so much as the result of external influences, but as the result of internal spiritual change. It is a perspective that can defy the common-sense logic that relies on material reasoning and instead can posit spiritual force as the basis of all change. In the words of Botanika members referencing the Prophet Muhammad's Hadith, 'Allah will not change the conditions of people, until people change themselves'. This is a narrative born in the spiritual journeys of Botanika; it is a new logic that emerged during crisis, a logic that reverses causality and places the metaphysical before the physical. As *davaatchis* frequently mention, the main purpose of going for *davaat* is to change one's *yakyn* (conviction), to remove from the heart the belief in the power of creation and replace it with a belief in the power of the creator. The main meaning of 'La illaha ilallah' (There is no God but God) in the *davaatchi*'s narrative is that everything that happens in our life, good and bad, happens only according to the will of God, and therefore, the only way to change one's *ahval* (conditions) is by improving one's morals and spiritual practice.

The implications of such a change might seem insignificant, but when we understand that it applies not only to Botanika, but also to a much larger group of the population of Kyrgyzstan, which is day by day growing in number and becoming more religious, then we see the Deleuzian 'unity that envelops multiplicity' (p. 128) and connects to nothing less than 'the soul of the world' (p. 26). This focus on the soul as the expression of the world relates the individual metaphysical experiences of human beings to the condition of the world in which they exist. Thus, we develop a new dimension of transition — the metaphysical. This can be seen in the narratives of Botanika members, both in their use of spiritual reasoning to explain their physical transformation, and in their numerous stories of spiritual miracles in their personal lives.

The metaphysical dimension of transition revives the power of individual and collective agency. Deleuzian individuals, or monads, are not passive objects of change — once they channel their internal spiritual forces, they become powerful agents, subjects, even 'superjects' (p. 20), working towards the improvement of their own lives and of the condition of the society of which they are a part. People describe themselves as becoming empowered: with the help of belief, prayers, supplication, *davaat*, and acts of piety, they contribute to changing the world for the better. According to this view, external factors, even such strong geopolitical actors as the US, Europe, Russia, and China, who are all competing for influence in Central Asia, become less influential: according to one of my interlocutors, 'George Bush and Vladimir Putin are both from Allah'.

The fold

The shift from materiality to spirituality discussed above does not have a clear border or threshold. Deleuze describes it as the fold — a curve with inflection points marking change. These inflection points are all unique for the different members of Botanika: they happened to them at different times and under different circumstances. Some of my respondents' stories that describe these inflection points — the times when their lives were taking significant turns — are very dramatic and illustrate very sharp changes, while others describe a more gradual transition. The most frequently mentioned inflection points for my respondents were their first three-day and forty-day *davaat* trips. For some, these resulted in their giving up alcohol, for others, in the resolution of life-threatening conflicts in the criminal world, and for others in finding a pious Muslim wife. For Deleuze, such inflection points are a 'point-fold' (p. 14), and the 'ideal genetic element of transition [...] authentic atom, non-conceptual point of non-contradiction, and a point of intrinsic singularity' (p. 14). They are also a 'pure Event' (p. 15), a 'weightless non-dimensional point between dimensions' (p. 15). This is exactly what that first experience represents: the transition from one mode of existence dominated by material animal instincts into another, characterized by spirituality and morality. The personal accounts of this point-fold in the stories of Botanika members are very rich, detailed, and well-imprinted on their memories.

If we project these individual trajectories of spiritual-material-spiritual change, mapping individual inflection points as they occur, we could envision the following diagram to illustrate these transitions from the Deleuzian perspective:

Fig. 10.8 Individual and collective trajectories: the Deleuzian perspective. Diagram © Emil Nasritdinov (2018), CC BY 4.0

This diagram allows us to discuss one last Deleuzian concept in the quest to debunk a linear perspective of transition — his idea of *texture*, which is freed from *structure*. Our understanding of the complexity of transition is limited by the rigidity of the structuralist perspective, which understands transition as the transformation of one structure to another, e.g., capitalism to socialism, a planned economy to a market economy, or atheism to religiosity. This is too rigid, too stiff, too essentialist. Instead, Deleuze draws an analogy with textiles, with cloth that covers the body. He describes how, in the baroque style, the shape of clothing is freed from the shape of the body; with its multiple and complex folds, it has a life of its own. Today, in Kyrgyzstan, the analogue of the multiple folds of the baroque style is the hijab and the long and loose Islamic dress. The primary aim of Islamic dress is exactly that — to hide the form of the body behind the infinite folds of the textile. It is an art of texture, not structure, which Deleuze calls the 'intensity of a spiritual force exerted over the body' (p. 122). It turns the soul inside out and it moulds the 'inner surfaces' of a person (p. 122). We can thus think allegorically about the drapery of the material world: the materiality of existence is covered with the spiritual layers of individual self-actualization.

Conclusion: fold, *hijrah*, and urban translocality

The fold is the transition from 'mundus' to 'cosmos' (p. 29) and it is the most interesting aspect of this research. How are materiality and spirituality connected? How does the internalization of external change happen? How does internal change affect external space? How can we understand the fold in the stories of Botanika? I suggest bringing to the discussion one additional Islamic concept — *hijrah*.

Hijrah is an important Islamic concept that is associated with the migration of the Prophet Muhammad (SAW) in 622 AD from Mecca, where Muslims were persecuted, to Medina, where the majority of residents at that time already accepted Islam. This migration was so important that it signified the beginning of the Islamic calendar. Traditionally, *hijrah* is perceived as a journey, a trip, a distance to overcome, and traditionally a person moves from a non-Muslim to a Muslim place (see Kamoludin Abdulaev, Chapter One). But the Prophet Muhammad (SAW) also described *hijrah* as leaving one's sins behind and beginning a new, pious life. This is a more complex understanding loaded with larger potential for interpretation, and it can help us to better understand what happened in Botanika.

Most of my interlocutors did not move from one place to another; for the most part their lives are tied to Botanika. Instead of changing their place of residence, they changed themselves, and because of their (and many other people's) internal evolution, a place that used to be non-Muslim became more Muslim in regard to the daily practices of its residents, including those of my main interlocutors. The Deleuzian fold is an excellent concept to understand *hijrah*: it is a membrane, an intermediate zone, a connection between two different worlds — non-Muslim and Muslim, materiality and spirituality, sin and piety. The fold helps one world to fold and unfold into another. It is a major zone of transition, a 'sinuous, zigzag, unlocatable primal tie' (p. 120). This *hijrah*-fold therefore becomes the main translocal connection.

However, this story is not just translocal, it is also significantly 'transtemporal'. It may be that a person remains in the same location, and perhaps that location does not even change significantly, at least not physically: all the old Soviet housing blocks are still there in Botanika. But the dynamic perception — the 'trans' — originates from a change within that person in that physical space. Translocality is not only the movement of people or goods or ideas across boundaries, as it is often understood, but it is also the transformation of place over time in tandem with the shifting spiritual perspective of its long-time inhabitants. 'Transtemporality' as a form of translocality within one place is exemplified by the lifecycles and biographies of my interlocutors, which, in turn, are closely related to the biography or lifecycle of the neighborhood as a very particular urban place and space. The main destination of the spiritual journeys of the 'Botanika boys' is Botanika itself as a 'Muslim place' (materially and immaterially). Individual biographies are thus connected to that of the neighborhood, thereby conflating both into Botanika as a single material-spiritual-spatial entity.

This seems like an apt point at which to end the story. However, let me add one final fold of thought, without which this conceptualization of translocality in Botanika will be incomplete. At the end of his book, when Deleuze applies his analysis of the baroque to the contemporary world, he suggests that today everything is in movement and thus 'monadology' becomes 'nomadology' (p. 137). All of my interlocutors mentioned that the key turning points in their transformation were their three-day, forty-day and four-month spiritual *davaat* journeys. Movement is crucial for transformation: at least for a short period of time, they all had to perform a real physical *hijrah* — to leave behind the environment of *duniya* (the worldly environment) and stay in the environment of *din* (religion) 'to clean the heart' (a phrase commonly used by *davaatchis*). Just as Joseph Campbell discusses in his 1948 work *The Hero with a Thousand Faces*, a person must leave his home, experience difficulties on the journey, and return transformed, enlightened and capable of changing the place from which he departed and to which he has returned. This is the most important understanding of translocality that this chapter contributes to the current volume: *hijrah* — the spiritual-physical journey of Botanika residents — becomes the fold that completely transforms the urban space.

References

Balci, B. 'The Rise of the Jama'at al Tabligh in Kyrgyzstan: The Revival of Islamic Ties Between the Indian Subcontinent and Central Asia?' *Central Asian Survey* 31.1 (2012): 61–76, https://doi.org/10.1080/02634937.2012.647843

Campbell, J. *The Hero with a Thousand Faces*. New World Library, 3rd ed. July 28, 2008 [1948].

Deleuze, G. *The Fold: Leibniz and the Baroque*. Minneapolis: University of Minnesota Press, 1992.

Heyat, F. 'Re-Islamisation in Kyrgyzstan: Gender, New Poverty and the Moral Dimension' *Central Asian Survey* 23:3–4 (2004): 275–87, https://doi.org/10.1080/0263493042000321371

Nasritdinov, E., and P. Schroeder. 'From Frunze to Bishkek: Soviet Territorial Youth Formations and Their Decline in the 1990s and 2000s'. *Central Asian Affairs* 3 (2016): 1–28, https://doi.org/10.1163/22142290-00301001

Pelkmans, M. 'Asymmetries on the 'Religious Market' in Kyrgyzstan'. In C. Hann, ed. *The Postsocialist Religious Question: Faith and Power in Central Asia and East-Central Europe*. Berlin and Münster: Lit Verlag, 2006, pp. 29–46.

Pelkmans, M. '"Culture" as a Tool and an Obstacle: Missionary Encounters in Post-Soviet Kyrgyzstan'. *Journal of the Royal Anthropological Institute* 13.4 (2007): 881–99, https://doi.org/10.1111/j.1467-9655.2007.00462.x

Afterword: On Transitive Concepts and Local Imaginations – Studying Mobilities from a Translocal Perspective

Barak Kalir

Translocality as an analytical concept appears to have ignited the imagination of many scholars who are considering and reconsidering multiple mobilities in space and time. In different academic quarters, there is a perceptible increase in the scope of social issues and the breadth of geographical locations that fall under a translocal magnifying glass. The conceptual appeal of translocality, I believe, has much to do with its transitive character. The seductiveness of transitive concepts was explained to me in a particularly convincing fashion by the late Gerd Baumann, an outstanding anthropologist, a gifted musician, and an inspiring teacher. 'Transitive concepts are good to think with' Baumann enthusiastically advocated, 'because they put the finger on processes and they capture the cadence of social change'. Indeed, a cursory view of the great contemporary and classic works that have had a lasting effect on the social sciences reveals the dominance of transitive concepts in shaping analytical frameworks. From the booming field of transnational studies to the importance of translation, and from transactional theories, transhistorical accounts, transborder movements, transcultural education, and transgender controversies, to all sorts of intriguing deviant transgressions, and to the divine evocations of the transcendental, one is easily left with the idea that all 'great transformations' are intimately linked to the vital prefix 'trans'.

  https://doi.org/10.11647/OBP.0114.11

Some of the most obvious advantages of using transitive concepts can be found in the ways they sensitize us to alteration and movement rather than to fixity and preservation. They pay heed to borders and boundaries precisely because they focus our gaze on their permissiveness and on the things that move across them (Kalir and Sur 2012). Transitive concepts foreground the condition of being betwixt and between (Turner 1975) when it comes to the identities, locations, and positions that actors occupy, embody, and enact in their everyday interactions with others. Transitive concepts, thus, make us attentive to potentialities and to creative processes that continuously make and remake our social as well as our material world.

Translocality, in particular, is a powerful analytical concept because it invokes the transitive features of locality. The notion of locality is intuitively and romantically associated with fixity, boundedness, tradition, and conservation. By adding transitive dimensions to the notion of locality we whimsically highlight and inventively break open the intricate links and productive tensions between mobility and motion on the one hand, and place and community on the other. Much of the budding literature on translocality in recent years has carved an large niche for the translocal (Brickell and Datta 2011, Freitag and von Oppen 2010, Greiner and Sakdapolrak 2013). It suffices here to recall how Freitag and von Oppen (2010:5), in their introduction to what is by now a seminal volume on translocality, dedicated a section to 'Translocality as an object of inquiry and as a research perspective'. This is understandable, as translocality seem to be the 'new kid in town', recently joining the much older and more established debates around processes of globalization and the omnipresence of transnationalism as an analytical framework for studying mobilities and flows.

There is something stimulating about the contributions in this book, which undoubtedly has to do with the exciting analytical originality and richness on offer, as scholars from different disciplinary backgrounds use a translocal magnifying glass to inspect very different empirical case studies. Yet this collection adds something else to the existing literature by revealing a compelling sense of maturity within the field of translocal studies. This refreshing sense of confidence in translocality as an established field of inquiry is demonstrated throughout this volume and is plainly proclaimed in the introduction, where the editors attest that all the contributions 'tackle "translocality" as a social reality' (p. 31).

By bringing together the work of scholars with very different disciplinary, empirical, and thematic approaches in an unapologetic manner, the editors make the merits of studying translocality instantly apparent to the reader. In what follows, I would like to highlight three major analytical advantages of working in a translocal vein, which are made evident in this book. The first has to do with the prime role of imagination in inspiring our interlocutors as they creatively contemplate and investigate translocal mobility. Since working with the imagination can (fortunately) be contagious, contributors to this volume appear to have been inspired to pursue their own 'sociological imagination' (Wright Mill 1959) in their analysis of translocal dynamics. The second advantage of a translocal approach is methodological in essence: the protracted engagement with localities as crucial research sites that register changes, which results from a concern with mobilities, immobilities, and the intersections between them. Finally, the role of emotion is central to many of the chapters, which causes me to ponder a possible link between a translocal perspective and the recent 'affective turn' in anthropology and other disciplines. Translocality can illuminate in its full colors the intimate and fascinating role that emotion can play in inducing motion.

But allow me to begin with what is probably the most arresting tension in this volume, namely the proclaimed openness that comes with a translocal approach and the regional focus of the collection. As the editors justly claim, the findings in the different chapters 'strikingly reveal the benefits of a translocal perspective for studying movements, transfers, and exchanges in Central Asia, the Caucasus, and beyond' (p. 30). It is 'and beyond' that saves this statement from becoming an oxymoron. As becomes apparent in many of the contributions, the vitality of a translocal perspective renders impossible a geographical focus on Central Asia and the Caucasus. For example, following the trajectories of Kyrgyz traders has taken Philipp Schröder all the way to south China as well as to the middle of Russia; the study of Tajik middlemen and students has taken Abdullah Mirzoev and Manja Stephan-Emmrich to

Dubai, Saudi Arabia, and the United Arab Emirates; and tracing the making of a new Kyrgyz 'globalizing ethno-nationalist' history has led Svetlana Jacquesson's account to the heart of Europe.

While a geographical focus can understandably provide coherence to a volume such as this, the editors are the first to point to its potential limiting effect. In situating the volume in the tradition of 'new area studies' the editors attempt to bring elasticity to the notion of an 'area' and to conceive of it as an idea rather than as a concrete territorial space. Notwithstanding this effort, one of the major achievements of this collection, in my opinion, is the wealth of connections — imagined and real — that are drawn by mobile subjects in making (sense of) their movements, circulations, and exchanges within trajectories that *do not* lend themselves neatly to any (political?) attempt at zoning.

This leads me straight to one of the palpable gains I see in translocality as a creative and critical approach that treats imagination as a crucial ingredient in understanding the role and experience of mobility in localities around the world. Although it is impossible to quantify the influence of the imagination on people's decisions, almost all of the contributions in this collection heed its importance in shaping people's aspirations for, and practices of, mobility: from Muslims moving within an imagined overarching global community of believers (*umma*) in the past (Abdullaev, Chapter One) and in the present (Mirzoev & Stephan-Emmrich, Chapter Three), to imaginings that relate to the past glory of a re-emerging Silk Road (Alff, Chapter Five, Fehlings, Chapter Seven, and Schröder, Chapter Eight), to an imagined global ethno-nationalist history (Jacquesson, Chapter Six), and sacred ancient lineages (Malikov, Chapter Three). Furthermore, Dungans in Kazakhstan seem to be under the spell of the (at least partly imaginative) promises of Chinese modernity (Alff, Chapter Five), while post-Soviet men in Kyrgyzstan are enchanted by reveries of Islamic purity (Nasritdinov, Chapter Ten), and hypermobile Tajik student travellers entertain imaginings of 'pious endeavours' (Stephan-Emmrich, Chapter Nine).

It was C. Wright Mills (1959) who argued for the importance of the 'sociological imagination' in tying everyday subjective experiences to social structures and historical developments. Following his cue, many scholars have since elucidated the pertinent role of the imagination in swaying the energies of individuals and groups towards the realization of major projects, for example, the fermentation of nationalism and the formation of nation states (Anderson 1983), the invention of traditions and histories (Hobsbawm and Ranger 2012), or the consolidation of geography as in the 'imagining of the Balkans' (Todorova 2009). More specifically, in relation to mobilities, the 'American dream' has (falsely) fuelled the imagination of millions with respect to socio-economic mobility (Hochschild 1996), while going overseas to promising destinations has always been a dominant image in metaphors of mobility (Cresswell 2006) and in propelling migration worldwide, not always in rational or predictable ways (Alpes 2014, Kalir 2010, Massey *et al.* 1999).

Translocality, being actor-centred and sensitive to the everyday nature of particular localities, causes the researcher to consider closely the agency of the researched. The translocal point of departure is therefore often the aspirations and inspirations of our interlocutors as they imagine, plan, and undertake different types of mobility in interaction with other relevant mobile and immobile subjects. The openness to the trajectories of our interlocutors, with no preconceived territorial parameters for what is to be considered meaningful mobility, appreciably distinguishes the creative potential of translocality from run-of-the-mill migration studies and from transnationalism in particular. Migration studies and transnationalism concentrate our attention on specific geographies (mostly international mobility) and prioritize certain subject of study (such as integration). Whether focusing on those who settle down elsewhere or those who move across national borders, these approaches to mobility are primarily informed by the researchers' ideas or paradigmatic analytical frameworks regarding the type of moving that matters (Kalir 2013).

Conversely, translocality is a creative approach that enriches our understanding of a changing world by exploring movement in ways and places that matter to those who engage in or experience mobility. Whether people move to a neighboring village, cross national borders, or take a flight to another corner of the world, translocality treats all these movements as equally meaningful and significant, both for the localities themselves and for those within them who move or stay put. The potential long-lasting contribution of translocality to the social sciences might very well be its ability to capture, and consider as meaningful, any movement that is conceived as such within a locality by our interlocutors. In this sense, translocality is neatly wedded to the creative capacity of 'grounded theory' (Glaser and Strauss 2009). Translocality allows our understanding to be directed by the experiences of those involved in movement and change, rather than by a top-down imposition of analytical schemes and methodological standards. There can therefore be little doubt that the gains of a creative bottom-up translocal perspective are maximized by studying movement without a geographic barrier, that is, without setting territorial limitations on our potential object of study.

There are obvious methodological and epistemological implications of approaching translocality as a bottom-up, actor-centered approach, which dovetail with longstanding debates about the production of knowledge in the social sciences and the humanities. Focusing on non-elite actors' accounts in rewriting history (Jacquesson, Chapter Six) or on narrating subjective aspirations for and experiences of historical mobilities (Abdullaev, Chapter One), calls to mind Spivak's (1988) disconcerting question about the ability of the subaltern to speak. Engaging in close encounters with interlocutors to co-produce our accounts of mobility (Schröder, Chapter Eight) invokes challenging discussion about the ownership of the text and the 'poetics and politics of ethnography' (Clifford and Marcus 1986). While these are important debates to be had when crafting translocality as a programmatic approach, I would like to highlight here another methodological aspect that has to do with its long-term engagement with specific localities.

The 'mobilities turn' (Urry 2007) has been widely welcomed as an overdue and updated way of doing research in a world that is increasingly in motion (Massey *et al.* 1999). Methodologically, the study of mobilities has contributed to a dominant social scientific inclination to move away from the anthropological tradition of studying neatly defined units: places, communities, sectors, and so on. Following people and commodities, studying flows, and capturing global encounters (Appadurai 1996, Burawoy *et al.* 2000, Tsing 2011), have become — methodologically and thematically — the order of the day. We are now at a point, I believe, when it is worth considering whether the pendulum has swung too far the other way. Do we too often study mobilities in ways that eclipse the intimate and patient examination of localities?

It appears that nowadays, 'deep hanging out' (Geertz 1998) with a certain group in a certain locality is increasingly considered by many researchers as limited and limiting (Wogan 2004). Bucking the trend, translocality thrusts our scrupulous inspection back to localities not simply as nodes in a wide network of mobilities, but as important research sites in their own right. Locality, then, is not simply a point of departure to study mobilities, nor is it a point of arrival in the sense of measuring the impact of economic and social remittances (Levitt and Schiller 2004) or of return migration (King 2015). Locality, rather than regaining its importance from the 'mobilities turn', has arguably always been a site where change is felt constantly and is registered in people's shifting practices, beliefs, and imaginations. In light of the contributions to this book, I would suggest that paying attention to the stationary should not be confused with entertaining a conservative perspective about fixity and permanence.

There are two exemplary contributions in this volume that illustrate the outstanding quality of a translocal perspective in capturing mobilities within a changing locality: Henryk Alff's (Chapter Five) examination of the changes in villages around Shortobe in southeastern Kazakhstan that result from Dungan relationships with China, and Emil Nasritdinov's (Chapter Ten) exploration of changes in Botanika in Bishkek. These fresh contributions are so telling about the potency of a translocal perspective because they root their detailed accounts of change in a long-term engagement with a particular locality. Both accounts take the reader on a trip across time that spans more than two decades and captures a transition from Soviet times to a new articulation of post-Soviet meta-narratives (religion, modernity) and everyday practices (pious deeds, consumption, trade, education). This long-term engagement with a locality is a rarity in much contemporary social scientific research, which is increasingly geared towards 'going with the flow' or is otherwise limited in its engagement with a single research site, not least due to budgetary and time constraints that have to do with the neoliberal restructuring of academic institutions (Holligan 2011).

Among other things, a protracted engagement with localities is effective in sensitizing us to the intricate relations between the mobile and the immobile. In recent years, attention has been increasingly drawn to ways in which mobile and non-mobile subjects are entangled in a web of connections that shape the possibilities for mobilities and the meanings they assume in different contexts (Kalir 2009, Porter *et al.* 2010). Adding to this growing body of literature, the contribution by Susanne Fehlings (Chapter Seven) exposes the increasingly restricted mobility of female petty traders in Georgia, and highlights a negative correlation between physical mobility and socioeconomic mobility. Given that structural market circumstances have changed in ways that disfavor petty trade, mobility either becomes immobility for some or leads to increased poverty for others. In her contribution, Elena Kim (Chapter Four) fixes her gaze on one village to account for the mobility-related impoverishment of already poor families who are made increasingly dependent on changing irrigation schemes. Both accounts demonstrate how a translocal perspective — with its attention to mundane changes in localities; to flows of ideas, subjects and objects; and to the interplay between mobile and immobile people — can reveal retrogression and stagnation as well as advancements in people's lives. This is a sharp correction to an implicit assumption about the positive effects of movement that underlies many migration and mobilities studies (Glick Schiller and Salazar 2013). Translocality can thus highlight the 'dark side' of mobility that affects millions of people who, although not necessarily 'on the move', are experiencing mobility in ways that spell disaster for their basic livelihood, family structures, and emotional ties.

Emotions are present in different contributions in this collection. This points us, potentially, in an exciting direction for the study of translocality. Emotions are clearly and intimately linked to the motivations that propel people to undertake mobilities, as well as the ways in which mobile and non-mobile subjects experience mobilities and their material and cultural consequences. It is less clear, however, whether there is a direct relationship between a translocal perspective and an awareness of the role of emotions. While the jury is still out, the contribution by Stephan-Emmrich (Chapter Nine) convincingly introduces the term 'emotional geographies' in examining how mobile Tajik students consider emotion in their experiences of 'good or bad Muslim places'. For his part, Philipp Schröder (Chapter Eight) recalls his interlocutors' and his own emotions of shame and embarrassment as crucial in the delicate negotiation of access to intimate spaces and moments in a translocal field(work). Many of the other contributions, although they do not discuss emotions directly, make recurrent references to desires, longings, nostalgia, pride, and other feelings in their investigations of interlocutors' dealings with (im)mobilities.

Hence, translocal studies can tap into a burgeoning debate about emotions among scholars who are swept up by the recent 'affective turn' in the social sciences (Clough and Halley 2007). Rather than thinking of feelings as 'autonomic processes that take place below the level of conscious awareness and meaning' (Leys 2011:437), translocality can show the value of 'ethnographic accounts that are specific about how humans' perceptions are social all the way down' (Martin 2013:157). In other words, translocality is positioned at a strategic spatial and temporal crossroads, allowing it to demonstrate that emotions — emanating from an individual sense of belonging or displacement, yet feeding collective negotiations of communal identities and traditions — are socially produced in particular contexts to manage tense and potentially jolting constellations of mobility and change. To this we can add the invaluable intersection between emotion and imagination, as well as the manner in which objects can produce feeling. Taking our cue again here from Stephan-Emmrich, the usage of iPhones by Tajik students is not simply a new medium to document and communicate their spiritual progress as they move between 'pious endeavours'. Instead, it is the very consumption of prestigious goods that largely produces emotions among these young and aspiring mobile subjects: a sense of progress, excitement and pride.

To conclude, the promise of translocality as an exciting conceptual framework to analyze mobilities is tremendous. Translocality provokes us to reconsider our study of mobility as an examination of an ongoing process of *em-placement* as well as of *re-placement*. It is a process in which ideas, goods, and people are changing places, moving from one location to another, transforming, and being transformed by both mobile and immobile actors. Crucially, translocality highlights and analyzes these processes of re-placement from a perspective that is grounded in the everyday and emotional experiences of those who are affected by (im)mobilities. A translocal perspective is vital because it allows us to interrogate mobilities without privileging physical movement between places as the thing that matters most. In other words, movement from a translocal perspective is measured not in meters but in matters.

References

Alpes, M. J. 'Imagining a Future in "Bush": Migration Aspirations at Times of Crisis in Anglophone Cameroon'. *Identities* 21.3 (2014): 259–74, https://doi.or g/10.1080/1070289x.2013.831350

Appadurai, A. *Modernity at Large: Cultural Dimensions of Globalization.* Minneapolis: University of Minnesota Press, 1996.

Brickell, K., and A. Datta. *Translocal Geographies. Spaces, Places, Connections.* Farnham: Ashgate, 2011, https://doi.org/10.4324/9781315549910

Burawoy, M., J. A. Blum, S. George, Z. Gille, and M. Thayer. *Global Ethnography: Forces, Connections, and Imaginations in a Postmodern World.* Berkeley: University of California Press, 2000.

Clifford, J., and G. E. Marcus. *Writing Culture: The Poetics and Politics of Ethnography.* Berkeley: University of California Press, 1986.

Clough, P. T., and Halley, J. *The Affective Turn: Theorizing the Social.* Durham and London: Duke University Press, 2007, https://doi.org/10.1215/9780822389606

Cresswell, T. *On the Move: Mobility in the Modern Western World.* New York: Routledge, 2006, https://doi.org/10.4324/9780203446713

Freitag, U., and A. von Oppen. *Translocality: The Study of Globalising Processes from a Southern Perspective.* Leiden: Brill, 2010, https://doi.org/10.1163/ ej.9789004181168.i-452

Geertz, C. 'Deep Hanging Out'. *New York Review of Books* 45.16 (1998): 69–72.

Glaser, B. G., and A. L. Strauss. *The Discovery of Grounded Theory: Strategies for Qualitative Research.* New Brunswick and London: Transaction Publishers, 2009.

Glick Schiller, N., and N. B. Salazar. 'Regimes of Mobility Across the Globe'. *Journal of Ethnic and Migration Studies* 39.2 (2013): 183–200, https://doi.org/1 0.1080/1369183x.2013.723253

Greiner, C., and P. Sakdapolrak. 'Translocality: Concepts, Applications and Emerging Research Perspectives'. *Geography Compass* 7.5 (2013): 373–84, https://doi.org/10.1111/gec3.12048

Hobsbawm, E., and T. Ranger. *The Invention of Tradition.* Cambridge: Cambridge University Press, 2012.

Hochschild, J. L. *Facing Up to the American Dream: Race, Class, and the Soul of the Nation.* Princeton: Princeton University Press, 1996.

Holligan, C. 'Feudalism and Academia: UK Academics' Accounts of Research Culture'. *International Journal of Qualitative Studies in Education* 24.1 (2011): 55–75, https://doi.org/10.1080/09518398.2010.485134

Kalir, B. 'Finding Jesus in the Holy Land and Taking Him to China: Chinese Temporary Migrant Workers in Israel Converting to Evangelical Christianity'. *Sociology of Religion* 70.2 (2009): 130–56, https://doi. org/10.1093/socrel/srp027

Kalir, B. *Latino Migrants in the Jewish State: Undocumented Lives in Israel.* Bloomington: Indiana University Press, 2010.

Kalir, B. 'Moving Subjects, Stagnant Paradigms: Can the "Mobilities Paradigm" Transcend Methodological Nationalism?' *Journal of Ethnic and Migration Studies* 39.2 (2013): 311–27, https://doi.org/10.1080/1369183x.2013.723260

Kalir, B., and M. Sur. *Transnational Flows and Permissive Polities: Ethnographies of Human Mobilities in Asia.* Amsterdam: Amsterdam University Press, 2012, https://doi.org/10.26530/oapen_464418

King, R. *Return Migration and Regional Economic Problems.* New York: Routledge, 2015, https://doi.org/10.4324/9781315722306

Levitt, P., and N. Glick Schiller. 'Conceptualizing Simultaneity: A Transnational Social Field Perspective on Society'. *International Migration Review* 38.3 (2004): 1002–39, https://doi.org/10.1111/j.1747-7379.2004.tb00227.x

Leys, R. 'The Turn to Affect: A Critique'. *Critical Inquiry* 37.3 (2011): 434–72, https://doi.org/10.1086/659353

Marcus, George. 'Ethnography in/of the World System: The Emergence of Multi-Sited Ethnography'. *Annual Review of Anthropology* 24 (1995): 95–117.

Martin, E. 'The Potentiality of Ethnography and the Limits of Affect Theory'. *Current Anthropology* 54.7 (2013): 149–58, https://doi.org/10.1086/670388

Massey, D. S., J. Arango, G. Hugo, A. Kouaouci, and A. Pellegrino. *Worlds in Motion: Understanding International Migration at the End of the Millennium.* Oxford: Clarendon Press, 1999.

Porter, G., K. Hampshire, A. Abane, E. Robson, A. Munthali, M. Mashiri, and A. Tanle. 'Moving Young Lives: Mobility, Immobility and Inter-Generational Tensions in Urban Africa'. *Geoforum* 41.5 (2010): 796–804, https://doi.org/10.1016/j.geoforum.2010.05.001

Spivak, G. C. 'Can the Subaltern Speak? Reflections on the History of an Idea'. In C. Nelson and L. Grossberg, eds. *Marxism and the Interpretation of Culture.* Urbana and Chicago: University of Illinois Press, 1988, pp. 271–313.

Todorova, M. *Imagining the Balkans.* Oxford: Oxford University Press, 2009.

Tsing, A. L. *Friction: An Ethnography of Global Connection.* Princeton: Princeton University Press, 2011.

Turner, V. *The Ritual Process: Structure and Anti-Structure.* Piscataway, NJ: Transaction Publishers, 1995.

Urry, J. *Mobilities.* Cambridge: Polity Press, 2007.

Wogan, P. 'Deep Hanging Out: Reflections on Fieldwork and Multisited Andean Ethnography'. *Identities: Global Studies in Culture and Power* 11.1 (2004): 129–39, https://doi.org/10.1080/725289021

Notes on Contributors

Kamoludin Abdullaev is an independent historian, affiliated with the Russian-Tajik Slavonic University (Tajikistan). He has taught at the Tajik State University, Ohio State University, Yale University and others. His research topics cover national and Muslim movements and migration in Central Asia, as well as contemporary developments and historical topics related to Tajikistan and Central Asia.

Henryk Alff is a research associate at the Leibniz Centre for Tropical Marine Research (ZMT) in Bremen (Germany) and is currently developing a new research project on materializations of China's Maritime Silk Road initiative. His research and numerous publications concentrate on migration, mobility, trading processes, and borderland studies in Kazakhstan, Kyrgyzstan, and China. He received his Ph.D. in human geography and migration studies.

Susanne Fehlings is a postdoctoral researcher at the Department of Social and Cultural Anthropology at the Universität Tübingen (Germany). Her research covers informal trading routes and markets, globalization from below, and urban anthropology in Armenia, post-Soviet Eurasia, and the Caucasus.

Svetlana Jacquesson is Director of the Central Asian Studies Institute at the American University of Central Asia (Kyrgyzstan) and Head of the MA programme in Central Asian Studies. Her recent research focuses on 'history making' or popular ways of re-emplotting history to support old and new identity claims. She has extensively published on this topic as well as on the legacy of nomadic cultures and renegotiation of this legacy in Kyrgyzstan and beyond.

Barak Kalir is Associate Professor in the Department of Anthropology and Sociology at the University of Amsterdam (the Netherlands) and co-director of the Institute for Migration and Ethnic Studies. His ethnographic work on migrants from Latin America and China has been published in leading journals including *International Migration*, *Journal of Ethnic and Migration Studies*, *Social Anthropology*, and *Sociology of Religion*.

Elena Kim is a post-doctoral researcher at the American University of Central Asia (Kyrgyzstan). She received her Ph.D. from Universität Bonn (Germany) and has previously studied in Hungary and Kyrgyzstan. Her current research and publications deal with gender development, women, natural resources, and violence.

Nathan Light is a researcher in the Department of Anthropology and Ethnology at Uppsala University, Sweden. He received his Ph.D. in the fields of Folklore and Anthropology from Indiana University in 1998. He has carried out field studies in Kyrgyzstan and the Xinjiang region of China since 1989, and published extensively on Central Asian history, narrative, performing arts, social relations and the economy. His current project 'Embedded in History' investigates the interrelations of historical knowledge and material and expressive practices in the Talas Valley in Kyrgyzstan.

Azim Malikov is a post-doctoral department member of the Institute of History at the Academy of the Sciences of Uzbekistan. His research interests cover ethnicity, identity, urban history, Islamic culture, and the transformation of society in Central Asia and Uzbekistan. He has worked as a research fellow at the Max Planck Institute for Social Anthropology in Germany.

Abdullah Mirzoev was a doctoral researcher in the Volkswagen-Foundation-funded research project 'Translocal Goods' from 2013 until 2016. Currently, he is a doctoral candidate at the Cluster of Excellence 'Asia and Europe in a Global Context: The Dynamics of Transculturality' at Universität Heidelberg (Germany). His research embraces the production, distribution and consumption of Islamic fashion in Tajikistan and the United Arab Emirates. He received his MSc from the Tajik National State University.

Emil Nasritdinov is Associate Professor in the Department of Anthropology at the American University of Central Asia (Kyrgyzstan). His three main areas of research and teaching expertise are migration, religion and urban anthropology. He has published several book chapters and articles on spiritual nomadism, migration, transnationalism, and regional change.

Philipp Schröder is a post-doctoral scholar and lecturer at the Institute for Asian and African Studies, Humboldt-Universität zu Berlin (Germany). His current research project is entitled 'The "China-Business" — An Ethnography of Kyrgyz Traders and their Translocal Livelihoods in-between "Home", China, and Russia'. He has published on the topics of identity and integration, urban spaces and mobilities, youth cultures and entrepreneurship, with a particular focus on Kyrgyzstan.

Manja Stephan-Emmrich is Junior Professor of Islam in Asian and African Societies at the Institute for Asian and African Studies at Humboldt-Universität zu Berlin (Germany). In her current anthropological book project, she is investigating the complex entanglements of translocal Islamic education networks, Tajik youth's work experiences, and reform-minded endeavours in Tajikistan, the Gulf, and the wider Middle East. She has published several articles and book chapters on Islamic lifestyles, youth and education, migration and mobility, and Muslim business networks in Dubai.

Index

Afghanistan 49, 65–67, 69–70, 76–80, 82–85, 182, 296, 298

agriculture 90, 142, 151, 155, 155–156, 157–158, 166, 166–167, 167, 171, 182
  collective farms 156, 182, 188
  farming 158, 170–171, 182, 187

Amu Darya 61, 64–66, 82, 154–155

Armenia 16, 229–230, 237, 242, 246–247, 249, 252, 274, 361

Basmachi 41, 63, 74, 77–78, 83–85

bazaar 94–95, 97, 105, 179, 187, 189–190, 233, 237–239, 244–245, 247–248, 250–251, 263, 265–266, 268–271, 275, 309

biography 45–46, 243, 304, 306, 346
  spatial 45

Bolshevism/Bolsheviks 62, 68, 73–74, 77–78, 80, 84, 86

borders 6, 16–17, 27–29, 31, 33–36, 39–43, 46, 48–52, 61–62, 65–67, 70–72, 74, 76, 78, 81–82, 85, 126, 133, 135, 138, 144, 159, 178, 182–183, 186, 188, 193, 196–197, 207, 219–220, 222, 229–231, 233–236, 242, 246–247, 251, 263, 267, 278, 281, 284, 295–296, 343, 349–350, 353, 361
  cross-border 16, 28–29, 33–36, 41–43, 46, 48–49, 52, 178, 188, 193, 196–197, 295–296
  policy 66

boundaries 10, 13, 20, 27, 29, 31, 33, 35, 37, 40, 42, 44, 46–47, 51, 59, 64, 72–73, 79, 86, 89, 91–92, 100–102, 112, 124, 131, 159, 185, 231, 233–235, 263–264, 270, 282, 296, 311, 322, 335, 346, 350
  crossing 35
  transgressing 33, 46–47, 50, 207

Bukhara 15–16, 63–66, 68, 72, 74–76, 80, 82, 84–86, 129, 132–133, 136, 138

capital 6, 8, 14, 29–30, 32, 37–38, 46, 48–49, 51, 65, 68, 73, 82, 90, 92, 94, 99, 105, 108, 112, 134, 137, 139, 153, 186, 188, 190, 196, 229, 236, 239, 245–247, 254, 256, 263, 266, 268, 278, 284, 291, 293, 296, 298, 319, 336, 339–340, 344
  cultural 196, 254
  economic 298
  social 112
  symbolic 82, 134, 137

capitalism 14, 30, 51, 153, 256, 263, 278, 284, 336, 339–340, 344

Caucasus, the 2, 5, 16–17, 27, 29–34, 40–41, 47–48, 50, 52, 72, 80, 105, 107, 229–232, 235–239, 244, 246, 249, 252, 254, 256, 268, 278, 351, 361

Central Asia 1–3, 5, 15–18, 27, 29–37, 40–41, 47–49, 51, 61–66, 68–86, 91, 95, 99, 104–105, 107, 110, 112–114, 121–125, 127–129, 131–135, 137, 139–141, 144–145, 151, 154, 178–180, 187–189, 194, 196, 207–209, 211, 217, 219–221, 229–232, 235, 244, 246, 252, 265, 268, 278–279, 292, 295, 298, 339, 341, 343, 351, 361–363

China 1–2, 16–17, 29–30, 35–37, 41,
    43, 48–50, 62, 64, 66–71, 76, 91, 125,
    165, 178–183, 185, 187–199, 210,
    218–219, 221, 231, 235, 243–247,
    250, 263–264, 267, 277–283, 297,
    309, 326, 343, 351, 355, 361–363
CIS (Commonwealth of Independent
    States) 91, 97–98, 108
clan 121, 123, 129, 132, 137, 140,
    208–210, 218
Cold War 69, 84
colonization 70, 72
    colonialism 29, 31, 43, 72
community 6, 13–14, 18, 35, 41, 46,
    70, 78, 81–83, 85, 102–105, 107–109,
    111–112, 123–125, 127, 132–133,
    155, 179, 182, 186, 193, 221, 246,
    254, 266, 270, 274, 277–279, 281,
    283, 296, 299, 302, 331, 335–336,
    339, 341, 350, 352, 354
construction 15, 41, 45, 89, 133–134,
    138, 183, 190, 199, 212, 219, 221,
    270, 310, 335
consumption 32, 91, 165, 247, 251,
    264, 302–303, 357, 362
corruption 94–95, 232, 268
    connections 94
culture 27, 36, 47, 51, 62, 69, 72,
    81, 84, 86, 91, 99, 104–105, 112,
    126, 135, 138–139, 141, 143, 145,
    154, 165, 170, 177–178, 181, 191,
    196–197, 217, 232, 235, 273, 297,
    299–300, 322, 327, 337, 361–363
    street 322, 327, 337
    youth 322, 327
development 8, 17, 27, 32, 36, 46, 51,
    84, 124, 126, 135, 153, 157, 159,
    184, 192–194, 196–197, 199, 252,
    268, 270
diaspora 9, 44, 46, 50, 62, 81–82, 96,
    99, 177, 213, 264, 268, 273–275,
    277–279, 281–283
digital 13–14, 49, 145, 276–277,
    291–294, 300–304, 307–312
    media 14, 302, 307, 309, 312
    practices 293, 301, 310–311

Dubai 36, 38, 46–48, 50, 89–93,
    96–101, 103–114, 196–197, 291–293,
    295, 297–298, 305–306, 308–309
economy 17, 30, 51, 90, 92–95, 99, 103,
    113, 156, 170, 195, 231, 235, 243,
    248, 252, 256, 268, 279, 336–337,
    344, 362
    economics 90, 102, 105, 232, 242,
    264, 281, 338
    informal 30, 90, 92, 94–95, 113, 231
emotion 3, 30, 37–38, 44, 82, 274, 276,
    285, 291–294, 300–304, 307–308,
    311–312, 351, 356–357
employment 27, 94, 98–99, 101,
    109–110, 154, 156–158, 182, 327
    contract 98, 102, 166, 169
entrepreneur 36, 49, 90, 93–95, 98–99,
    107, 109, 112, 178–179, 186–187,
    189–190, 192–193, 198, 230–233,
    241, 244, 249–251, 256, 263, 283,
    292, 298, 302, 363
    entrepreneurial 94, 107, 109,
    192–193, 230
    entrepreneurship 244, 283, 363
ethnicity/ethnic group 1, 30, 36, 40,
    74, 81–82, 86, 99–100, 103, 105, 107,
    121, 123, 132–133, 180, 271, 280,
    325, 362
ethnography 1, 28, 37, 45, 125,
    151–153, 155, 158, 160–164, 213,
    264, 276, 282, 299–300, 310–312,
    354, 363
Eurasia 15–16, 29, 36–37, 48–49, 65,
    96–97, 104–105, 112, 114, 182, 198,
    211, 222, 229, 263–264, 282, 296,
    361
exploitation 96, 105, 268
export 89, 108–109, 152, 155–156, 161,
    165–166, 189
Ferghana Valley 40, 123, 140
genealogy 123, 126, 128, 131, 133, 138,
    140, 143, 209
generation 8, 42, 44, 46, 48, 84,
    132–133, 138, 141–144, 188, 195,
    199, 243, 264, 266, 270, 273–277,
    281–283, 285

Georgia 31, 39, 50, 229–230, 232, 236–237, 242–243, 245–247, 249–252, 254, 256, 356

globalization 5–7, 29–34, 36, 42, 91, 112–113, 124, 139, 159–160, 186, 207, 223, 229–231, 233–237, 250, 254–256, 299, 350, 361

governance 16, 34, 50, 70–71, 90, 161, 166, 173, 339

Great Britain 65, 67, 71

guesthouse 92, 100–103

Gulf 91–96, 107, 111–114, 297, 363
  region 93

heritage 211–212, 219, 252, 270

hijra 35, 37–38, 41, 63, 76, 79–81, 294, 319, 345–346

historiography 34, 61, 77, 222

home 1, 14–15, 28, 31, 37, 42, 44, 46–49, 75, 81, 92–94, 98, 100–101, 103, 106–107, 109–110, 112, 114, 135, 152–153, 158–159, 164, 195–197, 236, 252, 255, 263, 269, 272–277, 281–283, 294–295, 301, 303–306, 309, 311–312, 319, 324, 326, 329, 333, 346, 363

homeland 42, 44, 81, 135, 197, 273–274, 282

identity 1, 30, 32, 36–37, 40, 42, 44–45, 47–48, 71, 76, 78–79, 81–82, 86, 99, 111–112, 121–126, 131, 133–136, 139, 144, 180, 205, 208, 252, 254, 263, 265, 269–270, 281, 299, 301, 303, 320, 322, 339, 361–363
  ethnic 269
  national 47, 133
  religious 45, 76, 81, 112, 134, 303

ideology 15, 125, 134–136, 142, 192, 242–243, 252, 268, 270, 337–339

imperialism 78

import 93, 189, 251

independence 37, 41, 68, 77, 86, 109, 134–135, 154, 166, 182, 217, 246, 252, 274

inequality 32, 173

informality 93, 98, 230–235, 237, 245, 250–251, 255–256

institutions 1, 6, 9, 20, 28, 30, 32–35, 38–39, 46, 50–51, 71, 78, 100, 102–103, 105, 122, 126, 136, 144, 151–155, 157–165, 167, 169, 173, 181, 185, 197, 220, 231–235, 238, 246, 251, 271, 281, 284–285, 297, 303, 355

integration 93, 95, 182, 273, 353, 363

internet 3, 14, 32, 37, 39, 42, 44, 48, 139, 145, 244, 274, 276–277, 305

Iran 17, 35–36, 48, 50, 61–62, 68–70, 76–77, 84, 89–91, 93, 97, 99, 101, 103–108, 111–112, 137, 230, 242, 245, 247, 291–292, 295, 297–298
  Persia/Persian 36, 50, 77, 84, 89, 94, 99, 105, 122, 127–128, 230, 298
  Turko-Iranian 68

Islam 1, 9–10, 15–16, 30, 33, 35–36, 48–49, 70, 72–73, 75–76, 78, 80–84, 90–91, 94, 99, 104, 111, 122, 129, 132–133, 135–136, 138, 142, 144, 183, 208, 274, 291–297, 302, 304–308, 331, 334, 341, 344–345, 352, 362–363
  holy group 121–129, 135, 139–140, 144
  mosque 31, 45, 142, 305–307, 319–320, 326, 331–333, 335–336
  piety 38, 48, 82, 105, 293–295, 300, 302, 305–306, 309–310, 312, 343, 345
  sacred lineage 121, 123, 125, 127, 131, 133–134, 136, 138–142, 144
  saints 121–123, 128, 132–134, 136, 140, 145
  Shia 99
  shrines 79–80, 123, 125, 132–134, 136–138, 140
  Sufi 121–123, 125–126, 129, 131–133, 135, 140, 144–145
  Sunni 36, 50, 75, 91, 99, 104, 112, 135

jihad 70, 76, 78, 80, 83–84, 331
  muhajeer/muhajed 76, 78, 80–83
  muhajeer/mujahed 83–84

Kazakhstan 16, 32, 35–36, 41, 48–49,
        69, 76, 95, 123–126, 131, 134–145,
        158, 177–183, 186, 188–192,
        194–198, 210, 278, 326, 352, 355,
        361
kin/kinship 99–100, 103, 105, 107, 123,
        138, 143, 188, 232–233, 235, 241,
        250, 303
Kyrgyzstan 1–2, 14, 16, 30–31, 34,
        37–38, 40, 45–46, 69, 76, 125, 153,
        177, 180–183, 189, 198, 205–209,
        211–213, 216–219, 221, 223, 263,
        266–268, 271–279, 281–283,
        319–321, 331, 338–339, 341–342,
        344, 352, 361–363
landowners 33
    smallholders 152–153, 156–159,
        161, 163–164, 166–167, 169–173
language 2–3, 48–49, 62, 69, 74, 81,
        89–90, 94, 104–105, 110, 112,
        123, 125, 133, 137, 143–144, 166,
        178, 181, 194–197, 205, 209–211,
        213–216, 219–220, 222, 235, 265,
        272–273, 277–279, 296, 298, 331
    linguistic 46, 104, 126, 136, 140, 182,
        188, 211–212, 215, 217–218, 221,
        264, 274
market 48, 50, 70, 90–91, 93, 95–97,
        103–104, 106–109, 111–112, 114,
        156, 165–166, 182, 187, 230–231,
        233, 235–247, 251, 253–256, 265,
        268, 279, 281, 297, 336–337, 344,
        356, 361
    informal 230–231, 236, 244
    labour 91, 103
media 2, 13–14, 18, 32, 37, 48–49,
        51, 76, 90–91, 94, 104, 107, 111,
        113–114, 122–123, 126, 132, 136,
        139, 144, 163, 173, 178, 196–198,
        206, 211, 219, 224, 232, 249, 256,
        277, 279, 282, 284–285, 291–294,
        297, 301–305, 307–309, 311–312,
        337, 345
    digital 14, 294, 302, 307, 309, 312
    technology 32, 293, 302
mediation
    material 293

methods/methodology 2, 6, 8–10, 12,
        19, 27–28, 30, 33–34, 36, 40, 42, 47,
        125, 144, 151–152, 159–160, 163,
        179–180, 186, 205, 207, 211, 215,
        220, 222–224, 264, 271, 284, 300,
        310–311, 351, 354
middlemen 48–49, 90–94, 101–109,
        111–114, 197, 246, 263, 277–279,
        281–282, 298, 351
migration 6, 16, 27–28, 32–33, 35–36,
        38, 41, 47, 49, 51–52, 61–63, 68, 71,
        73–79, 81, 84–86, 91–92, 95–96, 98,
        109–110, 112–113, 143, 151–153,
        160, 167, 194–196, 199, 232–233,
        282, 284, 293, 296–297, 299, 301,
        309, 345, 353, 355–356, 361–363
    emgration/emigrants 76
    emigration/emigrants 36, 38, 41, 62,
        73–75, 77, 79, 81, 84, 95
    immigration/immigrants 84, 110,
        153
    labour 6, 33, 38, 47, 51, 68, 91, 167,
        232, 296–297
    migrant guesthouse 92, 100–101,
        103
    migrants 32, 38, 44, 46, 48–49, 51,
        76, 80, 82, 84, 89, 92–97, 99–103,
        108–112, 158–159, 167, 196–197,
        234, 255, 266, 272, 274–275, 295,
        298, 301, 312, 327, 362
    regimes 109, 112
    student migrants 44, 295
    temporary migrants 100
    traveller 8, 13, 30, 36, 43–44, 48–49,
        51, 230, 247, 294–295, 297, 301–303,
        309–311, 352
mobility/mobilities 2–3, 5–13, 15–18,
        27–32, 35–36, 38–43, 46–47, 49–51,
        84, 92–93, 112, 153, 159–160,
        180, 184, 186, 190, 195–196, 199,
        229–230, 234–237, 242, 244–245,
        253–256, 279, 283, 293–294,
        296–301, 307–310, 312, 349–357,
        361, 363
    mobilities studies 356

modern 6–7, 11, 13, 18, 27, 29, 32–34, 43, 45, 49, 69, 71–72, 76–77, 84–86, 90, 94, 125, 129, 131, 133–134, 137, 139, 192–194, 198–199, 209, 212, 221, 239, 243, 251, 256, 272, 298–299, 309, 336, 352, 355
modernisation 192, 199
Moscow 16, 65, 67, 72, 89–90, 97, 105, 154, 213, 276, 296
nationalism 27, 30, 36–37, 40–41, 45, 62, 78, 81, 95, 134, 144, 186, 213, 217–218, 220, 270, 274, 284, 353
networks 9, 13, 17, 31, 35–36, 39, 46, 48, 50, 70, 83, 91–92, 98–100, 103–104, 107–108, 110, 112, 123, 125–126, 132, 139, 160, 178, 183–185, 187–188, 193–194, 196, 199, 219, 221–222, 231–235, 239, 241, 246, 250, 254–255, 268, 276, 279, 282, 284, 291, 296, 298, 363
  ethnic 99–100, 103, 105, 107
  kin-based 99–100, 103, 107
nomads 12, 17, 73, 85, 135, 270
  nomadic 17, 74–75, 85, 132, 139, 212, 218, 269, 361
  semi-nomadic 74–75, 85
  semi-nomads 85
place 3, 7, 10–14, 18–20, 28–29, 34–40, 42–47, 49–51, 61, 68, 71, 75, 80, 82, 84, 90, 92, 96–98, 100–103, 106, 108, 112–114, 121–122, 124–127, 132–134, 136–138, 144–145, 151–156, 158, 172, 178–179, 184–188, 194–199, 206, 210, 214, 218–219, 222, 230, 233–240, 244–245, 247, 251, 253, 255, 265, 268, 270, 272–273, 276, 279, 292–294, 297–298, 300–301, 303–307, 309–312, 320–321, 324, 326, 333, 335, 341–342, 345–346, 350, 353–354, 356–357
power 17–18, 28, 34, 42, 45, 50, 64–65, 68–69, 72, 74–75, 77–78, 81–82, 86, 105, 133, 139, 151–152, 154–155, 159–160, 162, 173, 178, 184, 198,

218–219, 230, 234, 276, 282, 284, 341–343, 350
refugee 6, 17, 51, 76, 82–83, 86, 178, 181–182, 188, 333
relations 1, 5–6, 13, 18–19, 28–37, 40, 43, 45, 50–51, 67–68, 70–73, 90, 92–93, 96, 99, 102, 108, 113–114, 122–123, 125–127, 132, 134, 137, 139–141, 151–154, 159–165, 177, 179–180, 182–187, 194, 196, 199, 209–211, 213–216, 219, 234–235, 241–242, 244–246, 249, 253, 255, 265, 271, 276, 278, 283, 296, 299, 310–311, 330, 335, 355–356, 362
  relationships 6, 19, 29, 33, 73, 93, 102, 123, 125, 127, 132, 137, 140–141, 160, 213–215, 244, 283, 311, 330, 335, 356
  ruling 151, 153, 162–165
  social 13, 18, 32, 34, 43, 122, 126, 154, 160–163, 235, 241, 362
research 1–3, 5–11, 14, 19, 27–29, 32–34, 37, 40, 42, 46, 49–50, 62, 77, 86, 90, 113, 123–126, 128, 131, 135, 140, 144–145, 152–154, 158, 160–164, 167, 177, 179–180, 185, 192, 195, 207–208, 213, 220, 222, 230, 234, 236, 253, 263–266, 268–269, 271, 277, 281–282, 285, 300, 310–312, 320, 322, 339, 345, 350–351, 353–355, 361–363
  methods 163
  perspective 5, 27, 33, 42, 86, 113, 144, 185, 207, 222, 300, 310, 350
resident 45–46, 50, 62, 78, 93, 97, 101–102, 155–156, 177, 179, 272, 295, 297, 320, 326–328, 335, 345–346
  residency permits 112
rural 17, 32–33, 36, 42, 50–51, 70, 110–111, 127, 129, 134, 151–152, 154, 156–159, 161, 166, 182, 186–187, 192, 195, 244
Russia 1–2, 16–18, 36–37, 41, 44, 46, 48, 50, 61, 64–74, 76–77, 83–86, 89–91, 94–98, 103–108, 110–113,

124–125, 137, 140, 158, 171, 178,
181, 189–190, 196–197, 205–206,
209–215, 219–221, 230–231,
244–246, 263–268, 271–279,
281–283, 292, 296–298, 306,
325–327, 329, 331, 343, 351, 361,
363. *See also* Soviet Union/USSR

Russian Empire 16, 71, 124, 178

Russian revolution 73, 77

Samarkand 132–133, 137–139

secular 63, 70–71, 78, 81, 291–292, 297

shame 42, 111, 268, 270, 356

Silk Road 5, 49, 70, 178, 198–199, 245,
252, 263, 352, 361

socialism 16, 31, 336, 340, 344

socioeconomic status/class 13, 61, 78,
91, 93–96, 99, 128, 243, 268, 273,
283, 324, 337

Soviet Union/USSR 15–16, 41, 61,
67–68, 78, 82, 86, 104, 134, 156, 165,
178, 181–183, 187–188, 208, 231,
252–254, 267, 272, 278, 296, 321,
326–327, 336, 338
   Soviet 14–17, 29–31, 35–36, 38–43,
   45, 47, 49, 51, 61–62, 66–70, 74–81,
   83, 85–86, 91, 96–98, 104, 113,
   121, 123–126, 129, 131–135, 137,
   140–144, 154, 156, 165, 178–179,
   181–183, 186–189, 194, 197, 207–
   208, 213, 216–217, 220, 222–223,
   229, 231, 239, 242–243, 246,
   252–254, 263, 265–267, 269–273,
   278–279, 284, 291, 295–296, 319,
   321–322, 326–327, 330, 335–339,
   346, 352, 355, 361

spatialisation/spatiality 30, 33–34,
37–38, 51, 186, 311

spirituality 340, 343–345

state 1, 6, 28, 30–31, 33, 39–42, 50–51,
68, 70–72, 78, 80–82, 93–94, 99,
112–113, 123, 125, 133, 136, 142,
152–156, 159, 161, 165–166,
169–170, 177–178, 182–183,
187–188, 193–195, 197–198, 208,
217, 220, 231–233, 235, 238–240,

242, 245, 247, 256, 264, 281, 284,
291–292, 296–297, 299, 305, 319,
329–330, 338, 341, 361–362

status 71, 74, 82, 98–99, 107, 110, 112,
121, 123, 125, 128–129, 131, 134,
141, 158, 223, 242, 253, 271, 279,
310

students 1, 16, 46, 179–180, 182,
194–196, 199, 242, 279, 292–296,
299, 302–303, 305, 307–309, 320,
326, 328, 351, 356–357
   student migrants 44, 295

Tajikistan 1, 16, 30, 36, 44, 66–69,
74–77, 79–80, 82, 85, 89–96, 98–99,
101, 105–108, 110–113, 125, 143,
210, 272, 291, 293, 295–297,
303–307, 309, 361–363

Tashkent 64–65, 68, 74, 124–126, 129,
132, 134–135, 137–144

technology 13–14, 32, 41, 139, 190,
293, 300, 302, 309, 312

texts 2, 13, 31–32, 36–37, 40, 47,
73, 122, 127, 154, 161–164, 167,
170–171, 173, 197, 217, 232, 236,
252, 254, 294, 308–309, 356–357

tourism 6, 15, 41, 48, 90–91, 93, 95–96,
101, 103, 111, 191–192, 233, 246,
297

trade 1, 12, 15–17, 30–31, 33, 36, 39,
41, 44, 46, 48, 50–52, 68, 90, 92–93,
95, 98–99, 101, 103–104, 106–109,
111, 159–160, 165, 170, 178–180,
182, 186–187, 189–190, 192–193,
195, 197, 229–256, 263–266,
268–271, 283, 294, 298, 309, 327,
335, 351, 355–356, 363
   business people 48, 50, 90, 92,
   99, 109, 177, 179, 189, 194, 230,
   243–244, 246, 250, 252, 270,
   277–278
   female traders 92, 243
   petty trade 39, 50, 229–230,
   232–234, 236, 242–243, 246, 249,
   252–256, 356

transformation 6–8, 10, 13, 19, 29–30, 37, 42–46, 70, 78, 84, 123–124, 127, 134, 185–186, 194, 199, 239, 266, 268, 278, 311, 321, 336–337, 340, 342, 344, 346, 349, 362

transgression 31, 39, 42, 48, 185, 220, 234, 264, 349

transition 38, 80, 156, 243, 297, 311, 321, 336–337, 340–345, 355

translation 31, 46–52, 179, 185, 212–213, 220, 278, 285, 349

translocal 1–3, 5–6, 8–12, 15–19, 27–34, 36–52, 61, 63, 68, 83–84, 89–94, 101, 107, 109, 111–113, 121–122, 124–127, 131–134, 136, 138–139, 141, 144–145, 151–153, 159–162, 164, 169–170, 173, 177–180, 184–186, 189–190, 193–194, 196–197, 199, 205, 207, 218–220, 222–223, 229–231, 234–237, 241–242, 244–245, 250, 254–256, 263–264, 271, 278, 281–282, 284–285, 291, 293–295, 299–300, 302, 304, 309–312, 319–321, 336, 345–346, 349–357, 362–363

practices 8, 11, 15–16, 31

studies 350, 357

translocality/translocalism 2–3, 5–6, 8–10, 12, 18–19, 27–34, 36–39, 41–45, 51–52, 84, 109, 111–113, 122, 124–127, 132, 138, 144, 159–160, 184–186, 199, 207, 229–231, 234–235, 237, 242, 254–256, 281, 299–300, 304, 311–312, 320–321, 336, 345–346, 349–357

transnationalism 5–7, 28, 33, 62, 109, 159, 234, 350, 353, 363

transtemporality 18–19, 44–45, 312, 346

Turkey 18, 50, 62, 76–78, 84, 95, 231, 235, 243, 245–247, 249–250, 252, 295, 326

Turkistan/Turkestan 16, 63, 65–66, 68–69, 72, 83–84, 124–126, 129, 131–132, 135–138, 140–143

Turko-Iranian 68

umma 35, 50, 81–82, 185, 235, 281–282, 296, 331, 352

United Arab Emirates 1–2, 89–90, 92–95, 98, 101, 107, 109–112, 291, 293, 295, 298, 303, 307, 309, 311, 352, 362

urban 17, 28–29, 36–38, 45–46, 70, 72–73, 75, 91–92, 94–95, 97, 100–101, 110–113, 127, 132, 134, 156, 158, 186, 189–190, 192, 236, 239, 244–246, 272, 282, 296, 305, 319–322, 331, 336, 338, 345–346, 361–363

Uzbekistan 32–34, 36, 50–51, 66, 69, 74–76, 85, 123–124, 126, 129, 135, 138–139, 142, 144–145, 151–152, 154–158, 161, 165–166, 170, 173, 210, 232, 272, 362

water 32, 34, 42, 50–51, 66, 152, 154–158, 161, 164–173, 332

irrigation 86, 152, 155, 157–158, 165–167, 170–171, 356

management 34, 51, 157, 164, 170, 173

This book need not end here…

At Open Book Publishers, we are changing the nature of the traditional academic book. The title you have just read will not be left on a library shelf, but will be accessed online by hundreds of readers each month across the globe. OBP publishes only the best academic work: each title passes through a rigorous peer-review process. We make all our books free to read online so that students, researchers and members of the public who can't afford a printed edition will have access to the same ideas.
This book and additional content is available at:
https://www.openbookpublishers.com/product/603

Customize

Personalize your copy of this book or design new books using OBP and third-party material. Take chapters or whole books from our published list and make a special edition, a new anthology or an illuminating coursepack. Each customized edition will be produced as a paperback and a downloadable PDF. Find out more at:
https://www.openbookpublishers.com/section/59/1

Donate

If you enjoyed this book, and feel that research like this should be available to all readers, regardless of their income, please think about donating to us. We do not operate for profit and all donations, as with all other revenue we generate, will be used to finance new Open Access publications.
https://www.openbookpublishers.com/section/13/1/support-us

You may also be interested in:

Frontier Encounters
Knowledge and Practice at the Russian, Chinese and Mongolian Border

Edited by Franck Billé, Grégory Delaplace and Caroline Humphrey

https://www.openbookpublishers.com/product/139

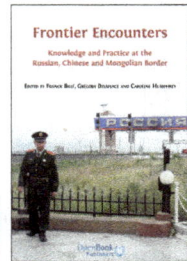

World of Walls
The Structure, Roles and Effectiveness of Separation Barriers

By Said Saddiki

https://www.openbookpublishers.com/product/635

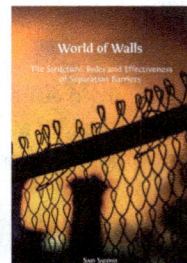

Complexity, Security and Civil Society in East Asia
Foreign Policies and the Korean Peninsula

Edited by Peter Hayes and Kiho Yi

https://www.openbookpublishers.com/product/326

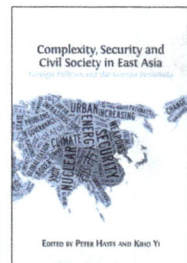

www.ingramcontent.com/pod-product-compliance
Lightning Source LLC
Chambersburg PA
CBHW051949270326
41929CB00015B/2584